The Legacy of Iraq

From the 2003 War to the
'Islamic State'

Edited by
Benjamin Isakhan

EDINBURGH
University Press

Edinburgh University Press Ltd
The Tun – Holyrood Road
12 (2f) Jackson's Entry
Edinburgh EH8 8PJ
www.euppublishing.com

Typeset in 11/13 Adobe Sabon by
IDSUK (DataConnection) Ltd, and
printed and bound in Great Britain by
CPI Group (UK) Ltd, Croydon CR0 4YY

A CIP record for this book is available from the British Library

ISBN 978 0 7486 9616 1 (hardback)
ISBN 978 0 7486 9617 8 (webready PDF)
ISBN 978 1 4744 0500 3 (epub)

Contents

Part III: The Plight of Iraqi Culture and Civil Society

Part IV: Regional and International Consequences of the Iraq War

Acknowledgements

In mid-2014, as the final edits were being made to each of the chapters included in this volume, the situation in Iraq changed dramatically. Within a matter of weeks, the Sunni fundamentalist terrorist network, the Islamic State of Iraq and Syria (ISIS), had taken several important cities across northern and western Iraq and declared an independent caliphate. They quickly imposed their deadly and austere vision on local populations and a sequence of dramatic humanitarian disasters unfolded, to the horror of the international community. With a mixture of surprise and fury, militias claiming to represent the Shia majority of southern Iraq surged north and the nation spiralled, once again, into a period of horrific sectarian violence. The Kurds of northern Iraq capitalised on the ISIS advance to seize new territory, including the important city of Kirkuk, and once again threatened to secede from the rest of the country. Meanwhile, the Iraqi government in Baghdad floundered under international scrutiny before a rapid sequence of political negotiations saw Prime Minister Maliki ousted and a new Iraqi government emerge.

While the chapters collected here did not predict this rapid turn of events, they do point to several of its root causes. There is simply no way to fully comprehend the 'Islamic State' advance, the spike in sectarianism, the most recent Kurdish push for independence and the political rotation in Baghdad without coming to terms with the complex legacies of the 2003 Iraq War. This book therefore not only documents several of the more troubling legacies, but also argues that key mistakes made by the US-led occupation and the fledgling Iraqi government since 2003 set in train a sequence of events that have served as the collective catalyst for the crisis that began in mid-2014. To ignore the legacies of the Iraq War and to deny their connection to contemporary events means that vital lessons will be ignored and the same mistakes will be made in the future. Each of the contributors to this volume was therefore asked to reflect on a key legacy of the Iraq War of 2003 and to document the trajectory of a given issue from the time of the intervention through more than a decade of failed projects and broken promises, through trauma, displacement, violence and disorder. I would like to thank each of them for the timely delivery of quality chapters. The professionalism and calibre of the authors involved and their detailed knowledge of the subject matter made the job of editing this volume a pleasure.

    This book would not have come to fruition without the generous support of four significant institutions and their staff. Firstly, the Australian Research Council and their Discovery Early Career Researcher Award (DE120100315), a fellowship which has enabled me to complete this volume. Secondly, the Middle East Studies Forum within the Centre for Citizenship and Globalisation at Deakin University, with special mention going to Fethi Mansouri. Thirdly, the Middle East Institute at the National University of Singapore and the kind support of Michael C. Hudson and Peter Sluglett. Finally, thanks also go to Gareth Stansfield at the Institute of Arab and Islamic Studies at the University of Exeter where I undertook a brief visiting research fellowship while putting the finishing touches on this volume. Among many other colleagues, I am also indebted to Amin Saikal and Liam Anderson for their enthusiasm and support for the project from its inception. In addition, I owe thanks to the administrative talents of Cayla Edwards, the research assistance of Kelsie Nabben and Verena Woeppel, the expertise and organisational skills of Wael Elhabrouk and the editorial acumen of Jennifer Kloester. I am also grateful to the anonymous referees who read earlier versions of the chapters as well as the staff of Edinburgh University Press who have contributed to the production of this book, particularly Nicola Ramsey and John Watson for their initial interest and confidence in the work.
    On a more personal note, I would like to thank my family and friends for their much-needed words of encouragement and love. Special mention must go to the ever-supportive and always patient Lyndal Isakhan and little Thomas Isakhan, who makes all the hard work so worthwhile.

Notes on Contributors

Howard Adelman was most recently a research professor at the Key Centre for Ethics, Law, Justice and Governance at Griffith University, Australia. He has authored and co-authored hundreds of publications, most relevantly *No Return, No Refuge: Rites and Rights in Minority Repatriation* (Columbia University Press, 2011) and *Protracted Displacement in Asia: No Place to Call Home* (Ashgate, 2008). In addition to his numerous writings on refugees, he has written articles, chapters and books on the Middle East, multiculturalism, humanitarian intervention, membership rights, ethics, early warning and conflict management.

Ranj Alaaldin is a doctoral candidate at the Department for International History at the London School of Economics and Political Science, United Kingdom. He is also a visiting scholar at Columbia University, United States. His research focuses on Iraq, looking in particular at Shia mobilisation, sectarianism and the Kurds. The author has conducted extensive fieldwork throughout Iraq and has published widely on Iraq and the Middle East region.

Nicholas Al-Jeloo has recently graduated with a PhD in Syriac studies from the University of Sydney, Australia. Among his publications are *Modern Aramaic (Assyrian/Syriac) Phrasebook and Dictionary* (Hippocrene, 2007), as well as a number of articles in peer-reviewed journals documenting his empirical research on the history and culture of Assyrians in Iraq and other countries. His research interests concern Eastern Christianity, minorities and Semitic languages, and he conducted numerous field trips to Iraq and among Iraqi refugee communities in Syria, Jordan and Lebanon between 2002 and 2010.

Liam Anderson is Professor of Political Science at Wright State University, United States. His research interests focus on issues of constitutional design, particularly with reference to ethnically divided states, such as Iraq. His publications include *The Future of Iraq: Dictatorship, Democracy, or Division?* (Palgrave Macmillan, 2005 – with Gareth Stansfield), *Crisis in Kirkuk: The Ethnopolitics of Conflict and Compromise* (University of Pennsylvania Press, 2009 – with Gareth Stansfield) and *An Atlas of Middle Eastern Affairs* (Routledge, 2011). His most recent book, *Federal Solutions to Ethnic Problems: Accommodating Diversity* (Routledge, 2013), examines the efficacy of different models of federal design to alleviate ethnic conflict.

Aloysia Brooks is a torture prevention advocate and lecturer in public policy and human rights. She has worked for more than ten years in human rights advocacy organisations, including Amnesty International Australia, and has worked with survivors of torture and trauma. Aloysia completed her doctorate at the University of Sydney, Australia. It included research on torture that has occurred as a result of the War on Terror, US foreign and national security policy and international human rights law.

Joseph A. Camilleri is Emeritus Professor of International Relations at La Trobe University, Australia. He is the author of some twenty books and more than 100 book chapters and journal articles spanning the entire spectrum of international relations. His recent publications include *Worlds in Transition: Evolving Governance across a Stressed Planet* (Edward Elgar, 2009), *Religion and Ethics in a Globalizing World: Conflict, Dialogue and Transformation* (Palgrave Macmillan, 2011) and *Culture, Religion and Conflict in Muslim Southeast Asia: Negotiating Tense Pluralisms* (Routledge, 2013). Professor Camilleri is a fellow of the Australian Academy of Social Sciences and has been awarded the Order of Australia medal.

Perri Campbell is an Alfred Deakin research fellow in the School of Education at Deakin University, Australia. Her work is situated at the crossroads of gender studies, critical social theory, media and youth studies. Dr Campbell's forthcoming publication *Digital Selves: Iraqi Women's Weblogs and the Limits of Freedom* (Common Ground, 2015) explores women's everyday experiences of war in Iraq and the use of digital communication technologies in post-conflict zones. Her current research explores young people's civic engagement and use of social media during the global Occupy movements and the Arab Spring uprisings.

Luke Howie is senior lecturer in the Behavioural Studies Department and the deputy director of the Global Terrorism Research Centre at Monash University, Australia. He is the author of three books that each explore the role of witnessing in understanding terrorism and the threat it poses: *Terrorism, the Worker and the City: Simulations and Security in a Time of Terror* (Gower, 2009), *Terror on the Screen: Witnesses and the Re-animation of 9/11 as Image-event, Popular culture, and Pornography* (New Academia, 2011) and *Witnesses to Terror: Understanding the Meanings and Consequences of Terrorism* (Palgrave Macmillan, 2012). In addition to his work in terrorism studies, Dr Howie's research interests include social theory, media and society, psychoanalysis and cultural sociology.

Benjamin Isakhan is Australian Research Council Discovery (DECRA) Senior Research Fellow at the Centre for Citizenship and Globalisation, and convenor of the Middle East Studies Forum at Deakin University, Australia. He is also adjunct senior research associate in the Department of Politics, Faculty of Humanities at the University of Johannesburg, South Africa. He is the author of *Democracy in Iraq: History, Politics, Discourse* (Ashgate, 2012) and the editor of five books including *The Edinburgh Companion to the History of Democracy* (Edinburgh University Press, 2015). Dr Isakhan's current research includes the ARC-funded project 'Measuring the Destruction of Heritage and Spikes of Violence in Iraq' (DE120100315), which involves several field trips to Iraq.

Binoy Kampmark is a lecturer in the School of Global, Urban and Social Studies, Royal Melbourne Institute of Technology, Australia. He is the author of *Victim and Executioners: American Political Discourses on the Holocaust from Liberation to Bitburg* (Nova, 2013) and *The Sacred Child: The Politics of Child Abuse and Abusers in the Twenty-first Century* (Nova, 2012). He has also published many journal articles on security matters relating to terrorism, war and refugees. He is a contributing editor to CounterPunch, and was a Commonwealth scholar at Selwyn College, Cambridge, United Kingdom.

Philippe Le Billon is a professor at the Department of Geography and the Liu Institute for Global Issues at the University of British Columbia, Canada. Working on links between environment, development and security, he has published widely on natural resources and armed conflicts, the political economy of war, resource governance and corruption. His two most recent books are *Wars of Plunder: Conflicts, Profits and the Politics of Resources* (Oxford University Press, 2013) and *Oil* (Polity Press, 2012).

Diane C. Siebrandt is a PhD candidate at the Centre for Citizenship and Globalisation at Deakin University, Australia. She has presented at numerous conferences and symposiums, highlighting her efforts to protect heritage sites across Iraq during her work overseeing the US embassy's Cultural Heritage Program between 2006 and 2012. She was repeatedly recognised for her achievements with numerous awards from the US military and US embassy in Baghdad, and in 2010 was honoured with the Archaeological Institute of America's Outstanding Public Service Award.

Ronen Zeidel is a research fellow and Iraq analyst in the Moshe Dayan Center for Middle East and Africa, and convenor of the Iraq and the

'Islamic State' Forum at Tel Aviv University, Israel. He is the editor of *Iraq between Occupations: Perspectives from 1920 to the Present* (Palgrave Macmillan, 2010). Dr Zeidel is also the author of many articles on Iraqi history, society and culture, as well as on the nation's diverse national and sectarian identities. His articles on the Sunnis were the first to concentrate on the problems faced by the Sunnis as an obstacle in the construction of a 'New Iraq'.

Introduction

The Iraq Legacies – Intervention, Occupation, Withdrawal and Beyond

Benjamin Isakhan

In March of 2003 the world's last remaining superpower launched a pre-emptive strike on a sovereign nation without UN approval or popular global support. The justification given to the world for such an attack was twofold: Iraq was accused of harbouring weapons of mass destruction (WMDs) and having links to al-Qaeda, neither of which could be permitted in a post-9/11 world. When, in the wake of the invasion, evidence failed to emerge for either Iraq's WMDs or links to terrorism, the Bush administration was forced to reframe the war and redefine the parameters of what would constitute victory. To do this, the United States and its Coalition partners undertook an ambitious and unprecedented project to turn Iraq into a liberal democracy, underpinned by free-market capitalism and constituted by a citizen body free to live in peace and prosperity. But the realities of Iraq fell well short of this idealistic vision. The Iraq War rapidly descended into chaos, causing heavy civilian losses and military casualties, along with shaky progress towards increasingly elusive goals. In 2006, any hopes that the world may have held when watching the ascension of Iraq's first democratically elected government were quickly dashed as a brutal and deadly ethno-religious sectarian conflict took hold. In the US, as well as in other Coalition countries, wide dissatisfaction with the motives and outcomes of the war brought heightened calls for a complete withdrawal. As Iraq's new political elite began to reveal their distaste for democracy, as violence continued, as supposedly vanquished enemies resurfaced and the people of Iraq struggled with poor electricity, limited potable water and crumbling infrastructure, the United States began withdrawing its forces. By December 2011 the US military had left Iraq, having failed not only to find WMDs or links to al-Qaeda, but also to deliver on their promise of a democratic, peaceful and prosperous Iraq.

Now, more than a decade after the war began and as Iraq faces the very real prospect of disintegration due to the devastating advance of the Islamic State in Iraq and Syria (ISIS) and the Kurdish seizure of

Kirkuk and other 'disputed territories' (see the concluding chapter for a discussion of these events), it is imperative to measure the costs of the intervention, to assess the successes and failures of the goals of the war, and to reflect on the difficulties that Iraq has faced beyond withdrawal. But before doing so, any robust discussion and thorough analysis must first acknowledge that the Iraq War means many different things to many different people. The legacies of the Iraq War are much more than a collection of facts about the merits and drawbacks of the intervention and everything that has happened since – they are also a collection of people's lived realities and strongly held opinions. Anyone who has spent time in Iraq or with Iraqis since 2003 will not only have been touched by people's tragic and deeply personal experiences of the war, but also by the diversity of opinions they will encounter (Kukis 2011). In the Kurdistan region of northern Iraq, for example, while most acknowledge the tragedies that have followed the war, they also describe it as a 'liberation' from the oppression of the Baathist regime and as ushering in a period of relative peace and prosperity. Many Shia Arabs of southern and central Iraq also emphasise the oppressive nature of the Baathist state and the fact that they have experienced unprecedented freedom and a degree of influence never possible under the former regime. Where they generally differ from the Kurds is in their discussions of the suffering they have experienced since 2003 and the fact that many of them have inadequate access to basic needs like water, sewerage, electricity, health care and education. In the central and western provinces, dominated by Iraq's Sunni Arab minority, which had held power since the creation of modern Iraq in 1921, the situation is even grimmer. For many of them, the 2003 war was an 'invasion' which saw them not only toppled from power, but also become increasingly marginalised and subject to unprecedented violence. Beyond these broad generalisations are the many nuanced and highly personal experiences of all those Iraqi people who have suffered loss, upheaval, trauma and persecution since 2003. Although much less is at stake, divisions similar to those found across Iraq can also be found in the West, especially within those countries which fought in the war. In the United States – as in other Coalition countries – there are sharp differences of opinion between, for example, those who protested against the war in 2003 and the military personnel who did tours of duty in Iraq.

These diverse personal experiences and opinions illustrate the fact that the Iraq War has not left behind a monolithic legacy that can be retold in a singular, linear narrative, but rather a multifaceted and intersecting set of legacies which must be sensitively and carefully examined if we are to ever understand the consequences of the war. To date, however, very little scholarly attention has been paid to the difficult legacies of

Iraq. While, in the lead up to and in the wake of the intervention, much was written on the motives and merits of the war and its effort to bring democracy, free-market capitalism and peace to the long-suffering Iraqi people (much of this literature is discussed later in this chapter), there has been no substantive study or sustained analysis of the legacies of the Iraq War or of the challenges and opportunities the nation faces beyond the withdrawal.

While acknowledging that not all of the consequences of the Iraq War can be addressed in a single volume, this book will nonetheless be the first to dissect and discuss some of the Iraq War's more complex legacies and the varying analyses, debates and discussions they have stimulated. This tightly structured edited volume follows the trajectory of these legacies back to the earliest days of the US intervention and examines the extent to which key decisions and errors of judgement on the part of the Coalition and the Iraqi political elite have had unexpected and devastating consequences for Iraq today. The book examines how the war dramatically altered the lives of ordinary Iraqis and led to many of the most deep-seated and intractable problems facing Iraq, the region and the world today. Indeed, while the chapters collected here did not predict the rapid turn of events that transpired after the dramatic advance of ISIS in mid-2014, they do point to several of its root causes, the argument here being that the Iraq War of 2003 has left behind a sequence of deeply felt but rarely examined legacies and that together these legacies have served as the catalyst of Iraq's current chaos. In a broader sense, this study also addresses some of the most significant problems of our time: democracy in the Middle East, foreign intervention in the region, sectarian politics and violence, the rise of Islamic fundamentalism and terrorist organisations, and the decline of US power and influence in the region and the world. Therefore, this volume is not only timely, but it also addresses a significant lacuna in academic and policy debates by addressing a series of urgent questions concerning the legacies of Iraq.

Intervention

Key to understanding the 2003 intervention in Iraq is coming to terms with its broader context and central motivations. To do so, one must begin by mentioning the events of 11 September 2001: the attacks on the World Trade Center in New York and the Pentagon in Washington by the international Islamist terrorist network, al-Qaeda. In reaction, the George W. Bush administration declared a global 'War on Terror'. This war began a few weeks later in Afghanistan where a US-led international coalition undertook a mission to overthrow the Taliban and hunt down al-Qaeda. The US was able to get UN support for the war and secure military commitments from many traditional allies and new friends. The US toppled the Taliban and, after more than a decade of relentless searching, assassinated Osama bin Laden. However, both the Taliban and al-Qaeda proved more sophisticated, more resilient and more capable than had been anticipated by the architects of the war. Today, as the thirteen-year military intervention in Afghanistan enters its final stages, we are left to reflect on the lack of tangible successes and the fact that Afghanistan faces a very uncertain future beyond occupation.

As the war in Afghanistan continued, the Bush administration began building its case for a second major military intervention, this time against Iraq. In his 2003 State of the Union address, President Bush drew attention to Saddam Hussein's brutal oppression of the diverse Iraqi people, and Iraq's continued defiance of various UN resolutions and initiatives, including that of the International Atomic Energy Agency. Crucially, he alleged links between the Iraqi government and terrorist networks such as al-Qaeda. Thus, President Bush not only set the stage for a war with Iraq, he also erroneously linked Saddam's regime with the September 11 attacks and thereby invoked the collective wrath of the American people. As Bush put it:

> Before September 11, 2001, many in the world believed that Saddam Hussein could be contained. But chemical agents and lethal viruses and shadowy terrorist networks are not easily contained. Imagine those nineteen hijackers with other weapons, and other plans – this time armed by Saddam Hussein. It would take just one vial, one canister, one crate slipped into this country to bring a day of horror like none we have ever known. We will do everything in our power to make sure that day never comes. (Bush 2003c)

These sentiments were quickly reiterated by the leaders of the United States' most adamant supporters across the globe. Most notably, British Prime Minister Tony Blair addressed the House of Commons, stating that 'Saddam's weapons of mass destruction and the threats they pose to the world must be confronted' (Blair 2003). Australian Prime Minister John Howard parroted in a ministerial statement that Iraq's 'possession of chemical and biological weapons and its pursuit of a nuclear capability poses a real and unacceptable threat to the stability and security of our world' (Howard 2003).

Despite their best efforts, however, these leaders failed to convince the UN, many long-standing European allies or a sceptical global public. The lack of support was also felt on the streets as many people across America and around the world rallied against this pre-emptive war on a sovereign nation (Ali 2003). In February 2003, this led to 'perhaps the biggest anti-war protests in human history' with approximately six to ten million people marching in 600 cities across the globe (Hil 2008: 28). This widespread opposition was also reflected in the small number of countries willing to send troops to the war. The US was able to assemble a 'Coalition of the Willing' which included an initial military commitment from just four countries: the United States (148,000), the United Kingdom (45,000), Australia (2,000) and Poland (194).[1] On 19 March 2003 Bush addressed the US and the world, stating:

> At this hour, American and Coalition forces are in the early stages of military operations to disarm Iraq, to free its people and to defend the world from grave danger. On my orders, Coalition forces have begun striking selected targets of military importance to undermine Saddam Hussein's ability to wage war. (Bush 2003a)

This marked the beginning of the 'shock and awe' campaign. Conceived by senior military personnel, designed by Pentagon war planners and put into practice by Defence Secretary Donald Rumsfeld, this campaign was to be a brief and explosive demonstration of the scale and precision of US military power (Ullman & Wade 1996). It was ostensibly orchestrated to destroy the entire apparatus of the Baathist state as quickly as possible and to usher in a new era of freedom and democracy. Instead, not only did the war ultimately destroy considerable public infrastructure (such as roads, sewerage and water), but it also led to a devastatingly high number of civilian casualties and injuries. Nonetheless, on 9 April 2003 US-led Coalition forces seized Baghdad with very little resistance, much of the Republican Guard having disbanded during the earlier phases of the war. To celebrate the victory and to write the moment of Saddam's downfall into the annals of history, US marines and a group of apparently jubilant Iraqis tore down the giant bronze statue of Saddam in Firdos Square in central Baghdad. Portrayed to the world as the spontaneous actions of a people's liberation, the scene was in fact carefully choreographed by the US Psychological Operations Unit, designed to serve the twin purposes of a mass media spectacle and to promote the legitimacy of the war across a sceptical globe (Rampton 2003: 1–7). A similarly manufactured moment occurred on 1 May 2003 when President Bush arrived via fighter jet on the USS *Abraham Lincoln*. Under a banner proclaiming 'Mission Accomplished', the US President announced the completion of major military combat in Iraq (Bush 2003a). Whatever one thinks of the war and whatever criticisms one might make of the ways in which it was conducted, the 'shock and awe' campaign will go down in history as one of the most successful military interventions of all time. It took just six weeks to topple the 35-year reign of the Baathist regime and to declare victory in Iraq.

Occupation

The declaration of victory soon proved premature. In the immediate aftermath of the war, Coalition forces failed to secure the country beyond Baathist rule and Iraq quickly descended into chaos (Bensahel et al. 2008). As is by now well known, massive looting took place across the country including at important cultural sites such as the Iraq National Museum and the Iraq National Library and Archive (Isakhan 2013b; Stone & Bajjaly 2008). To some extent order was restored with the arrival of the Coalition Provisional Authority (CPA), which governed Iraq on behalf of the Coalition immediately after the war (21 April 2003–28 June 2004). However, the CPA left behind its own complicated legacy and among its many controversial moves was the wholesale de-Baathification of Iraq. This had a series of immediate and devastating consequences for Iraq, most notably the marginalisation of the minority Sunni Arab population and the fact that it left many people – including many very well-armed and well-trained members of the military and security apparatus – without an adequate source of income, leading to an upsurge in violence (Barakat 2005; Hatch 2005).

In addition to the failures of de-Baathification, the US and its Coalition partners also had to face up to the fact that they had not been able to find any evidence for either Saddam's alleged stockpile of WMDs or his links to terrorist networks such as al-Qaeda. The Coalition thus came under fire for having deliberately misled the public and the Bush administration was forced to articulate a set of three new and inter-connected goals: to topple Saddam Hussein and bring peace and stability to the long-suffering Iraqi people; to replace the autocracy of the Baathist regime with the Western liberal model of democracy; and to transform Iraq into a prosperous state governed by a free-market economy. This three-pronged goal was clearly articulated by Bush in a speech presented before the National Endowment for Democracy in November 2003. In terms of the second key goal – to bring the Western liberal model of democracy to Iraq – Bush claimed that, although bringing democracy to Iraq would be a

> massive and difficult undertaking, it is worth our effort, it is worth our sacrifice, because we know the stakes. The failure of Iraqi democracy would embolden terrorists around the world, increase dangers to the American people, and extinguish the hopes of millions in the region. Iraqi democracy will succeed – and that success will send forth the news, from Damascus to Teheran – that freedom can be the future of every nation. The establishment of a free Iraq at the heart of the Middle East will be a watershed event in the global democratic revolution. (Bush 2003b)

However, when the US began talking about bringing democracy to Iraq they did not expect the Iraqi people to hold them to their word. In fact, the original plan of the CPA was to install a puppet Iraqi government that would write a constitution under American auspices and be pliable to their interests in the region. When news of this plan reached the people of Iraq they took to the streets in a series of massive nationwide protests throughout 2003 and 2004. They demanded democracy and called on the US to make good on their promise to see Iraq transform from an oppressive dictatorship into a modern representative democracy governed by the principles of justice and equality. These early protests were but a forerunner to a movement – particularly supported by the majority Shia Arab population of Iraq – that gathered enormous momentum over the ensuing months. Indeed, senior Shia religious figures such as Grand Ayatollah Ali al-Sistani took the unprecedented step of issuing politically motivated fatwas which argued that the US lacked the appropriate authority to install a government in Iraq and demanded that they instead hold national elections so that the Iraqi people could nominate their own representatives (al-Sistani 2010). Under the weight of such criticisms, in June 2004 the US-led CPA transferred sovereignty to the Iraqi Interim Government (Isakhan 2013a). This body had limited powers but was designed to prepare the way for the democratic transition.

On 30 January 2005 some 8.5 million Iraqis voted in the nation's first free and fair elections. The elected assembly was charged with the task of drafting a permanent Iraqi constitution. This, along with the need to position the candidates within the new government, brought with it the kind of political in-fighting, jostling and rhetoric that is typical of a fledgling democracy. There remained much friction among the groups and lengthy debates ensued over key issues such as the official role of Islam in the new constitution as well as extended deliberations over the merits of regional autonomy versus a federated state (Dawisha 2005). The new Iraqi constitution was finally delivered on 28 August 2005 before being ratified via a national referendum six weeks later, on 15 October. With the constitution officially accepted, the Iraqi people were invited to visit the polls again on 15 December 2005, this time to elect a 275-seat government. This was arguably the most successful of Iraq's recent forays into democratic practice, with strong Sunni participation, very low levels of violence and an estimated eleven million people participating in the election. However, the election did see a six-month political stalemate set in with the various factions divided over who should lead Iraq. The impasse was eventually resolved and the little-known Nouri al-Maliki of the Shia Islamist Da'wa party was eventually nominated as Prime Minister, his government finally taking office in May 2006 (Stansfield 2007: 183–9).

The series of elections and the referendum held in 2005 were remark-able accomplishments in and of themselves. The fact that millions of Iraqis – men and women, young and old, Sunni and Shia, Kurd and Arab, Christian and Muslim – literally risked their lives to vote is a strong testament to the political determination of the people and the degree to which they rapidly embraced democracy. Another strong tes-tament is the often overlooked fact that in the immediate aftermath of a brutal and oppressive dictatorship and under a violent military occupa-tion, Iraq developed its own vibrant civil society. Since 2003, political parties of all shades have (re)emerged and developed complex policy agendas; civil society organisations and workers' union movements have advocated on behalf of the Iraqi people; and media outlets have been enthusiastically produced and consumed by a populace thirsty for uncensored news. In addition, various protest movements have taken to the streets *en masse* to air their concerns about everything from the ongoing US-led occupation to the government's failure to provide basic security and infrastructure (Isakhan 2006, 2008, 2012b).

However, one of the unfortunate consequences of the US effort to bring democracy to Iraq was that many key ethno-religious political factions viewed it as an opportunity to peddle their own relatively nar-row and very divisive political rhetoric (Davis 2007). Overwhelmingly, Iraq's key political parties failed to unfold a vision for a united and pros-perous Iraq. Similarly, when Iraqis took to the polls, most of them voted along ethno-religious sectarian lines. This meant that the 275-member government they elected was constituted not so much by a body who wanted to draw Iraq together behind a common ideology and work towards a collective and egalitarian future, but rather by representa-tives who had been given a mandate by their constituents to fight in the interests of their ethnicity or religion.

These political divisions soon manifested in violence. Between 2006 and 2008 Iraq descended into a dark and unprecedented period with grim and complex battles fought between the occupying forces, the Iraqi armed services, various insurgent groups and terrorist organisations, as well as between competing ethno-religious sectarian militias (Dawisha 2009: 258–71; Isakhan 2012c). In the so-called 'Sunni triangle' a web of insurgent groups (made up of former Baathists, Iraqi nationalists and al-Qaeda in Iraq (AQI)) stepped up their attacks on the US and on vari-ous Shia militias. The tide of violence was stemmed somewhat with the assassination of the head of AQI, Abu Musab al-Zarqawi, by the US in June 2006, and also with the rise of the Awakening Council ('Sons of Iraq'), a Sunni alliance of tribal sheikhs mostly from the Anbar prov-ince who fought the insurgency on US salaries. In the Shia-dominated south, powerful militias – such as Moqtada al-Sadr's Mahdi Army and the Badr Brigade of the Supreme Council for Islamic Revolution in Iraq (SCIRI) – waged a series of deadly attacks against the US, the Iraqi government, Sunni insurgents and each other. The violence peaked after the February 2006 attack on the al-Askari mosque in Samarra, an iconic edifice highly revered by the Shia population and deliberately targeted by Sunni insurgents. The Sunni–Shia bloodbath that followed led many commentators to argue that Iraq had in fact slipped into a civil war (Fearon 2007). By 2008, however, the violence had calmed considerably following the 2007 US troop surge and the increased effectiveness of the Iraq Security Forces (ISF).

Although things were much more peaceful in the Kurdish north, the two key political parties, the Kurdistan Democratic Party (KDP) and the Patriotic Union of Kurdistan (PUK), sought to utilise their influence over Baghdad not only to press for increasing degrees of autonomy, but also to try to bring the oil-rich but ethnically diverse province of Kirkuk under their jurisdiction. Such obstinacy aside, the Kurdistan Regional Government (KRG) has emerged as a bastion of relative peace and freedom (Stansfield 2003) despite some worrying signs concerning crackdowns on intellectuals, dissenters and journalists and occasional waves of harassment. Other concerns include the fact that the KDP and the PUK dominate the politics of the region and have proven themselves capable of manipulating the practices and institutions of democracy for their own ends.

The KRG's actions, however, pale in comparison to the increasingly authoritarian nature of the Shia-dominated government in Baghdad and especially of the Prime Minister (Dodge 2012b). To consolidate his grip on power, from 2006 Maliki instigated a four-pronged approach. Firstly, he cracked down hard on Iraqi civil society, even going so far as to close down media outlets and political parties that dared to criticise his government. Secondly, he successfully harnessed the increasing strength of the ISF, transforming it into a force directly under the control of his office and loyal to himself, sometimes using it to target and undermine his opponents. Thirdly, he broadened his political support base by installing those loyal to him in key positions. Finally, Maliki has routinely intimidated and undermined key state institutions and mechanisms of public oversight including the judiciary, the electoral commission and those responsible for investigating corruption.

Perhaps the most telling sign of Maliki's increasing autocracy came in the aftermath of the 7 March 2010 elections. Neither of the two frontrunners – Iyad Allawi's Iraq National Movement or al-Iraqiyya, and Maliki's own newly founded State of Law Coalition – had managed to secure the 163 seats needed to form a government in the 325-member parliament. Nonetheless, Maliki was determined to cling to power. This led to nine months of crippling political deadlock until a new government was finally announced in December 2010 and – to the grave disappointment of many Iraqis – much remained the same: Maliki retained the position of Prime Minister (and actually extended his portfolio to include the powerful defence and interior ministries), while many other key positions would rotate among a handful of familiar players (Ottaway & Kaysi 2010a). For his troubles, Allawi was invited to enter a power-sharing arrangement with the government as the head of a new National Security Council. However, it was not long before Allawi was complaining that there was no real 'power-sharing' in Iraq and he withdrew from the post.

Withdrawal

The political stalemate of 2010 was just the latest challenge to the US plan to install the liberal model of democracy in Iraq, raising deep questions about the successes and failures of this effort. However, the Iraq War brought additional challenges to the United States and its Coalition partners, including: the failure to maintain order and achieve decisive progress in the face of ever-shifting goals; the devastating death toll of Iraqi civilians and Coalition troops; the resurgence of violence especially by al-Qaeda; and the shocking events at Abu Ghraib prison. These and other problems converged to make the war remarkably unpopular across the globe and arguably fostered rising anti-Americanism and a deep cynicism about US leadership – even among America's staunchest allies. Indeed, from the beginning of the intervention various individuals and political groups within Iraq and across the world were calling for the complete withdrawal of all Coalition forces (Isakhan 2014b). In Iraq, these ranged from terrorist groups such as al-Qaeda to non-partisan civil society organisations, and from 'ordinary' Iraqis to senior political figures.

In the West, a handful of scholarly and policy-oriented studies suggested possible drawdown options. These included detailed proposals for a phased withdrawal commencing as early as 2006 through to warnings about the dangers of premature withdrawal, especially the possible damage to critical US strategic interests in the region and to the social and political reconstruction of Iraq (Cordesman & Mausner 2009; McGovern & Polk 2006; Perry et al. 2009). Despite the significance of these studies, the Bush administration succumbed to increasing pressure from both their domestic constituents and from the Iraqi government to finally negotiate the Status of Forces Agreement (SOFA) in 2008. This document, drafted and ratified in the twilight of the Bush administration, set out the legal framework and precise timeline for a gradual US withdrawal from Iraq by 31 December 2011. Despite much popular opposition to the SOFA in Iraq on the grounds that it legitimated and prolonged the occupation, the SOFA was officially ratified by the Iraqi parliament on 27 November 2008.

Just weeks after the final confirmation of the SOFA, Barack Obama assumed office as the new President of the US. Yet, while Obama campaigned on a platform of 'change', and despite wide expectations for a significant rethink of US foreign policy regarding the Middle East in the wake of his Cairo address of mid-2009 (Obama 2009b), Obama confirmed early in his presidency that he intended to abide by Bush's withdrawal timetable (Obama 2009a). In accordance with the SOFA, in December 2011 the last US troops withdrew from Iraq, ending almost nine years of military occupation. To commemorate the event, Obama gave a speech at Fort Bragg military base in North Carolina. Unable to celebrate a military 'victory' or claim that the US had achieved its goals of a democratic, prosperous and peaceful Iraq, the speech emphasised the valiant efforts of the US military and highlighted their resolve in the face of mounting criticism and a prolonged and unpredictable conflict. Obama did, however, see the withdrawal as a 'moment of success' and argued that while 'Iraq is not a perfect place ... we're leaving behind a sovereign, stable and self-reliant Iraq' (Obama 2011).

Beyond

The evidence, however, does not support Obama's claim. Indeed, the final withdrawal of all US troops at the end of 2011 provides an opportunity to measure the costs of the war, to consider its aims and assess its successes and failures. In terms of the human cost, official figures indicate that 4,488 US military personnel and up to 3,418 US contractors died during Operation Iraqi Freedom along with a further 319 Coalition troops (Lutz 2013). To this can be added both the physical and mental injuries sustained during a protracted asymmetric war – costs which veterans and their families will have to bear for years to come. In financial terms, the Iraq War cost the US taxpayer $822 billion with an estimated total spend, actual and imputed, of $1.7 trillion (Crawford 2013). However, while the costs of the Iraq War were high for the US and its Coalition partners, they pale in comparison to the price paid by the Iraqis. Although estimates of those killed during the war vary, among the most conservative and most widely cited estimate is that of the Iraq Body Count, which asserts that approximately 162,000 Iraqi citizens have died since the war began in 2003 (Iraq Body Count 2013). In addition, an untold and unimaginable number have been injured. The war has also created approximately 2.7 million internally displaced people, 2 million refugees and countless migrants who have understandably chosen to leave Iraq since 2003 (Margesson et al. 2009). Beyond these figures are a series of very real, but far less tangible, costs such as the damage done to Iraq's rich cultural heritage or its sensitive ecosystems, or the deep emotional scars that come from a decade of war. Such costs will be felt by generations of Iraqis as yet unborn. They will grow up in a country riven by divisions and violence, with insufficient public infrastructure, with poor sanitation or education, with polluted rivers and soil, with looted museums, libraries and archaeological sites, and – most devastating of all – with little hope for a brighter future.

What makes these costs so alarming is that, while some measurable progress has been made, by and large the Iraq War abjectly failed to achieve the goals articulated early on: to topple Saddam Hussein and bring peace and stability to the long-suffering Iraqi people; to replace the autocracy of the Baathist regime with the Western liberal model of democracy; and to transform Iraq into a prosperous state governed by a free-market economy. In terms of the first key goal, it is certainly true that Coalition forces terminated the 45-year reign of the Baathist state in just six short weeks. Saddam was later captured before being put on trial and finally hanged on 30 December 2006. As we have seen, however, Coalition forces failed to adequately secure the nation beyond Saddam's rule and, from 2006, a brutal and bloody sectarian conflict took hold. In the wake of the 2007 US troop surge and subsequent calm came premature and self-congratulatory rhetoric that the US counter-insurgency strategy had defeated al-Qaeda in Iraq once and for all (Phillips 2009).

Today, Iraq remains one of the most violent places on earth. Ethno-religious sectarian factions and tribal warlords continue to wield significant power over their local constituents and terror is a part of daily life, with various factions capable of launching devastating attacks on a whim. At the end of 2011 when the US troops withdrew, they did so after three successive years in which the civilian death toll had been significantly lower than any year since the start of the war – though still alarmingly high. Between 2009 and 2011 the annual death toll was approximately 4,500 civilian casualties, much lower than the peak figure of 29,296 civilian casualties in 2006 (Iraq Body Count 2012b). Following the final withdrawal of all Coalition troops, however, violence escalated again. In 2013 civilian casualties jumped to 9,472, a figure comparable to the final brutal days of the 2008 civil war (Iraq Body Count 2014). Due to the sudden advance of ISIS (an al-Qaeda offshoot) and the sectarian backlash it unleashed, 2014's death toll is likely to be much higher again. The irony here barely needs to be stated: there was no credible al-Qaeda presence in Iraq before the Coalition forces staged the intervention but today large swathes of the country are held by one of its more nefarious offshoots.

The second key goal, to bring the Western liberal model of democracy to Iraq, created a complicated legacy. On the one hand, as we have seen, the Iraqi people are to be admired for having embraced democratic mechanisms and institutions, for producing a rich variety of media outlets, a complex array of political parties and civil society organisations and a strong culture of dissent – none of which were permitted under the former regime. On the other hand, Iraqi politics has become deeply divided along ethno-religious political lines and dominated by a series of factions who care little for democracy and have undertaken a number of draconian measures to tighten their grip on power. Today, the irony of having replaced the Baath with an Iraqi political elite who look more like authoritarians than democrats is not lost on the Iraqi people – even if it gets little mention elsewhere.

Iraq's troubled democracy also faces other threats. Today, Iraq is in the grip of three fundamental stalemates which are crippling the nation's fledgling democracy. The first is the deadlock between various elements of Iraq's dominant Shia Arab religio-political movements. While they hold a great deal of power in the new Iraq, there is certainly no love lost between Maliki's Da'wa party and other Shia Arab political factions such as the Sadrists or SCIRI. There is also the long-standing but increasingly tense stalemate between the central government in Baghdad and the KRG of northern Iraq. In 2014 the Kurds capitalised on the ISIS advance to seize Kirkuk and other disputed territories and have become increasingly assertive in their quest for increased autonomy and independence. Thirdly, the continued marginalisation of the Sunni Arab minority, who have been largely disenfranchised since 2003, has led to popular Sunni resentment of the Shia-dominated government – something ISIS have been able to exploit during their rapid expansion. The key questions that emerge from this series of complex political deadlocks are whether the modern nation of Iraq can sustain a unified state under a central government elected via nation-wide elections; whether it will devolve into a federated system with increased regional autonomy; whether current authoritarian tendencies will see the re-emergence of a fully fledged dictatorship; or whether Iraq will disintegrate altogether under the weight of secession, contestations, division and violence. Whatever the future holds, the current state of Iraq's troubled politics speaks volumes about the merits or otherwise of imposing a top-down model of democracy (Ghanim 2011).

The third and final goal, to transform Iraq into a beacon of prosperity driven by a free-market economy, also has a complicated legacy. Under the Baathist regime Iraq was a command economy, tightly controlled by the state. During the 1970s and 1980s Iraq was among the most prosperous of Arab countries, 'boasting a sizeable middle class, technical capacity, and, compared to other Middle Eastern countries, relatively high standards of education and health care, as well as high numbers of women educated and contributing to the economy' (Crocker 2004: 74). However, the Iran–Iraq War of the 1980s, the Gulf War of 1990–1 and the international sanctions which followed saw Iraq's economy decline severely. By 2003, Iraq lacked all of the economic infrastructure necessary to transform it into a free market. Nonetheless, in the wake of the intervention, the US and its Coalition partners poured millions of dollars of taxpayer money into various post-conflict free-market economic projects (Savage 2014). Most such projects were an abject failure. This is mainly because the US and its allies believed that by converting Iraq to a free-market economy and strengthening key institutions of the state, Iraqis would be implicitly better off. In other words, they privileged the macro level of a neo-liberal free-market economy over the existing local structures and community needs. Therefore, such projects in fact served to widen the gap between the 'new Iraq' and the people. As just one example, a 2011 report from the Centre for Global Development ranked Iraq as the worst performing middle-income country in the world on all eight of the Millennium Development Goals (extreme poverty, hunger, education, gender equality, child health, maternal health, HIV/AIDS, and water) (Leo & Thuotte 2011). Yet, over the years that have elapsed since the 2003 war, Iraq's economy has rapidly improved, mostly due to oil revenue. In 2001 – before the war – Iraq's gross domestic product (GDP) stood at US$29 billion and, following the first few years of the occupation, rose modestly to US$36 billion in 2005 (World Factbook 2007). However, with the signing of several lucrative oil contracts from 2008 onwards, Iraq's GDP skyrocketed and has followed an ongoing upward trajectory ever since. In 2013 – a decade after the war began – Iraq's GDP was USD$222 billion, nearly ten times the 2001 figure (World Factbook 2014). Thus, while Iraq generates billions of dollars in revenue from the nation's rich natural resources, Iraqis continue to live in destitution among the nation's crumbling and insufficient infrastructure.

The foremost reason for this is that the political turmoil and security vacuum have proved a catalyst for rampant corruption, allowing the political elite to empty the nation's coffers and cripple Iraq's economy (al-Ali 2014). Since the onset of the war, Transparency International has consistently ranked Iraq as among the most corrupt countries in the world. In 2003, Iraq was 113th out of 133 countries surveyed and by 2013 it was 171st out of 177 (Transparency International 2014). While such figures indicate that levels of corruption in Iraq have remained consistently poor, when viewed in relation to the ever-escalating GDP, one is left to wonder how many billions of dollars have been siphoned away from urgently needed public support and infrastructure via corruption. To give a sense of the scale of the problem, one report showed that in 2005–7 (referring only to those indicted) '111 electricity ministry officials were convicted of various corruption-related offenses for sums totalling more than $250 million [and] 319 defence ministry officials were convicted of crimes involving sums totalling more than $1 billion' (International Crisis Group 2011). Iraq is also hostage to its large, ineffective and inefficient bureaucracy. This bureaucracy is equal parts a legacy of the Baathist state, in which all decision-making was tightly controlled and highly centralised, and the US model of governance that was imposed with little consultation or consideration of existing Iraqi bureaucratic structures. Among the questions facing Iraq today are how to root out corruption and how to reform and streamline Iraq's bureaucracy without ousting capable workers from gainful employment. Despite being a free-market economy, corruption and a sluggish bureaucracy have left most ordinary Iraqis with sporadic electricity, limited potable water, few working sewerage systems and inadequate health care and education.

Chapter Summaries

In assessing the Iraq War according to its three central goals, it becomes clear that, despite the enormous human and financial costs, little has been achieved. Iraq is neither more peaceful nor prosperous, and only marginally more democratic, than the nation that was so violently invaded more than a decade ago. It is this failure to deliver on the key goals of the Iraq War which underpins each of the chapters that follow. Together they seek to address some of the manifold legacies of the Iraq War, place them in their appropriate context and discuss their continuing significance. Thus, this volume aims to set the framework for an ongoing debate, but one based not so much on the merits or drawbacks of the US-led intervention as on its myriad consequences for Iraq, the Middle East and the world.

In Part I ('The Aftermath of War: Strategic Decisions and Catastrophic Mistakes'), the contributors address the legacies of several strategic decisions and catastrophic mistakes made by the US and their Coalition partners in the earliest days of the war. In his chapter, Benjamin Isakhan examines the ongoing legacy of the CPA's plan to de-Baathify Iraq. He argues that de-Baathification has since become a powerful political tool in the hands of the Shia Arab-dominated Iraqi

government, who have utilised it to oust political opponents and ostracise Sunni politicians – sometimes with only the most tenuous links to
the former regime. Another potent political tool of the incumbent Iraqi
political elite is Iraq's vast oil wealth. After decades of nationalisation
and the crippling international sanctions of the 1990s, Iraq's oil sector was not ready for the US plan to rapidly privatise the industry and
welcome major foreign multinational companies eager for the massive
profits that Iraqi oil would bring. As Philippe Le Billon demonstrates in
his chapter, Iraq's oil sector has in fact become a deeply divisive issue
in Iraqi politics (especially between the Kurds and the central government), it has operated without an appropriate legal framework, it has
been exploited by corruption and – worst of all – the profits have not
been used to improve the lives of ordinary Iraqi citizens. While Western
profiteering from Iraqi oil may have left a bitter taste in the mouth of
both Iraqis and those in the West who opposed the war, nothing ener-
gised and galvanised anti-war sentiment as much as the shocking and
graphic photos of US military personnel torturing Iraqis at Abu Ghraib
prison. As Aloysia Brooks demonstrates in her chapter, not only were
the brutal images stingingly ironic in that the Coalition had in part justified its war by promising to end Saddam Hussein's brutal regime, but
they also put the lie to the notion that the Coalition were liberating the
Iraqi people in the interests of freedom, justice and democracy.

Part II ('Iraqi Politics since Saddam') sheds light on the complex political landscape of Iraq since the toppling of the Baathist regime in 2003.
In his chapter, Benjamin Isakhan documents that, in addition to Nouri
al-Maliki's well-known strategy of ostracising and even actively targeting Sunni Arab and Kurdish politicians, he has also sought to fracture
the various Shia political entities, pitting them against one another so
that he maintains the veneer of stability and secular nationalism in contrast to his avowedly religious and endlessly bickering Shia Arab opponents. Following on, Liam Anderson examines the complex trajectories
of Kurdish politics since 2003 with an emphasis on the problematic legacy of the 2005 Iraqi constitution, which was hastily designed under US
tutelage but which has left the issue of regional autonomy and federalism
open to huge variations in interpretation, causing great friction between
the KRG and Baghdad. As Ronen Zeidel documents in his chapter, the
toppling of the Sunni-dominated Baathist government in 2003 and
the subsequent Shia Arab and Kurdish power grabs has left the Sunnis
at the political margins. This sequence of events has fostered a growing
Sunni resentment of the central government and left an entire segment of
the population susceptible to the promises of religious zealots and violent fundamentalists such as ISIS. Similar marginalisation has confronted

Iraq's 'ultra-minorities', such as the smaller numbers of Turkmens, Assyrians, Chaldeans, Yazidis, Sabaeans and others. As Nicholas Al-Jeloo suggests in his chapter, these smaller groups have been routinely caught in the cross-fire since 2003 and are the subjects of sustained oppression and active persecution. They have also, like the Sunnis, been marginalised by the US imposed model of democracy and by a newly empowered elite who care little for Iraq's rich and delicate cultural mosaic.

Part III ('The Plight of Iraqi Culture and Civil Society') looks more deeply into this rich cultural mosaic by examining the consequences of the Iraq War for civil society, women and cultural heritage. Here, Benjamin Isakhan examines Iraq's largest workers' union, the Iraqi Federation of Oil Unions, and argues that, despite difficult circumstances and oppressive measures, it has served as one of the few bulwarks against a return to authoritarianism. In their chapter, Perri Campbell and Luke Howie focus on the plight of Iraqi women since the 2003 war. In the face of a host of difficulties, many Iraqi women turned to the internet and wrote detailed blogs which revealed an alternative, feminist vision of the Iraq War that highlighted the irony of a military intervention premised on democracy and freedom but that largely ignored women's rights. A similarly devastating legacy of the Iraq War has been the systematic looting and destruction of Iraq's rich cultural heritage. In her chapter for this volume, Diane C. Siebrandt focuses specifically on the use of fragile archaeological sites such as the ancient city of Babylon as major US military bases. Her chapter not only documents the damage done at such sites but also argues that when such sites were converted into military bases, the US effectively turned once-popular public spaces into zones of exclusion, thereby contravening the basic human right of Iraqis to access their own heritage.

The final section of this book, Part IV ('Regional and International Consequences of the Iraq War'), begins with a chapter by Howard Adelman that documents both the internal and external displacement of Iraqis since the onset of the war and relates their plight today – amounting to one of the largest people movements in modern history with profound effects for the demography and social landscape of Iraq, as well as its neighbours. The legacy of the Iraq intervention for its neighbours is the focus of Ranj Alaaldin's chapter, which examines the ripple effect it has had across the Middle East. The particular focus of Alaaldin's chapter is the extent to which Iraq's sectarian in-fighting has spilled across borders and had a direct and tangible effect on the civil war in Syria. Taking a much broader approach, Binoy Kampmark discusses the legacy of the Iraq War for the doctrine of humanitarian intervention and the extent to which the war brought into question its logic and popularity in international affairs. Kampmark's critique highlights the fact that notions of humanitarian intervention (and especially 'responsibility to protect') have in fact achieved renewed vigour in the wake of Iraq, which has been retrospectively understood as an intervention that underemphasised the humanitarian dimension. Finally, Joseph A. Camilleri examines the legacy of the Iraq War for two further global concerns, which he refers to as the 'globalisation of insecurity' and the 'limits to empire.' Underpinning his sophisticated analysis is an examination of the extent to which the Iraq War in fact served to strengthen the enemies of the US and created a less secure global environment. Paradoxically, the US also saw their economy falter during the war, giving way to rising cynicism about their status as a super-power and leaving them isolated with few supporters and little legitimacy even in the eyes of Coalition partners.

The chapters presented as part of this collection are underpinned by a unifying argument: that the Iraq War not only failed to deliver on its key promises to the Iraqi people but also had a series of very specific consequences for Iraq, for the region and for the world that have been underacknowledged. To demonstrate this, each chapter approaches the issue from a different perspective and draws upon different sets of empirical data, all of which point to the complex legacies of the Iraq War and the ways in which they have been actively marginalised or slowly forgotten in public, policy and political discourse. Threaded through each of the chapters are implicit questions about the political responsibilities and moral obligations of those who undertook the war and promised so much to the Iraqi people.

While there is no way to avoid the fact that the Iraq War has left behind a set of complicated and problematic legacies, the ultimate purpose of this volume is to apply fresh thinking to the many challenges that plague Iraq today and to identify new opportunities towards creating a peaceful and democratic future. In doing so, this volume hopes to move intellectual enquiry, political debate and pragmatic policy-making one step closer to fulfilling the promises of the intervention itself – to encourage peace, democracy and prosperity in Iraq. We owe the Iraqi people that much at least.

Note

1. In total, thirty-six countries participated in the 'Coalition of the Willing' in Iraq but, aside from the four countries mentioned, their troops arrived after the initial battle phase of the war.

Part I
The Aftermath of War: Strategic Decisions and Catastrophic Mistakes

Chapter 1

The De-Baathification of post-2003 Iraq: Purging the Past for Political Power

Benjamin Isakhan[1]

Following the toppling of the Baathist regime, in May 2003 the United States established the Coalition Provisional Authority (CPA), which was to serve as the occupational authority and interim government of Iraq under the leadership of Lewis Paul Bremer III. Despite the fact that Iraq had just endured a spectacular military defeat, the death of untold thousands of civilians and the devastation of much of its civil infrastructure and was in the grip of lawlessness and disorder, Bremer's foremost concern as head of the CPA was to de-Baathify Iraq. Indeed, Bremer's first official act was to issue Order Number 1: De-Baathification of Iraqi Society, written only three days after his arrival in Baghdad. The order sought to disestablish the Baath party by 'eliminating the party's structures and removing its leadership from positions of authority and responsibility in Iraqi society' (Bremer 2003a: 1). Specifically, this order prescribed the wholesale exclusion from public service of individuals who had occupied any of the four uppermost membership levels of the Baath.

A week later, on 23 May, Bremer continued the de-Baathification effort with Order Number 2: Dissolution of Entities, which ordered the dismissal of thousands of Iraqis from paid employment and the disbanding of several key Baathist institutions. This included important ministries, every arm of Iraq's extensive military machine, certain bureaucratic and governmental mechanisms, and even seemingly innocuous bodies like the National Olympic Committee (Bremer 2003b: 4–5). Two days later, Bremer issued two further edicts that supported this process of de-Baathification. The second of these was titled Order Number 5: Establishment of the Iraqi De-Baathification Council, which created an entity that was to be officially responsible for overseeing the de-Baathification of Iraq. This body was to be made up entirely of Iraqi nationals hand picked by Bremer, and headed by a controversial Shia Arab Iraqi exile who had provided suspect information to the US in the lead up to the intervention, Ahmed Chalabi.

During the first months of the occupation, the De-Baathification Council (DBC) was charged with advising the CPA about individual Baath party members as well as investigating 'the extent, nature, locations and current status of all Iraqi Baath Party property and assets' (Bremer 2003c: 2). Under Chalabi's leadership, however, the DBC implemented the CPA's de-Baathification programme in a hardline and uncompromising fashion, even adding additional tasks to its remit beyond what the CPA had stipulated. For example, while Order Number 1 had maintained a verifiable framework relating to party rank and government position, the DBC went as far as excluding those who were simply accused of crimes during the period of the Baath. By late 2003, even the CPA realised things were getting out of hand, but attempts to curtail the witch-hunt-like activities of the DBC were only partially successful. In January 2004 the Iraqi Governing Council (13 July 2003–1 June 2004), which governed Iraq under the jurisdiction of the CPA, changed the name of the DBC to the Higher National De-Baathification Commission (HNDC) and began eradicating certain organisations which had been associated with the former regime, such as trade guilds and private-sector companies (Hatch 2005: 105).

These early efforts to de-Baathify Iraq – and the fact that they were so central to the beginnings of governance beyond the former regime – left behind one of the most complex and troubling legacies of the Iraq War. It is important to note that the de-Baathification project was conceived by Bremer in consultation with a handful of leading neo-conservatives who were determined to oust the quasi-socialist Baathist state and to demonstrate not only their military might, but also that their model of free-market democracy was the ultimate form of human governance (Pfiffner 2010). These neo-conservatives found natural allies in several high-profile Iraqi expatriates, especially Shia Arabs such as Chalabi, who had long urged the US to end Saddam's dictatorship and his sectarian policies with a view to creating a more democratic and egalitarian Iraq. The plan was loosely based on earlier transitions from tyrannical rule to democracy after major military operations such as the de-Nazification of Germany after the Second World War (Porch 2003). As with de-Nazification, the US not only prescribed a formal legal apparatus for ousting the Baath (as above), but also ensured that justice was served on some of the most senior members of the former regime via public war crimes tribunals – most spectacularly the televised trial of Saddam Hussein throughout 2006.

In drawing inspiration from de-Nazification, however, the US had failed to learn critical lessons from several subsequent post-conflict environments of the second half of the twentieth century (Stover et al. 2005).

In the most successful cases, transitions to democracy were underpinned not only by strict laws to oust the former regime and public trials for senior members, but also by various forms of a truth and reconciliation commission (Humphrey 2002). While such bodies varied according to their respective context, they shared the principle that the only way to move beyond the tyranny and violence of the past was to establish an open forum in which all sides shared their 'truth' under amnesty and with a view to fostering reconciliation and social cohesion. However, neither the CPA nor subsequent Iraqi governments implemented such a process in Iraq (al-Marashi & Keskin 2008). The people of Iraq were not given any opportunity to deal with the traumas inflicted on the populace by the Baath and to address the divergent public narratives of suffering and remembrance.

The choice of de-Baathification over a potentially lengthy and emotive truth-and-reconciliation process in Iraq has had a host of unintended, immediate and devastating consequences. It not only failed to address deep sectarian divides that widened rapidly after 2003 and which have left Iraq on the brink of civil war ever since, it also marginalised the Sunni Arab population, who had ruled the modern nation state of Iraq since its founding in 1921; it forced thousands into unemployment and poverty; it prevented experienced bureaucratic and administrative, as well as dedicated security, personnel from helping to stabilise Iraq; it ousted functioning, if sluggish, institutions such as the judiciary, state media and public oversight bodies that might have helped build Iraq's new democracy; it saw the destruction of an entire epoch of state-produced murals, statues and symbols; and it brought about the disbanding of every tier of the Iraqi army, which in turn created an immediate upsurge in violence (Barakat 2005; Hatch 2005; Isakhan 2011b; El-Khawas 2008). More recently, several studies have noted that Iraq's de-Baathification also played directly into the hands of Iraq's Kurdish and especially Shia political authorities, who had both been routinely marginalised and actively persecuted by the former Sunni-dominated regime. This is particularly true of the Shia Arabs, who have been accused of utilising de-Baathification as a 'sectarian instrument wielded to prevent the Sunnis from participating in political life' (Sissons & al-Saiedi 2013: 17).

Thus, while de-Baathification was initially designed to rigidly preclude the former regime from participating in the mechanics of the state, over time it has become a flexible tool, unevenly applied by those who wield it. In terms of links to the former regime, de-Baathification has been passionately invoked against political opponents who may have had only the most tenuous connection to the Baath, while at the same time being routinely deployed in a sectarian manner – to marginalise and persecute members of the Sunni Arab minority even if their personal links to the Baath are limited, while Shia politicians who are known to have been active members of the former regime have been left unscathed. However, as this chapter demonstrates, such inconsistent application of de-Baathification cannot easily be distilled down to claims of political favouritism or blatant sectarianism. Instead, de-Baathification has become part of a broader political landscape of complex, overlapping and often shifting loyalties and personal political aspirations. This is broadly consistent with sociological patterns reported in Iraq in the twentieth century, where scholars such as Hanna Batatu and Nikolaos van Dam identified apparently Sunni sectarian loyalty as more parochial local, tribal or personal loyalty (Batatu 1978; Dam 1980).

In addressing the broader de-Baathification question at the intersection between politics and law in post-2003 Iraq this chapter outlines the efforts by Iraqi lawmakers to codify de-Baathification in Iraq's new constitution of 2005 as well as in subsequent pieces of more detailed legislation. The chapter then goes on to study the actual implementation of these laws in relation to the Iraqi parliamentary elections of 2010 and 2014, as well as the local elections of 2013. Throughout the chapter, special emphasis is given to the considerable discrepancies between the principles enshrined in the formal de-Baathification legislation and the way those principles are applied in practice. Finally, this chapter concludes by suggesting that Iraq needs to openly and honestly deal with its Baathist past if it is ever to move beyond patterns of political sectarianism, violence and autocracy.

The Legal Framework of De-Baathification

Following the election of January 2005, the Iraq Transitional Government (May 2005–May 2006), led by Prime Minister Ibrahim al-Jaafari, designed and ratified the Iraqi constitution in October 2005. The document enshrined the principles of de-Baathification with reference to key political positions, with Article 7 outlawing the party in all its manifestations. Surprisingly, given its context and timing, Article 7 of the constitution proved more lenient than one might expect. It makes clear that mere membership of the Baath does not constitute a crime. It also requires that Iraqi members of parliament must have 'quit the defunct Party ten years prior to its fall, in case [s]he was a member of the dissolved Baath Party' (Iraqi Constitution 2005: 134:3:C). In other words, the possibility of a former Baath party member holding a seat in the parliament was acknowledged by the framers of the Iraqi constitution. Despite the relative leniency of the constitution, hardliners such as Chalabi made a concerted effort to use the de-Baathification process against aspiring political opponents in the lead up to Iraq's 15 December 2005 parliamentary elections. An important key distinction between this and later elections was that the Iraq Higher Electoral Commission (IHEC) successfully stood up against pressure from HNDC efforts to ban candidates with loose affiliations to the former regime (Sissons & al-Saiedi 2013).

The December 2005 elections led to the formation of a new Iraqi government under the leadership of Prime Minister Nouri al-Maliki in May 2006. Very early in Maliki's incumbency – partly as a result of US concerns about the lack of progress in accommodating disgruntled Sunni Arabs with ties to the Baath – the issue of reframing de-Baathification came to the fore. This led to an attempt to move emphasis away from de-Baathification as the central thrust of the program – mostly because it had become synonymous with 'de-Sunnification'. The HNDC was rebranded as the Higher National Commission for Accountability and Justice (typically referred to in English as the Accountability and Justice Commission, AJC). The AJC continued under the leadership of Ali al-Lami, a prominent Shia politician with close ties to Iran, although Chalabi continued to play an active role. Under their leadership the AJC drafted the Accountability and Justice Law (AJL) and, after eighteen months of political wrangling within the Iraqi parliament, it came into effect in January 2008 (Sissons 2008). The AJL reversed several of the harsher elements of de-Baathification such as allowing some military personnel previously excluded to re-enter the Iraqi Security Forces (ISF) (Fantappie 2013: 7). Also, in moves similar to the CPA orders of 2003, the rule barring former Baath members from government service regardless of Baath membership rank was abolished, and some low-level Baath members were allowed to return to service everywhere except in key security and intelligence positions (Law of the Supreme National Commission for Accountability and Justice 2010). Overall, the AJL saw the parameters of exclusion based on Baath party affiliation shift in a more liberal direction.

De-Baathification at the 2010 Parliamentary Election

The first big test for the implementation of the new, more liberal AJL of 2008 came during the run-up to the parliamentary poll held on 7 March 2010. At this time, the two leaders of the AJC – Lami and Chalabi – were both candidates and part of the Iraq National Alliance (INA), the major Iran-sponsored pan-Shiite umbrella coalition headed by former PM Jaafari. Despite this serious conflict of interest, Lami and Chalabi had no qualms in unleashing a major push to exclude candidates with links to the Baath, including key political opponents. In January 2010, two months ahead of the election, the IHEC published a list containing the names of 511 election candidates disqualified by the AJC. Of these, 182 had belonged to the secret and special security agencies of the old regime, 216 had been members of the Baath, 105 were recipients of various medals of honour (including the prestigious Mesopotamia Order), five had participated in repressing the 1991 anti-Saddam intifada following the Gulf War, while three were described as 'propagandists' in favour of the Baath.

There were several problems with the list of banned candidates. Firstly, it is clear that the list represented an attempt by the AJC to ignore the new AJL and instead revert to the hardliner guidelines of the 2003–5 period. Closer scrutiny of the initial batch of 511 names indicated several contraventions of the 2008 AJL, such as the exclusion of candidates who were past low-level Baath members. Additionally, the AJC also put pressure on the IHEC to exclude some fifteen political blocs on the basis of unspecified ties to the Baath (Ottaway & Kaysi 2010b). This included an initial attempt to ban the Iraqi Front for National Dialogue, the party of the prominent Sunni politician Saleh al-Mutlaq. In effecting these draconian measures, the AJC relied less on the AJL and more on a 2004 CPA order that gave the IHEC the power to decide on matters of political party exclusion – even though it had been superseded by subsequent laws (Visser 2010: 226–38).

Secondly, the list prompted immediate criticism from both Western analysts and Iraqi politicians, who claimed that it framed the election as a sectarian contest with a clearly anti-Sunni agenda (Katzman 2010: 10–11). What the list actually showed was a far more complex, yet typically Iraqi, picture. There is no denying that the list contained mostly Sunni names and explicitly targeted the Sunni- and secular-dominated blocs. Together, former PM Iyad Allawi's secular- and Sunni-dominated bloc, the Iraq National Movement (INM or al-Iraqiyya), and the political bloc representing key Sunni tribes, the Unity Alliance of Iraq (Wassat), accounted for a third of all exclusions. Additionally, in their cases, it was often top candidates in key constituencies that were struck from the blocs. These parties were followed by other, smaller secular parties that also experienced problems disproportionate to their size. There were, in fact, eight lists about which little is known other than that they had a secular and/or nationalist orientation. Some of them, with a particular strength in Sunni tribal areas, accounted for another third of the list of those banned from the election. Geographically speaking, the patterns of discrimination seem clear, with Sunni-dominated provinces such as Anbar, Salahaddin and

Kirkuk targeted in a way that was disproportionate to their population size, while the Shia-dominated provinces south of Baghdad were left comparatively untouched.

However, Shiite and Kurdish candidates were also banned. Notably, Maliki's State of Law Coalition (SLC) suffered a few high-level casualties, as did the INA, who controlled the whole process. Both parties had candidates banned, but it is noteworthy that most bans applied to low-level candidates or to those from governorates dominated by other parties (such as the banning of INA candidates in Kurdish-dominated governorates). It is therefore reasonable to assume these bans were implemented less for de-Baathification purposes and more to counter claims that the entire effort was motivated by sectarianism.

A third significant problem was that this round of aggressive electoral de-Baathification was enthusiastically endorsed by most Shia factions, despite the lack of a legal basis. Indeed, some Shia politicians were at the forefront of widespread ad-hoc de-Baathification measures in the Iraqi provinces, beginning with a heated public debate about the appropriate response of the Shia to the legacy of the Baath. This soon led to anti-Baathist politicians as well as government officials implementing their own private agendas for the appropriate punishment of past Baathists, which developed into full-blown witch hunts in several governorates south of Baghdad. These included attempts to disarm people suspected of links to the Baath, the physical expulsion of past Baath party members from entire governorates, and other kangaroo court measures. Even Maliki's SLC eventually joined this descent into lawlessness, posing a major contradiction given Maliki's relatively moderate attitude to many Baathists in the armed forces and the judiciary during his expansion of power after 2008 and the SLC's non-sectarian platform of national unity at the 2010 election (Dodge 2012b).

A fourth and final problem was that the actions of the AJC met with very little resistance. Unlike in the December 2005 elections, when the IHEC had put up some resistance to the banning of candidates, by 2010 the IHEC was relatively weak and did not challenge the decisions of the AJC. The Iraqi judiciary did attempt to offer a counterweight in the shape of a special appeals court for de-Baathification cases as well as a special electoral judicial council, but this proved ineffective. It is also worth noting that the international community, and in particular the US and the United Nations Mission in Iraq (UNAMI), generally turned a blind eye to the enormous infractions of due process during the de-Baathification witch hunts. Instead of posing critical questions, both the US ambassador in Iraq at the time, Chris Hill, and the Dutch head of UNAMI, Ad Melkert, issued what amounted to clean bills of health at critical junctures, effectively rubber-stamping the hardline approach of the AJC.

When the US eventually put pressure on Iraq to lift the ban on former Baathists, the Iraqi Appeals Court acquiesced on 3 February 2010, causing Shia factions to respond furiously and Moqtada al-Sadr, a prominent Shia religious and political figure, to denounce it as 'a betrayal of the people and the blood which poured in Saddam's era and after the occupation' (cited in Cogan 2010). Maliki went even further, claiming that Iraq would not bow to US pressure. He insisted that the US were interfering in the national elections, which a Maliki spokesman described as 'illegal and unconstitutional' (cited in Cogan 2010). Maliki then used his executive powers to demand that Iraq's highest judicial authorities come to a decision and called a special parliamentary session to make sure the decision was enforced ('Maliki won't allow,' 2010). Eventually, on 12 February 2010 – less than a month before the election – the IHEC confirmed that a total of 458 candidates had effectively been barred from participating (AFP 2010; Mohammed 2010). Despite this final decision by IHEC, however, the AJC continued in its efforts, sending cases of potential disqualifications to IHEC just days before the elections. As late as 4 March 2010, sources in the AJC said they had written to IHEC to have the name of a candidate from the SLC in Najaf struck from the ballot paper.

Overall, the de-Baathification measures of 2010 were driven not so much by systematic and overt sectarianism or partisanship as by despotism, albeit clearly with the ulterior aim of perpetuating a sectarian political atmosphere. The basic problem was the attempt by the AJC to portray its decisions as 'legal' and 'constitutional' when they clearly were not – and the failure of the rest of the 'democratic' system in the new Iraq (or for that matter the international community) to offer any meaningful resistance.

Nonetheless, the elections went ahead as planned on 7 March 2010 and, despite the ban of many of its key candidates, Allawi's secular-Sunni al-Iraqiyya won the greatest number of seats (91) and Maliki's SLC came a close second (89), followed by Jaafari's Shia-dominated INA (70) ('Legislative Election of 7 March' 2010). However, none of these coalitions had won the 163 seats needed to form a government in the 325-member parliament. Despite having narrowly lost the election, both the SLC and the INA were determined to cling to power. To achieve this goal, a renewed de-Baathification effort was launched immediately after the election. The JAC once again attempted obvious infractions of the AJL in their quest to ban candidates somehow linked to Saddam's regime, forcing them to forfeit their seats (Ottaway & Kaysi 2010d). The damage was done, however, and the process of de-Baathification had significantly undermined Allawi's chances of forming a government. Iraq's political deadlock was only finally resolved in December 2010 when, despite having narrowly lost the election, Maliki managed to retain the position of PM.

A few months later, in May 2011, the head of the AJC, Lami, was assassinated in eastern Baghdad. Maliki then appointed his close ally Shia al-Sudani, the Shia minister for human rights, as head of the AJC, a position he held until the election of Falah Hasan al-Shanshul, another prominent Shia politician and a member of Sadr's political party. With Shanshul at the helm of the AJC and Maliki returned for a second term, the Iraqi government continued its aggressive de-Baathification campaign, using it primarily to target the minority Sunni population. Indeed, by December 2012, Iraq's Sunnis had a long list of grievances that included their political marginalisation since 2003, the continuing de-Baathification, including the use of the JAL to prevent Sunni politicians from competing in the 2010 election, mass unemployment, insufficient infrastructure and public services, the arrest and detention of thousands of Sunnis without trial, the overly harsh treatment of female prisoners and – most dramatically – the issuing of arrest warrants and later death sentences for high-profile Sunni politicians, including Vice President Tariq al-Hashemi and Iraq's finance minister, Rafie al-Issawi. From 21 December 2012, growing outrage at the Maliki government's actions triggered mass social unrest in the Sunni-dominated Anbar province. Although these protests gradually descended into the 'Anbar crisis' that began in late 2013, in which Sunni militias of various shades were pitted against the ISF, it is important to note that the initial impetus behind these protests had centred around calls for the annulment of the AJL and the ousting of Maliki.

To address these concerns, Maliki set up a high-level committee headed by his long-time Shia political ally Hussein al-Shahristani, deputy Prime Minister and minister for energy. Under Shahristani's orders, Shanshul received new directives to return 4,200 seized properties and pay nearly 3,000 pensions annulled by the AJC (Sadah 2013b). By March 2013 the Iraqi government had sought to address further inequities dealt out under the auspices of the AJC and in early April they approved a draft law amending the AJL (Sadah 2013a). Nonetheless the protests continued – in part because it was very difficult to gauge the sincerity of these initiatives and whether they could reverse the systemic effort to ostracise Iraq's Sunni population.

De-Baathification at the 2013 Provincial Elections

In mid-February 2013, in the lead up to the 20 April provincial elections, Shanshul sought to use the AJL to oust Chief Justice Midhat al-Mahmoud, head of the Supreme Court and a key Maliki ally. The move was clearly a political one, as Maliki had come to rely heavily on the senior judge and had been able to influence him to make several key decisions in Maliki's favour. Maliki immediately reacted by sending an official letter to the AJC stipulating the dismissal of Shanshul and appointing a temporary replacement, even though the commission was ostensibly an independent oversight body and Shanshul had been elected to the role by the AJC's members (Sadah 2013c, 2013e). Although Shanshul eventually returned to his post after his reinstatement was approved by the Iraqi parliament in July 2013, he had learned the hard way that de-Baathification was not a neutral law to be applied evenly, it was a political tool to be used at the government's discretion and to undermine or oust opponents of the Maliki government (Visser 2013a).

It is therefore not surprising that one of the key differences between the application of de-Baathification before the 2010 election and its application ahead of the 2013 election is that in the latter instance Maliki's SLC was virtually untouched by the AJC. The SLC only had a problem with a single candidate in Basra who was initially suspended and then reinstated after an appeal. Otherwise, the extent to which de-Baathification affected the different political entities and geographical regions of Iraq reveals a pattern that is remarkably similar to that seen in 2010 (Visser 2013b). In terms of party allegiances, the Shiite Islamists and Kurds generally had fewer problems with de-Baathification than their Sunni counterparts. In the Shia heartland south of Baghdad, there was virtually no de-Baathification at all after the witch hunt staged during the months prior to the 2010 parliamentary election had ousted any hopeful candidates with Baath party affiliations. The few cases of Shia de-Baathification that did occur happened in the Kurdish-dominated north – in governorates where the Shia parties did not stand to win key sets. It is also worth noting that the few cases of excluded Shia candidates were far down on their respective electoral lists and may have related to sloppy documentation and oversight by the party leadership.

On the other hand, the secular and Sunni-dominated parties were represented disproportionately among the entities targeted for de-Baathification. Indeed, the overwhelming bulk of de-Baathification cases were from the Sunni-majority areas as well as Baghdad, with Nineveh taking the biggest share of the total. In terms of Sunni or secular parties, al-Iraqiyya stood out, accounting for the lion's share of all de-Baathification cases, with many of their top candidates eliminated from the electoral lists in what amounted to a highly symbolic move against their leadership. For example, al-Iraqiyya splinter groups such as parliament speaker Osama al-Nujaifi's Mutahidoun (United) block and Deputy prime Minister Saleh al-Mutlaq's Arab al-Iraqiyya, did suffer some discrimination against their candidates. They did, however, have some success in their appeals, including the reinstatement of Arab al-Iraqiyya's top candidate in Baghdad and Mutahidoun's number three in Nineveh. However, Allawi's mainline al-Iraqiyya list did not share these successful reinstatements – despite appeals its top candidate in Anbar, its number five in Nineveh and its number six in Karbala were all excluded. Conversely, the National White bloc, a Shia-dominated breakaway group from al-Iraqiyya, which ran as part of Maliki's SLC and was headed by Shia politician Hassan Alawi, did not experience any nomination trouble at all.

As with the 2010 elections, the banning of candidates with alleged links to the Baath party defies easy categorisation. On the one hand, the 2013 effort was clearly more sectarian in nature, while on the other, if the AJL had been applied evenly there would probably have been greater numbers of disqualifications on both sides among both Sunnis and Shiites. Many ex-Baathists of either sect were probably able to run thanks to *wasta* (informal patronage) rather than fulfilment of the judicial requirements. This certainly implies that de-Baathification is being manipulated by a Shia-dominated Iraqi political elite determined not only to oust political opponents and wage a sectarian campaign, but also to privilege their political comrades regardless of their ties to the former regime.

De-Baathification at the 2014 Parliamentary Election

By December 2013 the unrest in Anbar, which had emerged initially in response to general Sunni marginalisation and suffering and evolved into a protest against the continued attack on senior Sunni political figures such as Hashemi and Issawi, had been crippling Iraq for a year. The situation descended rapidly into a complex series of skirmishes between the ISF and the various terrorist cells and tribal networks of Anbar and other-Sunni dominated regions. This meant that by the parliamentary elections of 30 April 2014, the ISF had lost territory and suffered heavy casualties (Abbas 2014b, 2014c). Perhaps because of this mounting crisis, de-Baathification was less prominent at these elections than at either the 2010 or the 2013 campaigns. While heated debate about the legacy of the former Baathist regime and candidates' affiliations with that regime had been the primary driver of disqualifications during the previous two elections, the focus was now split between de-Baathification and whether candidates were of 'good reputation' (Visser 2014c). This dual focus reflected the fact that, according to recent amendments to Iraqi electoral law, all prospective candidates must 'be of good conduct and shall not be convicted for a dishonourable crime' (cited in Abbas 2014a). However, it remained unclear exactly what constituted either 'good conduct' or a 'dishonourable crime', how these ought to be measured and the extent to which the law was to be applied to potential candidates.

The interpretation of the 'good reputation' clause brought about a dispute between the parliament and the IHEC (which deals with such requirements in the first instance) over how it ought to be applied to electoral candidates. Instead of drafting new, clearer laws and attempting to pass them through a divided parliament, various MPs decided to issue their own interpretation of the clause. They sought to prohibit the IHEC from excluding any candidate who had not yet been found guilty of an alleged crime (Hasan 2014a). This was a clever move as, due to Iraq's complex and sluggish judicial system and MPs' immunity, few existing candidates would be banned. The Iraqi parliament lacked the constitutional authority to limit the powers of the independent IHEC, which simply ignored the parliament's interpretation. At the same time, and probably under influence from Maliki's office, the Electoral Judicial Committee, an affiliate of the IHEC, issued what they deemed an unchallengeable edict outlining their interpretation of the law. Consequently, some MPs and many candidates were disqualified from running in the elections. In total around 400–500 candidates were initially excluded by the AJC because of their ties to the former regime, while the IHEC delisted a further seventy candidates because they failed to fulfil the 'good reputation' requirement. Unsurprisingly, many of the banned candidates reacted by filing a case with the Iraqi Supreme Court and some fifty-two candidates were subsequently reinstated during the appeals process. These cases of banning and then reinstating certain candidates are particularly interesting for studying the question of political influences over administrative and judicial processes in the 'new Iraq'.

Most revealing of all is the way in which the 'good reputation' clause was cleverly manipulated by Maliki's office. Initially, the amendments to Iraqi electoral law were designed by Maliki's opponents in the lead up to the election in the hope that they could be used against him and his affiliates (Visser 2014a). Nonetheless, Maliki was able to capitalise on the situation, moving beyond his earlier strategy of blatantly employing de-Baathification to oust prominent Sunnis and other opponents, to use the 'good reputation' clause in an attempt to disqual-ify several candidates who were all vocal critics of his regime. These included prominent Sunnis such as Issawi (Mutahidoun), the former minister for higher education and scientific research Abd Diab al-Ojaili (Al-Iraqiyya) and vocal Sunni secularist Mithal al-Alusi (of the small secularist and communist bloc the Civil Democratic Alliance), and also prominent Shia members of al-Iraqiyya such as Haider al-Mulla. Other Shia politicians were also marginalised, including Jawad al-Shahyla and Sabah al-Saadi – two prominent members of Sadr's al-Ahrar bloc who had also served as members of the independent corruption watch-dog, the Parliamentary Integrity Commission. What all of these indi-viduals had in common was not their sect or political affiliation, but their active and public criticism of the Prime Minister (Niqash Special Correspondent 2014). Maliki's hand in the banning of candidates based on the 'good reputation' clause becomes especially clear in the case of Sunni politician Mishan al-Jubouri (a member of Mutlaq's al-Arabiyya coalition). Jubouri was initially ousted under the 'good reputation' clause because he faced charges of corruption and financial support for terrorism. However, the charges were acquitted under review, most likely because Mutlaq had reconciled with Maliki (Hasan 2014b).

As with the 2010 and 2013 elections, those excluded from the 2014 election under the de-Baathification programme and via the 'good repu-tation' clause defy the easy black-and-white classification so popular with the Western media. Neither de-Baathification nor 'good reputation' can be reduced to simple sectarianism by proxy, nor can they be seen to have exclusively affected the Sunni Arab minority because of its ties to the former regime. In fact, the ousting of candidates in 2014 crossed geographical, sectarian and party lines, as did their reinstatement. To the extent that some parties stood out for being targeted disproportion-ately, it is true that the Sunni-secular parties were predominant. It is also clear, however, that Sunni-secular politicians in many cases managed to seek legal redress for what was perceived as political targeting by Shiite Islamist circles.

Conclusion

Of the manifold legacies left behind by the US in Iraq, the CPA's deci-sion to rapidly de-Baathify Iraq without a substantive parallel truth and reconciliation campaign ranks among the most problematic and troublesome. In the hands of the new Shia-dominated government, de-Baathification has become a highly politicised tool that has been used to undermine political opponents, privilege allies and isolate

Sunnis from the state – often irrespective of actual connections to the former regime. There is more than a little irony in the fact that de-Baathification – designed in Washington to end authoritarian rule underpinned by sectarianism – has been manipulated by Maliki's increasingly dictatorial government not only to marginalise Sunnis and remove them from positions of influence, but also as a part of his broader campaign to undermine his political opponents, centralise power and prolong his incumbency (Dodge 2012b).

In addition the above analysis of de-Baathification in relation to the three Iraqi elections between 2010 and 2014 also reveals how capriciousness and the absence of due process affected all political blocs in Iraq to some extent and did not discriminate among sects in the way many outsiders claim. Indeed, de-Baathification has affected people across the board in Iraq, with both unsuspecting allies of the incumbent government and major Shiite Islamist blocs sometimes subjected to it. This is not surprising given the complex political history of Iraq where sect, patronage, tribe and personal ambition constitute an intricate matrix of ever-shifting political allegiances – as witnessed by the fact that many Shiites were once tightly connected with the former, Sunni-dominated Baathist state.

If there is any hope for reform of the de-Baathification issue, it lies in the fact that many Iraqi politicians from all sides of politics remain concerned about how to resolve the traumas of the past and finally put to rest the legacy of the Baath. Some advocate a softening of the AJL with respect to reinstating governmental bureaucrats and administrators along with withdrawn pensions. This, it is claimed, would play an important role in bringing about national reconciliation following the years of discord born of war and regime change. Others maintain that Iraq must utilise Article 7 of the 2005 constitution, which prescribes the drafting of an additional set of laws to address the final ousting of the Baath as well as all forms of racism and sectarianism. Work has begun on this law, but parliament has yet to pass it largely due to its sensitive nature and the fact that any perceived support for the Baath has led to political shouting matches. Until the law is passed, however, de-Baathification will remain the subject of political manipulation, sectarian discrimination, demagoguery and vigilantism. Only when Article 7 is fully implemented will Iraqis be able to effectively and finally address the question of continued government employment of Iraqis with Baathist pasts dating from the pre-2003 era.

Beyond the necessity for such a legal framework it is also imperative that Iraq learn from twentieth-century examples in which people have attempted to forge new versions of national identity and solidarity that openly engage with the traumas of the past. Such truth-and-reconciliation approaches would not only move Iraq beyond simplistic responses like total de-Baathification but also discourage reductive political ideology which emphasises schisms rather than breaks them down. If Iraq is to ever develop a unified post-Baathist national identity then it must stage a bold engagement with the sufferings of the past. This would not only create avenues of inter-community dialogue, help placate ethno-religious violence and sectarianism, and facilitate the establishment of an inclusive political order; it could also ensure that the Iraqi people are not destined to repeat a pattern of ethno-religious sectarian discrimination and violent authoritarianism.

Note

1. I am indebted to Reidar Visser for supplying a great deal of primary data for analysis and inclusion in this chapter as well as his thoughts on earlier versions.

Chapter 2
The Contested Politics of Iraq's Oil Wealth

Philippe Le Billon

The Iraq War of 2003 set in motion a series of events that was to have enormous consequences for Iraq's oil sector, its use by political factions and the distribution of its revenue to populations. The US destroyed much of the Iraqi state, turned the country towards ill-defined constitutional federalism, failed to provide a stable security environment, and pushed hard for a liberalisation of the oil sector. Within this broader context, inadequate infrastructure and legal and administrative frameworks for the management of the Iraqi oil sector have meant that recovery in oil production was slow, that much of the revenues did not benefit the population, and that major uncertainties remain over relations between the federal government and regional authorities and over the legality of contracts passed with international oil companies. These legacies will continue to affect the politics and economy of Iraq for decades to come.

On 15 February 2003, millions of people gathered in hundreds of cities around the world to oppose a US- and British-led military invasion of Iraq. Among their main slogans was 'No more blood for oil'. War, early critics argued, would bring a US-compliant regime and open up to US and British companies Iraq's massive oil wealth: the world's fifth largest oil reserves at 140 billion barrels, and potentially among the most profitable given their relatively low technical production costs (Xu & Bell 2013). Six years after the fall of Baghdad to US troops in April 2003, American and British oil companies were indeed signing major oil exploitation contracts in Iraq for increasing the production of three 'super-giant' Iraqi oil fields – Rumaila, West Qurna and Majnoon – while junior oil companies had already taken the opportunity of investing in the Kurdistan region of Iraq at the invitation of a largely autonomous regional government. Concern at a US 'oil grab' was also broadly shared within Iraq, where the oil nationalisation of the 1960s remains widely perceived as a proud historical achievement and a guarantee of future sovereignty.

As discussed in this chapter, a foreign take-over of Iraq's oil wealth and the application of neo-liberal policies – premised on the failure of statist policies, the inefficiency and corruption of the public sector, and the need for foreign capital – were at the core of the contested politics of Iraq's oil wealth (Mahdi 2007b; Muttitt 2012). But contestations extend well beyond the role of BP, Exxon, Shell, or Occidental, and whether the US invasion was indeed an 'oil grab'. Iraq's vast oil wealth is unevenly distributed territorially, and as sectarian issues grew in prominence, so did the politics of revenue distribution among the different regions. The contested politics of oil are often seen through a regionalist lens due to various interpretations of the new Iraqi constitution, approved by referendum in 2005, which sought to secure an even distribution of oil revenues to all Iraqi people. A simplistic and dangerous narrative associates the largest oil reserves with the Shiite areas of southern Iraq, and to a lesser extent with the borderlands of the Kurdish region, raising concern that Shiites and Kurds would thrive in the event of Iraq's dismemberment at the expense of the Sunnis.

Beyond regionalism is the very concrete issue of oil management and revenue spending. The Iraqi government and many foreign governments have been keen to rapidly increase oil production, hoping to turn Iraq into another 'swing state' able to sustain global economic growth and buffer price fluctuations. Many Iraqi oil experts contest this policy, preferring to see a gradual and long-term increase rather than a 'big push' that risks damaging fields and exhausting reserves within a few decades while justifying the major role now taken by foreign oil companies. If Iraq needs more reconstruction its absorptive capacity is low, especially given the initial dismemberment of its state apparatus, and high levels of insecurity and out-migration. The 'big push' is thus deepening oil dependence and raising concerns over wasteful spending, high corruption and capital flight. The long-term contestations around Iraq's oil wealth will increasingly centre on resource control by producing regional entities and the translation of this wealth into broad development for the Iraqi population, a process that has so far been greatly undermined by continued hostilities diverting monies to the security sector but also by mismanagement and corruption (al-Ali 2014).

Oil Wealth and Regional Politics

Iraq's vast oil wealth has long constituted a major dimension of its domestic, regional and international politics. Since their 'discovery' by competing British and German commercial interests in the first three decades of the twentieth century, Iraq's massive petroleum reserves and revenues have made the country both an opportunity and a threat to the region and to Western interests generally. Commercial oil discoveries exacerbated the struggle over the spoils of the Ottoman Empire, and the economic and geopolitical significance of the reserves reinforced a Western security imperative to prevent the (re)emergence of a powerful regional rival (Atarodi 2003). Oil has not only motivated Western interests in the region, but has also significantly affected the balance of power within and between regional states. The vast revenues available to states and the elites have increased inequalities in wealth and power which, despite religious or nationalist ideologies and populist economic measures, have often exacerbated internal dissent and instability.

Oil figured prominently in explanations of the US invasion of Iraq in 2003, yet it long remained a taboo subject for the US and British administration. US Secretary of Defense Donald Rumsfeld did not list Iraq's massive oil wealth among the eight reasons motivating its 'pre-emptive war' against the regime of Saddam Hussein, although his then deputy, Paul Wolfowitz, falsely argued (2003) – in light of the devastating effects of the sanctions – that the US 'had virtually no economic options with Iraq because the country floats on a sea of oil'. Despite official arguments to the contrary, Iraq was obviously a militarily weakened but economically very promising target of US intervention (Le Billon & El Khatib 2004). At the heart of the policy change on the 'Iraqi issue' were two strategic decisions. First, the Iraq 'problem' had to be solved, not simply managed as it was during the previous two US administrations. The 9/11 attacks provided the justifying context of the US strike, while false allegations of an imminent WMD threat helped to construct the justifying motive. Second, the Bush administration was prepared to push beyond the limitations imposed by international (including Arab) public opinion and the UN Security Council. The idea that the US-led forces were invading Iraq to secure oil interests was repeatedly denied by the US administration and the British government, although they rarely elaborated on the reasons why such a factor was discounted – simply asserting instead that Iraq's oil reserves would not be exploited for the United States' own purpose but 'be held in trust for the Iraqi people, to benefit the Iraqi people', as legally required from occupying powers (US Secretary of State Colin Powell, cited in Vieth 2003).

Several elements point to the place of oil interests in the motive and outcome of the war, including the preferential awarding of Iraqi-paid reconstruction and oil infrastructure rehabilitation contracts to US firms close to the administration, the cancellation or significant modification of current oil development contracts with (non-US) companies, the non-competitive awarding of contracts to US/UK oil companies, and attempts to foster the privatisation and internationalisation of the Iraqi oil sector through legal changes (BBC 2003). Yet, given the huge investments required in the Iraqi oil sector, the risks involved and potential image problems, US oil companies were unlikely to monopolise the sector. Indeed, their contracts gave access to just eight billion barrels of reserves, compared to twenty billion for UK companies, twelve billion for Chinese and about ten billion for Russian ones.

Iraq's oil wealth *per se* may not have been the primary motive of the US administration, but it 'greatly increase[d] the incentives to topple Saddam, by any means possible' (Duffield 2012: 145). From this perspective, invading Iraq and toppling Saddam Hussein meant ending the uncertainties of sanctions and raising Iraq's oil production for the benefit of US and British companies while doing so at limited cost given the expected rapid victory and an Iraqi self-funded reconstruction of the country. It also offered the prospects of bringing cheap oil to international markets, thereby increasing the profitability of Western oil companies struggling to access new reserves, and of moving beyond a containment regime based on UN sanctions. Securing a long-term partnership with the new regime of a key oil-producing country would also allow more room for manoeuvre with Saudi Arabia and Iran. Specific oil goals were to some extent reached: Iraq is producing more, while US and British oil companies are among the large 'players'. Still, US and British broader interests have been undermined, through a costly war, reputational damage and a large net benefit for some of its key economic competitors – especially China – in terms of oil supply, prices and economic competitiveness resulting from US and British investments in a military campaign rather than domestic investments. This damage, however, pales in comparison to the dramatic suffering that most Iraqis have endured since 2003.

Who Owns the Oil?

The control of Iraq's oil wealth has been disputed not only internationally, but also domestically between federal and regional authorities. Geologically, Iraq's proven oil reserves are massive, but unevenly distributed, with about 60 per cent of reserves located in the south-eastern Shiite areas around Basra and 17 per cent in the borderlands areas of the Kurdish region in the north-east (EIA 2013). Most of the production comes from super-giant fields in the Basra area in the south and Kirkuk in the north, further exacerbating regional unevenness. Historical patterns of oil revenue distribution have also privileged some populations over others, notably in Baghdad and in Sunni areas in the centre of the country. Together, these issues have left certain groups, notably the Kurds and the Shiite population in the south, with feelings of dispossession. Further oil exploration and production, and clearer rules of revenue distribution, could change this picture, but the current distribution of reserves, production and revenues has not yet fully addressed regionalist issues over resource ownership, control and revenue allocation.

Past constitutional arrangements officially sought to maintain unity and centralisation, with the Iraq interim constitution of 1970 stating in its Article 13 that 'national resources and basic means of production are owned by the People. They are directly invested by the Central Authority in the Iraqi Republic, according to exigencies of the general planning of the national economy.' Kurdish parties, which had long sought greater autonomy from Baghdad, resisted this centralisation, while some Shiite groups also suffered from past marginalisation and repression. Sectarian divides between Shia and Sunni were exacerbated by the Gulf War in 1991 and have been even more so since the US-led invasion in 2003. The 2005 constitution, with its federalist framework, its openness to decentralisation and its attempt to redress historical wrongs, has partly addressed these tensions, but paradoxically it has also exacerbated them – largely due to a lack of clarity resulting in diverging interpretations. The longest and most institutionalised identity divide separates Kurds from the rest of the Iraqi population, yet Kurds have secured a large degree of autonomy mainly through the responsibilities placed under the Kurdistan Regional Government (KRG). Shiite groups may perceive in the declaration of Prime Minister al-Maliki and his Islamist Da'wa party an insurance against Sunni dominance, while Sunni Arab groups, in turn, have expressed feelings of political and economic marginalisation (Haddad 2011). The country is increasingly torn apart as identity politics become reified and groups hope that autonomy will help them escape what they see as the failings of the federal state.

With regard to oil, Mishkat Al Moumin (2012: 413) has argued that constitutional provisions 'have created a vague and conflicting legal system that has pitted government agencies, levels of government, and religious and ethnic groups against one another, threatening the entire peacebuilding process.' Under the 2005 Iraqi constitution, oil and gas are 'owned by all the people of Iraq in all the regions and governorates' (Art. 111), suggesting that oil revenues from *all* oil fields are to be distributed to all Iraqis. In contrast, 'the management of the oil and gas extracted from *present* fields [emphasis added]' shall be undertaken by the 'federal government, with the producing governorates and regional governments' (Art. 112). Thus, other fields (whether undiscovered or undeveloped is not clear) supposedly fall under the management of regional governments and perhaps even governorates. Furthermore, this joint management is conditional upon the federal government 'distribut[ing] its revenues in a fair manner in proportion to the population distribution in all parts of the country' (Art. 112). This suggests that if the distribution is unfair, management would thereby possibly fall under the exclusive mandate of the producing governorates and regional governments, especially in light of Article 115, which states that 'priority shall be given to the law of the regions and governorates not organized in a region in case of dispute'. The revenue distribution is also determined by a special allocation for regions 'damaged' under Saddam Hussein and during recent hostilities, thereby potentially entitling Kurdish and Shiite regions to a greater share of revenues (Art. 112). Although President Bush's emphasis in 2007 on the necessity to 'share oil revenues among all Iraqis' was a foundation for a national-level sense of fairness and inclusion, the US administration had initially separated oil management and the privatisation of the oil industry – its priority – from the more 'domestic' issue of revenue distribution. The result was two separate pieces of legislation – the Oil Law and the Oil Revenue Distribution Law – progressing at different speeds and blocking each other (see below).

Some Sunni groups are concerned that this system will evolve into a federation of oil-rich and oil-poor regions privileging Kurdish and Shiite populations – a prospect antithetical not only to their economic interests but also to their preference for a unified and highly centralised Iraq based on the supposed 'golden days' of state-led Arab nationalism in the 1970s, in which the Sunni political community played the major role. Such a threat seems very tangible as regions can easily be constituted: a Kurdish region already exists, and after 2003 the Islamic Supreme Council of Iraq sought to form a Shiite region of nine provinces (Haddad 2011; Kane 2010).

The KRG indeed moved 'swiftly to develop an investor-friendly legal regime for petroleum exploration and development' (Cameron 2011: 83), using the (temporary) protection afforded by the foreign military presence and thereby avoiding possible federal military action against unwanted oil development in the Kurdish region. Federal authorities did not move militarily against such parallel development, but they leveraged their control of the pipeline network, blocked oil payments back to the KRG, and barred some companies, such as Sinopec and Exxon, from collaborating with the KRG without the authorisation of the Federal Ministry of Oil (Cameron 2011). In response, the KRG reinforced its links with Turkey by welcoming Turkish investments and setting up its own oil pipeline to Turkey to reduce leverage from Baghdad, much to the ire of the federal government. The KRG is supposed to receive 17 per cent of Iraq's federal budget, in proportion to its population – this is far more than it has generated even after the federal government authorised Kurdish oil exports. This proportion, however, has been eroding, with estimates for 2013 of only 10.4 per cent (Kurdish Globe 2013). Yet the prospect of a 'big push' in oil production in the rest of Iraq (see below) should entice the KRG to remain within this demography-based revenue distribution scheme; even if the it is hoping to boost its own production from 250,000 bpd (barrels per day) in 2013 to 2 million bpd by 2020.

What Governs the Oil Sector? Politics around the Oil Law

Not only does the 2005 Iraqi constitution lack clarity and details on the governance of oil, it also remains contentious. By 2013 specific federal-level oil legislation still had not been passed, nor had the constitution been revised to address its main points of contention. Early consideration for reforms pre-dated the 2003 invasion, with the US State Department Oil and Energy Working Group devising a draft framework for Iraq's oil policy that would rapidly open the sector to international oil companies. The framework was further refined under contracts by USAID during the administration of the Coalition Provisional Authority (CPA). In 2004, six months after the dissolution of the CPA, the Iraqi finance minister announced plans for a new oil law that would be 'very promising to the American investors ... certainly to oil companies' (US Department of State 2004). While US-hired consultants continued to work on a new oil law, the federal government officially started working on its law in May 2006, reaching Cabinet approval in July 2007 (Jiyad 2010a). Yet the Iraqi parliament – the Council of Representatives – refused to pass it. By 2009, the absence of new legislation motivated the Ministry of Oil to issue long-term service contracts to foreign oil companies (see below).

The contested politics of the 2007 draft Federal Oil and Gas Law resulted from a broad range of issues (Mahdi 2007a). These included the erosion of elected representatives' power over the oil sector; the tacit privatisation of the oil sector through production-sharing contracts fiscally advantageous to Iraqi oil corporations (IOC); the marginalisation of the national oil companies through the absence of preferential treatment over IOCs and uncertainties over continued control of fields already developed; fear in the KRG of a diminution in its control of oil should its autonomy under the constitution be reduced; the decentralisation, or even devolution, of the Ministry of Oil's extensive responsibilities to entities under the control of regional governments and oil-producing governorates – with the fear that such decentralisation reduces competence, aggravates the risk of corruption, and results in conflicts over the management of fields straddling provincial borders; the lack of comprehensiveness, with many areas of uncertainty and reference to complementary laws as yet undrafted on revenue-sharing, national oil companies and the reorganisation of the Ministry of Oil. To all of this were added allegations of grand corruption and oil theft, as well as uncertainties associated with US military withdrawal (Cameron 2011). Overall, the Oil Law has faced broad opposition, especially from Iraqi oil sector professionals, some of whom have described it as 'dysfunctional, inadequate, disadvantageous and unpatriotic' (Jiyad 2010a: 159).

While federal legislation faced broad and sustained opposition, by September 2006 the KRG had drafted its own Oil and Gas Law and had it approved by the regional parliament in August 2007 as the deadlock over the federal law became clear. The KRG based the legality of its legislation and its control of oil in the Kurdish region – including disputed areas – on Iraqi constitution articles 112 (regional co-responsibility for oil management), 115 (the priority of regional over federal legislation) and 121 (regional powers). The federal government declared these contracts – numbering about fifty by 2014 – illegal from a constitutional standpoint. Federal authorities also denounced the type of contracts passed by the KRG: production-sharing agreements (PSAs), which allocated a proportion of oil produced to investors rather than a service fee per barrel. There were also official critiques about contracts being awarded in secrecy, without public bidding and, at least initially, without content disclosure (Jiyad 2010a). The KRG was accused of giving 'away rights to oil and gas resources to foreign oil companies', although it did renegotiate the terms of contract to ensure greater control and benefits (Cameron 2011: 92; International Crisis Group 2012). Finally, there have been allegations of conflicts of interest within the KRG, as well as with former US ambassador and KRG adviser Peter Galbraith, who had strongly advocated a constitution based on a federalist 'bottom-up' system rather than regional autonomy status while being remunerated by the Norwegian oil and gas company DNO and holding a 5 per cent stake in its operations in the Kurdish region (Glanz and Gibbs 2009).

By 2014 the Federal Ministry of Oil and the Council of Ministers were in a difficult position with respect to the KRG. A legal argument against the Kurdish contracts is the need for the federal-level Council of Representatives to approve any contracts, a role that the executive branch of the government does not want to acknowledge for its own awards of long-term service contracts (LTSCs) in 2008 and 2009 (see below). The bargaining position of the KRG was bolstered by its success in attracting investments from major oil companies through generous tax incentives, the conversion of the Kurdish-controlled pipeline to Turkey from gas to oil flows, and difficulties encountered by federal authorities in getting non-KRG production and exports to grow, in part the result of deteriorating security. Prime Minister Maliki had long accommodated Kurdish interests to maintain his coalition in power. Yet, by the time of the elections in 2014, federal authorities were withholding budget transfers to the region while the KRG was committing to oil sales on the international market without Baghdad's approval, thereby heightening tensions. A legacy of the US intervention was thus even greater autonomy for the Kurdistan region of Iraq from Baghdad through the creation of a foreign-dominated oil sector.

Are IOCs Now in Control of the Oil Sector?

In 2008, and despite the absence of a new hydrocarbon law, the federal government invited foreign oil companies to invest in the country's oil sector through a first licensing round. By 2012, the federal government had offered 63 billion barrels of Iraq's proven reserves to IOCs through LTSCs, with low remuneration fees per barrel produced – an approach more within the norms of the OPEC-dominated region than the more controversial route of the PSAs followed by the KRG. This move towards relative 'foreignisation' has been broadly contested, most notably for limiting the ability of future development by the Iraqi national oil companies (INOCs), the Northern Oil Company and the Southern Oil Company. Critics argue that the Ministry of Oil created the necessity of bringing in IOCs through overambitious production targets that the INOCs could not reach, and through the 'deliberate neglect' or even impediment of INOCs and Iraqi-led development, notably through disruptive changes in management. A major legacy may thus be a weakening in or perhaps the demise of the IROCs as oil-producing companies, reducing them to a role facilitating the work of IOCs (Jiyad 2010a).

If the fees per barrel are indeed low, generally between US$1.15 and US$2, LTSCs are relatively close to PSAs. Service is not about technical assistance *per se* but about field development, and the duration of these contracts is much longer than usual – twenty years renewable for another five years, as against a worldwide average of nine years (Jiyad 2010a). Because exclusive rights are granted to all types of reservoirs and not only those already developed or identified, these contracts constitute a *de facto* concessional agreement with effective access to and control over reservoir development within the entire contracted area (Jiyad 2010a). Associated with weak relinquishment clauses, the contracts constitute for IOCs an opportunity to (speculatively) hold onto potentially lucrative fields. There is also a risk that IOCs may use their Iraqi oil assets as collateral for operations outside the country, while in turn any future overseas assets of the INOC (and more generally the Iraqi state) could be confiscated by an IOC successfully pursuing international arbitration against Iraqi partners or detrimental policy decisions by the Iraqi government. In other words, IOCs would be able to use Iraqi assets both in Iraq and abroad to pursue their interests. As such, these contracts are hybrid in nature, incorporating service contract elements with those of production-sharing contracts (Cameron 2011).

Other criticisms have included the reduced influence that Iraqi government partners in these ventures – mostly the regional oil companies and the State Oil Marketing Organisation – have over the management of the fields. Linkages with the domestic economy are not actively promoted, with contracts applying a principle of competition based on international market prices. While this may reduce cost inflation, it also reduces opportunities to support local industries and service providers that, while they may be more costly, are contributing to the broader Iraqi economy. Furthermore, the contracts have not been fully disclosed, thus generating concern about their precise implications. Many contracts also seem to have been renegotiated, with the deputy Prime Minister for energy, Hussain al-Shahristani, having confessed that 'our contracts have been very tight, perhaps the toughest the oil companies had to deal with ... We want the oil companies to make a good profit in Iraq and that is why we are willing to reconsider those contracts' (quoted in Defterios 2013).

Contracts are also legally contested as they were not approved by the Council of Representatives – with one critic noting that 'even the Ba'ath era oil and gas laws in existence required parliamentary acts to become valid' (Shafiq 2014). Moreover, currently there is not sufficient export capacity to meet production targets, and such capacity falls in part under the responsibility of the Iraqi government, which could thus be liable to pay IOCs the equivalent remuneration fees (Jiyad 2010b). Yet only the Sadrists have publicly refused these contracts, while other parties have requested to review them (Khadduri 2010). In short, although these services contracts are highly contested they have come to express the main oil policy in terms of relationships with IOCs, the role and future opportunities for Iraq's regional oil companies, and production targets.

What Production Targets?

Iraq has had by far the most volatile oil production in the world, the result of highly contested politics around its oil sector and the broader implications of three major international wars and chronic domestic civil strife. Iraq saw a very slow increase in oil production until the 1950s, partly due to British interests within the Iraq Petroleum Company that privileged production from more fully controlled assets in Iran than those in Iraq (Mitchell 2011). The war with Iran from 1980 affected Iraq's oil exploration, production and shipment, with production declining from an historical peak of 3.5 million bpd in 1979 to 0.9 million bpd in 1981. During the first years of UN sanctions following Iraq's invasion of Kuwait, nearly all exports and much production ceased, with an all-time low production of 0.3 million bpd in 1991 and gradual increases until 2001, before a decline to 1.3 million bpd in 2003 and a slow and erratic growth to 3 million bpd by 2013 (EIA 2013). In its geopolitical project to turn Iraq into an ally and 'beacon of democracy' in the region, the US administration supported plans to increase oil production from a level of roughly 2.4 million bpd in 2000 to 6 million bpd within about a decade. By 2011 the federal government still deemed it feasible to reach a production of 12 million bpd by 2017, a figure that was later reduced to 9–10 million bpd by 2020 (Salaheddin 2012).

This 'big push' approach raised several issues besides the resulting, and controversial, necessity of requiring foreign oil companies to boost production at such a rapid rate. The first issue was the long-term planning of oil production, or 'oil depletion policy', of the federal government. The current policy would see the likely exhaustion of fields within three to four decades rather than a century at lower levels of production. Some oil experts also contest the big push on a field production management profile, arguing that seeking to grow production too fast will bring an accelerated decline in oil recovery and fail to meet the optimal depletion rate for the fields (Jiyad 2010a). The second issue related to export policies and export route issues. Iraq is highly constrained by its political geography, with only a narrow and relatively shallow coastal area, and generally hostile or wary neighbours most of whom consider Iraq at best an oil competitor and at worst an historical enemy. Both oil terminals and international pipelines constrict production growth. The third issue is that of trans-border fields, twenty-four of which have been identified and fifteen are in production (Uqaili 2008). There have already been a number of open disputes (including with Iran over the Fakka oil field), but recently dispute resolution has been prompt – in contrast to the 1980s and 1990s when Saddam Hussein used such disputes to justify in part the invasion of Kuwait. Finally, a rapid growth in Iraqi oil exports would change the landscape of the oil supply market, which, along with the shale oil boom in the US and a possible easing of sanctions on Iran, could lead to declining prices. Iraq's oil production growth is slowly changing its relationship with the other members of OPEC – which, along with oil companies, gained massively from a decade of high oil prices (in part sustained by Iraq's slow production growth) – with a possible return of Iraq to the quota system if and when production eventually reaches 4–5 million bpd (Makan & Hume 2014). Such production levels would signal, among other things, a possible end to – or at least a pause in – the long history of (often-manufactured) crises that have kept Iraq underproducing and thereby sustaining scarcity and prices for the oil industry (Mitchell 2011).

Are Iraqi People Benefiting from Their Oil Wealth?

Iraq is among the world's most oil-dependent countries, with oil constituting 60 per cent of GDP and 94 per cent of government revenues over the 2009–13 period. The sector, however, employs only 1 per cent of the population. In March 2014, Iraq's oil production came back to its 1979 historical peak. By 1980 Iraq was at war with Iran and, from then on, an even larger proportion of Iraqi people were victims rather than beneficiaries of their oil wealth. Based on IMF country statistical figures, oil revenues for the government have amounted to about US$470 billion in the decade since the US invasion, or an average of US$1,500 per person – growing from a figure of an estimated US$500 in 2003 to US$3,000 in 2012. Yet most Iraqi people have seen relatively little of that windfall. By 2007, an estimated 43 per cent of the Iraqi population lived on less than US$1 a day, with much of the poverty being due to high unemployment rates and little welfare (International Monetary Fund 2007). The mismanagement of reconstruction under the CPA, political violence, and priority spending on security and energy have meant that the daily lives of Iraqi people, at least outside the Kurdish region, have not improved.

In the first few years after the US-led invasion most of the budget was spent on salaries, but by 2012 about a third was being spent on investment, 33 per cent of which was dedicated to the oil sector. Investment in education, health, water and environment is about half of that invested in the energy sector. About 60 per cent of the government's operating budget went into civil servants' wages and benefits. The economic dominance of oil and the limits of fiscal linkages have incurred a cost on the population. Despite some progress – notably in terms of poverty reduction – by 2013 about a third of the population was still without sustainable access to safe drinking water, only half the secondary-school-age children were enrolled education, and 12 per cent of the population still lived on less than US$2.50 per day. Perhaps most striking, in the oil-rich governorate of Basra, 16 per cent lived below the poverty line and an estimated 21 per cent of the population suffered from food deprivation (Joint Analysis Policy Unit 2013; Joint Analysis Unit 2014).

There have been numerous instances of contestation over the management of oil revenues, most notably in relation to the removal of subsidies and allegations of corruption. Oil subsidies costing the government an estimated US$8 billion in lost revenues were removed between 2005 and 2007, at the express demand of the IMF and the US government as part of a debt cancellation deal – a very unpopular measure often perceived as a dispossession of the Iraqi people of their oil (Looney 2006). A second major area of contention has been corruption, which spread and increased in 2003 as a result of greater capital flows, threats against oversight agencies and the instrumentation of impunity – illicit capital flows between 2007 and 2011 alone may have amounted to US$80 billion, about a quarter of oil revenues (al-Ali 2014; Kar & LeBlanc 2013; Le Billon 2005; Looney 2008). More generally, critics have pointed at the rise of authoritarian tendencies on the part of the current federal government and, in particular, the Prime Minister, Nouri al-Maliki (Dodge 2013). Overall, Iraq's rising oil wealth has been of little benefit to the majority of its population given its continued import dependence, insecurity, low budget execution, and high levels of corruption and capital flight.

Conclusion

The US intervention in 2003 brought to an end the authoritarian rule of Saddam Hussein, but in a way that devastated and divided the country. Iraq's potential oil wealth is among the highest in the world, offering the government an opportunity to turn around its tragic history and improve the life of its population. Such an opportunity, however, not only rests on ramping up production and sustained high oil prices, it also relies on the much more difficult task of adequately managing oil revenues to broaden the scope and reach of an oil-fuelled economy. The legacy of the US intervention has been in both respects largely disastrous. A worsening of security, increased political tensions and widespread corruption, along with very slow and erratic oil production growth, have brought yet more misery for most of the people of Iraq.

In contrast with the rest of Iraq, the Kurdistan region has benefited from this intervention, further consolidating the economic and security gains made since the 'no-fly zone' was established in 1991 to secure it from Saddam's air force. The Kurdish people's own tragic history, years of experience surviving under a double-sanction regime, as well as their sense of national unity and purpose moved them away from the deadly path brought upon the rest of Iraq by the war and its legacy. The US intervention allowed the KRG to attract foreign oil companies that could provide the region with large production volumes and vast direct oil revenues. However, despite much official optimism and many impressive achievements, neither this economic windfall nor its translation into long-term and broadly shared economic benefits are much in evidence as Baghdad continues to oppose direct shipments, the economy shows signs of an unsustainable boom, inequalities are fast rising, and institutional reforms are only slowly taking place.

Most of Iraq has so far demonstrated some of the more dramatic symptoms of the so-called 'resource curse' (Le Billon 2012; Ross 2012), not least in terms of continued armed conflicts, widespread corruption, authoritarian rule and developmental underperformance. In this respect, much of the literature on the resource curse stresses the importance of strong institutions for managing windfall oil profits. One of the major legacies of the US in this respect was the dismantlement of the Iraq state apparatus and the failure to bring about effective alternative institutions. This played out in the oil sector, with neither a consolidation of the Iraqi national oil companies that could have followed a slower but perhaps more sustained growth in oil production, nor a liberalisation of the sector that would have brought greater investments by foreign oil companies. This compromise, arguably the result in large part of Iraqi domestic politics, was pragmatic, but it has so far delivered results well below Iraq's oil potential while exacerbating concerns over foreign control of the oil industry and the sub-national distribution of oil revenues. The legacies of the US intervention with respect to the oil sector have thus far been overwhelmingly negative for the Iraqi people, resulting in massive wastage and graft, the financing of a deadly civil war, and the loss of one of Iraq's major symbols of independence and status: control over some of the world's largest oil reserves.

Chapter 3
Torture at Abu Ghraib: Non-disclosure and Impunity

Aloysia Brooks

If there is any image that encapsulates the failures of the US-led invasion of Iraq, it is the pictures of the twisted and tortured men of Abu Ghraib. The image of a man standing on a small box with a black shroud across his body, hood over his face and electrical cords attached to his fingers, has now become a symbol of Western hypocrisy and injustice. There is no small irony in staging a major military intervention to 'liberate' the Iraqi people from their suffering under the Baathist regime, which included routine torture (Makiya 1998; Sassoon 2012), only to replace this regime with a military occupation that was responsible for the events at Abu Ghraib. Over a decade since the declared conclusion of the Iraq War, the Abu Ghraib prison scandal has led to adverse and far-reaching consequences, including the disintegration of international human rights standards due to the selective application of the rule of law and the breakdown in moral standing of the main governments involved in the war, and, most significantly, it has set back global strategies to prevent torture. This chapter discusses some of the long-standing social and political impacts of the torture of prisoners in Iraq by Coalition forces, and reflects on the consequences of the culture of silence and impunity that has typified torture in the so-called War on Terror. More specifically, it explores the culture of silence and non-disclosure that has led to further human rights abuses globally, including the exportation of torture techniques used at Abu Ghraib prison to different parts of the world, the increased public acceptance of torture in countries such as the US and Australia, and the marginalisation and vilification of certain groups within the global community. Finally, the chapter explores the importance of acknowledgement, transparency and accountability in relation to torture and for the broader promotion and protection of human rights and the achievement of long-standing peace in the region.

Background

The greater context of the War on Terror is integral in understanding the use of torture by Coalition forces during the Iraq War. Justification for torture was predicated on the notion that terrorism formed a 'new' type of threat, and that this 'new' nature of war meant that the ability to 'quickly obtain information' from those deemed terrorists was essential in order to protect the civilian population (Lazreg 2008: 261–2). However, while the war paradigm was set by the Bush administration post 9/11, the treatment of those detained was not in accordance with the Geneva Conventions, the binding international humanitarian protections enacted to protect both civilians and combatants in times of conflict.[1] Rather, the dichotomy of 'us and them' was firmly established in order to justify the inhumane treatment of those detained by dismantling the protections afforded to prisoners of war. Consequently, those detained in the War on Terror were placed in a separate category of humanity – on the side of the terrorists. This dangerous foundation set the scene for much of the torture that took place in Iraq.

In 2003, the Baghdad Central Confinement Facility, now more commonly known as Abu Ghraib prison, housed a growing number of detainees after a dramatic increase in Iraqi people detained by US forces, including women and children. There were several categories of prisoners: common criminals, those alleged to have committed offences against Coalition forces, and a small number of 'high-value' detainees who were detained in 'hard sites' (Hersh 2004). It was within the hard sites that much of the torture and ill-treatment was documented (Mastroianni 2013). Many of the soldiers sent to guard the prisoners had little to no experience working within a prison environment. This lack of experience, coupled with limited standard operating procedures and the pervading rhetoric of fear designating those detained as hardened criminals set on killing Americans (Gourevitch & Morris 2008), opened the way for appalling abuse.

There have been several accounts detailing the torture that took place within Abu Ghraib; however, its full extent will probably never be known. This is due to a number of factors, including the prevailing culture of non-disclosure, which sees the Obama administration continuing to withhold reports, photos and films depicting interrogations and the extent of abuse (Office of the High Commissioner for Human Rights 2013). In addition, the intense trauma and shame suffered by those who were on the receiving end means that many will never completely disclose what was done to them. For example, sexually humiliating torture techniques were intentionally used against Muslim men and women because of the profound cultural and personal implications.

Even without the full extent of the torture being revealed, a litany of abuses that contravene the Convention against Torture and other Cruel, Inhuman or Degrading Treatment or Punishment has been documented.[2] In a confidential report, the International Committee of the Red Cross (ICRC), the organisation tasked with ensuring compliance and respect for the Geneva Conventions during times of war, alleged serious mistreatment of those detained in Abu Ghraib prison. While the full contents of the ICRC report have not been released publicly,[3] some of the documented cases included: threats during interrogation; insults and verbal violence during transfer; sleep deprivation due to loud music or lights kept on in the cell at night; walking in the corridors handcuffed and naked except for female underwear over the head; and handcuffing either to the upper bed bars or doors of the cell for three to four hours at a time (Namey 2011c: 8). The ICRC noted that some detainees presented with physical marks and psychological symptoms which were compatible with these allegations. The ICRC delegates witnessed the following:

> Some detainees presented significant signs of concentration difficulties, memory problems, verbal expression problems, incoherent speech, acute anxiety reactions, abnormal behaviour and suicidal ideas. These symptoms appeared to have been provoked by the interrogation period and methods. Some detainees were kept in total darkness in their cells. Some detainees were kept naked in their cells. Obvious scars around wrists, allegedly caused by very tight handcuffing with 'flexicuffs'. Some detainees wore female underwear. Some were provided with one jumpsuit and no underwear; and, in some cells beds were without mattresses and blankets. (Namey 2011c: 8)

It was not just the ICRC that documented the abuses. The 'Taguba Report' was one of the most comprehensive accounts of the torture that took place in Abu Ghraib. Major General Antonio Taguba found that between October and December of 2003 there were incidences of 'sadistic, blatant and wanton criminal abuses' perpetrated by the 372nd Military Police Company and US intelligence personnel (Taguba 2004: 16). The report detailed incidents including sodomising of prisoners with a chemical light and broomstick, threatening detainees with loaded weapons, breaking chemical lights and pouring the phosphoric liquid on people, sexual humiliation that included forced nudity, prisoners being threatened with rape, allowing a military police guard to stitch the wound of a detainee after being slammed against the wall in his cell, the use of military working dogs to bite and terrify those detained, beatings with broomsticks and other implements, pouring cold water on naked detainees and hitting prisoners (Taguba 2004: 17–18).

The 2004 Fay report further documents:

The abuses spanned from direct physical assault, such as delivering head blows rendering detainees unconscious, to sexual posing and forced participation in group masturbation. At the extremes were the death of a detainee in OGA custody, an alleged rape committed by a US translator and observed by a female solider, and the alleged sexual assault of a female soldier. (Fay 2004: 71)

Evidently, many of the techniques used in Abu Ghraib formed part of the interrogation strategy already being employed at Guantanamo Bay (Fay 2004; Mayer 2008). The commander of the prison at the time, Brigadier General Janis Karpinski, recalled that General Geoffrey Miller, who was sent to Abu Ghraib from Guantanamo Bay on the orders of Secretary of Defense, Donald Rumsfeld, to reform interrogation methods at Abu Ghraib, stated that they were 'going to change the nature of the interrogation at Abu Ghraib' in order to obtain 'active intelligence' (Karpinski 2004; Karpinski & Strasser 2005). Indeed, in August 2003, Miller apparently submitted a report that suggested that interrogators at Abu Ghraib 'GTMO-ise' their approach – part of which included the use of military police to 'soften up' prisoners for interrogation (Mayer 2008: 241). Despite the obvious spill-over of techniques utilised in Guantanamo, George Mastroianni (2013: 56) suggests that some of the brutal acts committed by US troops at Abu Ghraib were in fact 'retaliation by guards for behaviour of which they did not approve or for their own entertainment'.[4]

However, it was not until some photos were leaked in April 2004 that the world was confronted with the realities of the torture experienced by the Iraqi people (Mastroianni 2013). US Army Specialist Joseph Darby, an military police officer at Abu Ghraib prison, was given a compact disc full of photos from a colleague, Charles Graner, that depicted the torture of prisoners (Bryan 2007). In a BBC Radio 4 interview, Darby described what he saw:

There were photos of Graner beating three prisoners in a group. There was a picture of a naked male Iraqi standing with a bag over his head, holding the head, the sandbagged head of a male Iraqi kneeling between his legs … Lynndie England … was leading prisoners around on a leash. She was giving a thumbs-up, standing next to Graner. Posing with one of the Iraqi prisoners who had died. (Quoted in Bryan 2007: 1)

After it became known that he leaked the photos, Darby experienced reprisals from his colleagues in the military and people in his local community – his home was vandalised, people from his hometown in Pennsylvania called him a traitor, and he and his family were under such threat that they had to change their identities and relocate as part of the witness protection programme (Bryan 2007).[5]

While the publication of the photos played a key role in exposing the torture and abuses at the hands of the US military and private security contractors in Iraq, the torture in Abu Ghraib was not an anomaly. In 2010, WikiLeaks released the Iraq War Logs, which contained classified military documents citing hundreds of cases of systematic torture, rape and murder in Iraq (WikiLeaks 2010). For example, in November 2003, an Iraqi major general was reportedly beaten and tortured for days by the US military. He was eventually suffocated to death after being 'stuffed into a sleeping bag, tied up with an electrical cord' and sat on by US soldiers (Mastroianni 2013: 54).

Transparency and Accountability?

In March 2013, the UN special rapporteur on human rights and counter-terrorism, Ben Emmerson, called on the US government to prosecute public officials found to be involved in gross or systematic human rights violations in order to secure the right to truth and the principle of accountability (Office of the High Commissioner for Human Rights 2013: para. 5). However, the Obama administration continues to hold a policy of moving forward and refuses to prosecute those who ordered the abuses because they acted 'in good faith', thus ensuring accountability remains elusive (Emmerson 2013: 5–6).

Some of the lower-level US troops who directly participated in the torture at Abu Ghraib were brought before a court martial and served prison time. As the ringleader of the torture, Graner was convicted of conspiracy, assault, maltreating prisoners, dereliction of duty and committing indecent acts. In 2005 he was sentenced to ten years – the longest sentence of those involved – but was released early in August 2012 for good behaviour (Deisher 2013). Some of the commissioned and non-commissioned officers involved were handed 'punitive letters', fined or relieved of their duties (Mastroianni 2013: 58). However, none received any judicial penalty.

In addition to higher-level government officials, the involvement of private military and security contractors has provided stumbling blocks to accountability. In June 2004, prior to their handover to the Iraqi government, the US-appointed Coalition Provisional Authority gave blanket legal immunity to civilian contractors operating in Iraq (Elsea 2010).[6] In effect this meant that any criminal activity carried out by these private security contractors was exempt from prosecution under US and local Iraqi laws. Thus, the Abu Ghraib dog handlers who were ordered by civilian contractors to use their dogs to terrify prisoners during interrogations were unable to be prosecuted.

Holding those responsible to account also continues to elude survivors. While international human rights law provides that victims of torture should be given compensation, the survivors have yet to see any form of recompense from the US government. Although Engility Holdings, a defence contractor involved in the torture of prisoners, settled a lawsuit brought by former detainees, another US military contractor, CACI International, audaciously began proceedings in 2013 to sue the victims of torture for the company's court costs (Deisher 2013). Legal proceedings against the US contractors were dismissed in 2011 on the grounds that the companies have legal immunity as government contractors.

Evidence of torture continues to be hidden from the international community. President Obama has refused to release photos and interrogation films depicting the torture of men and women in US custody (Open Society Justice Initiative 2013). The CIA has even admitted to destroying some of the 'interrogation' tapes which depict the torture of so-called 'high-value detainees' (Open Society Justice Initiative 2013). Indeed, the horrifying pictorial evidence viewed for the 'Taguba report', including tapes and pictures of women and children being raped, has remained classified.

The full circumstances surrounding the torture and death of one particular detainee, Mandel al-Jamadi, who was held by US Navy SEALs as a ghost prisoner, are yet to be released (Hibbitts 2005). News reports state that he died while being suspended by his wrists, which were handcuffed behind his back (Deisher 2013). While the UK government is currently holding an investigation into the murder and torture of prisoners in Iraq committed by its troops during the war (Bunkall 2014),[7] other Coalition governments remain silent.

Most worrying has been the conferral of rewards or promotions on those involved who held higher-level positions. Larry James, a former US Army psychologist and former head of the Behavioural Science Division who was involved in overseeing the 'interrogation' of prisoners at both

Abu Ghraib and Guantanamo Bay, was appointed dean of the School of Professional Psychology at Wright State University in 2008, and was selected by Michelle Obama to a head a White House task force entitled Enhancing the Psychological Wellbeing of the Military Family (Center for Torture Accountability 2013; Greenwald 2011). Jay Bybee, one of the authors of the now notorious 'torture memos' and the man who advocated legal immunity for acts that clearly amounted to torture, is now a sitting US federal judge (Cohen 2013). Disturbingly, he is ruling on cases involving the torture and cruel, inhuman and degrading treatment of US prisoners.[8] John Yoo, the man who attempted to manipulate the definition of torture to support the Bush administration's torture programme and who said it would be acceptable for the President to torture a child in the interests of national security, is now teaching law at Berkeley (Kulwin 2013). Finally, General Geoffrey Miller, who sanctioned harsh interrogation techniques in Guantanamo and exported them to Abu Ghraib, was promoted to deputy commanding general for detainee operations in Iraq. He received the Distinguished Service Medal at the Pentagon Hall of Heroes in 2006 (Spiegel 2006).

Legacies

What legacy has this inhumane treatment left for the governments involved, the wider community, and the men and women who were subjected to torture and cruel and degrading treatment? And most importantly, what are the long-term impacts of allowing those who order, sanction and fail to fully disclose the extent of torture to remain unaccountable?

The lack of respect for international law and the culture of silence and non-disclosure have serious consequences for the countries involved, and for the global strategy to eradicate torture. Internationally, the moral standing of the US government has declined immensely (Chaffee 2008) and not only in relation to torture, but also for its lack of regard for human rights and the selective application of the rule of law in countless other circumstances in the War on Terror. Any future US action in the Middle East will always be tainted by the powerful images depicting the torture of Muslim men at Abu Ghraib. And the images of torture as 'American justice' will forever remain as a powerful backdrop to any dealings with Middle Eastern countries and will continue to fuel anti-American activities (Karon 2004).

Truda Gray and Brian Martin (2007) argue that the release of the images provided some benefits, as they not only humanised those being tortured, but also exposed the deceitful rhetoric of the US government in relation to torture and provided evidence which supported the allegations of torture by detainees. While members of the Bush administration were publicly stating that the US was not engaging in acts amounting to torture and that those accusing them of such atrocities were dishonest, the photos and the disclosure of classified material by whistle-blowers exposed their lie.

However, the disclosures have delivered more broad-ranging problematic consequences. Although the release of the photos meant that the world had 'proof' that the US was engaging in torture and ill-treatment, the residual adverse effect was to provide an impetus for illegal actions that occur in war to be further hidden – whether they be in relation to the recording and storage of material that could provide evidence of human rights violations or the ability for ground forces to record incidents. This was compounded by Private Bradley (Chelsea) Manning's release of material to WikiLeaks that included a film depicting US troops killing unarmed civilians in Iraq, which WikiLeaks labelled 'collateral murder'. The easiest way to stop images like this becoming public again is to prevent the recording of incidents in the first place, or to have compromising footage destroyed. This tactic has already been employed by the US government in relation to the destruction of films depicting the 'interrogation' of terror suspects. With warfare now more commonly being fought remotely, for example, with drones in remote parts of Pakistan and Yemen, there are rarely any survivors to capture footage. The use of cameras in US detention facilities such as Guantanamo Bay is strictly forbidden, and documents taken to and from the prison are monitored for any content that may disclose information that compromises 'national security', including evidence of torture.

To date, the consequences for whistle-blowers have been harsh and in many cases excessive. More whistle-blowers have been prosecuted by the Obama administration using espionage laws than all other US administrations combined, in what some see as an attempt to send a severe warning to anyone thinking of disclosing evidence of government malfeasance (Currier 2013). The emerging consequence is that the atrocities of war become further hidden from public view. As governments become more careful about storing material that may expose acts of an embarrassing or potentially criminal nature, evidence of human rights abuses committed in the privacy of prison cells or secret interrogation facilities will likely remain concealed. This is particularly concerning given the importance of monitoring mechanisms being set in place to prevent torture. It has been well established that surveillance mechanisms serve to minimise the risk of acts amounting to torture from taking place (Asia Pacific Forum of National Human Rights Institutions et al. 2010).

One of the most worrying developments resulting from the torture of prisoners in Abu Ghraib and elsewhere in Iraq has been the lack of legal accountability. Some whistle-blowers who exposed atrocities have been prosecuted, while the failure to hold to account those who sanctioned torture and engaged in practices to prevent the full and frank disclosure of relevant material has paved the way for future human rights abuses to take place. If there are no consequences for the individuals or governments involved (except in some cases the lower-level soldiers), there is little incentive to discontinue such practices, and this has set a dangerous precedent. Transparency and accountability are essential to long-term and meaningful torture prevention as well as upholding long-established human rights (Asia Pacific Forum of National Human Rights Institutions et al. 2010).[9] Research has identified that if states condone torture, whether through silent complicity or by actively reframing the actions as less than torture, then this creates a precarious and dangerous situation in relation to torture prevention (Başoğlu 1993). Indeed, the current lack of transparency is antithetical to the established democratic principles which are deemed to form the basis of the US system of government (Linnartz 2008).

Further, the reluctance to implement legally enshrined human rights mechanisms remains pervasive. Although legal immunity was provided to those acting in Iraq, and the US government 'unsigned' the Rome Statute,[10] which would have brought them before the International Criminal Court, applicable legal mechanisms to address alleged breaches of human rights law were not implemented for political reasons. For example, Spain attempted to hold to account those allegedly responsible for ordering torture under universal jurisdiction provisions which, under international law, allow states to claim criminal jurisdiction over an individual for grave breaches of international law such as crimes against humanity or torture (Gallagher 2009). However, WikiLeaks cables reveal that the case was dropped after the US pressured the Spanish government to halt proceedings (Tremlett 2010).

Political pressure to prevent accountability also occurred in relation to investigations. While the UK government has taken several steps to reflect on the role it played in the torture and other atrocities that took place during the Iraq War, and in some cases prosecuted those involved, not all Coalition members have followed suit. In Australia, for example, successive governments have refused to acknowledge or investigate their own military. In 2011, it was revealed that an Australian military officer was involved in providing legal advice in relation to interrogation techniques, responding to torture allegations on behalf of the US and hiding some 'high-value' Abu Ghraib detainees from the ICRC (Namey 2011a, 2011b). Freedom-of-information documents revealed that the Australian government went to great lengths to protect the US government from any embarrassment and consequently failed to investigate credible allegations of torture (Namey 2011c). In addition, the Australian government has been named as one of fifty-four involved in the CIA's euphemistically named 'extraordinary rendition program' (Open Society Justice Initiative 2013). The Australian government's knowledge of the torture of Australian citizens by the CIA and in Guantanamo Bay is now well documented, yet there has been selective acknowledgement of the atrocities committed against those detained. This is not an anomaly, as many governments around the world appear to have unwritten policies of 'turning a blind eye' to atrocities committed by their allies. This has a detrimental effect on international human rights protections and mechanisms which work to prevent torture.

Other governments have used the War on Terror narrative and the impunity of US torture as an excuse to treat their own citizens in a less than humane fashion (Scahill 2009). This is of particular relevance in a country such as Iraq, as it is one of the few states not to have ratified the Convention against Torture (United Nations Iraq 2010). A UN report in relation to the human rights situation in Iraq specifically notes the importance of investigating reports of torture and deaths and ensuring US government contractors are held to account in order to strengthen human rights in the region (United Nations Assistance Mission for Iraq 2008: 7). The report further states that 'the lack of accountability of the perpetrators of such human rights abuses reinforces the culture of impunity' (United Nations Assistance Mission for Iraq 2008: 24). Indeed, human rights groups have noted that the continuing impunity 'sends a dangerous signal to government officials at home and abroad that there will be few consequences for torture and other brutality. Accountability today is critical to stopping torture tomorrow' (American Civil Liberties Union, n.d.: para. 4).

The Political Response and Legacy

It is not only the lack of legal accountability in relation to the torture that took place at Abu Ghraib that has left a destructive legacy. The dehumanising and apologetic language utilised by multiple administrations contributed to delegitimising the suffering of the victims and excused the actions of those involved. In the US, the atrocities were blamed on 'a few bad apples', while at the same time the higher echelons of the Bush administration engaged in debates to legally justify the use of 'enhanced interrogation techniques' as acceptable and necessary to protect the public (Lazreg 2008; Mayer 2008).

In Australia, former Prime Minister John Howard described the torture that took place in Abu Ghraib as an anomaly, and a 'misbehaviour' on the part of some US troops (AAP 2004: para. 9). In response to the released photos, Howard not only belittled the experience of the torture victims by saying that 'far worse' had been done under Saddam Hussein, but also defended and indeed credited the actions of the US by saying that they had admitted it was a problem and that those responsible had been court-martialled (AAP 2004: para. 5).

The relabelling of torture by senior political figures, and in turn by the mainstream media, was also used as a tactic to reduce the perception of suffering, and subsequently inhibited the humanisation of the victims. Research reveals that the US and Australian media used words such as 'abuse' and 'mistreatment' to describe the treatment of the men, women and children, rather than 'torture' (Bennett et al. 2006). Evidence has shown that the mainstream media in both countries provided largely uncritical reports of what the Bush administration said at the time and much of the language went unchallenged, thereby tending to downplay the reality of torture due to a perceived 'state of exception' (Doucette 2010; Rejali 2007). Judith Butler (2009: 1–32) describes this disavowal of suffering as a 'differential allocation of grievability' that 'operates to produce and maintain certain exclusionary conceptions of who is normatively human'. The devaluation of the lives of Iraqi men and women was reinforced not only in the act of torture, but also by the subsequent framing of the issue (human rights apply only if you are considered human).

The Cancerous Nature of Torture

It is vital to examine this issue while taking into account the long-term and widespread impact of torture. Researchers have long known the cancerous nature of torture: it spreads in unforeseeable ways. Torture does not cease at geographical borders. Luk Vervaet (2010) argues that the techniques used in Abu Ghraib and Guantanamo Bay appear to have also been used in European police stations and US domestic prisons. Research shows that torture techniques used in wartime are frequently imported into the domestic sphere, whether in relation to violence against women or returned troops working as security guards, police officers or prison guards (Rejali 2007; Sarson & MacDonald 2009).

At a community level, the legacy of torture has remained toxic, in relation to both social attitudes towards torture and pro-torture rhetoric. In particular, the establishment of a dominant culture that is more accepting of torture, both in Australia and the US, has become apparent since 9/11

(Australian Red Cross 2009; Gronke et al. 2010). While torture is most prevalently described as an abhorrent act that warrants accountability by the international community (BBC 2006b), the level of aversion appears to vary depending on who the victim or survivor is and which person or state is accused of perpetrating the torture. Research into public attitudes reveals a greater acceptance of torture in countries involved in the War on Terror and those experiencing violent political conflict, such as India and Israel (BBC 2006b).

Adverse reactions to torture have also been limited by the terminology used and the techniques employed, which has manifested in the general acceptance of what Darius Rejali (2007) calls 'clean' torture techniques – that is, techniques which leave no visible marks, such as forced standing and sleep deprivation. The culture of impunity and silence surrounding torture has contributed to creating and maintaining an 'us and them' mentality and, in the process, promoting the public message that 'torture is okay' where national security is at risk (Frow 2007).

Of the political and social legacies of the Iraq War, there was perhaps none more destructive than that experienced by the individuals tortured at Abu Ghraib and elsewhere in Iraq. The experience of the victims and survivors and their families has scarcely been reported or acknowledged. The trauma experienced by victims of torture is lifelong and never leaves the individual.

A decade after the US invasion, the individuals and communities of Iraq continue to live with daily violence and human rights violations. More recently, after bodies were found with brutal torture marks in Iraq, the former UN special rapporteur on torture, Manfred Nowak, described the situation as 'worse than it has been in the times of Saddam Hussein' (Guardian 2006: para. 2). Indeed, in 2014 the levels of violence have increased in many parts of the country, as conflict between insurgent groups continues to flourish (Human Rights Watch 2014b). Undeniably, the individual trauma experienced by those who were on the receiving end of the torture will only be exacerbated by the continued conflict and the torture that continues to take place.

Moving Forward?

In order to prevent the further denigration of existing human rights mechanisms and overcome the destructive legacy left from the torture of those in Iraq by Coalition forces, a solid international response is needed that sees transparency and accountability for torture as the norm across international boundaries, no matter who has carried out unlawful activities.

Cooperative political will to uphold human rights is therefore paramount in order to reverse this destructive legacy. Accountability is only one way to confront torture. Transparency and a willingness to reflect on past mistakes in the interest of long-standing peace in the region are necessary to prevent the furtherance of any narrative that sees torture as acceptable. Accountability and transparency are particularly important for the US government, as it has positioned itself as the global protector of human rights, and initially used human rights discourse to justify intervening in Iraq (Schwenkel 2009: 33).

Conclusion

Over a decade on from the war and the painful legacy of torture by Coalition forces in Iraq, the damage remains. By failing to hold to account those at the top who ordered the types of torture perpetrated against the Iraqi people, the governments involved have diminished their legitimacy as rights-respecting states and, in the process, have diminished human rights norms. The selective application of international law by some governments has set a dangerous precedent and opened the way for a repeat of similar serious human rights breaches. Additionally, the denigration of human rights protections in lieu of national security concerns has only served to further justify misconduct towards those who are deemed undeserving of safeguards against ill-treatment.

The ineffective response to Abu Ghraib in relation to global torture prevention strategies must also be acknowledged. Indeed the level of political non-disclosure and the protection of allies from scrutiny have paved the way for gross violations to occur again with few consequences. The way in which states record and store material that could potentially provide evidence of human rights violations has also changed, potentially reducing the chance for public awareness of illegal activity. The prosecution of whistle-blowers has also served as a detriment to those willing to expose the abuse of power in this way.

The extensive and longer-term consequences of the shift in attitudes to torture are yet to be seen. What will happen next time there is a war and immunity is granted in relation to atrocities committed against soldiers from coalition forces? The coalition countries involved will have little to complain about when the tables are turned and the Geneva Conventions manipulated and selectively applied to the detriment of their own troops. In this regard, the state of *unaccountability* has left a dark stain on all future military operations.

Despite the politics of accountability, the legacy of the events at Abu Ghraib is most destructive for the victims and their families. Their suffering has been minimised and barely scrutinised publicly. Their torture has been relabelled as 'abuse' or 'mistreatment', and they have been shown contempt by private security contractors attempting to sue them for court costs. Additionally, their sense of legitimate suffering has been denied by a blatant disregard for international human rights and humanitarian law standards, which in turn has set back international torture prevention strategies. The events of Abu Ghraib are worthy of reflection in relation to notions of shared responsibility and what it means to be a part of a global community. There are strong ethical imperatives to address the destructive legacy left by torture carried out during Operation Iraqi Freedom, as well as the legal commitments set out in human rights treaties and conventions.

Notes

1. Core rules of international customary law and the four Geneva Conventions are binding on parties acting in an armed conflict, irrespective of treaty ratification. However, the Bush administration argued that the Geneva Conventions did not apply to the conflict with 'al-Qaeda' for a number of reasons, including the failure to wear distinctive insignia or uniforms to identify themselves as combatants as required under the third Geneva Convention, and because they did not comply with the rules of international humanitarian law, such as the prohibition on the targeting of civilians. Apart from the obvious issues in relation to the treatment of those detained, this proposition was fraught with problems, particularly as the US government deemed those captured not entitled to go before a tribunal to prove they were not members of the terrorist group. Indeed, the argument that the attacks on the World Trade Center and the Pentagon in 2001 were an 'act of war', rather than a civilian criminal act, is also fraught with legal difficulties. For more see Duffy (2005: 225–6, 242–3, 249–73).
2. The UN Convention against Torture provides the most widely accepted definition of torture, including any act by which severe pain and suffering is intentionally inflicted on a person for such purposes of obtaining from him or a third person information or a confession. The action must be with the consent or acquiescence of a public official or other person acting in an official capacity. However, the Bush administration sought to lessen the scope to only include acts that would result in organ failure or death. For more see Rejali (2007).
3. Documents released under freedom-of-information legislation make reference to the report, and provide some detail with regard to its contents, e.g. Namey (2011c).
4. He refers to the alleged rape of a young boy and the incitement of a riot on 7 November 2003.
5. Although Darby handed the photos over on the condition of anonymity, his identity was publicly revealed by Donald Rumsfeld.

6. This immunity continued after the CPA was dissolved in June 2004.
7. At the time of writing the International Criminal Court has been asked to investigate more than 1,000 torture claims detailed against British troops.
8. In 2012, Bybee oversaw a case where a US prisoner had alleged his treatment amounted to cruel and inhuman treatment. In Bybee's ruling he stated that the guards did not have any reason to believe that a 'contraband watch' was unconstitutional. The man in question was subjected to 24-hour bright lighting and body cavity searches; he had no mattress to sleep on, was put in waist chains which prevented him from using his hands to eat, and was placed in a hot, unventilated cell for a week (Cohen 2013).
9. I refer to human rights norms here as a function of moral limitations that hold the inherent worth and dignity of all human beings at the heart of the conceptualisation. The notion of human rights as a function of empire, however, is important to acknowledge. The way that the US has situated itself as a 'global protector' of human rights makes the importance of accountability even more apparent. For more see Schwenkel (2009).
10. The Rome Statute was signed by the Clinton administration in 2000; however, in 2002 the Bush administration 'unsigned' the statute so that it could not be brought before ICC jurisdiction. The US remains steadfastly opposed to ratifying it (Duffy 2005: 127).

Part II
Iraqi Politics since Saddam

Chapter 4
Shattering the Shia: A Maliki Political Strategy in Post-Saddam Iraq

Benjamin Isakhan

In July 2001 three prominent Iraqi Shia Arabs in exile penned a manifesto known as 'The Declaration of the Shia of Iraq'. They criticised Saddam Hussein's avowedly sectarian brand of authoritarianism and highlighted the atrocities he had committed against the Shia Arab people of Iraq. They called for an end to Saddam's cruel dictatorship, advocating the 'establishment of a democratic parliamentary constitutional order, that carefully avoids the hegemony of one sect or ethnic group over the others' (al-Rubaie et al. 2010: 315). In the lead up to the 2003 US intervention, the declaration received wide support from Iraqi Shia clerics and US war planners alike. Not surprisingly, following the war and the toppling of Saddam's regime, it was arguably the Shia Arab majority and their leaders who were the most enthusiastic about bringing democracy to Iraq and the most determined to put US rhetoric on democracy promotion to the test.

Perhaps the best-known example came from the country's leading Shia cleric, Grand Ayatollah Ali al-Sistani, who issued a number of politically motivated fatwas that demanded elections and called upon the faithful (including women) to vote (al-Sistani 2010). Other members of the Shia Arab political elite also incorporated elements of democracy into their programmes: a complex array of Shia Arab political parties (re)emerged forming policy-driven campaigns and complex alliances; they organised major protests, civil disobedience campaigns and nationwide petitions; and they created news outlets and used them to disseminate information to their constituents (Isakhan 2013a, 2015b). In the lead up to the January and December 2005 elections, the key Shia Arab political parties – Da'wa ('Calling'), the Islamic Supreme Council of Iraq (ISCI), Moqtada al-Sadr's Sadr Trend, the Badr Organisation and al-Fadhila ('Islamic Virtue Party') – all came together under the banner of the United Iraqi Alliance (UIA). The negotiations were notably facilitated and encouraged by Sistani, who, with other prominent Shia Arab leaders, acknowledged that by bringing the varying Shia Arab factions together they stood a greater chance of winning at the polls and subsequently wielding unprecedented power. This was to pay dividends. On the back of democratic elections, the Shia Arabs ascended the political hierarchy to not only dominate Iraq but become the first ever Shia-led political authority in the modern Arab world.

Not surprisingly, a collection of scholarly studies have sought to address this phenomenon. Many of these works have focused on the relationship between the US's democracy promotion agenda and that of Iraq's Shia Arab religio-political leaders. Most notably, Juan Cole has argued that this period witnessed

> a remarkable development in Shiite religious and legal thinking about democracy in Iraq. The ideals of elections, representation of the people, the expression of the national will, and a rule of law are invoked over and over again by the most prominent religious leaders. Unlike Khomeini in 1979, they are completely unafraid of the phrase ... 'democracy', and generally see no contradiction between it and Islam. (Cole 2006: 24–5)

Focusing specifically on Sistani's religious edicts, Babak Rahimi has argued that he was in effect cultivating 'grassroots political participation to enhance civil society' that in turn could 'produce a democratic order in which public Islam is compatible with not only the principles of inclusion, competition and accessibility but also with the basic logic of democratic governance – namely accountability and popular sovereignty' (Rahimi 2004). In terms of the Shia Arab political parties and their rise to prominence since 2003, Vali Nasr has argued that they were 'injecting a robust element of real pluralism into the too-often Sunni-dominated political life of the Muslim world' and 'are also finding democracy appealing as an idea in itself, not merely as an episodically useful vehicle for their power and ambitions' (Nasr 2007: 180).

To a certain extent, this optimism is justified given the embrace of democratic ideals and institutions by the Shia Arabs immediately after the fall of the Baathist regime. However, very few studies have sought to question this optimism in the light of more recent events. Addressing this lacuna, and leaving aside Orientalist arguments that would imply that Shia Islam is antithetical to democracy, this chapter instead argues that one key legacy of the US effort to bring democracy to Iraq has been that many elements within Iraq's Shia Arab political elite have viewed democracy through the lens of a cynical majoritarianism and manipulated it to catapult themselves to power. This has had a further legacy, enabling the democratically elected government of Prime Minister Nouri al-Maliki to utilise his incumbency to maintain the veneer of democracy while becoming increasingly dictatorial and authoritarian. In doing so, Maliki's government shares much in common with other 'hybrid regimes' in which governments hijack nominally democratic mechanisms such as elections, media freedoms, political opposition and civil society as part of their strategy to retain, rather than diffuse, power (Dodge 2012b, 2013). Although Maliki has deployed a host of different strategies along these lines – including blatant sectarianism, undermining key state institutions, the creation of a shadow state loyal to himself, and the concentration of military and political power in his own hands – this chapter focuses on Maliki's less well-known efforts to shatter the unity of his Shia Arab political opponents. It focuses on his first two terms in power and examines the ways in which he has been able to systematically fracture the Shia political elite to such an extent that once tenuously united factions now stand bitterly divided. The chapter concludes by reflecting on the reasoning behind such an approach and the prospects of Iraq's democracy moving beyond the blatant power grab of the incumbent Maliki government.

Maliki's First Term: Emerging Anti-democratic Trends amidst Shia In-fighting

The story of the fracturing of the Iraqi Shia Arab political elite begins immediately after the December 2005 elections. The 128 seats (of 275) won by the Shia-dominated UIA were tightly divided among ISCI (30 seats), the Sadrist Trend (28), Da'wa (25) and a handful of smaller parties and independents (Katzman 2010: 21). It is at this point that the alliance began to falter, opening up a series of long-held divisions between the leaders of Iraq's Shia Arab community. The Sadrists and Da'wa joined ranks and suggested that Ibrahim al-Jaafari (then of Da'wa) retain his position as Prime Minister, while ISCI put forward their own candidate, Vice President Adel Abdul-Mahdi. This led to a deadlock, with the various Shia Arab factions divided over who should lead Iraq. Debates raged, sometimes to the exclusion of Kurdish or Sunni concerns or consultation. The impasse was eventually resolved – with the help of Sistani – and Jaafari stepped down as leader. The little-known Maliki was then nominated as his replacement by Da'wa. Maliki was quickly endorsed by the US and was supported by most Iraqi politicians because he was regarded as a quiet, hardworking moderate who posed little threat to the US plan for democratisation or to the interests of the nation's political elite. His appointment was quickly approved by the

Iraqi parliament in April before the new government finally took office in May 2006, six months after the election.

Upon coming to power, Maliki had to accept that his many years in exile meant that he had very little public recognition and, crucially, very little political support. He knew that if he was to stay in office he would need to create political entities that were directly loyal to him. In 2007 he began to build support within his own Da'wa party, first by being elected the party's general secretary in April – a post which he still holds today. He then built up a small but loyal group of family members, friends, technocrats and trusted advisers, mostly from within Da'wa, who have come to be known as the 'Malikiyoun'. Maliki placed members of this group in privileged senior positions across Iraq's vast bureaucracy and was thereby able to bypass Cabinet and his political opponents in making and enacting key decisions (Dodge 2012b: 158–9). Central to Maliki's inner circle was his own son, Ahmed Nouri al-Maliki, who was appointed to the position of deputy chief of staff inside the Office of the Prime Minister.

Beyond this, Maliki also initiated a series of independent tribe-based parliamentary units or 'support councils'. These loose political units are not democratic in the sense that they are not constituted by the elected representatives of the people, but are an appropriation of tribal forms of governance where hereditary factions wield significant power over local politics. These support councils are spread out across key southern Shia Arab provinces, northern Kurdish provinces and even in multi-ethnic Baghdad. They are ostensibly supported by Maliki in exchange for their loyalty and they answer directly to the Da'wa elite (Duss & Juul 2009: 3) Not surprisingly, the creation of these support councils has been controversial across Iraq, especially among key Shia Arab and Kurdish political organisations, who see it as a move to commandeer their political support base.

Despite Maliki's best efforts to garner new political support, not long after coming to power the incumbent UIA began to unravel. In March 2007, the Shia Islamist Fadhila party withdrew, followed in September by the Sadrists, who complained that, despite their holding a significant number of seats, the bloc was dominated by the members of Da'wa and ISCI (China Daily 2007). This deteriorating relationship – especially between Maliki and Sadr – was to culminate in the March 2008 'Basra offensive', a series of military manoeuvres orchestrated by Maliki in which the Iraqi Security Forces (ISF) undertook their first operations since 2003. This *Saulat al-Fursan* ('Charge of the Knights') saw the Iraqi army pitted against Sadr's own militia, the Jaysh al-Mahdi ('Mahdi Army') after Maliki's initial attempts to broker its disarmament failed. The operation was initially a disaster and came very close to failing altogether; it only succeeded when US forces decided to support Maliki. Although Sadr's forces were not easily beaten, Maliki's plan was ultimately successful and the few short weeks of fighting saw him defeat Sadr's militia and dramatically erode his organisational, military and political infrastructure. The Basra offensive was then followed by similar operations in other Sadr strongholds such as Sadr City (Baghdad), Amara and elsewhere (Duss & Juul 2009: 3, 14). Cleverly, Maliki utilised his alignment to ISCI to recruit members of the Badr Brigade (the former armed wing of ISCI which in 2003 changed its name to the Badr Organisation in order to relaunch itself as a political body) to fight in the Basra offensive. Due to their victory and their subsequent respect for Maliki, many Badr members joined the ISF. To an extent, this move undermined both Sadr and ISCI; Maliki had successfully used ISCI's militia against Sadr's, while at the same time creating a force loyal to himself.

Maliki's increasing support base and his military successes gave rise to growing concern among the Shia Arab political elite. Some members of the UIA even began to challenge his leadership, nominating Jaafari as the next leader of the coalition and nominee for Prime Minister. Despite the fact that Jaafari had won the internal UIA nomination by one vote, Maliki fought off the challenge and – in a sign of things to come – refused to stand aside. Instead, he responded by splitting those loyal to him in Da'wa from the UIA, while Jaafari formed his own party, the National Reform Movement (NRM), in 2008 (Ottaway & Kaysi 2010e). This was a calculated political move by Maliki. He knew that without Da'wa, the UIA would be in ruins and the constituent political parties would be forced to contest the 2009 provincial elections separately. This enabled Maliki to form the State of Law Coalition (SLC), which would be virtually unstoppable at the 2009 elections. While his Shia Arab political opponents bickered among themselves, Maliki worked hard to cobble together an odd array of smaller Shia Arab, Kurdish, Turkmen and Christian parties as well as Sunni independents. This enabled Maliki to adopt the guise of a non-sectarian pro-national unity platform, separating himself from Shia Arab ideologues and in-fighting. The SLC emerged the clear winner of the 2009 provincial elections, winning 126 of 440 seats, as well as being the largest list in Baghdad and in eight of the nine Shia Arab provinces. Running under new lists, ISCI secured fifty-two seats as part of the Martyr al-Mehraab list, the Sadrists won forty-three under the Independent Free Movement list and Jaafari's NRM received a paltry twenty-three. The SLC had not only won the election, they had delivered a decisive blow to the other Shia Arab political entities.

Given these disappointing results and the breakup of the UIA before the 2009 elections, the various Shia Arab political entities reignited negotiations with the view to forming a new coalition ahead of the 2010 national elections. Although Maliki was initially invited to join, he insisted that the Da'wa party should receive half of the seats won by the coalition and that he should retain the position of Prime Minister (Daily Telegraph, 2009). However, this was unacceptable to many elements of the Shia Arab elite, who had already tried to replace Maliki and were increasingly concerned about his tight grip on power. Thus, in September of 2009, the National Iraqi Alliance (NIA) was formally announced without Maliki or the SLC. It was headed by Jaafari and was made up of ISCI, Badr, the Sadr Trend, the NRM and other smaller political entities. This was an uneasy alliance – particularly between ISCI and Sadr, whose forces had clashed violently only the year before.

All of this meant that throughout 2006–9 and in the lead up to the 2010 national elections, Maliki was able to successfully increase his political support base and military might, develop his credentials as a nationalist non-sectarian leader and flag the strength of his central government and the ISF (Katzman 2010: 3). Maliki emerged as a strong and determined leader who was even prepared to take on toxic elements within his own Shia Arab population if it meant bringing security and stability to Iraq. In retrospect, however, Maliki's first term in office saw him tighten his grip on power. He built up a number of state apparatuses loyal to himself, routinely undermined his political opponents and demonstrated his emerging authoritarian tendencies.

Maliki's Second Term: Sectarian Populism and Fermenting Shia Disunity

At the 7 March 2010 elections, none of the political blocs won the 163 seats needed to form a government in the 325-member parliament. Despite the ban of many of its key candidates, former PM Iyad Allawi and his largely Sunni and secular Shia alliance, al-Iraqiyya (Iraqi National Movement, INM) won the greatest number of seats at the election (91 of 325). Maliki's SLC came a close second (89) followed by the Shia-dominated NIA (70, of which the Sadrists secured 39 and ISCI 18) ('Legislative Election of 7 March' 2010). This meant that the various blocs and their constituent political parties would have to cobble together a coalition government. This was never going to be an easy task, but it was made cripplingly difficult by the obstinacy and incompetence of much of Iraq's political elite, who routinely failed to encourage the mutually beneficial dialogue and debate critical to democracy. Foremost among these was Maliki himself, who was determined to cling to power and underwent an aggressive and multifaceted campaign to that end (Ottaway & Kaysi 2010c). Such misconduct saw the nation plummet into nine months of political stalemate: several long and complex political negotiations ensued; new alliances were forged and then broken; old enemies shook hands and discussed new pathways to peace only to fall back on pre-existing disagreements; and various models and options were tabled before being scrapped at the last moment.

Much of the stalemate centred on the division between the key Shia Arab political blocs. In the lead up to the 2010 elections ISCI, the Sadrists and the NRM had all been adamant that they did not want to see Maliki return for a second term. After the election, each of them met with Allawi, the Kurds and each other in the hope of forming a political alliance that would prevent Maliki from securing a majority. Eventually, Maliki's SLC formed a very shaky alliance with the NIA when ISCI and the Sadrists presented him with a fifty-article document that severely limited the role of the Prime Minister – reducing it to a type of managerial rather than executive role (Ottaway & Kaysi 2010c). With such provisions, and in moves reminiscent of those by the UIA, the two coalitions formally merged into the National Alliance (NA) on 11 June 2010. This new alliance now held 159 seats in the Iraqi parliament, catapulting the Shia Arab political elite of Iraq to within realistic reach of the 163 seats needed to form a government. However, the prospect of another term for Maliki appeared to prompt a response from Sistani, who had thus far remained silent on Iraq's protracted political stalemate. In what appeared to be a thinly veiled criticism of Maliki and his determination to stay in power, Sistani also met with Allawi, where, according to his spokesman, he stressed 'that the formation of the government is subject to dialogue between political blocs according to the mechanism set by the Constitution' (cited in Zahra 2010). In other words, Sistani believed that because Allawi had won the greatest number of seats at the 2010 elections, the constitution guaranteed him the prerogative to form the government, not Maliki. With such high-level interventions by Sistani, the various Shia Arab factions appeared to distance themselves increasingly from Maliki and in early August the INA broke off talks with the SLC, thus ending the National Alliance (Londoño 2010).

Iraq's political deadlock continued until early November 2010 when an agreement was signed during a high-profile meeting in Erbil which would pave the way for the formation of a government. The new Iraqi government was finally announced in December of 2010 and – to the grave disappointment of many Iraqis – Maliki retained the position of

Prime Minister and actually extended his portfolio out to include the powerful Defence and Interior ministries (Ottaway & Kaysi 2010a). For his troubles, Allawi was to enter a power-sharing arrangement with the government as the head of a new National Security Council, but it was not long before he was complaining that there was no real 'power-sharing' in Iraq and he withdrew from the post. Other high-profile resignations followed, including ISCI's Mahdi, who resigned just three weeks after being nominated as one of Iraq's three Vice Presidents because of Maliki's handling of the 2010 stalemate and his failure to abide by the Erbil agreement.

Despite the crippling political stalemate of 2010, Maliki's determination to retain office and the complex set of deep-seated problems facing the country, in December 2011 the US withdrew the last of its troops from Iraq, bringing to an end nearly nine years of military occupation. The US withdrawal meant that Maliki no longer had a major military presence that would defend his government at all costs. Although he had worked hard to bring the ISF under his direct control, the political situation in Iraq was fragile and members of the ISF could be easily swayed by populist ideology, threats or the promise of reward. Maliki urgently needed militant Shia Arab ideologues who would defend his rule. He found them in two key militias. Both had waged deadly attacks against the United States, both had deep ideological ties to Iran and had trained there, both were shadowy networks known for a long list of crimes and their cruelty, and, crucially, both were increasingly isolated from more moderate elements within their respective movements. The first, Asaib Ahl al-Haq ('League of the Righteous', AAH), is headed by a former senior member of the Sadrist movement, Qais al-Khazali; the second is Kataeb Hezbollah ('The Party of God Brigade', KH) headed by Abu Mahdi al-Muhandis, a former member of parliament and senior figure within both Da'wa and Badr. Although it is unclear whether Maliki directly controls the two militias or whether they simply share the same broad agenda, for the time being they appear content to do his bidding. Both AAH and KH have been rewarded with headquarters in the opulent mansions of the US-created government enclave, the International Zone, and with identification badges from the Prime Minister's Office that allow them through security checkpoints to conduct their operations (Filkins 2014; Parker 2014). More to the point, Maliki has been able to use these two militias to intimidate, undermine and directly attack his political opponents. This has included conducting sophisticated operations against Shia Arab enemies such as the Sadrists.

Maliki has also been able to intimidate and undermine his Sunni opponents. Indeed, the withdrawal of the US and the coopting of

Maliki's new militant allies, AAH and KH, meant that Maliki could demolish his democratic façade and reveal the full extent of not only his dictatorial ambitions but also his avowedly sectarian plan. Within days of the US withdrawal, Maliki began his carefully choreographed sectarian campaign to target senior Sunni politicians, to isolate Allawi and to fracture his INM. The most dramatic examples include the issuing of arrest warrants and later death sentences for some of the highest-profile Sunni Arab politicians in Iraq, including Vice President Tariq al-Hashemi in December 2011 and Finance Minister Rafie al-Issawi one year later. Both had joined al-Iraqiyya in the lead up to 2010 elections and had been vocal in their criticisms of Maliki. They were accused of having links to al-Qaeda and of being key orchestrators of various terrorist operations. Although the Maliki government claimed to have strong evidence to support the charges brought against the two men, this evidence has not been made public for fear that it would trigger a sectarian backlash – thus the strength of the cases is difficult to determine. Whatever the facts, these actions were certainly perceived as a sectarian issue by Iraq's Sunni population and were just the latest in a long list of grievances held by many Sunnis against the central government, including their political marginalisation since 2003, the ongoing de-Baathification, mass unemployment, insufficient infrastructure and public services, the arrest and detention of thousands of Sunnis without trial and especially the treatment of female prisoners. All of this triggered mass social unrest in the Sunni-dominated Anbar province from 21 December 2012.

In the context of such political unrest, Iraq held another round of provincial elections on 20 April 2013. These elections actually took place in only twelve of Iraq's eighteen governorates. The three Kurdish provinces controlled by the KRG held their own elections in September 2013. However, elections in three further Sunni Arab-dominated provinces were also delayed: in Anbar and Nineveh they took place on 20 June, while in the disputed and violent province of Kirkuk they were delayed indefinitely. Although the SLC was still the overwhelming victor, with 102 of the 378 available seats, and had secured seven of Iraq's provinces, this was a setback from the 2009 result of 126 seats and nine provinces.

Maliki's opponents had not been idle. Many political parties and key players experimented with different combinations in order to see if they could win seats and to test the political waters ahead of the 2014 national elections (al-Zeidi 2013). By doing so, both the ISCI-dominated Citizens' Alliance and the Sadrist movement rebounded significantly from the 2009 provincial elections: ISCI won sixty-five seats (compared to only fifty-two in 2009) and the Sadrists secured sixty (up from forty-three in 2009). These two traditional rivals then stood together to form a government in the crucial oil-rich and prosperous southern province of Basra. More importantly, in Baghdad, Hakim and Sadr joined forces with the prominent Sunni bloc Mutahidoun (United), led by the parliament speaker, Osama al-Nujaifi, and several members of al-Iraqiyya. This alliance came under the new title 'The Alliance for Baghdad' and saw a non-sectarian, multi-party at the helm in the capital.

By December 2013, the protests in Anbar, which had initially emerged in response to general Sunni marginalisation and suffering but especially to the continued attack on senior Sunni political figures such as Hashemi and Issawi, had been crippling Iraq for a year. What needs to be mentioned here is that the conflict in Anbar comprises a complex web of different groups whose interests are often competing and some-times overlapping. While providing a detailed assessment of the key protagonists and events of the Anbar crisis is beyond the scope of this chapter, it is worth mentioning that, despite several attempts by Maliki to end the conflict, by the time of the April 2014 national elections, the ISF had in fact lost territory and suffered very heavy casualties at the hands of the various terrorist cells and militants of Anbar and other Sunni-dominated regions. More to the point, the extremist al-Qaeda offshoot the Islamic State in Iraq and Syria (ISIS) managed to extend their power beyond the confines of Anbar to become an active threat in four additional Sunni-majority central and northern provinces (Diyala, Salahuddin, Nineveh and Babil) as well as parts of western and north-ern Baghdad (Abbas 2014a, 2014b).

The Anbar crisis compounded Maliki's sliding popularity in Iraqi polit-ical circles. His second term in office had been marred by his failure to abide by the Erbil agreement of 2010, his active persecution of the Sunnis, his inability to resolve the Anbar crisis and his lacklustre results at the 2013 provincial elections. Virtually every major figure from across Iraq's ethno-religious spectrum and ideological divides began to speak out pub-licly against Maliki using the strongest possible language – he was routinely referred to as 'sectarian', 'violent', 'tyrannical' and a 'dictator'. While such calls are to some extent expected from the Kurdish and Sunni Arab minor-ities who were being increasingly marginalised and undermined by Maliki, they also emanated from important Shia Arab figures. This became espe-cially apparent in the lead up to the 2014 national elections. As with the 2010 elections, both ISCI and Sadr were adamantly opposed to another term for Maliki. From as early as July 2011 the *ISCI Bulletin* had been insisting that the Maliki government was yet another example of 'strong iron fisted central rule'. ISCI warned that such a system had historically created a 'pattern of unfair and oppressive regimes' and 'totalitarian governments' that had led to 'the arbitrary exclusion and long marginalisation of the majority population of Iraq' (the Shia Arabs). For ISCI such a situation created a 'need to remove these types of unfair regimes that ruled Iraq and their damaging effects' (ISCI Bulletin 2011: 6). The Sadrists were equally scathing. When Sadr suddenly and mysteriously resigned altogether from Iraqi politics in mid-February 2014, he used his retirement speech in the Shia holy city of Najaf not only to encourage Iraqis to vote and his supporters to continue their hard work, but also to criticise Maliki. He argued that, while Maliki had come to power promising to improve the lives of the majority Shia Arab population, his government had turned out to be 'a group of wolves hungry for power and money, backed by the West [US] and the East [Iran]' and under his leadership 'politics became a door for injustice and carelessness' (quoted in Adnan 2014). Even Maliki's own SLC and Da'wa party indulged in a rare moment of dissent. In mid-August 2013 during a frank and heated meeting, various members urged Maliki not to run for a third term, arguing that his obstinacy embarrassed the political blocs and undermined their popularity and integrity (Sadah 2013d).

While to some extent such rhetoric might be expected from Maliki's political opponents (even if they are of the same sect or from within his own party), perhaps the best barometer of anti-Maliki feeling among the Shia Arab political elite comes from the religious seminary (*hawza*) headed by Sistani in Najaf. Throughout Maliki's second term, Sistani's spokespeople repeatedly issued statements commenting on various political developments and, although they did not criticise Maliki directly, many can be interpreted as thinly veiled criticisms of his regime. For example, in July 2013 when Maliki wanted to implement some changes to Iraq's electoral law, Sistani's spokespeople explicitly announced that they did not support the change – by implication saying that they did not want Maliki to succeed in a third term (Hussein 2013). Similarly, in the lead up to the 2014 elections, Sistani issued a fatwa on 24 February in which he not only encouraged his followers to vote but also to 'choose wisely' and 'distinguish the good from the bad, and differentiate between those who work to serve the people and fight corruption and those who work to benefit themselves and who they represent' (quoted in Mamouri 2014c). The most straightforward attack on Maliki, however, came when another prominent member of the *hawza* and one of the four leading Shia clerics in Iraq, Grand Ayatollah Basheer Nujaifi, issued a very direct and sharply worded statement in which he advised his followers not to vote for Maliki due to his failures in Anbar and the allegations of corruption and other abuses of power (Parker & Salman 2014).

Yet, once again, Maliki was able to counter his lack of support from the Shia religious authority. One month before the elections, on 30 March, a Shia Iraqi cleric and senior figure in the Da'wa movement, Grand Ayatollah Kazem al-Haeri, issued a fatwa banning the faithful from voting for non-religious candidates (in other words, for non-Shia – that is, Sunni Arab or Kurdish – candidates, or for secular nationalists such as Allawi). Parts of the fatwa were printed on large and intimidating banners that were strung up across Baghdad and elsewhere in Iraq (Mamouri 2014b). Indeed, despite his lack of popularity among Iraq's politico-religious elite, Maliki remains popular among his hardline Shia constituents.

To some extent, his unflinching approach to his Sunni opponents and the ongoing Anbar crisis has actually worked in his favour. Much of Iraq's Shia Arab majority view the ongoing chaos in Iraq and the broader Middle East as a product of fundamentalist Sunni Arab terrorism that is explicitly targeting Shia Arabs. In this context, Maliki has sometimes been called the 'modern Mukhtar' in reference to the seventh-century revolutionary Mukhtar al-Thaqafi, who avenged the killing by Sunni Arabs of a revered Shia leader, Imam Hussein, in Karbala – one of the founding events in Shia politico-religious history. Such Shiite sectarian populism centred around Maliki no longer perceives the Sunni population as fellow citizens but as enemies of the Shia Arab-dominated state. The Anbar crisis has also enabled Maliki to campaign once again as a 'wartime' candidate: a strongman who is capable of standing up to al-Qaeda. This is especially clear in his campaign for the 2014 national elections, which was launched on 10 April in Basra and followed by visits to several other Shia Arab-dominated cities including the holy city of Najaf. In language markedly different from his supposedly non-sectarian and unifying platform of 2010, Maliki attempted to portray himself as a strong leader who had prevented Sunni extremists from toppling the Shia Arab-dominated government and inflicting further death and destruction on his ethno-religious constituents (Parker & Salman 2014). Maliki's rhetoric relied heavily on sectarianism and on finishing the fight against – as he so often calls them – 'terrorists, Baathists and sectarians' (for which read 'Sunni Arabs') (Maliki quoted in: Abd-al-Amir 2013).

However, pure populism was not going to be enough to win the 2014 election. On 20 April – just over a week before the election – Maliki announced during an interview on the Lebanese television channel al-Manar that he wanted to form a 'majority government' in which the ministers would be appointed directly by him (Hasan 2014b). His justification for such a move was that a strong central government was the only way to deal with Sunni uprisings and Kurdish secessionist aspirations. However, Maliki's new 'majority government' was merely another strategy to retain power. In other words, while Maliki knew that the SLC was unlikely to secure the 165 seats needed to form a government, he was hoping they could increase their seats to over 100 (up from 89 at the 2010 elections). This would mean that Maliki could align his party with other smaller entities to form a government rather than enter into lengthy post-election negotiations with his rivals in the larger blocs and be forced into another cumbersome power-sharing agreement.

In order to achieve a 'majority government', Maliki was banking on the fact that his consistent efforts to undermine and fracture his political opponents had taken a heavy toll on their ability to come together in coherent and unified political blocs. Unlike the 2010 election, in which the major political entities in Iraq united under a handful of large blocs, the lead up to the 2014 elections saw the different parties and figures competing against each other on separate lists. Although this was partly a product of a recently adopted electoral system, much of the division was due to the successes of Maliki's 'divide and rule' strategy. This is certainly true of both the major Sunni and Kurdish blocs, who for the first time competed against each other. Allawi's secular Sunni-dominated INM had now split into three separate lists and several other, smaller, entities, and the former Kurdish Alliance was now divided between the two main Kurdish parties. The key Shia Arab political factions had also devolved considerably from being unified under the banner of the UIA in 2005 and the INA of 2010. By the time of the 2014 elections, aside from the SLC, the Shia parties had effectively been split into four major blocs: the ISCI-dominated al-Muwatin (Citizen) bloc, the Sadrist-dominated al-Ahrar (Free) bloc, Jaafari's NRM and al-Fadhila, as well as several smaller groups and independent candidates (Visser 2014b, 2014c). Only one political coalition stood strong and united – Maliki's own SLC. In the lead up to the election, Maliki had managed to bring together a dozen smaller parties and blocks including: his own Da'wa party; Badr; the Independent Bloc, led by Hussein al-Shahristani, the deputy Prime Minister for Energy and a close Maliki ally; and even some former al-Iraqiyya members such as Sunni politician Iskandar Witwit (Hasan 2014; Visser 2014c).

Despite the strength and unity of his SLC and the shattering of his opponents, Maliki also reasoned that, in order to create his new majority government, he would need to align himself with several successful candidates after the elections (to secure the 165 seats). To ensure such candidates were pliant to his interests, he set about dispersing his political support base across Iraq, planting those loyal to him in some unexpected quarters. These pro-Maliki politicians – which included around a dozen ministers and MPs who were once officially part of Maliki's SLC – entered the electoral race on separate lists. Throughout the elections, many of these individuals and groups were vocally pro-Maliki; their campaign posters often featured large portraits of the Prime Minister alongside their candidates and one even had the slogan 'Hand in hand with Prime Minister Maliki' (Visser 2014d). As just one example, the pro-Maliki militia AAH ran in several places across the country under the auspices of their political wing, al-Sadiqun ('Truthful') (Visser 2014c). It remains to be seen if this tactic will pay off and whether Maliki will be able to capitalise on these supporters in forming his next government. What is certain is that Maliki has once again out-manoeuvred his political opponents by diversifying the electoral lists (and thereby portraying an image of robust political competition) in order to stack the election in his favour.

The issue of sectarianism will rightly mar the legacy of Maliki's second term in power, especially in light of his treatment of the Sunni Arab minority and the crises in Anbar and elsewhere. What has mostly gone unnoticed in scholarly analysis of Maliki's rule, however, is the extent to which he has also systematically undermined his opponents among the Shia Arab political elite. He has done this by refusing to negotiate with other Shia Arab political figures to form a government after narrowly losing the 2010 elections, by building up deadly Shia militias directly loyal to himself and by manipulating religio-political rhetoric to hone a carefully crafted image of himself as *the* Shia Arab leader capable of defending his ethno-religious constituents against the horrors of terrorism and violence. All of this has sowed the seeds of bitter divides and violent clashes between the various Shia Arab political entities to the extent that they have descended rapidly to a point where they are no longer able to unite behind coherent political blocs and challenge Maliki's authority.

Conclusion

Approximately fifteen years after the publication of the 'The Declaration of the Shia of Iraq', the world is forced to confront the legacy of having replaced Saddam's Sunni Arab-dominated regime with the increasingly dictatorial Maliki government. The Declaration's call for a robust democracy that 'carefully avoids the hegemony of one sect or ethnic group over the others' (Al-Rubaie et al. 2010: 315) is painfully ironic given the power of Maliki's Shia Arab-dominated government and its systemic discrimination against the Kurds and especially the Sunni Arabs. While the earliest days of the post-Baathist state saw the Shia Arab political elite engage with the ideals and institutions of democracy in a way that gave cause for hope, the ill-conceived notion of imposing a foreign model of democracy by force and the Shia Arab abuse of this process towards their own ends have gradually been exposed. Also exposed is the fact that such events paved the way for Iraq's fragile democracy to devolve substantially to the point where the incumbent Maliki government has created a hybrid regime in which the mechanisms of democracy are routinely undermined or manipulated towards the singular goal of retaining power.

As this chapter has shown, Maliki's first two terms in office will be characterised by militarisation, the manufacture of crisis, meddling in legislative process and oversight mechanisms, sectarian politics and an increasingly authoritarian style of governance. What must also be included on this list is Maliki's parallel campaign to shatter the unity of Iraq's Shia Arab political elite. While it may at first seem counter-intuitive for Maliki to work to undermine politicians from his own ethno-religious group, one must remember that the Shia Arabs constitute some 60 per cent of the population. In other words, the greatest threat to Maliki's stranglehold on power in Iraq's fragile 'winner takes all' democracy may not be Kurdish secession or militant Sunnis, but an electoral challenge from a Shia Arab rival popular enough to secure the votes needed to form a government. Maliki has therefore done everything in his power to mitigate this prospect. If his strategy proves successful and he is able to retain power beyond the 2014 elections, then the prospects of a peaceful and democratic future for Iraq move one step further away from being a genuine legacy of the Iraq War of 2003.

Chapter 5

The Dangerous Legacy of a Flawed Constitution: Resolving Iraq's Kurdish 'Problem'

Liam Anderson

Relative to the rest of Iraq, the Kurdistan region is peaceful, tolerant and prosperous. The region provided an anchor of stability over the 2006–7 period as the rest of the country teetered on the brink of all-out civil war. More recently, the emergence of the liberal political party the Movement for Change (Gorran) in 2009 has challenged the dominance of the Kurdistan Democratic Party (KDP) and the Patriotic Union of Kurdistan (PUK), paving the way for a meaningfully competitive political system. Small wonder then that many view the Kurdistan region as the success story of the new Iraq and among the few unambiguously positive legacies of the 2003 US military intervention.[1] Unfortunately, this success rests on precarious foundations. The more enduring legacy of eight years of US occupation is a constitution that fails to define the political 'rules of the game', leaving the Kurds' autonomous status guaranteed by a founding document that is ambiguous, incomplete and currently unravelling at an alarming rate.

At the time that Iraq's constitution was drafted, few Arab Iraqis seriously questioned that a high level of autonomy for the Kurds was both justified and inevitable. What derailed the constitutional drafting process and has subsequently thwarted all efforts to clarify and complete this unfinished document was the refusal to limit this level of autonomy to the Kurds. The potential application of Kurdish levels of autonomy to an Iraq-wide system of federalism is deeply disturbing to many Iraqis and, so long as the constitution continues to allow for this eventuality, it cannot form the basis of durable sectarian reconciliation and a stable political order. There is no reason why a highly autonomous Kurdistan region cannot coexist with an otherwise unitary Iraqi state, or, for that matter, as one unit among many in a formally asymmetric system of federalism. There is no compelling necessity for a constitution to treat all groups in the same way. As shown below, there are many examples from around the world of ethnic groups being singled out for special protection via territorial autonomy in either constitutions or documents of equivalent legal standing. Most of these 'ethnofederal' arrangements work effectively. This chapter argues that this approach should have been, and should still be, applied to Iraq as a way to break a damaging impasse over the contents of the country's constitution. Ideally, the end product will be a document that safeguards Kurdish interests and simultaneously provides a viable foundation for sectarian reconciliation. In this way, Iraq's political leaders can finally resolve one of the most complex and destructive legacies of the 2003 war.

The Constitution: Imperfect Process, Imperfect Product

The process of drafting Iraq's permanent constitution was always destined to be challenging.[2] By the summer of 2005, a violent and escalating insurgency rooted in the disempowered Sunni Arab community had already claimed the lives of more than 1,700 US troops and approximately 25,000 Iraqi civilians, the reconstruction of the country's shattered physical and social infrastructure had barely begun, and the timeline for completion of the process was, in the view of many, being driven more by political calculations in Washington DC than the reality of events on the ground in Iraq. The most challenging task for the architects of Iraq's permanent constitution was how to craft a framework of political institutions that was sufficiently flexible to accommodate the demands of the Kurds for maximum autonomy, yet robust enough to deal decisively with the country's escalating security concerns and urgent reconstruction needs. Kurdish leaders came to the table with a set of 'red line', non-negotiable demands such as retaining their autonomy under a federal system and a referendum on whether the oil-rich city of Kirkuk would join their region, among others. They also came with the so-called 'Kurdish veto' outlined in Article 61 of the interim constitution, the Transitional Administrative Law (TAL), which allowed two-thirds of voters in three or more governorates to reject the permanent constitution. This gave the Kurds a vital strategic advantage during the drafting of the permanent constitution. In simple terms, it meant the Kurds could not be forced to accept a constitution that was inimical to their interests.

What emerged from the process was a package deal of trade-offs between the Kurdish and Shia political leaders that was acceptable to both, but which offered little to Iraq's embattled and embittered Sunni community. With respect to the Kurds, the constitution reiterated and reinforced many of the various rights and powers accorded them in the TAL. Thus, Kurdistan was formally recognised as a federal region (Article 117), the status of the Kurdish Regional Government (KRG) was recognised officially, albeit indirectly (Article 143), Kurdish remained one of Iraq's two official languages (Article 4), the KRG retained power over 'all administrative requirements of the region', and, critically, federal regions were empowered to administer all aspects of internal security, including the creation of 'guards of the region' (Article 121(5)). Hence, the Kurdish armed forces (Peshmerga) were accorded constitutional legitimacy. Additionally, the Kurds won some important new concessions. Unlike the TAL, which specifically listed oil and gas management as an exclusive power of the federal government, the constitution (apparently) allowed the Kurds (or indeed any region) to control the management and development of oil and gas reserves within their own region. The Kurds also won a seemingly important victory in their struggle to reclaim disputed territories. Article 140 incorporated the process outlined in the TAL's Article 58, but established a deadline of 31 December 2007 for the 'executive authority' to complete the process. Of all the main parties to the drafting process, the Kurds had the most reason to be enthused about the finished product; but while the constitution obtained almost unanimous approval among Kurdish voters in the October 2005 referendum, it was, and continues to be, a document that divides rather than unites Iraqis.

Unresolved Issues

The drafters of Iraq's constitution used a variety of tactics to deal with issues that proved too contentious to resolve. In some cases, they simply avoided the problem by handing it off for future resolution. Hence, intractable disputes over the composition of the Federal Supreme Court and the nature of representation in a second chamber of parliament (the Federation Council) meant that, while both are mentioned in the finished document (in Articles 92 and 65 respectively), their creation is contingent on the passage of enabling legislation through the Council of Representatives with a two-thirds majority of votes in each case. Needless to say, nearly ten years after the ratification of the constitution, Iraq is now no closer to creating these two key institutions – a failure that has important political repercussions (see below).

Textual ambiguity was another tactic used by drafters in an effort to deal with intractable issues. Hence, 'ambiguity of a rather extreme sort' (Hamoudi 2013: 71) was used to fudge the clauses dealing with oil and gas and, more broadly, those addressing the division of powers between federal and regional governments. The 'exclusive competences' of the federal government are listed in Article 110, while competences shared between Baghdad and the regions and governorates are detailed in Article 114. The oil and gas provisions are sandwiched between the two in Articles 111 and 112, indicating a different status for oil and gas than for other competences. Exactly what this status is remains unclear. The text of Article 112 states that the management of oil and gas from 'present' fields is the responsibility of the federal government *with* the producing governorates and regions, which implies a collaborative (that is, shared) competence. Article 115, meanwhile, reserves all powers not listed as exclusive to the federal government to the regions and governorates and gives priority to regional law over federal law in areas of shared competence in the event of disputes. To complicate matters further, a nullification clause – Article 121(2) – gives regions, though not governorates, the right to amend the application of federal law if it contradicts regional law in an area 'outside the exclusive authorities of the federal government'. The most straightforward and reasonable way to interpret these clauses is that, at least with respect to future oil and gas fields, a regional oil and gas law trumps a federal oil and gas law and this is certainly the meaning the Kurds (who insisted on Article 121) intended. Yet this is not an interpretation accepted by some legal experts or, more importantly, by Iraq's Oil Ministry.[3]

Ambiguities aside, another key issue that remains unresolved by the constitution is the status of the disputed territories of northern Iraq. Article 140 established a three-stage process – normalisation, census and referendum – for determining the fate of disputed territories and gave the 'executive authority' until the end of December 2007 to complete the process. Superficially, the language of Article 140 was straightforward and clear cut, but below the surface, the process was riddled with complexity. For example, part of the normalisation process required a reversal of the demographic manipulations of the previous regime, a task that would ultimately require relocating hundreds of thousands of Arabs to their place of origin and resettling an equivalent number of Kurds in their place. By the time the 2007 deadline expired, this first stage of the process had barely begun and Article 140 was effectively dead and buried (Anderson & Stansfield 2009: ch. 9). This left no accepted process in place for resolving the disputed territories issue.

'Whatever the Kurds Get...'

Beyond its failure to resolve issues that are pivotal to the design of the state, the other major defect of the constitution was the decision not to treat the Kurds as a separate and special case. Unlike the TAL, which singled out the Kurdistan region for special treatment, the far-reaching autonomy granted to the Kurds in the constitution is potentially available to any governorate, either singly or collectively, that successfully navigates the transition to regional status. The process of region formation is outlined in Article 119 of the constitution and fleshed out in the Law on the Formation of Regions, passed by the Council of Representatives in 2006. The process is straightforward and permissive. A request for a referendum to form a region can be made by one-third of the members of the governorate council, or by one-tenth of the population of the governorate; the Council of Ministers is then required to arrange a referendum within three months, and the region is formed if approved by a majority of voters. A failed referendum can be repeated annually ad infinitum. The same process can also be used by multiple governorates to join together in a single region, and whereas the TAL placed an upper limit on the number of governorates that could amalgamate into a region, the constitution contains no such limit. Article 119 may be the single most destructive provision in the constitution because it paves the way for the emergence at some point in the future of a system-wide federation of powerful regions that would each enjoy a level of autonomy equivalent to that of the Kurdistan region. Backed by the Kurds, the Supreme Council for the Islamic Revolution in Iraq (SCIRI, now ISCI) was the driving force behind the decision to allow any governorate, or group of governorates potentially, to enjoy Kurdish levels of autonomy. According to Feisal al-Istrabadi (2009), Abdul al-Mahdi summed up the sentiments of ISCI notables in the phrase 'Whatever the Kurds get, the Shi'ah should get'; Larry Diamond concurs, noting that 'the notion of a powerful regional government proved attractive to more than just the Kurds. Shiites began to ask, If the Kurds can have it, why can't we?' (Diamond 2005b: 167). The fear among Sunni Arab political leaders was, and still is, that Article 119 could be used to create an Iraq-wide system of federalism composed of powerful regions and an emasculated federal government. The initial concern was over the possible emergence of a nine-governorate Shia mega-region that would then control more than 90 per cent of the country's oil reserves. This fear was confirmed by ISCI's leader, Abdul Aziz al-Hakim, in an August 2005 speech in the holy city of Najaf and it is telling that it was this speech that, according to Haider Ala Hamoudi, prompted Sunni members of the Constitutional Drafting Commission to withdraw from the drafting process, thus ending any prospect, however remote, of a consensual document emerging (Hamoudi 2013: 79). ISCI's virtual annihilation in the 2009 governorate elections and Basra's failed referendum on regional status the same year both indicate a distinct lack of enthusiasm within the Shia community for the idea of powerful regions, still less for that of a single Shia mega-region. Yet the problem remains because these defeats are *'temporary and perpetually reversible'* (Hamoudi 2013: 174, original emphasis).

The tendency among most Western scholars and many of the Iraqis actually involved in the process is to view the constitution as fundamentally flawed, in terms both of drafting procedures and of the finished product.[4] Hamoudi is a refreshing exception to this. In his view, the presence of ubiquitous textual ambiguities and the framers' decision to leave many of the most contentious issues for future resolution are a source of the document's strength. Rather than the 'forced imposition of one vision onto one or more identitarian groups', the drafters created an 'incomplete constitution through the liberal use of capacious text' (Hamoudi 2013: 57). In turn this produced a document that was 'specific enough to govern' and could act as 'a unifying symbol for the nation' but that was also sufficiently imprecise 'to provide opportunities to develop consensual constitutional construction in the future on matters of irreconcilable division' (Hamoudi 2013: 57). The problem with Hamoudi's argument is that none of this has happened. More than ten years after the constitution's ratification, none of the most contentious issues has been resolved. So, why is it that Iraq's political leaders are incapable of developing 'consensual constitutional constructions' with respect to these issues?

The Article 142 process provided an ideal opportunity to complete an incomplete constitution. Included in an unsuccessful eleventh-hour effort to win over Sunni support for the constitution, Article 142 detailed a temporary procedure for constitutional amendment that was less onerous than the regular procedure outlined in Article 126. It allowed a Constitutional Review Committee (CRC) 'representing the principal components of Iraqi society' a four-month period to produce a package of recommended constitutional amendments that could then be approved by a majority vote in parliament (rather than the two-thirds vote stipulated in Article 126) and ratified by a majority vote in a referendum. The process was genuinely inclusive, it was shielded from the intense media scrutiny that had accompanied the original drafting process, and its four-month deadline proved to be conveniently flexible. Yet, by the time of the CRC's final report (July 2008), negotiators had been unable to make tangible progress on *any* of the constitution's most divisive issues.[5] The incapacity of Iraq's political elite to resolve contentious issues is easy to describe, but less easy to explain. Superficially, the Kurds are to blame in that most of these intractable issues relate in one way or another to Kurdish red-line demands. Understandably, the Kurds pursued maximalist demands with respect to the autonomous status of their own region and inevitably this involved control over the region's security and some control over the exploitation of oil and gas reserves. Armed with veto power during both the drafting process and the Article 142 negotiations, the Kurds were under no obligation to agree to anything that seriously compromised these vital interests. But the deeper problem with the constitution lies less in the high degree of autonomy afforded the Kurds and more in the fact that it does not reserve this level of autonomy *exclusively* for the Kurds. Those provisions that guarantee a high degree of autonomy for the Kurdistan region (Article 121, for example) also guarantee an equivalent degree of autonomy for any future region. Hence, during Article 142 negotiations, the determination of Kurdish leaders to protect the former necessarily entailed the preservation of the latter. With no compromise possible on the design of Iraq's federal system, agreement on a *package* of constitutional amendments (as required by Article 142) was all but impossible.

The Repercussions of a Failing Document

Subsequent to the ratification of the constitution, the Kurds have, understandably, used ambiguities in the document to help expand the frontiers of regional autonomy. For example, Article 121(2) (the nullification clause) has been interpreted by the Kurds to mean that any law passed by the Iraqi government since 1991 that falls outside its narrowly defined exclusive competences must be specifically approved by the Kurdish parliament before it comes into effect in the region. Article 121(2), or perhaps Article 115, can also be used to justify the KRG's enactment of a regional oil and gas law, despite the continued failure of the Iraqi government to produce a federal equivalent. Since passage of the law in 2007, the KRG has signed contracts with more than forty foreign oil companies, including majors such as ExxonMobil.[6] In late 2013, the completion of a new pipeline linking the region's producing oil fields to the Turkish export hub of Ceyhan finally provided the Kurds with an export outlet that bypasses the existing Iraqi pipeline system and paves the way for a degree of oil independence for the region. This is important because it decreases Baghdad's ability to use oil revenues as a weapon to bring the Kurds to heel. Finally, the constitutional right of a region to control internal security and provide 'guards of the region' translates, in the Kurdish case, to the Peshmerga: a *de facto* standing army of more than 100,000 well-trained soldiers dispersed throughout the recognised region and beyond. Peshmerga forces patrol the so-called 'trigger line' that defines the disputed territories of northern Iraq, and the deployment of Iraqi government forces above this line requires the consent of the KRG (at least according to the Kurds). In sum, since the ratification of the constitution, the Kurds have used its inherent lack of clarity to expand the boundaries of their own autonomy to the maximum. In so doing, they provide a blueprint for the autonomy demands of *any* future region. With respect to oil and gas, for example, the main problem for the Iraqi government is not the loss of control over the exploitation of the Kurdistan region's modest reserves, it is that, in the words of one Iraqi oil expert, 'other provinces who have oil potential will see this and say "Well, we're not getting what we want from the central government and we're going to demand the same thing that the Kurds have".' (Lando 2014) To avoid setting a dangerous precedent, the Oil Ministry in Baghdad has strongly contested the legality of the KRG's oil and gas contracts, denied the use of Iraq's oil infrastructure to transport Kurdish oil, blacklisted companies that sign contracts with the KRG, and threatened to reduce the Kurds' 17 per cent share of the annual budget. Each side relies on a different interpretation of the ambiguous oil and gas clauses and, without a constitutional court empowered to interpret the constitution (itself one of several institutions held hostage to the stalled Article 142 process), there is really no decisive way to adjudicate between rival political claims.

While the constitution accurately reflects the preferences of those in positions of power at the time of its drafting, it no longer reflects the preferences of a large majority of Iraqis – if indeed it ever did. This much is evident from the numerous opinion polls in which both Sunni and Shia communities have roundly rejected a federal system composed of powerful regions and a weak central government in favour of a centralised system with a strong leader. Simultaneously, the reinvention of Nouri al-Maliki as the strongman champion of Iraqi nationalism revealed a deep reservoir of support within Iraq for the vision of a strongly centralised Iraqi state. A one-time supporter of the constitution, and a participant in its drafting, in late 2008 Maliki began to rail against its provisions, calling for its amendment to strengthen the power of the federal government at the expense of the regions. Bolstered by the successful elimination of rival militias in the south and his willingness to challenge his one-time Kurdish allies in the north, Maliki campaigned in the 2009 governorate elections as an ardent Iraqi nationalist, determined to centralise power in Baghdad (and in himself) and committed to reining in the Kurds' territorial ambitions. His political vehicle for electoral purposes was a loose alliance of forces running under the State of Law (SOL) banner. The election results confirmed that the SOL had won decisive victories from Baghdad to Basra and all but eliminated ISCI as a viable political force in the south. The vote was a personal triumph for Maliki and a political disaster for ISCI, long the Kurds' most reliable ally in Baghdad.

Subsequently, Maliki has succeeded in consolidating his hold on power in Baghdad, helped in no small measure by the declining capacity of the constitution to serve as a meaningful check and balance on the exercise of the Prime Minister's power. In part this decline is institutional. Following the 2010 national elections, the temporary veto-wielding Presidency Council was replaced by a permanent ceremonial presidency stripped of veto power. At the same time, the two institutions that might have served as effective checks on the power of the Prime Minister – the Federation Council and a constitutional court – remain uncreated victims of the constitutional impasse. In place of a duly constituted supreme court, the body that is currently fulfilling the role of constitutional arbiter is the Federal Supreme Court (FSC), which was appointed and empowered during the transitional period under the terms of the TAL.[7] The nine-member court, headed by Judge Midhat al-Mahmoud, has since handed down a string of decisions, some more controversial than others. In 2007, for example, the FSC was asked to adjudicate on the constitutionality of certain provisions of the draft law on the powers of governorates. In its opinion, the FSC justified its legal competence to adjudicate by reference to Article 93 of the constitution. In other words, the court assumed for itself the powers assigned to an, as yet, non-existent supreme court to pass judgment on the draft legislation. Describing the court's opinion as 'curious and inexplicable', one legal expert concluded that, 'as a body that pre-dated the instrument, the Court ... cannot appropriate for itself the quite different jurisdictional authority that the Constitution earmarked for a different (though identically named) institution that has yet to be established' (Samaraweera 2007). Perhaps in tacit recognition of its dubious legal standing, the court has mostly avoided becoming embroiled in bitterly contentious issues, such as oil and gas, but this merely delays the day of reckoning. Moreover, the most predictable pattern that can be discerned from the court's judgments to date is that it will empower the federal government at the expense of the governorates, and that it will favour the expansion of prime ministerial power at the expense of other branches of the federal government.

Some of these court-sanctioned grants of power to Maliki have relied on highly creative interpretations of the constitution. In January 2011, for example, the court ruled that all key independent commissions, including the Iraqi High Election Commission and the Central Bank, were 'executive' in nature and should, therefore, be placed under the jurisdiction of the executive branch (that is, the Prime Minister). This extraordinary ruling, which constitutes a massive grant of power to the Prime Minister, is difficult to square with the constitution, which states that these various bodies 'are considered *independent* commissions subject to monitoring by the Council of Representatives' (emphasis added). Among other things, the FSC has also ruled that the parliament has no power to initiate legislation; that government ministers cannot be questioned by parliament (despite the constitution expressly allowing this) without evidence of malfeasance being produced; and that a law limiting the Prime Minister to two terms was unconstitutional. Whether due to the intrinsic merits of the case, or, more likely, a well-honed survival instinct, the court has consistently ruled in favour of Iraq's most powerful politician. Far from checking the power of the Prime Minister, the court has instead played the role of active enabler in Maliki's evolving system of 'competitive authoritarianism' (Dodge 2013). Unhindered by constitutional constraints and backed by a supportive court, Maliki has been able to exploit constitutional ambiguities to create a 'shadow state' staffed by loyal supporters and family members that circumvents or simply ignores established chains of command and existing institutions of state. This has allowed him to establish personal control over Iraq's most effective coercive forces, and thereby avoid any pretence of parliamentary oversight (Dodge 2013: 250). Unfortunately, the problem lies not just with the current Prime Minister. Maliki's actions set a dangerous precedent for the future exercise of executive power, and his elaborate framework of extra-constitutional coercive institutions will be inherited and can be used by any successor, if and when Maliki leaves office.

Along with Iraq's slow but steady drift toward authoritarianism, developments in the Kurdistan region have greatly increased the potential for friction, even military conflict, between Erbil and Baghdad. The electoral decline of the Patriotic Union of Kurdistan, and the long-term illness of its respected leader, the former Iraqi President Jalal Talabani, leaves Masoud Barzani's Kurdistan Democratic Party as the pre-eminent political force in the region and Barzani himself as the unchallenged 'face' of the Kurds. From 2003 until the onset of his debilitating illness in 2012, Talabani played an important role as mediator, both between Sunni and Shia leaders when, in 2006, Iraq was on the cusp of all-out civil war, and between Baghdad and Erbil. In his absence, relations between the Iraqi government and the KRG have deteriorated sharply. To an already combustible mix of military confrontations in the disputed territories and bitter disputes over oil and gas contracts can be added a deep personal animosity between Maliki and Barzani. The latter is President of the Kurdistan region and the son of Mustafa

Barzani, the father of Kurdish nationalism, the former a newly minted champion of Iraqi nationalism, so compromise over these issues is anathema to both. In most political systems, confrontations of this sort would be mediated by a shared recognition of the accepted 'rules of the game' (that is, a finished constitution) and by a duly constituted court with the acknowledged authority to interpret the rules. Iraq has neither. In their continued absence, the threat of military force remains the ultimate arbiter of relations between Baghdad and Erbil.

More than a decade on from Operation Iraqi Freedom, Iraq's political leaders find themselves at a crossroads. Many of the country's most divisive issues – such as the division of powers between Baghdad and the regions, management of the oil and gas sector, and the future status of disputed territories in northern Iraq – are inter-twined and relate in one way or another to the current and future status of the Kurds in Iraq. Iraq is badly in need of a new constitutional settlement that, first and foremost, clarifies the nature of the relationship between the Kurdistan region and the rest of Iraq, but also results in a document that can foster sectarian reconciliation and serve as a meaningful constraint on the increasingly arbitrary exercise of executive power.

A Way Ahead

Iraq is obviously not unique in the problems it faces. Across the world, minority ethnic groups continue to struggle against governments for recognition of cultural rights, territorial autonomy and self-government. In some cases, Sri Lanka for example, governments stubbornly resist granting autonomy to an ethnic group and the outcome is determined on the battlefield, but in many others, governments have conceded territorial autonomy in an effort to terminate costly civil conflicts or pre-empt potential escalation to conflict. The word 'ethnofederalism' is often used as a catch-all term to describe institutional arrangements in which autonomy is granted to territorially concentrated minorities. However, in so far as this implies that all such arrangements are structurally similar, the term is misleading. In some systems, the Soviet Union and Yugoslavia for instance, the grant of autonomy is system-wide and symmetrical. Such 'federations of ethnic homelands' are relatively rare historically and, as the examples above indicate, have a generally poor track record of success. Significantly more successful have been ethnofederal arrangements in which the autonomy of an ethnic unit has been granted within the confines of an otherwise unitary state (a federacy), or those in which ethnic units enjoy a higher level of autonomy than other units within system-wide federation (an asymmetric federation). Since 1945, there have been more than thirty ethnic units that fit either one of these two categories.[8] All share certain key characteristics of relevance the Kurdish case.

First, in every case, the relationship between the central government and an autonomous ethnic entity (or entities) is defined in a separate document. In the case of Gagauzia, for example, its relationship with the Moldovan government is anchored in the Moldovan constitution, but fleshed out in in a separate organic 'Law on the Special Legal Status of Gagauzia'. Italy's five 'historic' regions have their autonomy defined in 'special statutes' that distinguish them from the country's fifteen 'ordinary' regions, while Bougainville's autonomy is outlined in the 2001 UN-backed peace agreement signed with the government of Papua New Guinea. In all of these cases a specific ethnic group (or groups) enjoys a differently defined relationship with the central government from the rest of the population.

Second, this form of ethnic autonomy is compatible with any type of institutional arrangement applied to the rest of the country. A large majority of the world's ethnofederal arrangements involve autonomous ethnic units attached to otherwise unitary states, but other permutations are possible. Russia, for example, is a system-wide federation of eighty-nine sub-units, but power relations between Moscow and a number of ethnic regions are separately defined in bilateral treaties. Meanwhile, Italy's five special regions are part of a system-wide arrangement in which power is devolved to twenty regions, and Spain's State of Autonomies comprises three 'historical regions' alongside a country-wide system of autonomous communities that functions as a *de facto* federation. In these three cases, therefore, separately codified agreements with specific ethnic units exist within a system-wide federal or regional arrangement. Federacies are the most frequent form of ethnofederation, comprising approximately two-thirds of the total number.

Third, these systems are flexible with respect to how much 'extra' autonomy is granted to an ethnic unit and how well protected the arrangement is against unilateral revocation by the government. In the case of Bougainville, for example, the grant of autonomy is extensive and includes control over natural resources and the right to self-determination; in the case of Gagauzia, the grant of autonomy is mainly limited to language use and administrative matters. In terms of protection, the special law that details Gagauzia's autonomy can be amended by a three-fifths vote in the Moldovan parliament; the autonomy of the Swedish-speaking Finnish Åland Islands, conversely, is generally acknowledged to be 'deeply rooted in international customary law' (Hannikainen 1997: 78).

Fourth, and contrary to the claims of many critics of ethnofederalism, this form of centre–periphery arrangement has a good track record of success.[9] Since 1945, a number of ethnofederal arrangements have failed, in the sense that they have resulted in secessions or state collapse, but almost all of these cases were fully, and symmetrically, ethnofederal. Over this period, federacy has failed just once, in South Sudan;[10] indeed South Sudan's autonomous relationship with Sudan failed on two occasions between independence (1956) and its formal secession (2011). At the same time, a centralised unitary state, coupled with government-sponsored programmes of coercive assimilation fared no better, failing twice over the same period (1956–72 and 1983–2005).

Fifth, a valid criticism of using, say, the Åland Islands' autonomy as a template for the design of autonomous arrangements elsewhere concerns context. The success of an autonomy arrangement in the stable, peaceful, democratic and prosperous environment of Nordic Europe may tell us little about its likely prospects in less hospitable terrain. Yet the success of ethnic autonomy arrangements is neither culturally nor geographically contingent. Surviving examples exist in all corners of the world, from Central America (Nicaragua, Panama) to western and eastern Europe (Finland, Moldova, Spain) and south-east Asia (Indonesia, the Philippines). That this type of arrangement 'works' for Finland is less than surprising; that it can survive in places like Indonesia and the Philippines following enduring ethnic conflicts is more impressive.

Conclusion: Ethnofederalism Applied to Iraq

The absence of a constitution that clearly defines the rules of the game and that can serve as a vital source of national unity is one of the most pernicious and enduring legacies of the US intervention in Iraq. An ethnofederal arrangement is not a 'silver bullet' remedy for all the ailments of ethnically divided societies and Iraq is no different in this respect. Nonetheless, it seems clear that something decisive needs to take place if Iraq is to recalibrate its political system in a way that imparts stability and clarity to the conduct of politics. This requires, at a minimum, a finished constitution that is stripped of its more extreme ambiguities and that can serve as an arbiter of power relations and a meaningful restraint on the actions of political actors.

The key to breaking the constitutional impasse is to separate the Kurds legally and constitutionally from the rest of Iraq. This would require tacit acknowledgement that the Kurds suffered disproportionately *as a group* at the hands of a succession of Arab-dominated governments and are therefore entitled to special protection. An 'Act of

Autonomy for the Kurdistan Region' would allow the precise nature of the relationship between Erbil and Baghdad to be clarified and codified in a separate document. This document could then be anchored in the Iraqi constitution and, ideally, recognised by an international institution, such as the UN Security Council. Realistically, the Kurds are unlikely to settle for a level of autonomy less than that which they currently enjoy, which means control over internal security and the right to manage and develop the region's oil and gas reserves. In return, the Kurds would recognise Baghdad's right to disperse all revenues from oil and gas exports, in line with an agreed formula, and would give up their presumed 'right' to the Iraqi presidency and their 'right' to influence events in Baghdad out of proportion to their numerical presence in parliament. The future status of disputed territories will likely remain a sticking point, but a new constitutional settlement would mean there is at least some sort of *process* in place for resolving this issue. The logical solution is to separate security and governance from oil and gas, with Baghdad controlling the management and development of the latter, and Erbil providing the former.

To determine the extent of the territory governed from Erbil, Iraq could do worse than draw on Moldova's example. To determine the geographic extent of Gagauzia's autonomous region, in 1994 a series of referenda were staged down to village level in order to determine the will of the people. The result was an admittedly bizarrely and discontinuously shaped 'Gagauz Yeri', but one which included only those populations that wanted to be part of an autonomous region and excluded everyone else.

None of this will be easy, but the alternatives are all worse. If nothing is done, Iraq will continue its dangerous drift toward constitutional anarchy. As one Iraqi expert puts it,

> we now have no rules to govern our system of government. The fact that the constitution has not been revised since 2005 has meant that we are totally left at the politicians' mercy: they are making it up as they go along ... This is no way to run a state and we desperately need a solution to this problem.[11]

The benefits of the ethnofederacy approach, moreover, are considerable. The Kurds would gain clarity in their relations with Baghdad and, critically, a higher level of protection for their autonomous status than they currently enjoy – especially if the document that codifies this status is internationally recognised. At present, Kurdish autonomy is protected by a deteriorating balance of military power and by the text of a document that is steadily unravelling. For the rest of Iraq, the removal of the Kurds from the constitutional debate would pave the way for a new settlement more in line with the expressed wishes of the Iraqi people. A high level of Kurdish autonomy is entirely compatible with any form of arrangement for the rest of the country. An autonomous Kurdistan region can be grafted onto an otherwise unitary state, or it can constitute one region among many in a formally asymmetric system of federalism (as in Russia) or regionalism (as in Italy). An agreement on centre–periphery relations for Iraq as a whole opens the door for other constitutional compromises, which, hopefully, will include a duly constituted supreme court, meaningful institutional constraints on the arbitrary exercise of executive power and, eventually, the completion of a constitution that has become a virtual irrelevance to the conduct of political power relations in Iraq.

Notes

1. See for example Diamond (2011); Londoño (2012); Maher (2013).
2. Space precludes a detailed treatment of the various complexities and failings of the drafting process. These have been extensively and competently dealt with elsewhere; see for example Allawi (2007); Arato (2009); Deeks & Burton (2007); Diamond (2005b); Galbraith (2006); Hamoudi (2013); International Crisis Group (2005); al-Istrabadi (2009); al-Marashi (2005); Morrow (2005).
3. For legal opinions that challenge the Kurds' interpretation, see Bell & Saunders (2007); Zedalis (2008).
4. For generally critical assessments of process and product, see Arato (2009); Diamond (2005); al-Istrabadi (2009); Morrow (2005); Visser (2010).
5. For details see 'Final Report of the Constitutional Review Committee', available at http://www.gjpi.org/wp-content/uploads/2009/01/final-report-of-the-crc-report.doc (accessed 17 October 2014).
6. For details of the KRG's recent ventures in the oil and gas sector, see Alkadiri (2010); Mills (2013); Voller (2013).
7. The legal basis for the court is Order 30, an executive order issued by then Prime Minister Iyad Allawi.
8. For a full list of these, see Anderson (2013: 250–1).
9. The main criticism of ethnofederal system is that they are prone to secessions and/or state collapse. Prominent critics include Brubaker (1996); Bunce (1999); Cornell (2002); Roeder (1991, 2009).
10. At the time of writing the future of Crimea is unclear. If, as seems likely, Crimea becomes officially part of Russia, then it joins South Sudan as a second failure of federacy.
11. Zaid al-Ali, quoted in Musings on Iraq (2014).

Chapter 6
Between *Aqalliya* and *Mukawin*: Understanding Sunni Political Attitudes in Post-Saddam Iraq

Ronen Zeidel

The April 2003 American invasion turned the Arab Sunnis, once the hegemonic group in Iraq, into a marginalised group. Further steps by the American authorities, particularly the extensive measures of de-Baathification and the ban on the Iraqi army and security forces, added more fuel to the fire, culminating in a Sunni upheaval and later Iraq's first sectarian civil war (2006–8). The political process began to take root meanwhile, and the Sunnis finally joined it in 2005, voting against the approval of Iraq's permanent constitution in October and participating in the general elections of December the same year. Before 2010, Sunnis never fared well in elections. Despite that, they were pivotal in getting the Status of Forces Agreement (SOFA), the roadmap for American withdrawal, approved by parliament in 2008. In the 2010 elections, the Sunnis voted in large numbers for a non-sectarian Shiite candidate, Iyad Allawi, only to be disappointed by his failure to establish a coalition and his eventual mishandling of the party. From this point on, Sunni politics become overtly sectarian. This chapter will delineate the Sunni perception and its limitations.

Sunni integration into the political process in Iraq has been defined as a 'harsh readjustment' (Zeidel 2008). Today, the shadow of a resumption of civil war is looming high as the Sunnis, politically more disunited than ever before, conduct a struggle against the Iraqi regime in Baghdad along civil, sectarian but also provincial and regional lines. Despite their delayed inclusion in the political process, Iraq's Sunnis never accepted the cause of the upheaval, namely the American invasion, and consequently do not recognise the legality of the current Iraqi government. Only the threat of yet another sectarian civil war prevents a much deeper rift between Sunnis and Shias.

Fanar Haddad (2011: 25–31) offers a useful typology of sectarian behaviours: passive, assertive and banal. Passive behaviour backgrounds sectarian identity, assertive foregrounds it (not necessarily by violent means) and banal takes it for granted, 'like a flag hanging unnoticed on a public building' (Billig 1995: 8). Applying that typology to Iraq's Sunnis, one can discern a movement after 2003, and even more so after 2010, from banal sectarianism to a more assertive kind. This is due to the Sunni reaction to what they perceive as an increasing sectarianism on the part of the Shias, who now control the government and assert their numerical superiority in elections. As we shall see below, this process involves the Sunnis not only setting their own boundaries between the 'in-group' (Sunnis) and the 'out-group' (Shias), but also giving content and shape to their own group identity.

In 2014, as they face another general election and doubt is cast over Sunni secession as a valid option, Iraq's Sunnis appear doomed to being left in political limbo. Contemporary Iraqi political discourse offers two useful terms between which the Sunni appear to fall: *aqalliya* ('minority') and *mukawin* ('component'). *Aqalliya* can be defined as a 'smaller number, numerical inferiority or minority'(Hans Wehr 1976: 783). In current Iraqi political usage, it refers exclusively to the smaller minorities such as the Christians, Turkmens, Yazidis and so on (Salloum 2013: 12–16). The 2005 Iraqi constitution avoids the use of this term and substitutes it with the term *mukawin*, referring to all components of the Iraqi population, whether large or small. This was done to eliminate from the constitution any reference to the numerical inferiority of minorities and create a semblance of equality and possibly 'partnership'.[1]

Mukawin is a more egalitarian term, but, as Saad Salloum rightly demonstrates, it is not a 'magic solution' to the problem of the smaller minorities as the term is unofficially sub-divided into 'small components' and 'large components' (Salloum 2013: 15). Sunni politicians prefer the term to describe their constituency, referring to the Sunnis as '*mukawin min mukawinat al-Iraq*' ('one of the components of Iraq'). Today the term has become synonymous with the Sunnis and is rarely applied to the other major groups in Iraq, the Shia and the Kurds. It is used as a substitute for the word *ta'ifa*, which means 'sect, denomination, confession or religious minority' (Hans Wehr 1976: 574). This term focuses on the sectarian conflict and places the Sunnis on uneasy ground. As part of the dominant branch of Islam worldwide, Sunnis in Iraq and elsewhere have not been accustomed to consider themselves as a 'sect'. In religious terms, they consider themselves adherents of 'orthodox Islam' and in political terms, have a history as Iraq's political elite. As such, they had a share in shaping an anti-sectarian national identity throughout the twentieth century. For the Sunnis, accepting the term *ta'ifa* means accepting sectarianism in the political arena and the end of their anti-sectarian version of Iraqi nationalism. However, now that sectarianism is entrenched in Iraqi political life, the Sunnis are obliged to respond and craft their own sectarian identity. Nevertheless, they still do so with a measure of reticence. Sunni politicians are following the general trend and becoming less inhibited in using the term 'Sunnis' in reference to their constituencies, in an ongoing process of forging a distinctive Sunni identity (discussed below). Prior to 2006, they were much less inclined to do so. Using this term, however, does not resolve the difference between 'sect' and 'component', which is connected to the identity of the Sunni group.

In Sunni eyes, the term *mukawin* is not a substitute for *aqalliya* because they do not believe the latter word should be applied to them. The Sunnis correctly argue that this term applies only to the small minorities in Iraq and that they are on a different level. In general, they urge Iraqi politicians and those engaged in political discourse to refrain from calling the Sunnis *aqalliya*; even if technically they are a 'minority' they should not be associated with 'numerical inferiority'. However, their marginalisation pushes them towards the state of being a *de facto aqalliya*.

Underneath this semantic and legal dispute, there is a hidden debate over the significance of numbers in a political system based on democratic elections. Before 2003, Sunnis were a political majority and a numerical minority in Iraq. After 2003, they became a political as well as a numerical minority. While Shias after 2003 adopted the mantra of 'majority rule', Sunni Arabs reacted by rejecting the claim that they were a numerical minority, arguing that they form 42 per cent of the population (by adding the predominantly Sunni Kurds to the calculation) whereas the Shias make up only 41 per cent ('Alyan 2005: 196–8; Haddad 2011: 94). Faced with the new reality after 2003, the Sunnis reacted first by delegitimising the change of April 2003, then by denouncing the 'sectarianism' of the Shia-led government and finally by concentrating on their 'marginalisation' and asserting their claims as Sunnis.

From Semantics to Politics: The Sunnis in the Political Process

Accepting the consequences of change in 2003 was not easy for the Sunnis. After two years of fighting a crusade against the political process and boycotting the first general election in January 2005, the Sunnis finally got involved in the political process during the second half of 2005. First they demanded to take part in the draft committee of the constitution and were given the status of 'observers' there. Later they participated, for the first time, in the referendum on the constitution, held in October 2005, and voted against it. At the end of the year the Sunnis participated in the general election although the voting rates in Sunni areas were modest.

From then on, and despite the continuing American presence, the Sunnis were definitely in the political process. However, this came at a cost. The general election of December 2005 was conducted on clear ethno-sectarian lines, ending with a convincing majority for the Shia coalition. The Sunni parties, disguised as Islamic and national parties, but in one bloc, won only 55 of the 275 seats in parliament. This was the first time that the Sunnis had to cope with the significance of numerical inferiority. After the initial shock, Sunni politicians discovered the advantages of bargaining in the negotiations for the formation of a coalition. With the country rapidly deteriorating into a sectarian civil war in 2006, and despite their marginal number in parliament, Sunni politicians were invited to form the first 'Cabinet of National Unity' under Nouri al-Maliki in June 2006. It was during this troubled period that Shias, Sunnis and Kurds agreed to share key political positions. The most important political roles given to the Sunnis were the speaker of the parliament and the Minister of Defence portfolio. During the term of this government, Sunni politicians habitually complained of marginalisation and discrimination towards Sunni areas, and the Cabinet of National Unity came to an end in 2009 when the Sunni ministers resigned. However, the same period saw episodes of cooperation between Sunnis and Shias in parliament, especially in 2008 over the issue of signing the SOFA with the Americans, putting an end to the American military presence in Iraq. The fact that Sunni tribal militias, trained and financed by the Americans, were winning the battle against al-Qaeda also contributed to the sectarian rapprochement. In 2008 the Iraqi parliament approved the Justice and Accountability Law, limiting the purges against those who were suspected of membership of the Baath party – a Sunni request.

The first bad omens that Maliki was targeting leading Sunni politicians came with the sacking of Dr Mahmud al-Mashhadani, the parliamentary speaker and holder of the highest position among the Sunnis in early 2009. The 2010 election campaign was marred by the disqualification of hundreds of Sunni candidates due to allegations of previous membership in the Baath party. The most prominent was Saleh al-Mutlaq, who, thanks to American pressure, was allowed to return to his post. It seems that Maliki, encouraged by his success at the municipal elections of 2009, was eager to weaken the Sunni bloc as well. We may never know whether he was pursuing this policy simply for the sake of weakening the Sunnis or whether it was part of his broader goal to centralise power. Whatever Maliki's true intentions, the disqualification of candidates was certainly viewed as part of a broader sectarian agenda.

In the run-up to the 2010 elections the Sunni bloc, headed by the Iraqi Islamic Party, fell apart. The Sunnis tried to realign on a non-sectarian agenda. Rafi al-Issawi, who was serving as deputy Prime Minister at the time, expressed that disposition when he said: 'The project of 2005, having sectarian blocs in politics, is now over.' (al-Issawi 2009) The epitome of this trend was the formation of the Iraq National Movement, more commonly known as the al-Iraqiyya list. Headed by a Shia politician and former Prime Minister, Iyad Allawi, this party seemingly offered a non- and even anti-sectarian line, featuring an equal number of Sunni and Shia candidates. The Sunni voters pinned all their hopes on al-Iraqiyya and turnout in the Sunni areas reached an all-time high. Al-Iraqiyya was the sensation of the elections, winning the largest number of seats in parliament: 91 out of 325. Maliki's State of Law party came second with eighty-nine seats. With these two parties winning over half of the seats between them, and conservative sectarian parties seriously weakened, this could have been an opportunity for the non-sectarian 'grand coalition' which so many Iraqis desired – especially as the two parties had similar agendas on many issues. Ultimately, the two leaders, especially Maliki, could not overcome personal animosities and join forces. Maliki opted for a sectarian Shia coalition and dedicated much effort to successfully dismantling Allawi's party.

The 2010 elections represented the peak of Sunni electoral gains. Al-Iraqiyya won votes from Sunnis and Shias to become the biggest party in parliament. However, when this achievement failed to translate into political influence, the Sunnis began to despair, losing faith not only in this particular party, but also in the political process as a whole. The period following the swearing of the second Maliki Cabinet in September 2010 saw a loss of credibility for two leading Sunni politicians: Vice President Tariq al-Hashimi was accused in 2011 of instigating murders and fled to Turkey, and in Sunni eyes Mutlaq's reputation was irreparably tarnished by accepting the position of Deputy Prime Minister and deserting Al-Iraqiyya. The Sunnis also partially lost their most important ministerial job: Maliki seized the Ministry of Defence, sidelining the politically weak Sunni acting minister, Sadun al-Dulaymi. Only the speaker of the parliament, Osama al-Nujaifi, emerged as a possible electoral hope.

From 2012, Sunni fatigue with the political process was expressed by a rise in increased parliamentary protest, especially in Sunni provinces: marches, demonstrations, sit-ins and hunger strikes were held, led by local activists and targeting the Maliki government and Sunni politicians alike. Since April 2013, the government has shown signs of growing impatience and has frequently resorted to force to disperse these demonstrations. In Hawija, an area with a Sunni majority, there was a massacre when government troops shot and killed dozens of unarmed Sunni demonstrators. Extremists from the Islamic State of Iraq and Syria (ISIS) infiltrated Fallujah and Ramadi, and left only when a military operation was imminent. On the eve of the third general election, planned for late April 2014, the situation in the Sunni-majority province of Anbar was extremely tense.

The Sunnis and Federalism: A Double-edged Sword

Iraq is defined by its constitution as a federal state. The constitution enables three provinces to establish a 'federal region' (*iqlim*) if the provincial councils agree. At present, only the Kurdish provinces in the north enjoy federal status. Initially, Sunnis were apprehensive about federalism. The first Arabs to accommodate the idea of a federal status were those in the Shia provinces in the south and centre. The Shia claim for a federal status was related to material gains: retaining oil money in Basra and preserving the financial autonomy of the Shia religious establishment in Karbala and Najaf. Calls by the Islamic Supreme Council of Iraq (ISCI), a Shia party, to establish a Southern region (*Iqlim al-Janub*), consisting of nine Shiite provinces, were probably motivated by security concerns and an inflated sense of political power. By contrast, the Sunni areas had nothing to gain from federalism and feared that the dismemberment of Iraq would leave them without resources (especially oil) of their own.

The Sunni estrangement from Baghdad boosted provincial politics and an increasing support in the provinces for decentralisation, but not federalism. Since 2011, provincial politicians, headed by Atheel al-Nujaifi, the governor of Nainawa (Mosul) and brother of Osama al-Nujaifi, the parliamentary speaker, have become the foremost exponents of Sunni claims. The four Sunni provinces (Anbar, Diyala, Salah al-Din and Nainawa) are now a central factor in Sunni politics. Whereas Kurdish politics is ethno-national and Shia politics, despite the existence of regional issues, is predominantly sectarian and national, Sunni politics is becoming increasingly provincial.

This provincialism is also nurtured by the awareness that many problems are unique to each province. Thus, for example, the discovery in 2011 of large gas fields in the province of Anbar triggered a local struggle against the central government in Baghdad over future sharing of the gas profits (ARTE 2011). The province of Nainawa confronts Kurdish autonomy on several territorial issues. Salah al-Din and Diyala are multi-ethnic and multisectarian regions where Sunnis enjoy a narrow majority. Calls for the establishment of a united Sunni province or a federal entity are rare and inconsistent.[2] However, that the Sunni provinces support and champion almost every Sunni cause beyond their borders shows that the pursuit of a Sunni sectarian identity is not yet abandoned at the provincial level.

The Syrian civil war poses a real challenge to Sunni territorial tenacity. The occupation of neighbouring provinces in Syria by fellow Sunni rebels did not go unnoticed by Iraqi Sunnis. Moreover, the emergence of radical Islamic and jihadi forces on the Syrian side had immediate repercussions on Sunni areas in Iraq. The border is porous and jihadis easily cross it. The most daring challenge comes from ISIS, led by an Iraqi, Abu Bakr al-Baghdadi. A splinter group from al-Qaeda, this organisation has declared that it does not recognise the border between the two countries (as implied by their name). It has further declared that it intends to annex the Sunni province of Anbar to its holdings in Syria. Regardless of what Sunni Iraqis think about the war in Syria, the large majority expects to see an end to al-Qaeda violence in their areas and, if necessary, they are ready to fight the extremists. ISIS's declaration was not supported by the al-Qaeda leadership, let alone by the Sunnis of Iraq. However, the fact that ISIS manages to find some safe havens on Iraqi soil (in the Tharthar area, west of Tikrit) is cause for alarm.

Iraqi Sunnis in the provinces are calling for a larger measure of decentralisation rather than a federal status. Federalism is a divisive issue in Sunni provinces. Apparently, an increasing number of Sunnis in the provinces favour the formation of province-specific regions – an unconstitutional measure – instead of the unification of some provinces. Sunni politicians and Sunnis in Baghdad, still a significant part of the community, are more in favour of a central Baghdad-based government, but one in which the Sunnis would have more power. These politicians are conducting political manoeuvres to weaken Maliki and amend the constitution, mostly within the walls of the 'Green Zone' away from the public eye. So far they have been unsuccessful. By contrast, provincial politics are much closer to the ground. However, the politicians in Baghdad retain a unified vision of the Sunni cause, unlike provincial politicians, who fail to have influence in the capital; Baghdadi politicians can potentially have more impact on national politics. Eventually, these politicians will lead Sunni parties in the coming elections.

Forging Sunni Sectarian Identity

The Sunni reticence towards defining their group as a *tai'fa* (religious sect) implies that their sectarian identity has been feeble. In the first years after the occupation only the extreme organisations openly admitted to representing the Sunnis and fighting against the Shia. The introduction of Shia sectarianism into politics and the revival of Shia practices further aggravated the Sunni alienation. The sectarian civil war of 2006–7, especially in mixed areas like Baghdad, served as a 'laboratory' for the forging of a Sunni sectarian identity with its own symbols, practices and 'heroes'.

After the civil war Sunnis adopted a host of attributes that separated them from other groups (especially the Shia) and declared their 'Sunniness'. The Sunni writer Diyaa al-Khalidi lists these Sunni traits, mostly related to religious practices and Islamic history: the Sunnis pray in the Friday mosque (*jami*) and swear 'by God, the Khalifs and Abi Hanifa'. A stranger who finds himself in a Sunni quarter should recite the names of his Sunni friends and their tribal sheikhs, as well as sayings of the famous Islamic jurists Abu Hanifa and Ibn Hanbal. He should also be able to recite the *da'aa*: the ending of the muezzin's call in which Sunnis mention only the prophet while the Shia add his family (*ahl al-bayt*) (al-Khalidi 2012: 82, 93, 122). A major issue is the different mode of prayer: the Sunnis pray differently to the Shia. In addition, articles of clothing, such as the white or red and white *yashmagh* or *keffiyeh* (head covering), the short gown of the Wahabis and logos of organisations, are used to declare Sunni sectarian affiliation. Supporting certain Baghdadi football clubs (Mansur, Rashid) is another signifier which might also be related to sectarian violence. Sometimes Sunnis also use the previous Iraqi flag or pictures of Saddam Hussein as signifiers though *not* as expression of support for the former president and his regime.

To match the extravagance of the Shia holidays, the Iraqi Sunnis have turned *al-Mawlid al-Nabawi* (the Prophet's Birthday) into the major Sunni holiday (Haddad 2013: 108–10). The imitation of Shia rites in preparation for this holiday had already been seen in early 2010. Reporting the festivities in February 2010, the Sunni TV channel al-Baghdadiya focused on Aa'thamiyaa, Baghdad's most traditional Sunni quarter, which took centre stage in the celebrations, claiming an attendance of 'millions'. Interviewees wished that 'Iraq would be united and distant from sectarianism', which, in this context, should be explained as the end of the exclusion of Sunnis and sectarian violence. One might also notice the appearance of a new Sunni logo in the celebrations: a calligraphic version of the name of the prophet accompanied by the word *qudwatuna* ('our role model')

(Haddad 2013: 108). Compared with the Shia holidays, the celebration of al-Mawlid is rather dull, comprising speeches and some music.[3] However, visiting Baghdad in 2012, Fanar Haddad was surprised to see a band of Sunni youth carrying a large drum and marching in preparation for al-Mawlid in obvious imitation of Shia Ashura marches (*mawakib*, 'procession') (Haddad 2013:110).

This situation is very similar to other conflict areas (Bosnia, Rwanda, Northern Ireland) where two groups sharing many similarities and speaking the same language become segregated and choose a set of signifiers to create borders. Insignificant items from the past, a head cover or a mode of speaking, take on major significance as they become the markers for deciding who people are. In this situation, al-Qaeda and the other jihadi organisations are also filling a certain function and consequently find followers and a place. As Haddad shows, sectarian civil wars create 'warlords', but they also generate a certain understanding and even a need for such 'warlords' who 'protect' the community and revenge the actions of their rival 'warlords' (Haddad 2011: 187–99). The jihadis are also signifiers of extreme devotion to the Sunni cause. They are like the 'ultras' in a football club: marginalised but adored, vilified and feared but also touching a common chord, yet always few in number. Their invitation, by the local population to Fallujah and Ramadi in January 2014, as part of the struggle against the Iraqi government was an admonition to the government.

The Sunni sectarian cause is not composed solely of religious and historic aspects or particular clothes. Contemporary Sunni identity is also constituted by grievances: being dismissed from the army, the security services or government solely for being Sunnis; purged for being junior members of the Baath as part of the process of de-Baathification (Zeidel 2014); being held in secret detention centres and tortured on suspicion of terrorist activity; and suffering from discrimination in the allocation of resources. All these, and many more, advance a common secular Sunni identity, which is more relevant to Sunnis who are neither religious nor interested in the sectarian issue per se.

Significantly, the Sunni religious establishment has largely been absent. The Iraqi Islamic Party, once a leading Sunni party and now in decline, was a party of politicians rather than clergymen. With the demise of the Association of Muslim Scholars (*Haiat al-Ulamaa al-Muslimin*), who in any case boycotted the political process between 2003 and 2005, the Sunni political scene was left in the hands of traditionalist or even secular politicians who abhorred the idea of turning Iraq into a theocracy or a Sharia state. The only official Sunni institution in Iraq today is a religious institution: the Sunni Waqf, established after 2003 and headed since

2005 by Shaykh Ahmad Abdel Ghaffour al-Samaraai. Efforts to unify the Sunni clerical establishment by renewing the position of the Grand Mufti, which was vacant for many years (some say since 1955), failed. The Sunni Waqf is state controlled and, as such, cannot provide political and spiritual guidance. In addition, the Sunni clerical world has so far not created leading charismatic personalities to match Shia's Grand Ayatollah Ali al-Sistani (Rabkin 2014; Zeidel 2009: 20–35). Similarly, neither the Sunni tribal world nor the provincial council of the Sunni provinces has produced politicians of a national calibre (Marr 2006, 2007; Zeidel 2010: 159–73)

The 2014 Elections

The end of April 2014 saw Iraq preparing for a general election, the first national election to take place since the American withdrawal. None of the existing Sunni parties expected to fare well in the polling given that al-Iraqiyya was split and the Iraqi Islamic Party had not recovered from the resignation of its head, Tariq al-Hashimi, in October 2009.[4] In December 2013 Sunni politicians decided to run in three blocs, headed respectively by the parliamentary speaker, Osama al-Nujaifi, Saleh al-Mutlaq and Iyad Allawi (a Shia who appeals to Sunni voters). Each bloc is composed of smaller political groups. The biggest block is Nujaifi's, which includes tribal and provincial groups as well as Turkmen parties. Of the three, only Allawi's remains loyal to al-Iraqiyya's anti-sectarian line (Habib 2013b).

To evaluate Sunni options for the elections, one has to observe Sunni electoral behaviour in previous campaigns. The first elections in January 2005 were officially boycotted by the Sunnis, who, at that time, objected to the political process. The result was the election of a parliament lacking Sunni representation and their exclusion from the Draft Committee of the Permanent Constitution. The Sunnis realised that this was a mistake and the Sunni politicians responsible were ousted. In the following months, the Sunnis gradually joined the political process and participated in the elections of December 2005 and 2010 as well as in provincial elections. However, Sunni parties understand that boycotting the 2014 elections would repeat the error of January 2005 with serious consequences to the community and therefore refrain from issuing such calls. Nonetheless, a low Sunni turnout would mean a decline in Sunni representation in parliament and might be translated into an increase in extra-parliamentary activity and the de facto delegitimising of the political system.

In the second campaign of December 2005, the first in which Sunnis participated, a large number of Sunnis voted for political Islam, represented by the Iraqi Islamic Party. This may have been a Sunni reaction to Shia voters voting for their representatives of political Islam. It is interesting that, at that stage, the immediate response to sectarianism in politics was expressed in terms of political Islam. However, perhaps due to the weakness of the Sunni clerical establishment, the performance of political Islam in politics left the Sunnis unenthusiastic, to say the least. On the sidelines of the Sunni community, Sunni Islamists are radicalising and tilting toward the Salafi or even the jihadi options.

One thing that still sustains the anti-jihadist and anti-sectarian line is that the bulk of Sunni intellectuals refuse to adhere to a sectarian identity and continue to background their Sunni affiliation. In his novel *Qatala* ('Murderers'), the writer Diyaa al-Khalidi harshly criticises the rise of Sunni identity during the sectarian civil war and attributes it to a perpetual Iraqi need to cling to grand ideologies in order to explain reality: communism, Baathism and pan-Arabism in the past and now political Islam and sectarianism in the present. He alleges that the communists and Baathists of yesterday are the sectarian militiamen of today (al-Khalidi 2012). The book was a bestseller in Iraq. Intellectuals are often unjustly ignored in the discussion of political patterns. Sunni intellectuals could have been instrumental in the forging of Sunni identity, but so far they have preferred not to be part of the process. Apparently, sectarian identity is an alien idea to those who had nothing to do with its creation and who have always dissociated themselves from it.

Finally, though some regional, provincial and tribal alignments show up in Sunni politics, they never stand by themselves as an option for the entire Sunni constituency, but rather always shelter under bigger coalitions. These alignments fail to exceed their parochial agendas and present a national and sectarian agenda that would appeal to Sunnis across Iraq. If, however, Sunnis voted in large numbers for their tribal, regional or provincial parties, the Sunni cause would be 'privatised' and lose much of its resonance. The common denominator of Iraqi Sunnis would disappear in an ocean of local and tribal claims. At present it seems that the future of Sunni Arab politics in Iraq lies in two potential options: the openly sectarian option and the anti-sectarian option, represented by the declining al-Iraqiyya. A third option, of non-participation in the elections and radicalisation, might also have an impact on Sunni politics in the longer term.

Legacy

The Sunnis in Iraq were closely associated with the state. Moreover, they were associated with a highly centralised state, run from Baghdad.

During the decades under Saddam the state was a 'Leviathan', employing many and dispensing favours to those close to the leadership. After the 2003 invasion, the Sunnis could no longer preserve their hegemony. Hasty steps by the Americans, such as the dissolution of the armed forces, contributed to the creation of a Sunni cause which was predominantly civilian and best summarised by the word 'marginalisation'. All this still lacked an ideological dimension that would give context to this group. With the rise of ethno-sectarian politics after the invasion, the Sunnis first faced an uneasy situation, since years of being in power had weakened their sectarian identity. In retaliation against the increasing sectarianism of the Shia, the Sunnis first opted for political Islam, then in 2010 voted for an anti-sectarian party headed by a Shia. When all these options failed, Sunnis discovered their Sunniness.

This newly found sectarian identity is still rather poor in comparison with Shia identity and rituals. It also fails to evoke the same emotions. Within this identity and within Sunni politics, diverse forces are working in different directions, hindering the emergence of a vision common to all the Sunnis. Are Sunnis still in favour of a centralised state or do they prefer a decentralised one? Do they accept the rule of the ballot box? As of mid-2013, the Sunnis were in a rebellion against the central government, refusing to accept its rulings or acknowledging its legitimacy. This represents a step back from participation in the political process. The central government, on its part, would like to resume dialogue with the Sunnis but shows little tolerance of Sunni protests. It is this state of affairs that is driving Iraq into a quagmire. If anything is to be learned from the re-emergence of this schism following the invasion, it is that in the absence of a fully fledged democracy based on a civil pact, politics in societies riven with ethno-religious divides can arouse latent conflicts in which previously amicable factions can descend into the worst kinds of sectarianism.

Conclusion

Returning to the discussion of the terms in the first part of the chapter, the Sunnis justifiably reject the term *aqalliya* (minority) in reference to their community. Technically, Sunnis are an *aqalliya* in Iraq but their numbers equal those of the Kurds and they have a majority in four provinces, while the Kurds control three provinces. Moreover, the Sunnis' political influence and their historic role in Iraq that preceded the formation of the new state make them a central actor and certainly not a small minority. Any attempt to exclude or marginalise the Sunnis harms the process of peace and stability in Iraq.

Nevertheless, the Sunnis are taking the first steps towards adjusting to the new realities. Of all the major actors in Iraqi politics, only the Sunnis refer to themselves as a *mukawin* (component). This is significant. It implies not only that the Sunnis consider themselves equal to the other major groups, but also that they are not alone in Iraq. A component is always part of a whole and if the components can come together – by cooperation and consent – then there will be a stable future. In this context, developing a Sunni sectarian identity is not necessarily a negative trend. Sectarianism has a bad name in Iraq and many still wish it to disappear, at least from the political sphere. However, knowing who you are as a Sunni and what it means greatly helps to define the Sunni role in Iraq. Sunni sectarian identity is not only an esoteric invocation of the distant past, it also includes the Sunni role in the formation of Iraq as well as their many grievances since 2003. The final outcome of Sunni identity may not be as historically rooted and rich in emotions as the Shia identity, but that is hardly the point.

Finally, Sunnis should not 'arm' themselves with a solid sectarian identity in preparation for a sectarian civil war. They should develop a sectarian identity as their input for a pluralistic and inclusive Iraqi national identity that would embrace all of Iraq's components and find a protected space for the smaller minorities. At the end of the process, the Sunni sectarian identity should be banal and not have political connotations: a Sunni should be able to say, 'I am a Sunni, but it does not affect my vote.' For this to happen, Sunnis need to make certain that forging their identity is left neither to the extremists nor to the politicians, both of which groups have a blatant agenda. It should be the task of the Iraqi Sunni Arab intellectuals.

Notes

1. The Iraqi constitution of 2005 is available at: http://www.washington-post.com/wp-dyn/content/article/2005/10/12/AR2005101201450.html (accessed 17 October 2014).
2. The Sunnis failed in their bid to follow the letter of the constitution and form federal regions in the provinces of Salah al-Din and Nainawa.
3. See al-Baghdadiya's report of 25 February 2010 from the main scene in Aa'thamiya and celebrations in Fallujah.
4. In October 2009 al-Hashimi resigned from the Iraqi Islamic Party to establish a new party, the Renewal List (al-Tajdid), which joined al-Iraqiyya.

Chapter 7
Post-withdrawal Prospects for Iraq's 'Ultra-minorities'

Nicholas Al-Jeloo

The signing of Iraq's Transitional Administrative Law (TAL) on 8 March 2004 ushered in a new, more pluralistic era for Iraq. It was now a 'country of many nationalities' (Article 7B). Minority languages such as 'Turcoman, Syriac and Armenian' were now allowed to be officially taught in government institutions (Article 9) and 'the administrative, cultural and political rights of the Turcomans and ChaldoAssyrians and all other citizens' were now guaranteed by law (Article 53D). In addition, all Iraqi citizens were equal in their rights 'without regard to gender, sect, opinion, belief, nationality, religion, or origin'; 'discrimination on the basis of gender, nationality, religion, or origin' was prohibited (Article 12); and it was outlawed for any Iraqi to be discriminated against in election voting 'on the basis of gender, religion, sect, race, belief, ethnic origin, language, wealth, or literacy' (Article 20B).

'Ultra-minorities' have often been regarded as the proverbial canaries in the coal mine (Griswold 2010) – a barometer of pluralism and democracy in the 'new Iraq' (Chung 2012; Lewis 2003). In a speech delivered on 7 October 2002, prior to the United States-led military intervention, President George W. Bush stated: 'The oppression of Kurds, Assyrians, Turkomans, Shia, Sunnis and others will be lifted.' During the years since then, however, Chaldo-Assyrians, Turkmens, Shabaks, Yazidis, Sabaean Mandaeans and others have emerged as among the most vulnerable of the country's citizens, and their prospects after the withdrawal of Coalition troops remain bleak. This chapter will explore the successes and failures of this period with regard to Iraq's ethnic, linguistic and religious minorities, referring especially to recent human rights reports, making for a valuable case study in the way contemporary states deal with their minority groups.

Iraqi Elections and the Quota System

In January 2005, Iraq experienced its first democratic elections. During this process, however, Chaldo-Assyrian, Shabak, Turkmen and Yazidi villages around Mosul experienced interference and injustice due to fraud, intimidation, and the refusal by Kurdish security forces to permit ballot boxes to be distributed in their areas (United States Commission on International Religious Freedom 2008). Moreover, some villages received no ballots, and others that did receive them were not given their designated boxes. In other areas, the buses promised for voter transportation failed to materialise. In one place, the polls opened from 11 a.m. to 2 p.m. only. In others, ballot boxes were found stuffed before voting even started. The provincial authorities, dominated by members of the Kurdistan Democratic Party (KDP), blamed the lack of security in the area (Christian Peacemaker Teams in Iraq 2005: 2).

Additionally, the provincial elections law, passed in late September 2008 by the Iraqi parliament, was, at the last minute, stripped of Article 50 – a provision that would have guaranteed a set number of seats in provincial councils for minorities (al-Laithi 2008). On 3 November of the same year, however, Iraqi leaders ratified an amendment guaranteeing a quota of six seats in parliament for 'minority groups' out of a total of 325, with Christians allotted three and Yazidis, Shabaks and Mandaeans one each, ignoring the original UN recommendation of twelve seats (Reuters 2008). This outraged the Christians and Yazidis since these quotas did not adequately reflect their actual population, or comply with the new law stipulating one seat for every 100,000 people. The number of Christian seats was increased to five in June 2010 (Leichman 2010). The Yazidis, however, believed that they should have also been granted five seats (Taneja 2011b: 216).

The Iraqi Constitution

The new Iraqi constitution was adopted by referendum on 15 October 2005. There were only two Christians and one Turkmen on its drafting committee – out of a total of sixty-nine officials. To begin with, the preamble of the constitution is quite vague and makes no explicit reference to the pioneering civilisations of Sumer, Akkad, Babylonia and Assyria, which the Chaldo-Assyrians, Sabaean Mandaeans and some Yazidis perceive as their ancient heritage. It also makes mention of Iraq's martyrs as being 'Shiite and Sunni, Arabs and Kurds and Turkmen' – relegating those non-Muslims who gave their lives for the country to 'all the other components of the people' as if they are not as important (Republic of Iraq 2005: 2). Furthermore, it speaks of but says nothing of Iraq's first racially motivated genocidal campaign, namely the 1933 massacre of 3,000 Assyrians in and around the town of Summayl, nor of any other sufferings relating to Iraq's ultra-minorities (Benvenuto et. al. 2013). Ironically, the preamble extols the creation of a new Iraq: 'the Iraq of the future free from sectarianism, racism, complex of regional attachment, discrimination and exclusion'. Yet it gives clear prominence to Shiite and Sunni Arabs, Kurds and Turkmens, while completely ignoring the country's other vital ethnic groups and its non-Muslim heritage, effectively excluding them from the national narrative.

> the ravage of the holy cities and the South in the Sha'abaniyya uprising ... the mass graves, the marshes, Al-Dujail ... the sufferings of racial oppression in the massacres of Halabcha, Barzan, Anfal and the Fayli Kurds and ... the ordeals of the Turkmen in Bashir. (Republic of Iraq 2005: 2)

Additionally, by establishing Islam as 'the official religion of the State' and a fundamental source of national legislation the constitution failed to guarantee its citizens the individual right to freedom of religion or belief (Article 2(i)). Furthermore, constitutional provisions that establish Islam as 'a foundation source' of legislation, prohibit the passage of laws contrary to 'the established provisions of Islam' (Article 2(i)(a)) and 'guarantee the Islamic identity of the majority of the Iraqi people' (Article 2(ii)) could result in human rights abuses and discrimination against non-Muslims, non-conforming Muslims, women and others (Jawad 2013: 15). Also, the 'Islamic identity of the majority' could be used to justify violations of the individual's right to freedom of thought, conscience, religion or belief under international law (United States Commission on International Religious Freedom 2006). Indeed, members of non-Muslim minority groups are concerned that there can be no meaningful religious freedom in Iraq as long as the law, and in particular the constitution, is based explicitly and solely upon Islamic principles.

Moreover, the same article guarantees the full religious rights of Christians, Yazidis and Sabaean Mandaeans, yet there is no mention of smaller religious groups such as the Baha'is and Kaka'is. It is even contradictory since the Yazidis are not recognised as *Ahl al-Kitab* (People of the Book, meaning followers of the monotheistic faiths of the Abrahamic tradition) in either Islam or Islamic law and jurisprudence. In addition, Article 3, while stipulating that 'Iraq is a country of many nationalities, religions and sects', also emphasises, above all, the country's Arabic and Islamic identities (Republic of Iraq 2005: 3). Article 41 states that Iraqis are free in their commitment to their personal status according to their religions, sects, beliefs or choices (Republic of Iraq 2005: 13), yet it does not make it clear that the default system for personal status cases in Iraq is civil law, and Muslims who convert to Christianity continue to be unable to change their identity cards to reflect their newly adopted faith. Baha'is, on the other hand, are still recorded as Muslims and have not been granted any sort of constitutional recognition at all (Bureau of Democracy, Human Rights, and Labor 2008).

With regard to language, some members of minority groups have claimed that Article 4 of the constitution is discriminatory and, while recognising their native languages, it attempts to emphasise the role of Arabic and Kurdish. For example, one section unreasonably dictates the huge numbers of government documents to be published in Kurdish (Article 4(ii)). Another (Article 4(iv)) complicates native language educa-tion for many groups, requiring population density before recognising a particular language as official in any region (Republic of Iraq 2005: 3–4). It does not describe, however, what constitutes such density. This is dangerous for the Assyrians, who no longer have a large population density in any one area.

Meanwhile, judges appointed to courts (including religious courts) and adjudicating personal status matters are not required to meet inter-national standards with respect to judicial training. For instance, the constitution makes it possible to appoint judges with training only in Islamic jurisprudence to the Federal Supreme Court so long as they have a minimum of training in civil law, including a law degree (Article 92(ii)). Additionally, the constitution also provides for only *limited* freedom of expression, freedom of the press and freedom of assembly (Article 38). Conversely, Articles 68 and 77 of the constitution do not stipulate that either the President or Prime Minister are required to be Muslims (Republic of Iraq 2005: 22, 25), thus flagging the way for Iraq to have a non-Muslim leader in the future.

Finally, Article 125 dangerously divides Assyrians and Chaldeans into two separate ethnicities while, at the same time, vaguely promis-ing to guarantee each their administrative, political, cultural and educa-tional rights, which will be 'organised by law' (Republic of Iraq 2005: 37). This has led to fears that the conditions enshrined and legalised in Iraq's constitution will lead to the persecution and marginalisation of ethnic and religious minorities.

Minorities since 2003

Iraq's minority groups, many of which are non-Muslim, have partic-ularly suffered from attacks and other abuses. They are subsequently fleeing the country at rates far disproportionate to their numbers and this has seriously threatened these communities' continued existence in Iraq, unlike the country's 'major players' – Shiite Arabs, Kurds and

Sunni Arabs – and despite the common discourse of 'all Iraqis are suffering' (Lamani 2009: 3, 5). Lacking militias and tribal ties and, in the case of the Sabaean Mandaeans, being unable to defend themselves for religious reasons, they have become easy prey for extremists, insurgents and criminals. Moreover, they do not receive adequate protection from local authorities and are not legally allowed to organise their own armed militias for self-defence. Many of these minorities find themselves caught in the midst of a struggle between Kurds and Arabs for control of disputed territories in the Kirkuk and Nineveh governorates. A significant number of minority groups are concentrated in these areas and it is alleged that they have, therefore, been specifically targeted. In addition to lacking adequate security, these communities are legally, politically and economically marginalised (Omestad 2012). Additionally, their members have reported routine and systematic discrimination in being denied essential government services and reconstruction and development aid (Taneja 2011a: 15–22).

Currently, roughly 3.5 million Iraqis (12 per cent of the population) belong to various ethnic, linguistic or religious minorities. Prior to 2003 they were purported to have numbered 4 to 4.5 million (18 to 20 per cent). After the US-led intervention members of many minority groups placed high hopes in the creation of the 'new Iraq' and fought successfully for their inclusion among the cultural and religious groups protected by the new constitution. This recognition, however, has not necessarily guaranteed their collective futures in the country which they consider their homeland.

Chaldo-Assyrians

The Chaldo-Assyrians are largely Christian and constitute the majority of Iraq's Christian population. They belong to the Chaldean Catholic Church, the Syriac Orthodox Church, the Syriac Catholic Church, the Assyrian Church of the East and the Ancient Church of the East, as well as to some Protestant denominations. Despite their status as *Ahl al-Kitab* mentioned in the Qur'an, Christians are at particular risk because of their perceived religious ties with the West and thus, by association, with the multinational forces which were present in Iraq from 2003 (Ferris & Stoltz 2008: 12). Widely believed to be the descendants of ancient Mesopotamian peoples, the Chaldo-Assyrians live mainly in major Iraqi cities, as well as in rural areas of northern Iraq. They tend to be professionals, businesspeople or independent farmers and, for the most part, speak mutually intelligible dialects of Neo-Aramaic as their native language.

Since 2003, Chaldo-Assyrian churches, businesses and homes throughout Iraq have been the target of coordinated attacks (Hanna 2013).[1] Kidnappings, as well as verbal and written threats to convert to Islam, pay *jizyah* (a tax imposed upon non-Muslims), leave the country or else suffer death, have also been commonplace (Freeman 2013). In February 2008, the Chaldean Catholic Archbishop of Mosul, Mar Paulus Faraj Rahho, was abducted and killed (Goode 2008).[2] At least 413 Christians were killed between 10 April 2003 and 23 March 2012, and forty-six churches were attacked or bombed, leaving ninety-five dead (BetBasoo 2012: 34–68). Prior to 2003, between 1 and 1.5 million Assyrians lived in Iraq, comprising roughly 5 per cent of the country's total population (IRIN 2006). Today no more than 500,000 remain – down to less than 2 per cent (BBC 2013). The Christians form an incongruously high proportion of Iraqi refugees – nearly 40 per cent in 2007, according to the United Nations High Commissioner for Refugees (Sabah & Jervis 2007). Of the 750,000 Iraqi refugees in Jordan, almost 150,000 (20 per cent) are Christian (Ireland 2007), and of the 1.2 million in Syria, up to 550,000, or 46 per cent, are also Christian (Lattimer 2006).[3] In 2011 they made up the majority of Iraqi refugees in Lebanon and 46 per cent of all Iraqi refugees in Turkey (Office for the Coordination of Humanitarian Affairs 2011: 66, 91). According to the Iraqi Ministry of Displacement and Migration, only seventy-one Christian families returned to Iraq from Syria between 2008 and 2013 (Assyria Council of Europe 2012: 7, 24). Perceived insecurity and the fear of being caught in the Syrian civil war have generally contributed to an increase in Iraqi returnees, but this has not included Christians. Most of them currently await resettlement in Western countries.

As a consequence of the partial success of the US military's 'surge' in central and southern Iraq, there has been a heavy concentration of insurgents in Mosul, which is perceived as the traditional Assyrian heartland. Despite dramatically lower levels of violence nationwide, Mosul and the surrounding Nineveh governorate remain one of Iraq's most violent areas, accounting for nearly a fifth of all civilian deaths in 2012, according to the Iraq Body Count monitoring group (Iraq Body Count 2013). A Chaldean Catholic priest from a village near the city mentioned that he had not been there for seven years, as a result of the security situation. He conceded that peaceful coexistence was no longer possible in Mosul, with the result that there is no longer any future for Christians there today. At the local level, moreover, Nineveh's government was perceived to be failing in its security duties to guard and protect churches, convents and monasteries, with Kurdistan Regional Government (KRG) authorities filling the security vacuum in the countryside

(ACE et al. 2011: 17). When, in 2006, the establishment of a locally manned police force was suggested, it was thwarted by the KRG, which instead created and funded its own illegal Christian militia to 'protect' the Nineveh plain (Assyria Council of Europe & Hammurabi Human Rights Organization 2010: 46–7). A Christian official in that governorate summed it up best: 'many Christian families' have fled. 'They have lost confidence in everything,' he said. 'The government is incapable of doing anything to protect them. What future do non-Muslims have in countries where violence reins [*sic*]!' (Asia News 2013).

Yazidis

The Yazidis are an ancient and distinct religious group. They are concentrated around Sinjar, 150 kilometres west of Mosul, with communities in the Shaykhan district to the east, as well as in Dohuk governorate. The majority of them speak Kurdish, with a significant number of native Arabic speakers. According to radical Islamic belief, their belief system is not regarded as a 'heavenly religion'. They are instead classified as 'unbelievers' and have no rights under Islamic law (Taneja 2011a: 27). Since 2003, Yazidis have faced increasing persecution. Islamist groups have declared them 'impure' and called for the death of all members of their community (Chapman & Taneja 2009: 8). Significantly, many Yazidis in Iraq do not identify with the nation-building projects of Kurdish political parties, and instead prefer to be considered as a distinct ethnic group (International Crisis Group 2009: 32–3). This has led to some tension between them and the Kurdish security forces, which have employed a system of patronage and intimidation in order to coerce them into submission (Human Rights Watch 2009: 4, 9, 26, 42, 44–8).

The Yazidis' numbers have reportedly fallen from 700,000 in 2005 to approximately 500,000 in 2009 (United States Commission for International Religious Freedom 2009: 40), when it was reported that Mosul had been emptied of its Yazidi population (Lamani 2009: 7). According to the United States Commission for International Religious Freedom, this was caused by targeted attacks and the fact that so many had fled into exile. In mid-August 2007 Yazidis suffered the most devastating single attack on any group in Iraq when four coordinated suicide truck bombings destroyed the towns of al-Jazirah and al-Qahtaniyah, near Sinjar, killing 796 civilians and leaving more than 1,000 families homeless (Maisel 2008). Since then, despite the general reduction in violence in Iraq, attacks against Yazidis have continued (United States Commission for International Religious Freedom 2013: 1, 6).

Sabaean Mandaeans

Sabaean Mandaeism is one of the oldest surviving Gnostic religions in the world, dating back to ancient Mesopotamia (Chapman & Taneja 2009: 7). The Mandaic language is a later development of Babylonian Aramaic and is still spoken by a small number of Mandaeans as their native language (Macuch 1965). Prior to 2003, Mandaean communities were concentrated around major urban centres in central and southern Iraq. Since then, sectarian violence and political strife have placed them in jeopardy, forcing many to flee.

According to the Mandaean Human Rights Group, from 23 April 2003 to October 2009, the community in Iraq suffered 163 killings, 271 kidnappings, 11 cases of rape, 10 threats, 21 attacks, 41 cases of forced displacement and 33 cases of forced conversion to Islam, including forced circumcision of males (Mandaean Human Rights Group 2009).[4] It was also noted that some of the killings and kidnappings were conducted not in order to obtain ransom money, but rather to terrorise the families involved. Significantly, a substantial number of the victims were women and children. In many cases the families were forced to sell everything to pay for the release of their loved ones. Despite these ransoms being paid, in some cases the hostages were killed anyway. A number of Mandaeans were issued threats to convert to Islam, leave the country or else be killed – in clear contradiction of the status of Sabaeans in the Qur'an as *Ahl al-Kitab* (Vahidmanesh 2010).

There are thought to be fewer than 150,000 Mandaeans worldwide, 80,000 of whom lived in Iraq prior to 2003 (Reuters 2001). Today there are an estimated 8,000 to 10,000 left in Iraq (Contrera 2009), including some 5,000 who are reported to have sought refuge in the Iraqi Kurdistan region (UNAMI 2008: 17–18). Their situation is made more fragile by the fact that their religion is pacifist, forbidding them to use violence or carry weapons (Lupieri 2002: 91). Consequently, its adherents are effectively prevented from defending themselves from the violence being inflicted upon them. Furthermore, one can only be born a Mandaean as the religion is matrilineal, and marriage (particularly of males) outside it is perceived as akin to religious conversion (Taneja 2007: 11). Hence, the likelihood of a Mandaean eradication from Iraq seems realistic.

Turkmens

The Turkmens claim to be the third largest ethnic group in Iraq, with a history of settlement dating back to the seventh century (Taylor 2004: 30). Apart from residing in the country's major urban centres, a number of rural Turkmen communities are found in the north of the country, in an arc of towns and villages stretching from Tal-A'far, west of Mosul, through Erbil, Altun-Kopru, Kirkuk, Tuz-Khurmatu, Kifri and Mandali (Anderson & Stansfield 2009: 16, 57). This area, wedged between majority Arab and Kurdish towns and well within the 'disputed territories', has been promoted by them as *Turkmeneli* ('land of the Turkmens'). Estimates of their population in Iraq before 2003 have ranged between 500,000 and three million (Jenkins 2008: 6). Approximately 60 per cent of Turkmens are Sunni, while the rest are Shiite (Jawhar 2010: 6). Although some have been able to preserve their distinct language, it has been reported that the Iraqi Turkmens today are rapidly being assimilated into the general Arab and Kurdish populations and are no longer tribally organised (International Crisis Group 2006a: 5).

From 2003 tensions between Kurds and Turkmens escalated, with clashes in Kirkuk (Chapman & Taneja 2009: 8). The Turkmens view the city as being historically theirs and have received significant assistance from Turkey in order to prevent it falling under Kurdish control (Taneja 2007: 18). Since 2006, reports by the United Nations and others have documented that the KRG and the Peshmerga (Kurdish armed forces) are illegally policing Kirkuk, abducting Turkmens and Arabs and subjecting them to torture. Car bombings, believed to have been carried out by extremist groups, have claimed the lives of many more (SOITM 2011). A referendum on Kirkuk was set to take place in 2007, but has not yet been held (Taneja 2011a: 9). Beyond competition for Kirkuk, both Sunni and Shiite Turkmens have been targeted on sectarian grounds (Human Rights Watch 2009: 30). Additionally, between 2003 and 2006, reports emerged of Kurdish oppression of Turkmens in Tal-A'far, leading to an estimated 1,350 dead, 2,650 wounded, 3,658 houses and 563 shops damaged, 500 houses completely demolished, 1,468 houses robbed, and 4,685 families displaced (Telaferli 2007).

Shabaks

The Shabak people have lived mainly in the Nineveh plains, east of Mosul, since 1502 and were first officially recognised as a distinct ethnic group in 1952 (Taneja 2007: 19). They are culturally distinct, have their own traditions, and speak an Iranian language called Shabaki. Roughly 70 per cent of them are Shiite, while the rest are Sunni. Estimates place their numbers in Iraq at between 100,000 and 500,000 (Bruinessen 2000: 259). Currently, their status and lands are being disputed by both Kurds and Arabs who wish to extend land claims into the Nineveh governorate. Like other minorities in this position, the

Shabaks have suffered targeted persecution and forced assimilation. In 2003, there were about 60,000–70,000 Shabaks living in Mosul. By 2008 this number had been reduced to less than 10,000, with over 1,000 of them having been killed (Eibner 2008: 9). In 2005, two Assyrians were killed and four Shabaks were wounded when Peshmerga militiamen belonging to the KDP opened fire on a demonstration organised by the Democratic Shabak Coalition – a group advocating separate representation for the Shabak community (AINA 2005). Attacks against this group have continued. On 27 October 2012 a number of Shabaks in Mosul were killed by gunmen who invaded their homes (BBC 2012), and on 13 September 2013 a female suicide bomber killed twenty-one people attending a Shabak funeral near the city (Reuters 2013a).

Armenians

Armenians have lived in Iraq from as early as the mid-fourteenth century (Wilmshurst 2000: 219). The roots of the present community, however, stem from seventeenth-century merchants and their families, who hailed from Isfahan in Iran (Hovannisian 1997: 427). After the Armenian genocide, committed during the First World War, more Armenians settled in Iraq. Important communities exist in the cities of Basra, Baghdad, Kirkuk, Mosul and Zakho, as well as in rural parts of Dohuk governorate. Since 2003, Orthodox, Catholic and Protestant Armenians have been targeted like other Christian groups. Grass-roots organisations have reported that at least forty-five Armenians have been killed, while another thirty-two people have been kidnapped for ransom (AFP 2009). Armenian churches in Iraq have also been targeted and bombed. Armenian numbers today are estimated at between 12,000 and 15,000, from a pre-2003 population of 20,000, including those who are internally displaced in the north (PanArmenian.Net 2007).

Jews

The history of the Jewish community in Iraq goes back to the Biblical Babylonian Captivity (c. 605–538 BCE). Traditionally, they were farmers, tailors, goldsmiths and traders in spices and jewellery. Since the outbreak of the Second World War, however, and as a result of Arab nationalism, they have suffered persecution and almost all of them have either left the country voluntarily or were forced out. The United Nations High Commission for Refugees has reported that, since the fall of the Baathist regime in 2003, the situation of Jews in Iraq has worsened dramatically. It states that, 'given the ongoing climate of religious intolerance and extremism, these Jews in Iraq continue to be at risk of harassment, discrimination, and persecution for mainly religious reasons' (Chapman & Taneja 2009: 7). Today, the tiny community no longer has a rabbi in Iraq (the last one died in 1996), and its last active synagogue was closed in 2003 (Graff 2008). Since 2003, their population has been reduced considerably, from thirty-five to no more than ten people in Baghdad, with some families reported in the north (Lalani 2010: 6). Most of these essentially live in hiding due to their fear of being targeted (Taneja 2011a: 9).

Because of their relation to the state of Israel, the Jews have been largely excluded from any discourse relating to ethnic or religious minorities in Iraq. While they had previously formed a cultural and intellectual vanguard, numbering around 150,000 throughout the country prior to their mass-evacuation in 1951 (Hobson 2013), and constituting 40 per cent of Baghdad's population in the 1920s and 1930s (al-Haidari 2012), they are not mentioned anywhere in the TAL, the Iraqi constitution, legislation and so on. Nor did the Iraqi government do anything to curb the evacuation of elderly Jews to Israel by international Jewish organisations after 2003 (Farrell 2008). Thus it seems that the Iraqi Jews, who have a history spanning more than two and a half millennia, are not welcome. A law was even passed in March 2006 precluding Jews who immigrated to Israel from regaining Iraqi citizenship (United States Commission on International Religious Freedom 2008). The Iraqi government has additionally authorised the annexation of former synagogues to be used as mosques (Myers 2010).

Conclusion

The current plight of Iraq's minorities is directly relevant to the legacy of the 2003 US-led intervention in Iraq and the subsequent toppling of the Baathist regime. As the evidence has demonstrated, several key decisions made by the United States administration, in the early days after the intervention, set in process a chain of events that have since had profoundly negative consequences for Iraq's varied and vulnerable minorities. The administration clearly failed to understand the true complexity of Iraq's diversity, reducing the country's ethnic makeup to just three key groups. They advocated the drafting of a haphazard constitution, the holding of elections, and a quota system for representation of minorities in the country's Council of Representatives and provincial councils – all of which have left minorities disadvantaged when compared with the 'major players'.

The Iraq case study offers evidence that minority rights are generally neglected in complex conflict scenarios. The empirical material gathered shows that larger groups tend to oppress smaller groups in order to establish and expand their power-base, and maintain for their own benefit a firm hold on key government institutions and organisations. This oppression is exacerbated by sectarianism, a lack of education and security, and intense power struggles between various political and religious leaders.

In 2014, the prospects for minorities in Iraq remain grim. Reports from as October 2012 indicate that

> civilians continued to suffer from attacks based on their ethnic, religious and other affiliations ... Members of the Christian community were also targeted – as were members of the Turkoman community (particularly around Kirkuk) and members of religious and ethnic minorities, such as Yezidi, Shabaks, [and] Sabian Mandaeans. (UNAMI Human Rights Office & Office of the High Commissioner for Human Rights 2012: vii)

Members of Iraq's diverse ethnic and cultural groups continue to face attacks directed against them. In November 2013, the new Chaldean Catholic Patriarch, Raphael-Louis I Sako, requested 'practical measures' be taken to deal with an issue that 'threatened the existence' of Iraq's Christians, underlining that the deteriorating security situation in the country and 'spread of a culture of majority and minority' were key causes behind the Christians' migration (Nasrawi 2013). The following month, on Christmas Day, reports emerged of car bomb attacks, targeting Christians in Baghdad, in which up to thirty-eight people died (Ghazi 2013). The violence and discrimination have impaired these minorities' full and equal participation in the economic, political and social life of the country.

Minorities widely perceive themselves as being gradually excluded from society. Unless the current trajectory of persecution changes radically, Iraq's ancient non-Muslim religious communities will become virtually extinct within one generation. The ability of these and other minorities to live in peace and security in their own home will indicate the success of the United States' Operation Iraqi Freedom.

At present, the Iraqi state has demonstrated that it is neither fully functional nor able to fulfil its most basic purpose – security for all citizens. The Iraqi government needs to provide a mechanism of checks and balances which would protect national minority communities. It needs to declare and establish a proportional allocation of foreign assistance funding for its various ethnic, linguistic and religious groups, ensuring that the use of these funds is determined by independent national and local representatives for each group – separate from the central government or

KRG. This is in order to ensure that assistance benefits all of the country's diverse groups, and is not being withheld by Arab and Kurdish officials, or other local and regional stakeholders.

Primarily, urgent steps need to be taken in order to build trust and foster mutual respect between minority groups and the major ruling powers. The federal government in Baghdad and the authorities in the Iraqi Kurdistan region also need to establish self-governing local administrative units for all national and religious minorities, as permitted by Iraq's constitution, as well as programmes designed to advance the security, administration and economic development of those units. This includes the training of local police forces and army units to guard areas with minority populations. Moreover, safe and fair elections and general security and safety should be ensured for all Iraqis, regardless of their ethnicity or religion. The prevention of abuses against religious minorities should be a high priority, with religious extremism countered and respect for human rights promoted in both word and deed. The Iraqi authorities should, furthermore, actively punish clerics who preach against other religions or call for religious discrimination. Above all, they should recognise the country's minority groups in the constitution, and guarantee that their rights are preserved according to international law. This is the only way in which these minorities will ever be able to survive in the new Iraq and continue to form a vital part of its national fabric.

Notes

1. According to the Assyrian International News Agency (AINA 2013), there were as many as seventy-three recorded attacks on churches, monasteries and convents in Iraq between 26 June 2004 and 25 June 2013 – with some structures suffering more than one attack during that period. The worst of these occurred at Our Lady of Deliverance Syriac Catholic church in Baghdad on 31 October 2010, in which fifty-eight people died (Surk & Jakes 2010).
2. The kidnapping and murder of Christian clergymen began on 15 August 2006. Since then, six priests have been murdered in Iraq (BetBasoo 2012).
3. Rita Zekert, coordinator of the Caritas Migrant Centre in Damascus, said that the wartime influx of Iraqi refugees in 2003 included Sunni and Shiite Muslims, Christians and Kurds in percentages roughly proportionate to their numbers in Iraq, 'But nowadays, 95 percent of the people coming to us are Iraqi Christians' (quoted in Zoepf 2004).
4. It should be noted here that circumcision is strictly forbidden in the Mandaean religion and is tantamount to apostasy, such that circumcised males are excluded from all religious ceremonies.

Part III
The Plight of Iraqi Culture and Civil Society

Chapter 8
Doing Democracy in Difficult Times: Oil Unions and the Maliki Government

Benjamin Isakhan

Following the intervention in Iraq by Coalition forces in 2003, the Bush administration undertook an enormous and unprecedented project to bring the liberal model of democracy to Iraq. Driven by a top-down model of democratisation, the occupational authorities set about creating the formal institutions and mechanisms of a modern representative democracy. For example, they revitalised Iraq's judiciary, invested millions in reforming various arms of Iraq's sprawling bureaucracy and created various public oversight mechanisms that, in theory, would prevent the abuse of power. They also put in place an interim government that would go on to organise national elections. In 2005 these officials drafted the Iraqi constitution under US tutelage and paved the way for national elections and the subsequent appointment of a democratically elected government in 2006 (Isakhan 2012b). However, while the US went to great lengths to build the formal mechanisms and institutions of Iraq's new democracy, they both neglected and actively suppressed the local level of civil society that is so critical to the function and stability of democracy. To be effective and sustainable, democracy must be premised on much more than periodic elections, the rule of law, competition between parties and institutions which ensure effective oversight and accountability (Isakhan 2012a; Isakhan & Slaughter 2014; Isakhan & Stockwell 2011). Democracies must also rest on the negotiation of power between the state and civil society – defined here as the network of social and civic institutions that are distinct from the state and which represent, advocate for, and defend the rights and interests of the people (Keane 1998a, 1998b).

The Bush administration demonstrated a startling gap between rhetoric and action on the issue of democracy and civil society in Iraq. On the one hand it argued that the success of Iraq's democracy was central to its broader geopolitical agenda, and on the other it repeatedly tried to silence dissent, to limit democratic freedoms and to interfere in due process. In fact, the Coalition Provisional Authority (CPA), which governed Iraq on behalf of the US immediately after the 2003 invasion, was quick to nullify the results of a whole series of spontaneous local elections that sprang up across Iraq. Unfamiliar with such lively grass-roots democracy, the US outlawed these elections and the officials who had been elected by their own constituents were promptly replaced. The US also went to great lengths to ban several political parties and civil society organisations and forcibly shut down several of Iraq's independent newspapers once they proved too critical of the occupying forces and their military operations. All of this occurred despite the fact that Paul Bremer, the head of the CPA, famously stated that 'democracies don't work unless the political structure rests on a solid civil society ... They protect the individual from the state's raw power' (Bremer 2006: 19).

Bremer's observation proved prescient. Today, Iraq suffers not only from the legacy of the top-down model of democracy imposed by the US in the form of the increasingly authoritarian political elite that governs the country, but also from the legacy of the failure of the US to foster a genuine civil society that could adequately confront the 'raw power' of the current Iraqi government. Since coming to power in the wake of the 2003 intervention and the 2005 elections, both the central Shia-dominated government in Baghdad and the Kurdish Regional Government (KRG) of northern Iraq have cracked down hard on Iraq's fledgling civil society. This has included the forced closure or banning of media outlets that have dared to criticise the government or their policies or to expose the corruption and nepotism that is emptying the state coffers (Isakhan 2009: 17–18; al-Marashi 2007: 113–17). These governments have also taken a hardline stance against the many unions, protest movements and civil society networks that have sprung up across Iraq and represent the interests of a broad cross-section of Iraqi society, including women, the disabled and the working class. Journalists, civil society workers and protestors have been harassed, threatened, beaten, arrested, detained, sentenced to prison and fired on in broad daylight for daring to criticise the government and advocating for a more democratic future (Isakhan 2011a, 2014c; Schmidt & Healy 2011).

In this context, this chapter focuses on the specific case of the Iraqi Federation of Oil Unions (IFOU), Iraq's largest and most powerful independent workers' union. Leaving aside IFOU's resistance of foreign occupation and its fight against privatisation, this chapter focuses on the tensions between IFOU and the Maliki government and examines the extent to which IFOU has served as a bulwark against the state's rising authoritarianism. The chapter begins with a brief history of Iraqi trade unions under the Baathist regime and concludes by arguing that examples of civil society movements such as IFOU are perhaps Iraq's only real hope for genuine democratisation.

Iraqi Trade Unions and the Foundation of IFOU

Following its rise in 1968, the Baath party sought to quash Iraqi civil society and cracked down hard on media outlets, protest movements or labour unions that proved too critical of their agenda. With the ascendency of Saddam Hussein in 1979 this trend rapidly expanded as his leadership effectively eroded much of Iraq's long-established civil society. Members of political parties other than the Baath were detained, tortured and executed; the media was coopted as a loyal servant of the regime; and trade union movements were governed by 'Decree 150' (issued in 1987), which stripped workers of their basic rights: abolishing the minimum wage, and quashing any effort to bargain collectively, to organise and to strike (Muttitt 2012: 53). From the very beginning of his regime, Saddam made certain that the state presided over a vast public infrastructure and controlled key industries such as the oil sector. Consequently, an ever-increasing proportion of the population became 'citizen-employees' and could thus be easily threatened and controlled via their fear of dismissal without monetary compensation – or much worse –either for demanding better working conditions or for airing any opposition against the state (Sassoon 2012: 249–53). By the late Baathist period, the state-sanctioned General Federation of Trade Unions (GFTU) was Iraq's only union and the body was little more than a rubber stamp for government policy.

Despite all their rhetoric about bringing democracy to Iraq and despite the fact that they went to great lengths to overturn many other Baathist-era laws, the US-led coalition that occupied Iraq after 2003 not only failed to develop a new framework for union activity, they also failed to lift the draconian Baathist restrictions (including Decree 150). According to one recent study, US policy-makers failed to overturn these restrictions because they feared that a strong Iraqi oil union would stand in the way of their plans to privatise Iraq's state-owned oil sector (Muttitt 2012). Despite their being officially illegal, however, the collapse of the Baathist regime did bring about a dramatic upsurge in trade unions and workers' movements across Iraq. They represented the interests, among others, of Iraqi doctors, nurses, taxi drivers, university staff, police, electricians, engineers, journalists, teachers, carpenters, customs officers and emergency service personnel. Since then, they have repeatedly used non-violent protests, strikes, sit-ins and walk-outs to draw attention to important issues such as their poor working conditions, the interference they are subjected to from various forces, the pressures under which they work, unfair dismissals, ineffectual government regulation and the dangerous nature of their jobs. One of the earliest and strongest of these was formed by the thousands of Iraqis who worked for the state-run Southern Oil Company (SOC). Under the leadership of President Hassan Juma'a Awwad al-Asady they formed the Iraqi Federation of Oil Unions (IFOU)[1] immediately after the fall of Baghdad in April 2003.

It is important at the outset to note three substantive facts about IFOU. Firstly, it largely represents the interests of Iraq's Shia-dominated southern regions, which are also home to the vast majority of Iraq's oil reserves. The three provinces of Nasiriyah, Maysan and Basra alone hold around 71 per cent of Iraq's oil – literally billions of dollars' worth of natural resources (Munson 2009: 185). Secondly, it is important to note that because of IFOU's sheer size (over 26,000 members) it has managed to retain its political independence from the many major political parties or movements that have jostled for power since the fall of the former regime. Thirdly, despite being based in the Shia-dominated south and founded by former members of the Iraqi Communist Party, IFOU is neither ideologically nor ethno-religiously exclusive. As one commentator has put it, 'the new union attracted communists, democrats, Islamists, and others. The only political rule was that party and religious affiliations must be left at the door when doing union work' (Muttitt 2012: 57). For the first few years, IFOU undertook a valiant campaign to oppose the US occupation and to protect Iraq's oil sector from privatisation and international plundering (Isakhan 2011a, 2014c). However, as will be detailed below, its greatest challenge has come in the form of the increasingly dictatorial and oppressive nature of many of Iraq's political elite, particularly the Maliki government and its severe crackdown on civil society.

IFOU and the Maliki Government

Following the December 2005 elections, the little-known Nouri al-Maliki of the Shia Islamist Da'wa party was sworn in as Prime Minister in May 2006 (Stansfield 2007: 187–9). However, while the ascension of Iraq's first democratically elected government in many decades ought to have been cause for celebration, 2006 also saw Iraq descend into a bloody and protracted period marred by ethno-religious sectarian violence (Dawisha 2009: 258–71). Deliberately targeted for their ideology and actions, Iraq's various unions came under attack: members were kidnapped, detained, tortured and killed by a host of different factions, their offices were repeatedly bombed or looted and their activities were severely limited. Despite the pressure, IFOU continued its work among the oil workers of the south and gathered increasing momentum as its membership swelled to more than 26,000.

In late 2006, without any consultation with IFOU or Iraq's oil sector, the Iraqi government endorsed the Iraqi Oil Law. This law had originally been commissioned in 2004 by the US administration and designed by the US consulting firm BearingPoint. The IFOU leadership vehemently opposed the law because it would see up to two-thirds of Iraq's natural resources signed over to international companies on twenty-year contracts (AFL-CIO 2006). The issue here was a particular clause of the draft law which would allow for production-sharing agreements with foreign oil companies. IFOU saw such a law as a throwback to colonial exploitation of Iraqi oil and a blatant attempt by the US to commandeer Iraq's oil wealth for its own profit. However, when the Iraqi government continued to ignore IFOU's objections to the draft law, the union sent two public letters to the Iraqi Oil Ministry (on 27 April and 5 May 2007) in which it outlined a list of seventeen demands. These included improvements to wages, health benefits and other working conditions, as well as consultation on the proposed Iraqi Oil Law ('Iraqi Federation of Oil Unions Strike Demands' 2007). It also called for the sacking of the SOC general manager and for the company's financial and administrative independence from the Baghdad-based ministry ('Iraq: Oil workers on strike in Basra' 2007).

IFOU gave the ministry until 10 May to respond before they would go on strike – effectively stopping production in major southern oil-rich provinces. The power of IFOU meant that at the time a strike would have blocked an estimated 93 per cent of the federal government's budget. Not surprisingly, Maliki panicked and the strikes were delayed when he and delegates from the Ministry of Oil organised a meeting with members of IFOU, including Asady. This resulted in the formation of a committee tasked with working to find solutions acceptable to both sides. However, when the government failed to deliver on any of its promises by June, some 600 IFOU members went on strike across southern Iraq, bringing an immediate halt to the free flow of oil to much of the country. A few days later, Maliki responded by stating that he would 'strike with an iron fist anyone that would tamper with the public order or carry out evil schemes undermining the state's higher interests', labelling the IFOU leaders 'outlaws and saboteurs' (cited in Cogan 2007). These were not empty threats. Within days the Iraqi military surrounded the oil workers and arrest warrants were issued for several IFOU leaders including Asady in an attempt to clamp down on industrial action. At the time, Sami Ramadani, who runs IFOU's support committee in the United Kingdom, pointed out that 'issuing a warrant for the arrest of the oil workers' leaders is an outrageous attack on trade union and democratic freedom' (cited in Common Dreams 2007). Nonetheless, the union held

firm and, after several days of meetings and much political delibera-
tion, Asady released a statement claiming:

> Finally the workers have won in demanding their legitimate rights ...
> And after deliberations ... the two sides agreed to halt the strike and
> to use dialogue in dealings to resolve the outstanding issues ... There-
> fore we would like to say to all that the workers' will is indestructible.
> The workers can achieve what they want by the means available to
> them and their strength. And the oil workers are very strong, because
> they have a legitimate right ... Long live the Iraqi working class.
> (al-Asady 2007)

However, the fight was far from over. In the following month (July
2007), IFOU conducted further rallies in Basra in protest against the
draft Iraqi Oil Law. Even the state-sanctioned General Federation of
Iraqi Workers (GFIW) indicated their strong opposition to the law. They
demanded that the government consult with and include members of
the union in the discussions and adamantly rejected the privatisation of
Iraq's national oil wealth (General Federation of Iraqi Workers 2007).
Indicating his disdain for any critical union movement, the Iraqi Oil
Minister, Hussain al-Shahristani, issued a statement in which he ordered
the Ministry of Oil to immediately halt any 'cooperation with any member of any union in any of the committees organised under the name of
the union as these unions do not enjoy any legal status to work inside
the government sector' (cited in Solidarity Center 2007).

By May 2008, while the Iraqi Oil Law had not been officially ratified, the Iraqi government had begun courting several large international oil companies including Chevron and ExxonMobil in the hope
of securing lucrative contracts. In perhaps his most provocative move
to date, Asady responded by issuing a statement to the annual shareholder meetings of both Chevron and ExxonMobil. It is worth citing
at length:

> We call upon the governments, corporations and other institutions
> behind the ongoing occupation of Iraq to respond to our demands
> for real democracy, true sovereignty and self-determination, free of
> all foreign interference. Five years of invasion, war and occupation
> have brought nothing but death, destruction, misery and suffering to
> our people ... Our union offices have been raided. Union property
> has been seized and destroyed. Our bank accounts have been frozen.
> Our leaders have been beaten, arrested, abducted and assassinated.
> Our rights as workers are routinely violated. This is an attack on our

rights and the basic precepts of a democratic society ... We call upon you ... to end the nightmare of occupation and restore our sovereignty and national independence so that we can chart our own course to the future. (al-Asady 2008)

The statement goes on to list four key demands: the immediate withdrawal of all foreign troops; the passage of a labour law to protect the rights of the workers; an end to meddling in Iraq's economic affairs by foreign powers and multinational corporations; and that the 'US government, oil companies and others immediately cease lobbying for the oil law which would fracture the country and hand control over our oil to multinational companies like ExxonMobil and Chevron' (al-Asady 2008). Despite such vehement opposition and the lack of an appropriate legal framework, British and US oil companies including Chevron and ExxonMobil were awarded a series of lucrative oil contracts on 30 June 2008, fuelling the notion that the war was all about Western profiteering from Iraqi oil.

In the round of oil contracts awarded by the Iraqi government a year later (June 2009), BP and China National Petroleum Company bid for sites such as the Rumailah oil field in Basra, the country's largest producing oil field (Alsumaria 2009). IFOU threatened to escalate their opposition and a senior member of the union, Falih Abboud Imara, commented at the time: 'If the Ministry of Oil insists on executing the agreements with the foreign companies, we will work on making the deals fail' (cited in Al Jazeera 2009). To do so, IFOU would once again shift from peaceful demonstrations to complete strikes across all of Iraq's southern oil refineries controlled by IFOU, totally halting production. Given this environment, it is hardly surprising that the Iraqi Ministry of Oil stepped up its crackdown on the rights and freedoms of Iraq's oil unions. Shahristani employed several key tactics: he continued to maintain that union activity was in fact illegal because the 1987 Baathist law prohibiting unions had not been overturned; he threatened to sue the IFOU leadership for provocations against the government and foreign companies if they continued to create obstacles to reaching agreements with international oil firms; and he ordered the forced relocation of many IFOU members and activists throughout 2008–10, including union leaders such as Vice President Ibrahim Radhi (Norton-Taylor 2008; Solidarity Center 2010). The latter response was particularly harsh not only because it represented a major breach of civil rights and a blatant attempt at union-busting, but also because it was very dangerous for Radhi as union members were usually transferred to unsafe areas or to those with different ethno-religious or tribal affiliations.

At the March 2010 elections no one Iraqi political bloc managed to secure the 163 seats needed to form a government in the 325-member parliament. The nation plummeted into nine long months of political stalemate. In the middle of 2010, as the government deadlock continued and Iraqis sweltered in the heat of summer with only sporadic electricity to fuel their air conditioners and poor access to drinking water, frustrations reached boiling point. Several protests and sit-ins erupted across Iraq, the largest and longest of which were held in the south at Nasiriyah and Basra. In reaction to the protests, the Iraqi government introduced a set of regulations that severely limited the ability of Iraqis to organise peaceful protests. The new regulations also permitted the Iraqi Security Forces (ISF) to use 'all known methods to disperse protestors', including unlimited force, which led to intimidation, the arrest of protest organisers and to injuries and deaths (Human Rights Watch 2010). Under these new oppressive measures, it was not long before the Iraqi government brought charges against IFOU and issued arrest warrants for Asady and other senior members such as General Secretary Faleh Abood Umara, on the grounds that they had urged strikes and spoken to both the Iraqi and international media about the poor conditions suffered by Iraq's oil workers (Gentile 2010; Iraqi Federation of Oil Unions 2010).

Iraq's 2010 political deadlock continued until early November when an agreement was signed which would pave the way for the formation of a government. Finally, a government was announced in December of 2010; Maliki had succeeded in his campaign to retain the office of Prime Minister and many other key positions would rotate among a handful of familiar faces (Ottaway & Kaysi 2010a). One substantial change was the appointment of Shahristani as Deputy Prime Minister for Energy. It seems that his heavy-handed approach to cracking down on unions, protests and civil society had impressed Maliki and he was duly rewarded. At the time of his appointment, Shahristani boasted of the fifteen oil and gas contracts that had been signed with major international energy companies, despite the fact that Iraq had not officially ratified its Oil Law and the move had been strongly resisted by the sector, especially IFOU (UPI 2010).

As Shahristani took up his new post in Baghdad, the very first protests of the so-called 'Arab Spring' were occurring across Tunisia (Isakhan 2014a; Isakhan et al. 2012). As long-lasting and deeply entrenched regimes fell across the region and citizens embraced a new era of dissent and democratisation, Iraqis were confronted with the failures of their own democracy to deliver on the many promises made to them since 2003. This led to weeks of scattered protests across Iraq, culminating in the 'Day of Rage' (25 February 2011), in which thousands of protestors took to the streets in at least seventeen separate demonstrations across the country following Friday prayers. In Baghdad's own Tahrir Square thousands of Iraqi protestors gathered to voice their concerns and air their frustrations, with many calling for an end to Maliki's leadership (Al Jazeera 2011a, 2011b).

Predictably, Maliki reacted to these events in ways similar to dictators and autocrats across the region: he ordered a brutal crackdown on the Iraqi protestors, journalists and political actors who had been involved in the events and on Iraqi civil society. The ISF and the protestors clashed frequently, leading to many arrests, beatings and deaths. This also included a crackdown on the nation's oil sector. In February, the Ministry of Oil issued official penalties of around US$50,000 each to several refinery employees for having delayed production – for less than twenty-four hours – in order to protest against conditions and pay ('Minister of Oil' 2011). Such figures are exorbitant by international standards and impossible to pay for average Iraqis – the daily wage for skilled labour is around US$10, for unskilled labour as low as US$4.50. Similar fines were also issued to organisers of a combined IFOU and GFIW protest of more than 300 oil sector employees staged outside the headquarters of the SOC in May. They had rallied against the deep-seated corruption among management and demanded their pay rate match that of employees of foreign oil companies. One oil worker, Assad Abu Hussein, said:

> If the Southern Oil Company does not give us our rights of profits and bonuses, we will stop production. Just because we are poor and our field was not developed by a foreign company like the rest of the oil fields, we are being treated unfairly. (Quoted in Bedford 2011)

In response, the Iraqi government issued Decree 95 and Decree 97, which officially withdrew their recognition of the once state-backed GFIW, immediately appointing its replacement in the new Ministerial Preparatory Committee (MPC). In one swift manoeuvre the Iraqi government had rid themselves of any troublesome union movement in favour of the unelected and politically partisan MPC, which took over the supervision of Iraq's official trade sector, including the forthcoming union elections (International Federation of Chemical, Energy, Mine and General Workers' Unions 2011). It almost goes without saying that such moves are not only profoundly anti-democratic, they also speak to a complex Iraqi political landscape in which the ruling elite are becoming increasingly authoritarian and oppressive.

Given this political climate, it is not surprising that Iraq's trade unions have continued to suffer since the final withdrawal of all Coalition troops at the end of 2011. For example, from 24 June to 2 July 2012 the Iraqi Ministry of Labour and the MPC held a series of sham elections for positions on the executive of the state-approved GFIW. These elections were held behind closed doors with the result that a handful of specially chosen individuals – most with no union affiliation, credentials or experience – were 'elected' to positions of leadership in various Iraqi trade unions (US Labor against the War 2012b). The aim here was to undermine the legitimacy of Iraq's union movement and to create client unions rather than legitimate and democratically elected workers' representatives (Iraqi Civil Society Solidarity Initiative 2012). This is a typically authoritarian approach in which the role of civil society is inverted: rather than represent the interests of the people to the state, it is coopted by the state and forced to represent its interests to the people.

The government's action led several trade unions (including IFOU and the GFIW) to issue statements – including joint statements – which detailed their various grievances and demands as well as documenting their abhorrence of the sham elections (US Labor against the War 2012a, 2012b). In one such statement they called on the Iraqi government

> to address these violations; to support Iraqi workers' rights to legitimate, independent and democratic trade unionism as enshrined by Iraq's permanent constitution; and to further stop interfering in the internal affairs of the unions and instead provide legal and political space for the Iraqi trade union movement to constitute its internal democracy independently and transparently. (Iraqi Civil Society Solidarity Initiative 2012)

Further still, a federation of more than thirteen trade union movements (including IFOU and the GFIW) filed a lawsuit against the government to challenge the violations made by the Ministry of Labour and the MPC (General Federation of Iraqi Workers 2012). In what appears to be a clear retaliation for their outspoken criticisms of the government, the headquarters of the GFIW in Basra were raided in mid-September 2012, most likely by government forces, with computers, reports and meeting minutes confiscated (General Federation of Trade Unions and Workers' Councils in Iraq 2012). This was followed later the same month by an attempt by 'government thugs' to occupy the headquarters and take over the union (Iraqi Civil Society Solidarity Initiative 2012).

In early February 2013 another round of protests erupted among the oil workers of southern Iraq. For several weeks, hundreds gathered at the headquarters of the state-run SOC in Basra and at oil fields across the south. In Nasiriyah workers protested against a decision by the Ministry of Oil to alter their work hours and shift schedules; at the West Qurna 1 oil field they demanded that ExxonMobil and SOC make good on their promises for additional jobs for locals and compensation for farmland ruined or appropriated due to oil development; and at the

Basra headquarters of the SOC around 500 oil workers carried placards alleging nepotism and corruption before demanding payment of two years' worth of bonuses that had not been forthcoming (Iraq 2013a, 2013c; Oil Workers' Rights Defense Committee 2013). At the time of these protests, a federation of Iraqi unions (including IFOU) issued a joint open letter on the 18 February 2013. It made the following seven demands of the Iraqi government and the international oil companies currently operating in Iraq. It is worth citing at length:

1. Respect the sovereignty of the Iraqi people over their natural resources, and noting the lack of legitimacy of their contracts, to relinquish any claims to rights over Iraqi oil.
2. With oil companies now having taken the place of foreign troops in compromising Iraqi sovereignty, set a timetable for their withdrawal, while transferring technology to Iraq's national oil companies.
3. Stop exacerbating tensions between the Kurdistan Regional Government and the central Government of Iraq, by ceasing to exploit oil until a stable national accord has been achieved, supported by all Iraq's citizens.
4. Promote transparency in the oil sector in Iraq, by publishing details of all contracts and ensuring Iraqi citizens' access to information about Iraqi oil resources and their development. This is vital to end the corruption that has become rampant as a result of the presence of international oil companies in Iraq.
5. Support the passage of an Iraqi Labor Law that guarantees all Iraqi workers' rights that are in accord with the highest, international standards and that protects their freedom of association and their right to strike.
6. Adopt clear policies to protect the Iraqi environment and agree to utilize appropriate, advanced equipment to monitor the effects of your companies' activities on the soil, water and air in Iraq.
7. Agree that the security and protection of personnel and equipment in all Iraqi oil fields should be exclusively under the authority of national Iraqi security forces. These responsibilities should not be assigned to private security companies that are based in other nations and that undermine the sovereignty of Iraq. (Iraqi Civil Society Solidarity Initiative 2013)

When the Iraqi government continued to ignore their demands, the protests took an aggressive turn. On 28 February 2013 700 oil workers stormed the gates of the SOC headquarters and on 4 March 400 residents of nearby villages raided the West Qurna 2 site, wrecking offices but doing little substantial damage (Iraq 2013b; Reuters 2013b). In April, after these drastic actions failed to produce a tangible solution, around 1,000 oil workers created a tent city outside the SOC headquarters. This was followed by further oil union protests in Basra in August and September 2013 and culminated in a 3,000-strong IFOU-led rally at the SOC headquarters in December followed by two weeks of strikes (Bacon 2013; Ghanim 2013; Heuvelen & Iraq 2013).

Meanwhile, the Maliki government continued their crackdown on Iraq's civil society, including the issuing of more than US$600,000 in fines against sixteen union activists (Clarion 2013). Not surprisingly, these activists included Hassan al-Asady, who was also arrested, to be tried under the 1987 Baathist decree banning union activity. He stood accused of organising strikes and protests with the express intention of deliberately harming Iraq's economy and, if found guilty, faced up to five years in jail (Iraq & Lando 2013). The trial was postponed several times throughout April, May and June 2013 as the Ministry of Oil and the SOC consistently failed to produce evidence to support their case. Asady's defence maintained that his activities were the legitimate work of a union official and that he had sought to help the Iraqi people rather than to undermine their government. At the trial in Basra on 1 July 2013, the court took less than thirty minutes to acquit the case and formally drop all charges against Asady (IndustriALL 2013). However, both the Ministry of Oil and the SOC appealed the decision and the charges were reinstated before several further delays and another court hearing on 10 November 2013. Once again the case was acquitted for lack of evidence and all charges were dropped (Clarion 2013). At the time of his release, Asady stated:

> Iraq calls for democracy and is trying hard to reach a deal in state institutions on the principles of democracy, but regrettably [the Iraqi government is] ... overriding the Iraqi constitution, which gave the right to protest and strike, and which acknowledges the right of any citizen to express his opinion in a civilized manner, provided there is no damage to public property. (Quoted in Iraq & Lando 2013)

Conclusion

While Asady survived the trial and can return to his valiant fight on behalf of the oil workers, his comments strike at the heart of the central argument of this chapter. To be specific, Asady draws attention to the fact that, in the struggle of the Iraqi people towards democracy, they are confronted with the 'raw power' of a political elite who are manipulating and undermining Iraq's fragile democracy towards their own increasingly authoritarian ends. To mitigate against such a scenario a modern representative democracy is supposed to foster a vibrant and robust civil society which works on behalf of the people and serves as watchdog over those in power. As has been demonstrated in this chapter, however, Iraq's civil society groups, such as IFOU, have suffered immensely at the hands of Iraq's current government. Both Iraq's increasingly authoritarian government and their treatment of Iraq's civil society are a direct legacy of a military occupation which sought to impose a top-down model of democracy with little regard for the grassroots level of civil society.

It is remarkable that, in such a context, IFOU has been able to maintain its struggle. This is, however, a critical time for Iraqi civil society movements such as IFOU. They continue to endure poor conditions, low pay and little safety, and have virtually no rights. In the eight years that have elapsed since they came to power, the Iraqi government have not made any substantive effort to overturn the oppressive Baathist laws which restrict the rights of unions to advocate on behalf of the workers. Similarly, the lack of an appropriate legal framework governing foreign oil investment has left billions of dollars of Iraq's oil wealth exposed to foreign exploitation and rampant corruption. In addition, unions like IFOU have been actively suppressed by military force and the strong-arm tactics of an increasingly oppressive state that has mastered the manipulation of democracy for authoritarian ends.

Despite all of this, there are several very interesting points to be made about the struggle between trade unions and the current Iraqi government. First, these indigenous, localised and highly coordinated movements reveal the strength of the Iraqi people's will towards democracy and demonstrates that they are more than capable of utilising democratic mechanisms in the face of authoritarian forms of power. Second, while the participation and engagement of the Iraqi citizenship with democratic mechanisms such as unions does not qualify Iraq as a democracy, it is a positive milestone towards such an end. Civil society groups such as IFOU are critical in holding the Iraqi government to account; they are an informal network of power that have proven themselves capable of advocating for democratic change in the face of various forms of tyranny and oppression. Whichever way Iraq turns from here, Iraqi trade unions and workers' movements such as IFOU will be critical to the nation's stability and may well be the only real hope for a robust democracy.

Note

1. In its first iteration in 2003, IFOU was in fact named the Southern Oil Company Union. It then changed its name to the General Union of Oil Employees in June 2004 before a final name change to IFOU in 2006.

Chapter 9

'If You're a Female, You Risk Being Attacked': Digital Selves, Warblogs and Women's Rights in Post-invasion Iraq

Perri Campbell and Luke Howie

The intervention of 2003 and several key decisions made by the United States-led forces in the early days of the war set in process a chain of events that have had profound consequences for Iraq's women. In many respects the US-led invading forces failed to understand the complexity of Iraq and to adequately advocate for women's rights and freedoms. Women in Iraq now live in times characterised by surges in violence and state executions, illegal detention and abuse, political unrest, under-age marriage, chronic housing shortages and so-called 'honour' crimes (Bassem 2013; Smith et al. 2013). Media reports indicate that Iraqi women are 'victimised' and have become increasingly unsafe in the streets (Archer 2013; Barwari 2013; McGeough 2014). Zillah Eisenstein (2013) notes that, more than ten years after the invasion, for the most part 'women in Iraq are left to fend for themselves'. In this time of crisis, women cannot rely on the justice system in Iraq to uphold their rights. As the 2014 elections unfold in Iraq a new bill will be voted on. The 'Jafari law', as it is being called, would effectively legalise the marriage of minors (children as young as nine) and marital rape. Further legal injustices are highlighted by the Human Rights Watch report titled 'No One Is Safe'. The report describes illegal arrests and 'violations against women at every stage of the justice system ... Women are subject to threats of, or actual, sexual assault sometimes in front of husbands, brothers, and children' (Human Rights Watch 2014b: 2). This confirms what has long been denied by Iraqi officials – including the justice and human rights ministers – that women are being taken into custody and tortured, in many cases to coerce relatives into confessing to crimes they may or may not have committed (Human Rights Watch 2014b: 6; Zangana 2013). 'No One Is Safe' is but one record of the ways in which Iraqi women continue to face the consequences of the US-led invasion and occupation of Iraq, many of which have been denied, lied about and concealed from the broader public and

Western audiences (Carr 2008; Tessier 2007–8). This chapter attempts to contribute to the understanding of Iraqi women's lives, at a time when many people are asking questions about what violence against women means for broader Iraqi society. As one respondent says, 'normally, in Iraqi society, a man beating a woman in public is impossible. What's happening to women shows that no one is safe' (Human Rights Watch 2014b: 2).

For those witnesses[1] living outside Iraq – including these authors – the ability to understand women's lives in Iraq is determined by the information made available in media and academic spaces. Judith Butler (2009) argues that these sources present mere fragments or 'frames of war' which determine how external witnesses are able to imagine life in Iraq during this period in time. These 'frames' have an important function as they determine not only how people understand the war as an historical event, but how *life itself* is understood and recognised in this context. The argument, as Butler puts it, is that viewing and witnessing war involves the deployment of 'frames of recognition' – pre-conceived ideas of what constitutes life (Butler 2009: 5). Butler's theory has consequences for how Iraqi women's accounts of war matter and can be understood. Of particular interest to this chapter are the ways in which witnesses are able to understand women's lives in Iraq and how this is influenced by the discursive project of framing. This chapter focuses on the ways in which Iraqi women bloggers contribute to Western audiences' understanding of what it means to be a woman in post-invasion Iraq. Bloggers' stories contest existing – historical, political, news-media – frames of life, such as the 'struggling' Iraqi woman, or normative ideas of what it means to be an Iraqi woman. Bloggers give movement to and complexify the category 'Iraqi woman'.

This chapter engages with the stories told by two female Iraqi bloggers, who write a digital self online: 'Riverbend', as she is known, whose blog is titled Baghdad Burning, and Faiza al-Araji, whose blog is titled A Family in Baghdad.[2] Riverbend's and Faiza's blogs tell the story of women growing up and working (before the war) in Baghdad. Faiza and Riverbend are tied together by friendship. They are digitally networked, prominent figures in the Iraq War blogosphere, due partly to their position as two of the first female Iraqi bloggers, and partly to their ability to capture their audience with eyewitness accounts of life in Iraq. Many of Faiza's posts are translated by Riverbend. Many of Riverbend's stories and calls for justice are echoed in Faiza's own blog. These blogs, written in English, provide international audiences with an alternative narrative of events in Iraq, and at same time contribute to understandings – frames – of women's lives and rights.

Witnessing War Zones from Digital Fields of Possibility

The Iraq War has been recorded in a number of ways that will shape how it is remembered in the years to come. But, as Butler (2009) has argued, who gets to do the recording matters. Some witnesses' versions of events, it seems, matter more than others. In times of war witnesses can 'start with the numbers, counting the injured and the dead as a way of taking stock of the losses'. But this should never be the end of the process. Numbers can mean different things to different people in different contexts. The number of lives lost at the hands of nineteen terrorists on 9/11, for example, was far smaller than in many other violent events and attacks, including the United States-led invasion and occupation of Iraq – as Iraq Body Count attests.[3] As the sections that follow will demonstrate, to witness is to have a particular, situated view of events and their meaning.

The stories that we tell in this chapter take place online in the Iraq War blogosphere in what we will refer to as 'digital fields of possibility', a term drawn from the later work of Michel Foucault (1982a, 1982b). Fields of possibility are shaped by non-digital – offline – events and occurrences located in places such as the university or school, the market or the workplace. Digital fields of possibility are written into existence online and are shaped by personal experiences, conversations and images, all the while drawing on other, typically online, media discourses (Campbell & Kelly 2013). Digital fields embody the storytelling possibilities afforded by the relatively 'safe' spaces of the internet (safe when compared to the street corner or stopping at traffic lights). It is a space where people who are 'interested in the same issues pull together into networked neighborhoods of densely interconnected bloggers' (Whitaker & Varghese 2009: 6).

Iraqi women joined the Iraq War blogosphere documenting the challenges they faced in their everyday lives. In a time of war, weblogs allowed women to force 'out into the open issues that patriarchal societies would rather keep hidden' (Loewenstein 2008: 9). For those Iraqi women with access to the internet, this was a space to speak out and share fears in a public space relatively free from violent consequences. This was a space to ask 'Who takes responsibility for the spilt blood?' – to communicate personal and political perspectives, and to vent frustrations – 'or is this blood worthless because it is not American?' (al-Araji 2004a).

In the blogosphere individuals create and encounter certain types of self: 'digital selves'. These are selves that are written online, captured as they unfold in necessarily fragmented ways, mediated by digital communications technology. If it were not for the digital selves of the bloggers, the authors of this chapter would not encounter these women in the same ways, outside the corporatised, tightly managed, glossy productions of mass media news networks (Zhao 2005: 387). In this sense, this chapter is a story is about *connections* and points of contact between people who would otherwise not encounter each other (Kroker 2012: 2). In this context, it could even be argued that there is often something more authentic happening when digital selfhood is in play, contradicting some of the more traditional notions of online social encounters (Turkle 1999).

The following sections present an account of the selves that are written and given shape online by women in war zones and how these online or digital selves provide witnesses in distant locations – a window into life in Iraq during a particular time in one of the 'contact zones' of world affairs (Haraway 2008: 205; Torre & Fine 2008: 23). With heavily censored reporting from embedded journalists as the norm, the war blogs were a place to glimpse the war through the eyes of Iraqi people (Loewenstein 2008: 9). These weblogs continue to provide opportunities for challenging established channels through which Iraqi women's lives have been understood.

Riverbend's and Faiza's stories are not necessarily representative of women's experiences in Baghdad or other locations in Iraq. Their blogs communicate their lived experiences and realities. Their stories are often familiar in the ways they mirror news reporting (war, violence, chaos), but they also contradict these reports with accounts of women's social and emotional well-being, as well as their experiences of rights and freedoms. While the administration of George W. Bush promoted the improved condition of women post-invasion, these women bloggers tell stories of new, worse challenges in Iraq (al-Ali & Pratt 2009: 10).

Women's Rights and Lives in Iraq

Women's rights and lives in Iraq have developed in particular ways in different locations throughout the country's long history. Many positive stories of women's lives have emerged – from the nineteenth-century pioneering Iraqi women, to stories of women's rights groups and progressive state policies in the twentieth century (Efrati 2004: 154; Hourani 1991; Ingrams 1983: 85; Mernissi 1991: 90). Within this literature on Iraqi women's rights there is also debate over what women's rights mean and their particular connection to the West. For some, frames of women's rights include contradictory fields produced through the language of liberalism and an understanding of Muhammad as 'one of the greatest supporters of women's rights' (Mernissi 1991: 90). The challenge, in many instances, lies in how the rights and freedoms that women have (or desire) can be discussed and understood without imposing ideals about what rights women should have.

In many instances, the stories that audiences in the West encounter about women's rights in Iraq are strongly linked to Iraqi women's educational opportunities and political processes. Albert Hourani (1991) argues that women's rights became communicable to Western audiences particularly in the 1950s through the activities of women's liberation groups such as the Iraqi Women's League. However, Suad Joseph suggests that 'these rights and responsibilities have been defined mainly top down' (2000: 9) such as during the regime of Abd al-Karim Qasim (1958–63) and the Baathist governments of Al Bakr and Saddam Hussein (al-Ali & Pratt 2009: 33). Many accounts indicate that women's rights began to improve in 1959, when Qasim's government, 'supported by the Iraqi Communist Party[,] amended Personal Status Law' (PSL), and granted equal inheritance and divorce rights (al-Azzawi 2007: 4). In the 1970s, during Saddam Hussein's rule, women became part of a modernisation process through which they experienced greater educational opportunities and freedom in public spaces (al-Jawaheri 2008: 58). A decade later, educational opportunities were limited by the war with Iran (1980–8) and women were encouraged to participate in the labour force instead (al-Jawaheri 2008: 60).

Iraqi women have been, and continue to be, active in defining their rights and responsibilities as citizens. In the post-invasion era, many women attempted to shape Iraq's future 'by forming NGOs, advocating for women's rights and participating in the political process, whether as voters or candidates' (al-Ali & Pratt 2009: 8). However, they frequently operated within unsafe and unstable conditions. In 2007, Yanar Mohammed, the pioneer of the Organization for Women's Freedom in Iraq, received death threats for her work on women's rights and was forced to work in complete secrecy (Fang 2007).

It is in this context that one of the early justifications given for the invasion of Iraq can be situated: the so-called liberation of Iraqi women. In 2003, George W. Bush claimed that 'the advance of women's rights and the advance of liberty are ultimately inseparable' and that the occupying forces would support women's rights in Iraq (Bush 2003b). Despite this rhetoric, the early days of the occupation saw the issue of Decree 137, attempting to abolish the PSL, which had protected some of the 'most sensitive areas of women's lives, including marriage, polygamy, divorce, children custody, and inheritance' (al-Jawaheri

2008: 19). In the December 2005 elections women lost sixteen seats as numbers fell to the 25 percent minimum, effectively marginalising women from negotiations for government positions (Bechler 2006: 1). In the following years there was little evidence that the Bush administration had any particular interest in improving the rights of women (al-Ali & Pratt 2009: 11). This sentiment was expressed in 2011 'Day of Rage' protests (linked to the Arab Spring) where women took to the streets of Iraq and called for the 'rights' that the Bush, and subsequently the Obama, administrations had failed to deliver, including the right to work and equality (Organization of Women's Freedom in Iraq 2011). The protests provided an insight into the many challenges women in Iraq now face, including high unemployment rates and government corruption (Zangana 2013).

The following accounts from Iraqi women bloggers provide an understanding of what it means to be a woman in post-invasion Iraq, and the rights and freedoms that are relevant in Iraqi women's lives. It is to their stories that the remainder of this chapter is devoted.

'I'm Female, Iraqi and 24. I Survived the War. That's All You Need to Know': Riverbend

Riverbend began her blog Baghdad Burning after encouragement from Salam Pax (the original 'Baghdad Blogger') in 2003 (Riverbend 2003b). 'The 26-year-old computer specialist became distinct from other bloggers because she offered a refreshing woman's perspective of events in her city, Baghdad' (Al-Atraqchi 2005). As a testament to her popularity, extracts from Riverbend's blog have been published in two separate books: *Baghdad Burning: Girl Blog From Iraq* (2005) and *Baghdad Burning II: More Girl Blog From Iraq* (2006). Riverbend provides her readers with few personal details – her location, the names of friends and family. Since her blog is anonymous she is often accused by other bloggers of not being who she says she is (Bending Truth 2003).

Riverbend weaves the cultural significance of everyday experiences into her blog posts so that her readers might be able to understand the historical, cultural, religious, familial and cosmopolitan context in which she lives her life. She describes lying on the roof at night to escape the oppressive heat of the house, alert to the sounds of gunfire and tanks in the distance. The location of the rooftop provides an insight into the ways in which foreign troops flounder with particular Iraqi practices and cultural norms: women being dragged from their houses without time to dress appropriately and men pushed to the ground with a boot to their head. Fragments of the reality of life in a war zone begin to emerge.

This is an account shaped by Riverbend's morals, her family values, her fears and the uncertainty of the time in which she lives. Her blog offers personalised, time-stamped posts of what it means to be a child, an adult and a woman in post-invasion Iraq. Throughout her blogging career she has critiqued the various changes within the Iraqi government, the constitutional referendum and election, ethnic and religious conflict, the rise of militias and fundamentalists and how changes in Iraq have shaped her life, career and rights.

In Riverbend's Iraq, surgical or precision attacks inevitably kill 'civilians'. The newly formed security forces such as the Iraqi police cannot always be trusted. And women cannot walk the streets in Western clothes or without a male escort (Riverbend 2006b). In many ways her blog is a space to talk back when other possibilities for open dialogue are limited. It is a place to document the political interventions of the Bush administration and the Iraqi Governing Council. It is a space in which to communicate the personal costs of the war with people inside Iraq and people around the world. In late 2004, she wrote:

> Warning – the following post is an open letter of sorts to Americans ... I guess what I'm trying to say is this: Americans, the name of your country which once stood for 'freedom and justice' is tarnished worldwide. Your latest president has proved that the great American image of democracy is just that – an image. (Riverbend 2004)

Riverbend communicates the pain of relatives and friends whose families have been killed by foreign troops or cluster bombs or imprisoned in house raids. Hers is a voice against the occupation of Iraq.

Many days Riverbend stays at home. Her ability to move around freely in Iraq was diminished during the years of the occupation. She is told not to return to her job as a computing systems expert (in an undisclosed location in Baghdad). She says she was forced to quit her job on the grounds that it was too dangerous for her, a woman, to be there. At home, and without work, Riverbend uses her weblog as a form of escape. On one occasion when the family home had become confining and stifling she wrote: 'The Scene: Family Living Room; The Mood: Gloomy' (Riverbend 2003a). She reflected on the ways in which the war changed her life, her career prospects, even the clothes she wears and the public spaces she can occupy safely:

> There was a time, a couple of years ago, when you could more or less wear what you wanted if you weren't going to a public place ... For me, June marked the first month I don't dare leave the house without a

hijab, or headscarf. I don't wear a hijab usually, but it's no longer possible to drive around Baghdad without one. It's just not a good idea. (Take note that when I say 'drive' I actually mean 'sit in the back seat of the car' – I haven't driven for the longest time.) (Riverbend 2006b)

Elsewhere she wrote:

Sadr's militia control parts of Iraq now. Just a couple of days ago, his militia, with the help of Badr, were keeping women from visiting the market in the southern city of Karbala. Women weren't allowed in the marketplace and shop owners were complaining that their businesses were suffering. Welcome to the new Iraq. (Riverbend 2006c)

By writing about veiling and women's attire Riverbend enters into contested space. She says that women who have never worn veils are increasingly being persuaded to do so. She tells her readers about a story that has spread throughout her neighbourhood, about a young, unveiled women who was abducted. Her body was found in a veil – a warning to other women who refuse to comply with the demands of those whom Riverbend refers to as fundamentalists. In her blog she is (relatively) free to state that she should not have to wear a headscarf if she does not want to, and that she should not be glared at by others who choose to practise differently themselves (Riverbend 2003a).

Many bloggers write about veiling in post-invasion Iraq – some describe it as an everyday practice; others discuss it in response to questions and comments from Western readers. Veiling is one of the most written-about practices framing women's life in post-invasion Iraq. For some it is a controversial topic: as Joan Wallach Scott writes in *The Politics of the Veil*, it is 'the sign of something intolerable' (Scott 2007: 3). Much of the literature indicates that patriarchal power relations significantly shape women's lives in post-invasion Iraq and that, rightly or wrongly, veiling has been drawn into this narrative (Moghadam 2003: 4). Although women like Riverbend may be pressured to veil in public spaces by militant gangs, her actions and choices need not be understood as pre-determined by these power relations. Although choices are constrained and limited for women at this point in time, wearing the headscarf can be seen as a way of reshaping mobility in potentially dangerous social spaces.

As conditions in Iraq approached the peak of violence in 2007 and 2008 more everyday challenges emerged for Riverbend. In their homes and in the streets women faced the threat of violent encounters at the hands of different groups. Riverbend wrote the post 'The Rape of Sabrine' as a response to the sexual assault of one woman taken from her own home (these events were consequently denied by the Maliki government):

> They abducted her from her house in an area in southern Baghdad called Hai Al Amil. No – it wasn't a gang. It was Iraqi peace keeping or security forces – the ones trained by Americans? You know them. She was brutally gang-raped and is now telling the story. Half her face is covered for security reasons or reasons of privacy. (Riverbend 2007b)

As a discursive space Riverbend's blog becomes more chaotic and dark. Each entry is shaped in some way by the war, by the repercussions of enforced democracy and the experience of loss: loss of life, independence, rights, security and basic infrastructure. In 2006 electricity became a major concern as Iraq descended into what Riverbend avoids calling a civil war. And yet she believes a war had been provoked by neighbouring militant gangs under the instruction of corrupt politicians and religious fanatics. Riverbend and her family made the difficult decision to flee Iraq (Riverbend 2007a).

Writing from Syria, five years after the US-led invasion of Iraq, Riverbend feels more at home than she did in post-invasion Iraq. Her apartment block is full of Iraqi refugees who extend their hospitality to her and her family, creating a sense of unity and solidarity among the Iraqi families. Riverbend is very clear about the price Iraqi people have paid following the invasion. For Riverbend, the loss of her family house and her homeland in many respects symbolises a lost Iraqi way of life.

'Almost All the World Is Watching Silently': Faiza al-Araji

In April 2005, Faiza attended a conference for Iraqi women leaders organised by the US and hosted in neighbouring Jordan. This conference became a turning point for Faiza, who had, up until this point, been critical of the Bush administration's involvement in Iraq, yet hopeful that there would be positive outcomes for Iraq's social, cultural and economic future. For Faiza, the conference was not only patronising, it also exposed the ironies of promoting women's rights in a foreign culture following a major military intervention that had caused so much suffering. She wrote:

> During the opening session, a representative of the American Foreign office spoke, then two American women, (who work in American organizations propagating for Democracy in the world). The first one said, in meaning: Congratulations to you, Iraqi

women, for the decision of allotting 25% of the parliamentary seats and election lists to women, this was achieved by your struggle to obtain these rights ... I laughed ... smelling hypocrisy and adulation in the American woman's talk ... And so, the second woman came along, and spoke in smooth tones, as if she was an actress on stage: My dears, close your eyes and imagine your selves in Iraq, 2020. What do you see? The woman beside me, a Doctor from Hilla, in the south, said: Huh, I see naked, shameless women filling the streets ... ha, ha, ha. (al-Araji 2005c)

Sitting in the conference room with other professional women, Faiza listened to the 'smooth' voice of the American speakers telling her how Iraqi women have struggled for their rights. One speaker, representing the American State Department, congratulated the crowd of Iraqi women for establishing the 25 per cent quota ruling on women's involvement in government. The woman sitting beside Faiza commented: 'What struggle? The General Legation of Elections put these points. We didn't struggle.' Faiza wondered to herself: 'Why is she lying to us? Explaining things the way she likes?? Hummm ... to convince us we are strugglers, and she is showing us the right way. She must be enjoying this game' (al-Araji 2005c).

The delegation from the US Congress included an Iraqi women's committee. Faiza wrote:

This point drew my attention. So, there is a special committee thinking of the Iraqi Woman ... I understand why they cry upon the Iraqi women, giving them seats, and freedoms ... So they would become saleswomen for their thoughts; woman is half the society, she raises the generations, so, if we control her, control her mind, and brain wash it, she would become an excellent media tool, (cultural and social). I see now how many entry points there were, through which America entered to occupy Iraq. (al-Araji 2005c)

After sessions the following day, audience members attempted to voice their disapproval but were cut off and silenced by the chairperson. Faiza and the other women were enraged. Their questions had not been answered and they were not permitted to speak freely:

I went up to my room, and sat on the bed, putting my head between my hands, I thought quietly: what makes me stay, and listen to this empty talk, that burns up the nerves? ... I learned a lot ... I have seen the true face of those who occupied Iraq, and understood their plans about the future of Iraq. (al-Araji 2005c)

For Faiza, this conference, which was supposed to be concerned with women's rights, became a series of 'silly stories' about 'the oppressor or the oppressed ... these are their positions in life, swinging between two possibilities that have no third' (al-Araji 2005c). The language of 'the oppressor and the oppressed' is understood by Faiza as limiting the ways in which the conference conveners and the American spokespeople were able to imagine Iraqi women's lives and Iraq's future. It was a limiting frame that forced normative, Western borders around complex problems.

The digital self Faiza writes is sceptical, critical and passionate. She is willing to question the ideas she encountered at this conference. She does not imagine herself or other Iraqi women as oppressed. When one of her readers asked her how people could work to 'enhance the situation of Iraqi women in the next period', she explained some particular challenges she believes women face in post-invasion Iraq:

> Programs appeared since 2003 and enforced by a western funding agencies ... These are international resolutions and I certainly respect, but I don't find Iraqi women in need for. What is the purpose of giving her a lecture about women right and CEDAW [the UN Convention on the Elimination of all forms of Discrimination against Women] while she's being starved and deprived of basic human needs? ... In any way, I like to see that a woman is strong and has the ability to make decisions ... The local active Iraqi organization is usually poor and with limited resources. They tend to accept to implement any project from a western fund raising agency ... So if you look into the CV of these organizations, you will find strange activities that are implemented to pleas[e] the funding agency, but in reality, it didn't add anything positive to the community. (al-Araji 2010)

Despite these conditions, Faiza has lived some of the best years of her life in Iraq. She left Iraq in 1976 and came back after the First Gulf War in the early 1990s, got married and had three children. When she began blogging in 2003 after the invasion she had some hope for the future, for democracy and freedom. Faiza's blog is often about politics, women's rights, the future of Iraq, and the meaning of conflict in Iraq. Frequently, her reference point for political questions is local, family oriented, or informed by her frequent travels around the world. We see early on the challenges she is facing, not just as a politically active Islamic woman, but as a mother, a wife and an engineer. During bursts of electricity she goes online to research water purification and pollution and to answer her customers' enquiries. She instructs her driver on how to negotiate traffic jams, Humvees and armed soldiers on her way to work or to the shops.

Family is Faiza's sanctuary, but work can be a welcome distraction from tiresome relatives or strangers (Faiza 2004b). In her store in Baghdad she sells water purification systems. On an average day she works, shops, surfs the net and sometimes shares a story to entertain her neighbours (who, she tells us, are mostly 'housewives'). Faiza claims that she is a 'homebody', but she is still considerably more mobile than her female neighbours.

Working in Baghdad means travelling to and from the store, and travelling in Baghdad can be dangerous. For instance, returning home from work one evening Faiza decided not to call her son to open the garage door from inside the house as she usually does (Faiza 2004c), but instead to do it herself. As she attempted to open the door she was assaulted by an armed group who stole the car and her bag, containing valuable identification documents. This is one of the most traumatic moments Faiza describes in her blog. She wrote: 'Everything froze in that moment ... I saw myself dead, for sure. The street was empty, the wooden door of our house was closed, the buzz of the generator was filling the space with noise, and nobody knew what was going on here.' Faiza increasingly turned to religion for comfort and security in an environment of social upheaval. This was a pivotal time in which her faith and love for her family was strengthened, while her physical movements were increasingly limited.

Shortly after this experience Faiza and her family decided to leave Iraq and settle in Amman, Jordan. Life in Amman proved quiet compared to the everyday danger faced in Iraq, but having lived in a war zone for so long she could not escape the feelings of fear, danger, constant tension and anxiety. This is a powerful, less visible, legacy of war and violence. Faiza carried these emotions with her, jumping at the sound of fireworks in Amman, which reminds her of dangerous explosions. The sounds of celebration became confused with the sounds of war. War occupied Faiza's mind and continued to be the subject of her daily and weekly posts. From Amman, fragments of Faiza's digital self can be traced to Iraq.

In Amman Faiza's work for the Iraqi people took shape in January 2005. Like many bloggers writing about post-invasion Iraq, Faiza wants Iraqi voices to be heard. She wrote that she would like to do woman-oriented studies (Faiza 2005c), and that she could bring personal experience to this 'abstract' degree. Her first 'mission in life' was her family, but her focus now was on the women of Iraq. Faiza increasingly involved herself in conferences on the reconstruction of Iraq and women's rights. She spoke at the Congressional Forum on Iraq, at CodePink 'Women against War' rallies, and with Global Exchange and Democracy Now!

Conclusion

How is the legacy of the Iraq War represented by women's stories and what does it mean that these stories are captured online and written in contact with others around the world? The stories of Iraqi women, penned in a time of war, frame violence and chaos for an international audience. These eyewitness accounts enable distant others to become witnesses to women's everyday lives as they unfold in a time of war. For Judith Butler (2009: 1) particular *frames* produce recognisable figures and discourses for witnessing publics. She argues that 'if certain lives do not qualify as lives or are, from the start, not conceivable as lives within certain frames, then these lives are never lived nor lost in the full sense'. The epistemological problem of framing is a problem of vision, of language, and of the limits which shape people's ways of apprehending and understanding life. As Butler (2009: 9) suggests, by problematising the ways in which the war and its consequences for women's lives are framed, we 'show that the frame never quite contained the scene it was meant to limn, that something was already outside, which made the very sense of the inside possible, recognisable'. This critical engagement aims to open new spaces for recognising ways of being and lives practised outside normative frames. This is not just a question of recognising other persons within existing norms, but a critique of the ways in which being and women's lives are 'historically articulated and enforced' (Butler 2009: 5).

Riverbend and Faiza are only too aware of the ways in which Iraqi women's lives, experiences and rights have been framed and represented in a number of ways to Western audiences. In many cases women are seen to be 'struggling', without rights or the power to defend themselves against a rising tide of challenges. For Faiza, 'women's rights' have become a banner under which Western notions of development and 'democratisation' are imposed upon Iraqi people. In her post 'Overview on Iraq now ...' (al-Araji 2010) she comments on the ways in which women's lives have been understood and how the interventions deemed necessary by occupying forces are not necessarily what Iraqi women need. Along with Yasmin al-Jawaheri (2008) Faiza calls for local interventions, educational programmes, support and relief – particularly for those with limited resources and access to food, shelter or employment.

Faiza and Riverbend provide an opportunity for questioning what the war has meant for Iraqi women and what lessons can be learned. Iraqi women bloggers' stories break with the frames of war so often encountered in the mass media and in political discourse. They break with these frames by virtue of their weblog format: as stories told over a period of time, and as traces of lived experiences, and as digital selves. The women produce stories that they hope communicate a different reality – one which presents questions about the suitability of Western interventions into other people's lives and the everyday consequences this has for women. The legacy of the war for Riverbend and Faiza is one of estrangement from their homeland, of traumatic memories about the death of loved ones and about coming face to face with injustices tolerated on a global scale.

After six years' absence from her blog Riverbend returned. She is still living outside Iraq, but said she felt 'obliged' to comment on the lessons she has learned from the war 'Ten Years On'. She wrote to her international audience:

> We learned that while life is not fair, death is even less fair – it takes the good people ... Is it better now, ten years down the line? Do you feel safer, with hundreds of thousands of Iraqis out of the way (granted half of them were women and children, but children grow up, right?)? (Riverbend 2013)

Notes

1. It is argued that understanding what other people witness is like understanding someone else's pain – it holds a type of 'twilight status' between what can and cannot be known or understood (Thumim 2010: 291). 'Being a spectator of calamities taking place in another country', Susan Sontag wrote, 'is a quintessential modern experience' (Sontag 2003: 16) (on witnessing see also Howie 2011).
2. Faiza's blog was published in book form in 2008 (al-Araji et al. 2008).
3. Iraq Body Count is a 'public record of violent deaths following the 2003 invasion of Iraq' and can be accessed at: http://www.iraqbodycount.org

Chapter 10
The Impact of Coalition Military Operations on Archaeological Sites in Iraq

Diane C. Siebrandt

The creation of cities is only one example in a long list of cultural evolutions invented in Iraq. From Nineveh in the north, to Babylon and Ur in the south, the remains of ancient cities lie scattered across all of Iraq (Roux 1992). Ancient cities that flourished across Mesopotamia from 3500 BCE onwards were left largely abandoned and untouched for millennia until European explorers began excavations in the early nineteenth century. International excavations between Western and Iraqi archaeologists were eventually sponsored by Western organisations and the Iraqi antiquities authorities through the years (Bertman 2003). However, the Iran–Iraq War in the 1980s caused the cessation of most joint excavations, with only a slight reprieve between wars until the First Gulf War in 1990, which eventually led to UN sanctions imposed on the entire country. The sanctions caused further complications for cooperative work and, while local experts continued working on sites, cross-cultural relationships were hindered by a lack of international partnerships and an absence of communication with the West (Forsyth 2004; Palumbo 2005; Russell 2001).

The 2003 Iraq War further compounded problems by making it almost impossible for Western cultural heritage experts to engage one on one with their Iraqi counterparts. During the first several years of the war, the Westerners with whom Iraqis came into contact were mostly American combat troops, encounters that were often based on fear and suspicion of the US military's strong-arm tactics (Diamond 2005b; Fallows 2005; Hendrickson & Tucker 2005). With the spread of unrest throughout the country, Iraqi cultural heritage experts encountered difficulties travelling to and gaining access to sites, some of which were being used as military bases, leading to further problems of establishing rapport with the troops. This chapter therefore discusses how the disruption of access to sites by the Iraqi cultural heritage community contributed to a breakdown in social cohesion, as well as creating communal tensions.

Concern about the Iraq War and its impact on the country's cultural heritage sites began before the first US and Coalition troops entered Baghdad. Western cultural heritage experts warned US and UK leaders of the hazards that combat operations would pose to cultural heritage sites in the forms of looting and damage. Leaders were made aware of the list of international laws that call for the protection of cultural heritage, specifically the 1954 Hague Convention on the Protection of Cultural Property in the Event of an Armed Conflict (Gibson 2009; Stone 2009). The convention is founded on earlier laws, including the 1863 Lieber Code and the 1907 Hague Convention, which call for the protection of cultural property during times of conflict (Gerstenblith 2009). The 1954 convention has been widely cited as sound cause for the occupying forces to respect Iraq's cultural property (Gerstenblith 2009; Rutherglen 2006; Schipper et al. 2010; Thurlow 2005).

The convention's provisions only apply in armed conflict where two or more of the hostile countries are members of the convention and because neither the US nor the UK had ratified it by the start of the war, the convention did not govern the March 2003 invasion of Iraq (Forsyth 2004). In spite of this, Patty Gerstenblith points out that 'the policy of the United States was to view as binding those provisions of the Hague Convention that the United States regarded as part of customary international law'(Gerstenblith 2010: 11). It does appear that the articles in the convention were honoured, as no sites were damaged or targeted in the initial 'Shock and Awe' campaign. In May 2003 this was verified by a team of Western cultural heritage experts who travelled to Iraq in order to conduct site assessments; they found no evidence of damage caused by Coalition military munitions (Wright et al. 2003).

While these points are important for inclusion in any discussion about the war and its lasting implications on cultural heritage awareness programmes and future initiatives, one legacy that has rarely been considered is that the war made it hard for Iraqis to access their cultural heritage sites. Access to sites during all phases of the war was difficult due to the volatile and dangerous security environment across the entire country. In addition, Iraqis were directly barred from visiting sites due to foreign occupation. Being unable to access sites caused disruptions within the cultural heritage community and disconnected people from their shared history, caused communal tension and ultimately violated people's cultural rights.

Cultural Rights

Part of the preamble to the International Covenant on Economic, Social and Cultural Rights reads:

> In accordance with the Universal Declaration of Human Rights, the ideal of free human beings enjoying freedom from fear and want can only be achieved if conditions are created whereby everyone may enjoy his economic, social and cultural rights, as well as his civil and political rights. (United Nations 1966)

The difficulty for Iraqis wishing to engage in their cultural rights was a problem during all phases of the war. From 2003 traveling safely within Iraq was often difficult and at times impossible. When US and Coalition military forces (henceforth referred to as the Coalition or Coalition forces) entered Iraq on 20 March 2003, the only plan set in place appeared to be winning the war, with minimal consideration given to post-conflict operations. Coalition forces entered and occupied Baghdad on 9 April, encountering minimal pockets of Iraqi resistance along the way (Ballard 2010; Keegan 2004).

The Coalition Provisional Authority (CPA) took charge of the country in April, serving as temporary caretakers. One of the decisions that created devastating repercussions was the disbanding of the Iraqi army. Disbanding the army not only left Iraq without local military enforcement, which created a vacuum of order, it also caused massive unemployment within a community armed with weapons and little else. Many of the unemployed men joined the insurgency that followed the invasion, and went on to fight against the Coalition. Coalition forces were soon engaged in a brutal, unwavering insurgency, and as a result, the country became lawless (Aylwin-Foster 2005; Fallows 2005; Keegan 2004). Article 43 of the 1907 Hague Regulations requires that an occupying power restore and maintain public order and civil life in an occupied territory, but this was not done.

There was danger everywhere, from improvised explosive devices planted as roadside bombs to rocket attacks, suicide bombers targeting densely populated areas such as markets and mosques, as well as the specific threat of ethno-sectarian violence. Fake check points, car searches, kidnappings and assassinations were all used as weapons by the insurgents. Samarra is one example of the devastation that resulted from the conflict. The Askari, or Gold Dome Mosque and Shrine, a revered place of Shia worship, was targeted in 2006 and again in 2007 by the militant organisation al-Qaeda in Iraq, resulting in significant damage (Isakhan 2013b). Afterwards, the area became a hotbed of vio-lence which spread across the country, with retaliatory bombings and the loss of hundreds of lives (Bull 2007; Johnson 2008). This volatile environment rendered most Iraqi citizens housebound; the danger of travelling was too great for them to consider.

Because of the risks involved with travel, Iraqi cultural heritage spe-cialists were unable to visit many archaeological sites in order to assess site conditions, or attempt to engage in any preservation or conservation measures (Palumbo 2005). In addition, many sites in the south were left unguarded and were heavily looted by locals. Thieves indiscriminately dug holes in search of artefacts, leaving the remains of ancient cities riddled and destroying invaluable data in the process (Rothfield 2009; Russell 2008; Stone 2008). Some efforts were made by the Coalition to stop the looting, such as patrols carried out by the Italian Carabinieri in the southern province of Dhi Qar. However, mistrust between the local tribes and the Iraqi police force working with the Carabinieri, coupled with a lack of resources, eventually led to the termination of the patrols (Russell 2008).

Not being able to travel freely and safely to heritage sites and engage in their cultural patrimony was only one problem. Even if Iraqi heritage specialists were able to travel to a site, access was not always guaran-teed due to foreign occupation. When Coalition forces occupied Iraq at the start of the war, numerous bases and outposts were established across the country, often on or near archaeological sites. Article 5.1 in the 1954 convention requires that occupying powers safeguard and pre-serve occupied countries' cultural property. Despite this, between April 2003 and January 2005 the Coalition military base known as Camp Alpha was situated on the ruins of the ancient city of Babylon, caus-ing both direct and indirect damage (Moussa 2008). The topic of the occupation of Babylon has been covered by a variety of authors and the most comprehensive findings are compiled in a special report by the UNESCO International Coordination Committee for the Safeguarding of the Cultural Heritage of Iraq (International Coordination Commit-tee for the Safeguarding of the Cultural Heritage of Iraq 2009). John Curtis sums up the sentiment most commonly held among scholars and laypersons:

In the early days after the war, a military presence at Babylon served a valuable purpose in that it prevented the site from being looted. But it is regrettable that a military camp of this size should then have been established on one of the most important archaeological sites in the world. (Curtis 2005: 8)

Overall, archaeological sites suffered varying degrees of damage due to military occupation. Trenches were dug in the ground to create canals and dirt walls built for defence, large areas of soil littered with pottery fragments were used to fill sandbags, and the construction of buildings caused a variety of disturbances to the remains of the Sumerian city-state of Ur (modern Tell el-Muqayyar), to the undocumented sites of Tells Bahra and Oç Tepe in Kirkuk province, and, of course, to Babylon. At Babylon the weight of heavy vehicles, machinery and concrete barriers, and the seepage of hazardous chemicals into the ground, as well as the impact of large companies of personnel in concentrated areas, all contributed to damage to the site (Curtis 2009). The presence of foreign military units on historical sites not only caused physical damage to the sites, it also caused distress in the cultural heritage communities in Iraq. Whether or not Coalition military leaders coordinated with Iraqi antiquities authorities prior to the construction of Camp Alpha is unknown. Mesopotamian specialist Zainab Bahrani has described how military leaders assured her that plans for the base were mapped out with the full cooperation of Iraqi antiquities authorities; however, she was unable to find evidence of who the leaders were speaking with on the Iraqi side (Bahrani 2008).

Once a military base or outpost was constructed, it became a restricted area with access granted only to individuals holding US government-approved identification cards. Any individual not holding accepted identification could only enter as a visitor, and was subjected to a pat-down search of his/her person and an examination of all possessions brought onto the base. This was a security precaution put in place due to insurgent attacks against Coalition forces across the country and, while understandable, it served to anger and alienate the local community. Local caretakers and heritage professionals often felt offended and criminalised when barred from visiting sites near Coalition bases. John Curtis describes how he and the then director of the Iraqi State Board of Antiquities and Heritage, Abbas al-Husseini, tried to visit Ur but were unsuccessful in gaining entry to the site:

The site is incorporated within the perimeter fence surrounding Tallil Airbase, so all access to the site is controlled by US forces. When Dr al-Husseini arrived at the main gate, after having driven down especially from Baghdad, he refused to be searched and was therefore denied access. His entirely reasonable argument was that, as Director of Antiquities, he had responsibility for all archaeological sites in Iraq and should have unrestricted access to them. The stand-off lasted several hours, but Dr al-Husseini's protests were to no avail and he was unable to enter the site. (Curtis 2009: 4)

Abdulamir al-Hamdani, an Iraqi archaeologist and site inspector for Dhi Qar province, where the site of Ur is located, was also only able to gain access to the site by agreeing to be searched and then accompanied by an individual holding US-accepted identification. He and other Iraqi archaeologists were frustrated at not being able to provide conservation measures to the ruins due to the US-imposed restrictions (al-Hamdani 2008b). Numerous international regulations ensure that, even if cultural property is in the control of an occupying party, local authorities must be allowed to carry out their duties and responsibilities to sites. As Article 15 of the 1954 Hague Convention explains:

As far as is consistent with the interests of security, personnel engaged in the protection of cultural property shall, in the interests of such property, be respected and, if they fall into the hands of the opposing Party, shall be allowed to continue to carry out duties whenever the cultural property for which they are responsible has also fallen into the hands of the opposing Party. (UNESCO 1954)

In addition to the 1954 convention, other declarations and treaties serve to protect people's cultural rights, including the Universal Declaration of Human Rights, Article 27(1): 'Everyone has the right freely to participate in the cultural life of the community, to enjoy the arts and to share in scientific advancement and its benefits'. Article 15 of the International Covenant on Economic, Social and Cultural Rights also makes clear:

The States Parties to the present Covenant recognize the right of everyone (a) To take part in cultural life; (b) To enjoy the benefits of scientific progress and its applications. (3) The States Parties to the present Covenant undertake to respect the freedom indispensable for scientific research and creative activity. (4) The States Parties to the present Covenant recognize the benefits to be derived from the encouragement and development of international contacts and co-operation in the scientific and cultural fields. (United Nations 1966)

Further to that, Article 7(2) of the 1954 convention calls for cooperation between occupying powers and civilian authorities responsible for safeguarding cultural heritage. Because the Iraqi antiquities experts were greatly hindered and often unable to travel to and/or gain access to sites, there was little or no site management, which resulted in conservation maintenance neglect and continued looting (Wright et al. 2003). Heritage experts were denied their entitlement to carry out their required heritage preservation responsibilities and partake in research.

One small exception to difficulties with site access was at Ur, which was located inside the joint Coalition base Camp Adder/Ali Airbase (collectively known as Tallil Airbase). The base was established for the Iraqi air force in 1971, and was constructed about a kilometre from the archaeological remains of Ur. The Iraqi air force remained at the base until April 2003, when Coalition forces took over control. At that time, a fence was erected around the perimeter of the base, and included not only airstrips and living areas, but also the archaeological site. The inclusion of the site within the base perimeter garnered both the gratitude and the frustration of Iraqi antiquities authorities. They were thankful for the protection that the fence and Coalition guards provided from looters, but were frustrated at the inability of local staff to independently access the site for scientific purposes. However, a house belonging to the local site curator was included within the base perimeter. Because of this, the curator, Mr Dnaife Muhsen, was one of the few Iraqi heritage experts that had free access to a site.

Dnaife grew up on the ruins with a grandfather who had excavated with the renowned British archaeologist C. Leonard Woolley in the early twentieth century (Dnaife Muhsen personal communication 2009). Iraqi cultural heritage specialists are ethically bound by objectives in the Iraqi Antiquities and Heritage Law No. 55 of 2002, which mandates, among other responsibilities, that they protect sites from damage. However, Dnaife's connection to the site expanded beyond professional and scientific responsibilities. Familial ties to Ur further dictated his responsibility to keep the site free from harm, a task he could not fail at without losing face. Because restrictions to site access were not lessened, the Coalition forces looked as though they were not concerned with cultural attachments to local heritage. Damage to sites was detrimental, and not only affected the integrity of the site, but also devalued the meaning the Iraqis placed on the site. The occupation of the sites sent the message that is was acceptable to occupy and damage another's property.

Due to a complex history, many Iraqis view Westerners as spreading imperialism, with little regard for the local community. Westerners have been described as occupying the region to 'serve the marketing strategy of empires to interfere, infiltrate or invade the Near East at different times with overt benevolent concerns and excuses' (Mourad 2010: 155). Suspicions of Western intentions can be traced back to the 1916 Sykes–Picot Agreement, which divided up several Arab provinces. After World War I the country now known as Iraq fell under a British mandate and the Hashemite monarchy they installed, until the 1958 revolution brought independence and Iraqi control (Simon & Tejirian

2005). From the early nineteenth century, Western explorers began visiting Mesopotamia, exploring and revering Mesopotamian sites for their Biblical connections. However, until 1926, when Iraq Antiquities Law No. 40 placed restrictions on the export of artefacts, untold thousands of antiquities were transported to Europe and America. The long history of colonial powers manipulating Iraq and its people left the 2003 Iraqi population with suspicions about modern Western motives (Bahrani 1998).

The actions taken by Coalition forces during the Iraq War were seen once again as a Western power practising overtly colonial rule over Iraqi sites. This seemed to be confirmed when the local cultural heritage community was prevented from putting their practices to use when they were denied the right to access sites. Respecting and preserving cultural heritage is a significant element for successfully forming cross-cultural relationships. Unfortunately, there were few opportunities for cooperation between the Coalition troops and Iraqis.

Understanding and appreciating the value of a place varies depending on cultural and ethnic beliefs and background. Because the members of the Coalition and the Iraqis did not share a common belief system, there were differences in how archaeological sites were appreciated as significant. While the Coalition may have seen a site as strategically important for military operations – such as using an ancient *tell* as a lookout – the Iraqis valued the site as part of their collective history. Although many members of the Coalition recognised that they were on archaeological sites, this did not stop them from constructing bases on such sites. It is worth asking how Coalition forces might have felt if foreign forces had occupied and built on sites such as Mount Rushmore or Stonehenge (Isakhan 2011b). The lack of cultural awareness and communication between the two groups led to a series of misunderstandings about heritage and its contemporary significance to Iraqis. The planning that took place before the war never took into consideration the protection of cultural heritage sites or the importance of communicating with their caretakers or respecting their cultural rights (Fallows 2006; Rathmell 2005).

A large part of the misunderstanding between the different cultural groups was due to the reluctance of some Western cultural heritage specialists to work with the military. To their credit, the US Department of Defense (DOD) did attempt to engage with the local community via a programme called the Human Terrain System (HTS). This was designed to embed social scientists in Coalition forces to serve as cultural advisers (McFate & Fondacaro 2008). However, at its official 2007 start, the programme was overwhelmingly poorly received by Western anthropologists. In 2009 the American Anthropological Association (AAA) Commission on the Engagement of Anthropology, together with the US security and intelligence communities, released a report that asserted, among other issues, that anthropologists would not be able to follow the AAA's code of ethics if engaged in such a programme (AAA Commission on the Engagement of Anthropology with the US Security and Intelligence Communities 2009). The programme was also criticised by some military personnel who thought the teams were providing impractical direction, mainly due to their lack of regional knowledge (González 2008). Former HTS employees also expressed concerns over the deficiencies in the programme and personnel. During the 2007 AAA annual conference, Zenia Helbig told the audience: 'The program is desperate to hire anyone or anything that remotely falls into the category of academic, social science, regional expert, or PhD' (Helbig 2007).

Engaging with Iraqi cultural heritage experts was possible via contact with American experts in the same field. However, the controversy of AAA members working with the military hindered these efforts. A wide divide in opinion exists within the cultural heritage community as to whether or not partnering with military forces is ethical. Yannis Hamilakis argues against the efforts of the larger cultural heritage community in assisting the military to identify heritage sites that require protection. Hamilakis criticises Western cultural heritage professionals who cooperate with the military as being more concerned with material remains than human lives (Hamilakis 2010). John Curtis states he would not provide information pre-conflict, but would assist post-conflict because

> the pre-conflict situation is, in fact, governed by political considerations over which the army has no more control than archaeologists, but in the post-conflict situation, when the damage has occurred, both the army and archaeologists have an obligation to rebuild the infrastructure, including cultural heritage. Working with the army post-conflict is, therefore, a pragmatic solution. (Curtis 2011: 196)

Rene Teijgeler adds that archaeologists should only cooperate with the military if a peace mission is approved by a United Nations or 'generally accepted international body' (Teijgeler 2011: 210). Laurie Rush reminds us that 'unfortunately aggressive military actions take place whether archaeologists participate or not, and it is also critical to consider the importance of cultural preservation for the local inhabitants of an area in conflict'(Rush 2011: 142). No matter where one stands on the debate, it can be argued that one of the main elements left out of the

HTS programme was the lack of local engagement. The programme was designed and implemented by Westerners with little involvement from Iraqi stakeholders. Utilising Western social scientists years after the start of the war may have seemed advantageous at the time, but it did not produce the desired results of forming cross-cultural relationships.

Not involving the local cultural heritage community in 2003 was a significant mistake and a breach of the Universal Declaration of Human Rights, as well as the International Covenant on Economic, Social and Cultural Rights. Iraqi cultural heritage specialists were willing to cooperate with Coalition forces as early as 2003 in order to protect sites. Donny George, then the director of research at the Iraq Museum, is well noted for attempting to seek assistance from Coalition troops to assist with securing the museum from looters (George 2008). In the south, Abdulamir al-Hamdani was proactive in introducing himself to Coalition members in his bid to convince troops to carry out patrols near archaeological sites and work with Iraqi authorities to stop antiquity looters (al-Hamdani 2008a).

Awareness and Legacies

Fortunately, there are examples of positive engagements between Coalition forces and local specialists. In 2003 the ancient city of Kish (modern Tell Uhaimir), located approximately 12 kilometres east of Babylon, was occupied by Coalition and Iraqi forces. A radio relay outpost was constructed on top of the ruins of a Sumerian temple complex, its high vantage point in an otherwise flat landscape making it strategically attractive for military operations. Kish suffered damage from ground-penetrating disturbances and deterioration of the ruins due to heavy vehicle and pedestrian traffic. In 2007, an American military unit was tasked with dismantling the outpost and removing all occupation from the site. In order to prevent further damage to the site prior to the move, the unit sought advice and assistance from local heritage experts. While initially placing an outpost on the ruins was in violation of the 1954 convention, the awareness the unit eventually displayed in seeking expert advice is one positive example of cross-cultural cooperation (Siebrandt 2010).

Another positive example is the discovery of artefacts and archaeological features dating from at least 1300 BCE on al-Hurriyah air base, also known as Kirkuk Regional Air Base (KRAB), located in Kirkuk province. KRAB was established in the 1970s by the Iraqi air force, but was initially used as an air base by British military troops during the Second World War. Coalition forces moved onto the base in 2003, and constructed Forward Operating Base Warrior. The areas of archaeological interest on the base are represented by a total of six unexcavated sites, known by the local population as Tells Bahra and Oç Tepe. Because KRAB has been in use since at least the 1970s, there has been significant human encroachment on all archaeologically sensitive areas within the base boundaries (Siebrandt 2012).

American military personnel stationed at KRAB in 2008 discovered pottery during further base construction. Recognising the importance of the material, they halted the work and consulted local archaeological site inspectors. At the time, there were no contingency plans in place in the event that cultural property was located within base boundaries. Base personnel had to act ad hoc, and in consulting with the newly formed US Central Command Historical Cultural Advisory Group (now the Combatant Commanders Cultural Heritage Action Group or CCHAG), base personnel devised a plan to halt further construction and declare archaeologically sensitive areas off limits to all personnel (Pinckney 2010). Coalition personnel were also involved in a project to improve the tourist infrastructure around the remains of a Kassite-era ziggurat at Dur-Kurigalzu (modern Aqar Quf). Although plagued with inter-governmental issues, upgrades to the infrastructure were eventually completed (Roberts & Roberts 2013).

As mentioned previously, the ancient city of Ur was incorporated within the Tallil air base boundaries in 2003. In November 2008, Coalition forces announced that the border fence would be removed from around the site and the road leading to the ruins turned over to Iraqi control. Prior to the fence's removal, a site assessment was completed by a joint inspection team, which included American and Iraqi archaeologists and environmental officers from the ranks of the Coalition forces. The team was able to recommend conservation plans for the site and suggest future site management planning strategies. On 13 May 2009, control of the site was transferred from Coalition authority to Iraqi governmental authority. Before the site was fully turned over to Iraqi control, however, Coalition forces erected a new perimeter fence and four metal guard towers around the site (Siebrandt 2009). Each of these examples demonstrates that cooperation was possible between troops and civilian heritage experts despite the difficulties imposed by war. However, such positive examples are unfortunately not widely published.

Since 2003, changes driven by the legacy of the war have been proposed and implemented, one of which is the ratification of the 1954 Hague Convention. The US Senate finally signed the ratification in September 2008, providing the DOD with the policy necessary to ensure protection of cultural heritage sites during their operations (Gerstenblith 2008). Having the policy does not guarantee protection, but it is one of several tools that the DOD now have in place in order to protect sites. A second tool is the use of subject matter experts who provide pre-deployment cultural awareness training to military troops heading to overseas posts. The military training programmes cover topics ranging from how to identify a heritage site, to respecting cultural property (Rose 2007; Rush 2012; Zeidler & Rush 2010).

In addition, the Overseas Regional Cultural Heritage Integrated Data Project was formed in 2009 to create a cultural heritage resource database that could be used by US military planners. Although still in draft format, the database will contain information related to international and local laws, as well as cultural awareness planning strategies of any area outside the United States where military personnel are planning operations. So far project team members have created a number of country profiles which can be used to better understand protection issues when personnel conduct activities and mission-planning tactics across the globe (Green 2013).

Educational programmes in cultural property protection are also now included in the curriculum of the US Army Reserve Officer Training Corps (ROTC). The ROTC is a university-based programme whose graduates become commissioned officers in all branches of the United States armed forces. Providing such vital training to individuals who will eventually hold positions of authority ensures guidelines will be followed by subordinates (Valanis 2013). The implementation of cultural awareness training in the ROTC curriculum promises to have a long-lasting positive legacy. In addition, cooperation between civilians and military personnel in the cultural heritage sector and academia has resulted in the formation of several working groups. Most recently the Cultural Heritage by Archaeology and Military Panel partnered with the National Committees of the Blue Shield, the US Committee of the Blue Shield and CCHAG. The overall mission for these groups is to serve as sources of information-sharing among academics, archaeologists and governmental and military personnel in relation to the protection of cultural heritage during times of conflict. The successful implementation of progressive programing is a step, albeit small, towards the overall need for a greater awareness of the cultural rights of all peoples during times of conflict.

Conclusion

One of the major hindrances for the Coalition forces going into the conflict was the absence of methodological approaches for partnering with local cultural heritage experts. As a result of the war, the US Central

Command (CENTCOM) has amended its relevant contingency guidance practices for base camps. Prior to the war, the guidance in question, Regulation 202–2, only addressed environmental issues; it now includes a full chapter and guidelines on historical and best cultural preservation practices. Although the new guidelines were a direct result of the issues encountered in Iraq, the best practices are to be adhered to in any country in which CENTCOM is planning operations.

In 2008, the US and Iraqi governments signed the Strategic Framework Agreement for a Relationship of Friendship and Cooperation between the United States of America and the Republic of Iraq for political, economic, cultural and security ties between the two nations. Section IV of the document specifically calls for cultural cooperation, including forging strong, long-lasting bonds of friendship and mutual respect to promote international efforts and contributions to preserve Iraqi cultural heritage and protect antiquities. While these doctrines are a welcome step towards forming positive relations between local cultural heritage communities and occupying foreign forces, a great deal more remains to be done.

Protecting heritage sites is only one concern within the overall issues of conflict operation planning. Acknowledging relationships, concepts of identity and the sense of ownership that locals have towards heritage sites and respecting their cultural rights need more investigation. Many of the archaeological ruins in Iraq have existed for 5,000 years, and the damage inflicted on some of those sites due to the occupation is a legacy that cannot be reversed. The Coalition's poorly planned occupation strategy revealed serious faults in the military's ability to adhere to property protection laws. This eventually led to the US ratification of the 1954 Convention, increased training and awareness for military personnel, as well as some projects that restored and protected sites. Only time will tell if this more positive attitude will be held during the next conflict.

Part IV
Regional and International Consequences of the Iraq War

Chapter 11
Ethnic Cleansing in Iraq: Internal and External Displacement

Howard Adelman

The 2003 war changed Iraq forever because of the failure of the USA and its allies to provide stability and security for the people of Iraq, with the resulting separation of the major population groups within Iraq and the extrusion of minorities. Usually as a scapegoat for their own failings or as distractions to larger ambitions, regimes get rid of unwanted populations by extermination (genocide) or by ethnic cleansing. Societies, when they are insecure and feel threatened and in the absence of a strong governing authority, will do the same. If a population can move to another part of a state where they feel safe because they cohabit there in safety with members of their own ethnic or religious group, they become internally displaced. Minorities who lack any such safe haven in a polity try to cross a border if at all possible and become refugees. However, if an oppressed group cannot cross a border, forced migration easily leads to attempts at extinction.

The Iraqi refugee exodus has been examined at four-year intervals, beginning in 2002 before the onset of the Iraq War, then in 2006 before the upsurge in Sunni–Shiite violence that lasted until 2008. The 2010 examination took place after the separation of most Sunnis and Shiites and the flight of minority populations but before both the March 2010 Iraq elections and the outbreak of the Syrian civil war in 2011. In the final cross-sectional view in 2014, Iraqi refugees were expected to have returned; few did. In each temporal cross-section, specific groups become the focus – Kurds in 2002–3, Turkmens, Assyrian and Armenian Christians and Palestinians in 2006, smaller minorities in 2010, and refugees returning from Syria in 2014. These cross-sectional historical and ethno-religious slices dealing with internally displaced peoples (IDPs) and refugees over twelve years depict the dimensions and character of the Iraqi refugee problem and its legacy in Iraq. They also demonstrate that the war has changed the human geography of Iraq, probably for decades to come, as a direct result of the failure of the USA and its allies to provide a stable and secure environment for its people. Iraq was left with its small minorities largely extruded and its larger groups – Kurds, Sunni Arabs and Shia Arabs – mostly resettled within their own virtually homogeneous enclaves.

The Kurds in 2002

Kurds are one of three dominant groups in Iraq. As an ethnic minority, Kurds regard themselves as a distinct nationality with their own aspirations to statehood, a dream thwarted by the division of the Ottoman Empire after the First World War. The thirty million Kurds are the largest ethnic group in the Middle East without their own nation state. Spread among Iraq, Iran, Syria and Turkey, they speak an Indo-European language distinct from Arabic. The vast majority are Muslim, but their Sunni religious practices are distinctive. Kurdish Islamic schools have been centres of resistance to assimilation (McDowall 2004). To weaken self-determination (*kurayeti*), the Baathist state tried to replace Kurdish religious schools (*hujra*) with state-run Islamic schools (Rafaat 2012).

Kurds fought their subjugation in Turkey, Iran and Iraq (Stansfield 2003). After the collapse of the Ottoman Empire and the annexation of southern Kurdistan into Iraq in 1921, forcible assimilation into the Iraqi state included the systematic destruction of 4,500 Kurdish villages. After a successful *coup d'état* by Brigadier Abd al-Karim Qasim in 1958, Shaykh Ahmad Barzani, the Kurdish rebel leader, was pardoned; he and the Kurdish armed forces (Peshmerga) led a new revolt in 1961. In 1970 Saddam Hussein negotiated the March Manifesto with the Kurds, in return for a cessation of their rebellion, that allowed them to establish a semi-autonomous region in the north four years hence; in the interim, Saddam implemented Arabisation of the oil-rich Kirkuk region and then proclaimed the manifesto unilaterally in 1974.

Once again the Kurds revolted. The revolt was crushed when Iran stopped supporting the rebels. The first major outflow took place in 1975 when 210,000 Kurds fled to Iran. The following year, 70,000 fled, not only to Iran, but also to North America, Australia and Europe. Again, in 1979, 50,000 more Kurds fled to Iran. The Kurdish rebellion was renewed in 1980 following the outbreak of the Iran–Iraq War. Even though poison gas was used against the Kurds and they suffered 100,000 casualties, the rebellion was only repressed when Iran again ceased its support. In 1987, 50,000 fled and in 1988 the number increased to 100,000. In 1989, 60,000 fled to Turkey, a country that has a complicated relationship even with its own Kurdish population. That it should have become a destination of refuge for Iraqi Kurds indicates how difficult the situation was for them in Iraq.

Kurds had become a target of ethnic cleansing by Saddam Hussein. Human Rights Watch (1993) documented the systematic and deliberate murder of up to 100,000 Kurds between February and September 1988. In 1991, after American-led forces ousted Saddam Hussein from Kuwait, he regrouped to crush the renewed Kurdish uprising in the north (as well as a Shiite uprising in the south). Within forty-eight hours, almost two million Kurds fled: 800,000 to Turkey and one million to Iran, until the British Prime Minister, John Major, declared the Kurdistan region of Iraq (KRI) to be a no-fly zone to protect the Kurds from Saddam's vicious air campaign against the Kurdish civilian population. This humanitarian intervention was authorised by UN Security Council Resolution 668 in May 1991. The refugees returned. A KRI general election was held in May 1992.

The number of Kurdish refugees in the Middle East dramatically decreased after the establishment of a semi-autonomous Kurdish area in northern Iraq and Kurds acquired a degree of self-determination. The exodus and return of the Kurdish-Iraqi refugees in 1991 stands out as an excellent example of the truism that, in ethnic or religious warfare, refugees only return if they are a majority in an area and/or when they defeat the government that denies their self-determination (Adelman & Barkan 2011).

Since the Iraqi constitution confirmed the KRI as a self-rule region prior to the American invasion in 2003, the latter intervention simply strengthened Kurdish autonomy in northern Iraq. Iraqi Kurds then enjoyed de facto semi-statehood in spite of internal divisions between the Kurdistan Democratic Party and the Patriotic Union of Kurdistan, as well as pressures from Turkey, Iran and Baghdad. Baathist policies failed to temper the drive towards self-determination and even strengthened that trajectory (Laizer 1996; Yildiz & Blass 2004). Fawcett and Cohen (2002) in their report for the Brookings–Bern Project on Internal Displacement concluded that 'more than one million Kurds from the North ... had been deliberately expelled from their homes by the state policies of Saddam Hussein'. That million largely returned.

Kurds, once the largest group of refugees in the Middle East, managed to secure an enclave in the north of Iraq that has become a refuge for returning Iraqi Kurdish refugees, and for Kurdish refugees from other countries as well as other parts of Iraq. As a result of these political, economic and military changes, the part of northern Iraq controlled by Kurds has changed from a refugee-producing region for Kurds into a haven for Kurds from everywhere. Northern Iraq, however, became unsafe for other minorities. As the Kurds developed their relatively stable and prosperous autonomous KRI government and their own military – the Peshmerga, they consolidated control in law and also by the expulsion and assimilation of others.

Turkmens, Assyrians, Armenians and Palestinians in 2006

Following the 2003 American-led invasion, the US-appointed Coalition Provisional Authority (CPA) approved an interim constitution, the Law of Administration for the State of Iraq for the Transitional Period or the Transitional Administrative Law (TAL) (see Chapter 7). The TAL enabled compensation for returning migrants and a Property Claims Commission provided compensation or restored homes and properties to previously expelled inhabitants. Returning Kurds were provided with new employment opportunities and Kurds were given the right 'to determine their own national identity and ethnic affiliation free from coercion and duress'. Finally, Article 140 of the new constitution provided for a referendum in Kirkuk and the immediate surrounding region to determine whether that area would be part of the northern Kurdish semi-autonomous region.

Before that referendum could take place, measures were adopted to reverse Saddam Hussein's Arabisation policy, resulting in tens of thousands of Kurds returning to the region following the 2003 invasion (Naqishbendi 2005). Kurds in turn displaced Arabs who had been forced or subsidised to move to Kirkuk by Saddam Hussein (al-Khalidi & Tanner 2006). The Kurds did not restrict their 'ethnic cleansing' to Arabs; they also drove out Turkmens, Christian Armenians and Assyrian-Chaldeans (Associated Press 2007; Sirkeci 2005). An International Crisis Group report (2006a) documented the struggle over oil and identity among Kurdish, Turkmen, Arab and Assyrian-Chaldean communities. Turkmens not driven out were assimilated into the Kurdish majority in spite of Turkish efforts to fund their independence through the Turkmen National Association. In the new constitution for the KRI, the Kurdish President of Iraq, Jalal Talabani, promised 'Iraqi Turkmen autonomy in areas where they are a majority' (Cevik 2006). Unfortunately, this had no more effect than the Kurdistan Regional Council voting in the early 1990s to ensure that Christians had schools that taught in the Syriac language (Persecution 2014). Turkmen impotence was clear when they won only a single seat in the elections in Kirkuk (Anderson & Stansfield 2009; al-Hurmezi 2010). While Kurds were consolidating in the north and either assimilating (O uzlu 2004) or extruding the Turkmen population of over half a million (Sirkeci 2011), in the rest of Iraq Shiites and Sunnis were separating into enclaves. Other minorities, such as Assyrians and Palestinians, lacked enclaves where they lived in sufficient numbers to provide for their own protection.

Following the American-led invasion, a violent four-way conflict began. In addition to the Kurds consolidating in the north and pressuring Arabs and others to leave, there was the dramatic fight between the American-led forces and the Iraqi army. After the latter's defeat and the dismantling of the armed forces, this conflict morphed into a strong insurgency largely led and conducted by Sunni Iraqis who had been dislodged from power. There was even more dramatic inter-communal religious violence between Shiite and Sunni as well as an intra-communal conflict within the Shiite religious community between various Shia militias (International Crisis Group 2006b).

Moqtada al-Sadr's Mahdi Army consolidated their control of Sadr City in Baghdad, on which it imposed religious law. In addition to hunting down Sunnis with ties to Saddam Hussein's Baath party and enforcing Sharia law on other Shiites, they also engaged in a struggle with the 'moderates' led by Ayatollah Ali al-Sistani. On 29 January 2007, for example, the Shiite Soldiers of Heaven launched a large attack against Najaf, a holy city for Shiites, to occupy the sacred shrine and massacre the religious leadership there, including Sistani. They failed only because US forces intervened to reinforce the Iraqi army (Santora 2007). Minorities with no defence capability or opportunity to retreat to safe enclaves were forced to flee the country altogether.

As early as 2003, the International Federation of Human Rights recognised that ethnic and religious cleansing was under way in Iraq (FIDH 2003). Then, the main source of refugees had been officials and military officers with close ties to the former Baath regime (Ferris 2007c). In 2004, refugees fleeing violence from Anbar province and minorities under pressure followed. But the explosion in violence and the huge exodus really began in 2006 when, following the 22 February bombing of the Golden Mosque in Samarra, the level of assassinations, kidnappings and generalised violence made many neighbourhoods uninhabitable (al-Khalidi et al. 2007). Christians and Sabaean-Mandaeans were particularly targeted (Human Rights Watch 2006). Kälin stated unequivocally that 'minority communities have been particularly at risk and are reported to have left their communities in substantial numbers' (Kälin 2007: 14; see also Harper 2008). Scholars predicted that Iraq's demographic composition would change irreversibly as the extremists 'seek to consolidate "their" territory by expelling the "others"' (al-Khalidi and Tanner 2007: 8).

During 2006 and 2007, two million Iraqis were internally displaced while another two million fled: 1.1 million to Syria, mainly to Damascus and Aleppo (al-Miqdad 2007), and 750,000 to Jordan (al-Khalidi & Tanner 2007). At the beginning of 2007, UNHCR launched an appeal to raise an additional US$60 million to deal with refugees and IDPs in and from Iraq (Ferris & Hall 2007). The appeal covered Iraq and the five states with the bulk of the refugees: Syria, Jordan, Lebanon, Egypt and Turkey.

By 2005, 300,000 Iraqis had returned home to try to rebuild their lives. In 2006, that trend dramatically reversed. 'Spiraling levels of sectarian, political and criminal violence, dwindling basic services, loss of livelihood, inflation and uncertainty about the future have all contributed to an exodus now estimated at 40,000 to 50,000 a month fleeing their homes inside Iraq' (UNHCR 2007c). Resettlement seemed the only realistic option for a permanent solution for many refugees and certainly most minorities (UNHCR 2007b). The number of asylum seekers from Iraq in 2006 had escalated dramatically from the earlier years of the war (Ferris 2007a; Frelick 2007b). In Europe, a sharp increase took place in Iraqi asylum applicants with 22,200 cases from Iraq, 9,000 in Sweden alone (Ferris 2007b). Even though the USA was the main destination for asylum seekers (Frelick 2007a; UNHCR 2007a), US efforts to resettle refugees were too small given the enormity of the crisis (Cohen & al-Khalidi 2007). The Canadian record was even worse: in 2006 there were only 179 Iraqi claimants, fewer than when Saddam was in power.

UNHCR briefings especially stressed the plight of Palestinians from Iraq. As Andrew Harper, the Geneva-based senior Iraq operations manager for UNHCR, noted, 'Palestinians are the most vulnerable as they literally have nowhere else to flee, and in many cases have been denied travel documents' (UNHCR 2007c). Their persecution began in 2003.

> Palestinian refugees in Iraq became a target for violence, harassment, and eviction from their homes soon after the Iraqi government fell to US-led forces in 2003. Unknown assailants fired upon Palestinian housing projects with assault weapons and mortar rounds, and threw bombs into Palestinian homes. (Human Rights Watch 2006)

In Iraq Palestinians' housing had been subsidised at the expense of mostly Shia landlords who were paid a pittance by the government. After Saddam's fall, the landlords forcibly evicted their Palestinian tenants. On 23 January 2003, thirty Palestinians were abducted from the Hay el-Nidal apartments in Baghdad after they had been lodged there in a UNHCR 'safe' house since they had been evicted from their homes. The next day, ninety Palestinian men, women and children fled Baghdad in two rented buses.

By the end of 2006, only 15,000 of the 30,000 Palestinians who had been living in Iraq under Saddam Hussein remained and they lived in 'constant fear of harassment, killings and kidnappings in Baghdad' (UNHCR 2007c). In December 2006, UNHCR received a list of 161 who had been killed, but the Palestine Liberation Organisation's head of refugee affairs said the total was 520. Vincent Cochetel (2007: 21) reported that 'some 600 Palestinians have been murdered in Baghdad since 2003'. UNHCR recorded thirty-four Palestinian refugees killed and five kidnapped in the last two months of 2006. Despite their plight, no country would take the Palestinian refugees in (Harper 2008). Since April 2006, when Syria last allowed entry to a group of 287 Palestinians from Iraq, Syria has closed its gates to Iraqi-Palestinian refugees. Seventy-three Palestinians who arrived at el-Waleed camp were stranded at the Iraq–Syria border and were forced to join the 500-plus already living there. In 2007 the total number in both al-Tanf and el-Waleed camps was estimated at 1,600 (A'idoun Group 2007; IRIN 2007).

Iraqi Christians were worse off given their much larger numbers and history. The Assyrians have been the barometer of pluralism in Iraq, suffering three major disasters in the twentieth century. In 1915, 'up to two-thirds of the Assyrian community of southeastern Turkey and northern Iran was physically decimated in a matter of months' (Lewis 2003). An estimated 750,000 were slaughtered. In late summer of 1933, when an armed group of 800 Assyrians crossed from Iraq into Syria and were pushed back, they were attacked, crushed and slaughtered by the Iraqi military in the massacre at Simele and Assyrian villages around Simele were destroyed. Under Saddam Hussein, Assyrian religious and cultural life was severely repressed. In the Iran–Iraq War, Assyrians were drafted and sent as cannon fodder to the front lines. Denied their rights, hundreds of thousands emigrated.

Fifteen years before the 2003 American invasion and occupation of Iraq, Christian Assyrians constituted 10 per cent of the population or almost 2.5 million. After the 1991 Kuwait war, Iraqi Assyrians left in droves for Australia, Canada and the United States. In 2003, 400,000 Assyrians were living in North America, concentrated in Detroit, Phoenix, San José, Toronto and Windsor. At the start of the 2003 Bush war there were 1.5 million Christians still living in Iraq. Their exodus accelerated in August 2004 after Islamic terrorists bombed five churches in Baghdad and Mosul, killing seven and injuring more than forty. On 29 January 2006 the exodus turned to panic when six churches were bombed in Baghdad and the northern city of Kirkuk after protests swept through the Middle East over Danish newspaper cartoons depicting the Prophet Muhammad. In February, after the destruction of the Shia

Golden Mosque in Samarra, churches were burned. Christians were kidnapped, extorted, beheaded, raped and subjected to taxes because they were non-Muslims. These atrocities 'forced hundreds of thousands of Assyrians – together with other Christians – to abandon their ancestral land and flee to Jordan, Syria, Turkey and Lebanon' (Lamassu 2007: 44; see also al-Miqdad 2007: 20). Of the non-Chaldean Assyrians, two-thirds are Nestorians, who date back to ancient churches of Persia, and one-third follow the Syriac rite; they too have been persecuted.

A statement released by an American Catholic commission of bishops claimed that the community faced beheadings, rapes, crucifixions and other torture. The statement itemised recent atrocities, including a car bombing on 4 October 2006 with a dozen fatalities, a priest kidnapped on 9 October 2006 and beheaded in Mosul, and a teenager crucified in Basra. The most gruesome case was that of a fourteen-year-old boy, Ayad Tariq, in Baquba on 21 October 2006 in which a group of veiled Muslims attacked him after asking to see his identity card. They insisted that he was a 'dirty Christian sinner', and, screaming '*Allahu Akbar! Allahu Akbar!*' ('God is great!'), the assailants decapitated him.

Armenians constitute a small percentage of Christians in Iraq. As well as fleeing to other countries, they also returned to their homeland, Armenia, many assisted by the Danidh International Development Agency (DANIDA), the Armenian Red Cross, the NGO Mission to Armenia and even the Armenian Sociological Association. They live in rented flats and some have even purchased homes, especially if they were able to sell their property in Iraq. They have produced a disproportionate number of students studying at Yerevan Medical University.

The last remnants of a 2,000-year-old Christian community (a very small minority of Assyrians were and remain Arabic-speaking Muslims – the Mhallami in the Tur Abdin area) and the last Christian pocket of Assyrio-Aramaic-speaking people in the world – the Chaldeans and Syriacs – became victims of systematic religious and ethnic cleansing. Reputable authorities estimate that fewer than 200,000 Christians from this ancient community remained in Iraq in 2014, less than 10 per cent of the number living there in 1990 – despite legislation passed to secure their culture. This bears out the pessimistic prophecies of the great American writer William Saroyan, who foresaw in 1934 only a dismal fate for the Assyrian community after the 1933 pogroms. A 2004 UNHCR report on Iraqi Christians also proved prophetic: 'The days of officially preached religious tolerance during Saddam's rule are gone and freedom to worship now gives way to fear about an impending Islamisation of Iraq' (UNHCR 2004: 5). In May 2006, the United States Commission on International Religious Freedom warned that religiously motivated attacks would result in 'an exodus that may mean the end of the presence in Iraq of ancient Christian and other communities that have lived on those same lands for 2,000 years' (Wenski 2006).

After the bombing of the six churches, the European Parliament passed a resolution of strong condemnation with respect to the treatment of Assyrians (Chaldeans, Syriacs and other Christian minorities), urging Iraq to protect its Christian minorities. Christians have not given up entirely, however. Nor have moderate Muslims. On 16 August 2011, the Iraqi Parliament officially opened the General Directorate of Syriac Culture and Art, based on a curriculum recommended by the Council of Catholic Bishops of Iraq, and in 2014 Iraq's Ministry of Education decided to include Syriac and Christian education in 152 schools with 20,500 students in three of Iraq's provinces – Baghdad, Nineveh and Kirkuk – to preserve both the Syriac language and Christian denominations within Iraq. Either the entire curriculum will be taught in Syriac or only religious and language courses will be taught in Syriac with all other subjects in Arabic, depending on the school. In spite of such positive moves, prospects for Christians in Iraq remain dim. Half of the asylum seekers in Europe from Iraq are Christians.

Though the US State Department has made reconstruction projects a priority in areas with a dominant Chaldean-Assyrian population, only relatively small amounts are actually taken up by the Chaldeans. Of $1.2 billion allocated for projects in the province of Nineveh, only $33 million targeted the Chaldean-Assyrian population, who were once preponderant in that area. Within a very few years, Christian Assyrians, once the masters of the whole region, have been reduced to a rump in total disregard of the resolutions of indignant righteousness passed by the European Parliament.

What started with the seventh-century Muslim invasions of Mesopotamia and took off in the eleventh century when Muslims became the majority in what is now Iraq – the religious cleansing of Christians from Iraq – has been almost completed by 2014. Whether school reform and other measures will save the 200,000 survivors remains to be seen.

Refugees in Iraq 2010 – Mandaeans and Yazidis

On 16 July 2010, Canada's national public radio (CBC) broadcast a special on Iraqi refugees featuring Zakiya, a former Iraqi journalist and one of 1.1 million Iraqi refugees in Syria (of the 1.8 million who had fled since 2003). Zakiya is a Shia Muslim; her husband was a Sunni. Two of her daughters were killed in Iraq. Her husband, who returned to Iraq to retrieve money in 2009, was never seen again. Left with three children – a 12-year-old daughter, Huda, who suffers from panic attacks from her attempted kidnapping in Iraq, and nine-year-old twin boys – Zakiya lives in Jaramana, a low-rent suburb of Damascus and tries to survive on a UNHCR $200 monthly subsidy, food rations and her savings. Fortunately, Assad's Syria allowed the refugees free access to health services and education. Zakiya is unusual in rejecting a rare offer of resettlement to the United States; she blames America for the post-2003 chaos in Iraq. She still hopes to be selected for resettlement in Canada; given few openings, that hope may be dashed.

By 2010, with so many refugees unwilling to return home and with few opportunities to emigrate further west or north, and having totally exhausted their savings, the crisis had become perilous (Amos 2010: 67). The number of Iraqis resident in Syria had stabilised with 500 entering and exiting per day. UNHCR then supported their return but most international rights organisations, including the International Crisis Group, Amnesty International, the International Refugee Committee and Refugee International, considered the situation too perilous, certainly for minorities. Economic uncertainty prolonged the refugee situation; fewer and fewer refugees envisaged returning (Chatty 2010). Because UNHCR advocated return and because most refugees lived in cities rather than camps, UNHCR only managed to register 200,000 refugees even though the organisation provided support for 750,000. In 2010, only 273 Iraqi families returned to Iraqi under UNHCR's voluntary-repatriation programme.

Resettlement remained the only viable option for most non-Sunni and non-Shia refugees. Up to 2008, only 17,800 had been resettled (International Crisis Group 2008; Loughry & Duncan 2008). By 2010, more than 50,000 had been resettled. Minorities were especially in great need. One thousand Palestinian refugees from al-Tanf camp on the Iraq–Syria border were resettled in Europe with the rest moved to al-Hol camp in north-east Syria.

In addition to Palestinians and Christians, Mandaeans and Yazidis also fled to escape the increasingly sectarian violence. Of the overall refugee population in Syria, Christians were estimated to constitute 11 per cent, Mandaeans 2 per cent and Yazidis just under 1 per cent (UNHCR 2010). Discounting mixed marriages and Sunnis and Shiites in fear of human rights abuses, other than Palestinians, at least 14 per cent of the one million refugees (140,000) in Syria are in need of resettlement. Most live in the Jaramanah district of Damascus.

There are 40,000 Gnostic Mandaeans, a remnant of a once thriving ethno-religious sect in the Middle East who previously lived in southern Iraq and Baghdad. Most fled when militias attacked the Mandaean temple (Crawford 2007). 'Seventy-five percent of Iraq's Christian, Mandaean and Yazidi minorities have left their homes,' according to Michael La Civita, vice president for communications at the Catholic Near East Welfare Association (Bauman 2011). That 75 per cent included almost all of the Mandaean and Yazidi populations. Fortunately for the Mandaeans, the Mandaean diaspora sponsored the resettlement of Mandaean refugees.

The Yazidis have not been as fortunate. As documented in a Chapter 7, their persecution began in earnest in 2007. On 20 October 2010, the UN declared the first week of February Annual Interfaith Harmony Week in Iraq. It was inaugurated by the UN special representative to Iraq, Nikolay Mladenov, who attended services in St Joseph's Syriac Catholic Church, followed by special visits to Yazidi temples as well as Shiite and Sunni shrines. Mladenov attempted to counter the widespread Iraqi calumny equating the Yazidi religion with devil worship and satanic rites. Unfortunately, in terms of changing attitudes or even calming fears, his efforts proved ineffectual.

As long as Islam is the state religion of Iraq, as long as the constitution provides that no law can be passed in contravention of Islamic law, as long as there is no constitutional provision guaranteeing the protection of minorities, such symbolic gestures by the UN are futile. Since Iraq lacks a culture of press freedom and journalists have been consistently targeted for persecution and even death, the prospects for a culture of transparency and accountability seem slim, especially in light of the continued use of the media to advance government propaganda (Mamouri 2014a).

Iraqi Refugees Today

Because of the outbreak of the civil war in Syria, Syrian refugees flowed into Iraq and some Iraqi refugees returned home. Some went elsewhere. But most stayed where they were even though the war brought increasing insecurity to vast stretches of Syria. The positive inter-play of the refugees and the Syrian economy came to an end. With the influx of Iraqi refugees into Syria, its GDP doubled between 2004 and 2010 to $60 billion. Iraqis invested in Syrian businesses, creating an industrial and commercial boom. Syrian unemployment *declined*. However, the resultant inflationary pressures increased costs, especially for housing for Syrian consumers, and created widespread resentment. Further, by

2009, refugees were costing the Syrian government a billion dollars per year (Sassoon 2009: 61).

Within three years of the outbreak of the civil war on 15 March 2011, the numbers of Syrian refugees to Iraq exceeded those from Iraq over the previous ten years. So why then did the Iraqi refugees not return, especially in 2014? An important negative indicator for refugees was the enormous increase in attacks against the moderate cleric Grand Ayatollah Ali al-Sistani from other segments of the Shiite establishment who resented his refusal to make Sharia law supreme in Iraq, a position Sistani took in defence of human rights and the rights of non-Muslim minorities. The quietist *hawza* (Shia religious seminary) approach advocating moderation had always been attacked by figures such as Moqtada al-Sadr, who advocated a vocal *hawza* approach to push Sharia law on everyone. There were even more extreme approaches. Iraqi Shia militias such as Asa'ib Ahl al-Haq aligned themselves with Iran.

Since most of the persecution against minorities took place when Sistani was the Grand Ayatollah, though certainly without his blessing, what can be expected when he retires? Iraq may have human rights parliamentary committees, a ministry and NGOs to monitor human rights abuses, but it remains a significant human rights violator. The government systematically tortures prisoners, conducts arbitrary arrests and denies freedom of expression (HRW 2013a). Iraqi women are particularly targeted and subjected to arrests, illegal detention, rape, torture and even arbitrary killing (HRW 2013b).

The ongoing series of bombings in Iraq, particularly in Anbar province by al-Qaeda affiliates and other Sunni extremists against Shiite and government targets, escalated with a vengeance in December 2013. In January 2014 alone, the death toll exceeded 900. For example, in a terrorist attack on a transportation ministry building, twelve hostages were killed: four by terrorists and up to eight militants by Iraqi security forces (Casey & Haber 2014). On 24 February, shelling took place in Ramadi, and there were shootings in Mosul and bombings in Baghdad; seventeen people were killed.

On 20 January 2014 it appeared that the army were regaining control of Anbar, after they displaced Islamic State of Iran and Syria (ISIS) control of Khalidiya, which connects Fallujah with Ramadi. The ISIS military commander was killed along with dozens of his fighters. Though disowned by al-Qaeda on 3 February 2014, ISIS, led by Abu Bakr al-Baghdadi (Ibrahim Awwad Ibrahim Ali al-Badri al-Samarrrai), has for years had a strong presence in Anbar as well as in Baghdad and Basra. Previous attacks had come in late 2013 when the Maliki government used violence to disperse a Sunni sit-in; Nouri al-Maliki himself accused the Sunnis of using the peaceful sit-in as a base to plan and implement terrorist car bombings throughout Iraq.

ISIS saw its chance to position itself as the militant wing of the Sunni protest movement. However, this set off an internecine war between al-Qaeda and ISIS when the envoy to the Syrian rebel movement, Abu Khalid al-Suri, who had been close to Osama bin Laden, was murdered in a suicide attack soon after he was sent to mediate in the rivalry between ISIS and the official Syrian al-Qaeda offshoot, the al-Nusra Front. In late February 2014, Abu Mohammed al-Golani, the al-Nusra leader, accused ISIS of perpetrating the crime and sent a note to ISIS threatening to 'banish it, even from Iraq!' (Spencer 2014).

In 2006 the US Army general David Petraeus had aligned with Sunni traditional elders against the extremists. In early 2014 Maliki sought to end the crisis in Anbar using military and security resources and attempted to imitate Petraeus's tactics instead of waiting for the outcome of the coming parliamentary and presidential election in April. He miscalculated. Enough tribal leaders as well as Sunni clerics refused to cooperate (Abbas 2014d). This was helped by ISIS, which refused to harm religious or tribal leaders or even the police and instead concentrated on government targets. ISIS was also helped when Maliki ordered his military to shoot terrorists rather than take them prisoner (HRW 2013a). On 20 December 2013, Iraq Army general Abdul Amir al-Zaidi announced: 'I will kill any terrorist. I will not deliver him to justice' (American Civil Liberties Union n.d.). As a result of Maliki's poor decisions, clan leaders such as Shaykh Jassem al-Klabi emerged as independent actors in influencing election results. However, this still did not encourage Iraqi refugee return. Maliki's failures were accompanied by the rise of ISIS.

Thus, Sunni and even Shia refugees are reluctant to return home, let alone other minorities. Some have gone to Jordan, Lebanon, Turkey and elsewhere. Only 76,000 – that is 6 per cent of the Iraqi refugees in Syria – have returned. The vast majority remain in Syria, in spite of the civil war. The ratio of those who have stayed in Jordan is even higher; there have been very few returns from Jordan. By the end of 2013, UNHCR reported that almost 90 per cent of the refugees in Syria are Iraqis and two-thirds of those are from Baghdad (UNHCR 2013).

Conclusion

Small minorities in Iraq lacking a secure home were forced to seek refuge outside the country and could not return. Sunnis and Shias have largely decided not to return. Once the demons of ethnic and inter-sectarian violence were unleashed, the exodus by minorities could not be stopped, let alone reversed. Only the Kurds were able to consolidate their control in the north, including Kirkuk. Kurds returned in large numbers from abroad and from within Iraq. However erroneous the military mission in Iraq, however serious the strategic political errors of the US-led occupation forces, however inadequate and contradictory the humanitarian IDP and refugee support regime, the possibility of any significant numbers of returnees would most likely have been very low because of the extensive sectarian divisions within the country. By recognising this reality, romantic efforts at recreating a multi-ethnic and multireligious postwar society could have been avoided in favour of more realistic internal and external resettlement schemes.

Chapter 12

Shia Ascendancy in Iraq and the Sectarian Polarisation of the Middle East

Ranj Alaaldin

Central to the legacy of the US intervention in Iraq is the issue of sectarianism and the role it played in the reconstruction of the Iraqi state, as well as its impact on Iraqi society. Sectarianism was not a problem that emerged in post-2003 Iraq; its origins pre-date the modern Iraqi state and its relevance grew as a consequence of authoritarian rule and the emergence of parties and movements that drew their legitimacy and support from different ethno-sectarian communities. Events after 2003 exacerbated sectarian tensions and their significance for the political process and the Iraqi people. The 2006 sectarian civil war, the contestation of elections on the basis of identity and sect and continued sectarian violence are all symptoms of the post-2003 rise of sectarianism.

Sectarian polarisation in Iraq has also manifested itself on a regional scale. The removal of the Baath regime in 2003 has made a marked contribution to the polarisation of the Middle East along sectarian boundaries. Iraq's regional neighbours waged war on one another via proxies in Iraq. Jordan and Saudi Arabia, along with the Gulf states, opposed the replacement of Saddam Hussein's regime because of fears this would empower the Shias in Iraq and, therefore, Iran's influence in the region. To this day, Iraq's regional neighbours continue to influence rival political blocs and movements, prolonging the domestic polarisation in the country. Iraq's impact on the sectarian polarisation of the region was evident in the Arab Spring uprisings – particularly the civil war in Syria, which has transformed into a second front for Iraq's ongoing sectarian conflict. The overlapping and powerful combination of domestic and regional sectarian mobilisation means that sectarianism will continue to define the Middle East in the near and distant future.

The question of sectarianism and its contribution to the Iraqi state and society is a complicated one and, in addition to regional, domestic and pre- and post-2003 factors in Iraq, also encompasses other important questions including the role of symbolism, culture and geography. As such, the purpose of this chapter is to focus on the evolution of sectarianism in post-2003 Iraq, looking in particular at the issue of Sunni–Shia political relations and how sectarianism in the formative stages of the new Iraq has come to define the Iraqi state and society today. Against this backdrop, the chapter will analyse the impact it has had on the sectarian polarisation of the region. It will argue that the 2003 toppling of the Baath regime set in motion a series of events that, in the absence of authoritarian and violent containment, allowed pre-existing cycles of sectarian divisions and struggles to spin at a much more destructive rate, with far-reaching consequences for Iraq and the broader region. In this respect, the first legacy of the Iraq War is the intensification of sectarian tensions in Iraq, namely the divide between Iraq's Sunni and Shia communities; the second is the impact this has had on the definition and identity of the Iraqi state, as a result of the rise and liberation of the Shias and the Shia identity, and ultimately on sectarian polarisation in the Middle East.

Although this chapter is concerned with the broader empirical aspects of sectarianism in Iraq and its impact on the region, it is, nevertheless, worth pointing out that references to the concept can be misleading given its fluid nature. Its application to Iraq's Sunni and Shia communities can also be problematic as it simplifies and categorises heterogeneous communities into single actors, while pre-determining the attitudes and beliefs of individuals by virtue of their association with that community, regardless of the strength of the nexus between them. Broader socio-economic as well as political conditions underpin the relevance of sectarian identity. Further, Iraq has shown throughout its history that sectarianism and its impact on its society is determined by changing contexts, including civil strife (the 1991 uprising, the 2006 civil war), as well as inter-state conflicts such as the Iran–Iraq War. Despite the significance of sectarianism in Iraq and its legacies for the region, few accounts have dealt principally with sectarianism, with most Iraq-focused studies touching on the issue as part of broader research objectives. Fanar Haddad's study on the subject is the most recent and the most extensive, providing an in-depth and authoritative look at the history of sectarianism in Iraq with a particular emphasis on the 1991 uprisings and their impact on the post-2003 sectarian polarisation of Iraqi society (Haddad 2011). Other works are either outdated and concerned with pre-2003 Iraq and the history of the modern state more generally (Batatu 1978; Farouk-Sluglett & Sluglett 2003; Tripp 2007); are focused on the nation-building process in post-2003 Iraq and issues relating to post-2003 violence, political process and power-sharing (Anderson & Stansfield 2004; Dodge 2005; O'Leary 2009); or provide a history and dissection of the key political and religious actors in the country (Jabar 2003) and situate this against the backdrop of Iraq's recent history and post-2003 developments, namely its political process and US post-conflict reconstruction policies (Allawi 2007). In general, Iraq-focused studies have paid insufficient attention to the question of sectarian relations and their consequences for the Middle East. As a result, important dynamics and nuances have been missed. This chapter will address these dynamics in an attempt to provide a stronger understanding of sectarian relations in the new Iraq, as well as to better understand the impact of Iraq's domestic affairs on the broader region.

Sunni Arabs: Mobilisation and Marginalisation

In pre-2003 Iraq, identity politics helped mobilise communities in the effort to undermine Baathist rule and remedy political and social grievances. In the new Iraq, it has led to the mobilisation and unification of Shia and Kurdish populations for the purposes of contesting democratic elections and then, later, for the purposes of mobilising communities in the 2006 civil war between Sunni and Shia Arabs. For the Sunni Arabs, the overlap between the Shia faith and the Iraqi identity has been a source of agitation, regardless of the presence of Iraqi nationalism and patriotism among the Shias. This agitation has intensified as a result of the Shias' demographic superiority and their embracing of majority rule as well as fears that the new Iraq represents the rise of the Shias at the expense of the Sunnis, particularly after the toppling of the Baath regime in mid-2003, when millions of Shias poured onto the streets of the south to celebrate the Shia religious occasion of Arbaeen and called for the leadership of the ayatollahs and the clerical establishment (Rosen 2008).

The role and influence of the Shia clerical establishment is a central aspect of the overlap between faith and nationalism for the Iraqi Shias. The *marja'iyyah* has given the Shia community a far greater capacity to centralise the Shia voice because of the overarching and influential role it has in politics and the daily life of the Shias, although this has its limits. This influence increased from 1958 onwards with the demise of the communists and the advent of Shia political groups. Prior to this, the clerical establishment was able to mobilise merely hundreds for religious processions, as opposed to the tens of thousands they can mobilise today (Jabar 2003: 75). The Sunnis, by comparison, lack a centralised system of religious authority and jurisprudence. At the same time, Sunni Arabs found themselves lacking a political movement organised around and deriving its support from the Sunni community and Sunni identity.

As Haddad states, prior to 2003 Sunni Arabs largely saw themselves as 'sectless' in the sense that the Sunni identity manifested itself in and was 'validated in the daily reproduction of power relations' (Haddad 2013: 80). While there was a Sunni community to speak of, its identity was principally represented in the state, which over the course of the past eighty years embodied a combination of nationalistic, pan-Arabist and socialist ideologies that were at various points underpinned by ethnic chauvinism.

In post-2003 Iraq, the only Sunni Arab groups that possessed the capacity and experience to organise themselves politically and electorally were the Baath party and the Iraqi Islamic Party (IIP). The former was outlawed and the latter did not appeal to the broader and largely secular Sunni population. Iraq's Arab Sunnis were, therefore, unable to contest politics in the new Iraq in the same organised fashion as the Shias and the Kurds.

With the fall of the Baath regime came the fall of the Sunnis, as a UN report suggested in 2004 (United Nations Security Council 2004). However, while this may be a consequence of Iraqi history and politics itself, it is also rooted in a number of Sunni Arab miscalculations in the aftermath of regime change. A number of poorly managed post-conflict reconstruction policies exacerbated Sunni Arab apprehensions about the new Iraq – policies such as the reconstitution of the army and the process of de-Baathification. However, to attribute the descent into violence to the policies themselves or to suggest they were 'the central driver of conflict' misses some of the realities that preceded the Sunni insurgency and the civil war (Dodge 2012a: 462). While the case could be made that incompetent post-conflict management exacerbated Sunni Arab tensions and apprehension towards the new Iraq, it is not clear whether competent management would have placated Sunni Arabs. The dominant narrative in relation to the descent into chaos in Iraq is essentially that the Americans brought with them incompetent advisers and policy-makers, who then rushed the Iraqi constitution through and, consequently, left the Sunni Arabs disempowered and isolated. The implementation of the 2005 constitution is more broadly identified as the point at which the Sunni were marginalised, when they rejected the new Iraq and when violence started to escalate. What is missing here is the fact that the myth of Sunni disempowerment and marginalisation was already being propagated in 2003 and, therefore, from the outset of the new Iraq, too soon for it to be real. Further, while a UN report in 2004 noted that the Shias 'are committed to ... ensuring the political emancipation of the Shia community' (United Nations Security Council 2004), the trajectory of the new Iraq shows it was only after 2005 that a traditionally divided Shia community started to manage its internal differences, most notably with assistance from Grand Ayatollah Sistani. This came in response to the violent Sunni Arab mobilisation against the new political order in the country.

The notion of Sunni Arab marginalisation served a very specific purpose, namely the effective mobilisation of Sunni Arab support to oppose the US occupation, fight the occupying forces and delegitimise the new Iraq and its political process altogether. Sunni Arab militants and politicians also used it to conceal their own failures and strategic miscalculations, allowing the myth to spread exponentially. In other words, both politicians and militants looked to the concept of marginalisation for the purposes of winning local support. Its consequence, however, would be an increase in sectarian tensions and the destabilisation of the political environment. The first principal victim of this myth was indeed the constitution itself but not necessarily because of its merits or demerits. The momentum the misconception had generated meant that anything threatening the traditional identity of the state could be misconstrued as sidelining the Sunnis. Federalism, majority rule, Shia rule, decentralisation and the option of creating – rather than imposing – regions all threatened the old Iraq of centralised power, minority and dictatorial rule. Commenting in 2005, Saleh al-Mutlaq, one of the leading Sunni Arab representatives, warned:

> The issue of division through federalism is on the table. The Iraqi people have to give their word now and reject the constitution because this constitution is the *beginning of the division of the country* and the beginning of creating disturbance in the country. (BBC 2005, emphasis added)

The populist nature of the remarks is clear, particularly since the constitution *offered* rather than *imposed* federalism and ignored the fact that powerful Shia Islamic parties, like the Da'wa party and the Sadrists, were categorically against the idea of federalism and the regionalisation of Iraq. Partition, in other words, was unlikely, if not impossible.

Disingenuous Sunni Arab political participation in the post-conflict transitional process that was based around propagating the myth of Sunni marginalisation, mobilising local Sunni Arab support and challenging the new political order can only be inferred from actions and first-hand accounts that exist of the process, since the Sunni Arab elite have not alluded to this and are unlikely ever to do so. What we do know is that Sunni Arab politicians like Mutlaq and others – particularly those from the Iraqiyya bloc – who criticised the constitution and then withdrew from discussions and mobilised Sunni Arabs to reject it are today those that most often make reference to the constitution as the basis for their arguments and criticisms. As Haider Ala Hamoudi notes, 'the Sunni population no longer view the constitution as a foreign instrument imposed on them' and they have even gone as far as abandoning their plans to propose amendments to it (Hamoudi 2013: 4). We also know that Ayatollah al-Sistani, prior to the creation of the Shia United Iraqi Alliance, had made overtures to the IIP and al-Iraqiyya, asking them to join 'a broad, nonsectarian, national alliance to establish a founding assembly in charge of writing the constitution'. This was rejected (Hamoudi 2007: 1316). Far from having a new political order imposed on them and the Sunni Arab population, Iraq's Sunni Arab elite in effect torpedoed any effort to forge a post-conflict political and constitutional settlement, choosing instead to exacerbate existing apprehensions within the Sunni Arab population by asserting populist and sectarian discourses. Essentially, in targeting the constitution and adopting sensationalist positions, the Sunni Arab elite, above all, targeted the very bedrock of the new Iraq and, therefore, the legitimacy of the new political order. Hence, led by the Sunni Arab elite, Iraq's Sunni Arabs were mobilised to *exclude* themselves from the state, as opposed to being *rejected* by the new Iraq. Realising its miscalculations and that Iraq would move forward without them, Sunni Arab elites reversed their earlier election boycott to take part in the December 2005 elections.

The Insurgency

Combined with the Sunni Arab political mobilisation was a more effective and deadly mobilisation of violent Sunni Arab actors. The Iraqi insurgency comprised and continues to comprise a hybrid of disparate groups who have worked together at different points in the new Iraq. Despite their contrasting ideological and political visions they have been unified by a common goal of, firstly, forcing the Americans to withdraw from Iraq and, secondly, reversing Iraq's post-2003 political order. Generally speaking, the insurgency has been comprised of Sunni Arab groups including Baathists, Islamist radicals and petty criminals. They have been localised within the 'Sunni triangle', encompassing territories between Baghdad, Tikrit and Fallujah, but have also been able to conduct sophisticated operations beyond these areas (Anderson & Stansfield 2004: 232). The significance of the insurgency here relates to the overlap between the violent and political mobilisation of Iraq's Sunni Arabs and the space this provided for sectarian conflict.

The current understanding is that the post-2003 violence was largely attributable to the post-conflict collapse of the state, although some identify other reasons for it, such as the flood of jihadists entering the country before the collapse of the Iraqi state (Krepinevich 2005). In this sense, the insurgency is often described as being more reactive to the disbanding of the army and the collapse of the state, rather than proactive (Dodge 2005: 9). Referring to his time in Baghdad in 2003 and his interviews with senior Baathists, Toby Dodge notes how de-Baathification had bedazzled them, with one stressing: 'Why can't [Paul Bremer, the CPA Administrator] leave us alone? We are like the Communist Party of the Soviet Union, worn out and ideologically defeated.' Dodge goes on to argue that de-Baathification 'triggered a concerted attempt at organisation and then violent confrontation; the fight for a loser's peace had begun' (Dodge 2012a: 469). This is disputed by Allawi, who notes 'the oft-made claim that the disbanding of the army had released a flood of recruits for the insurgency was not the only, or even the main, underpinning of the insurgency' (Allawi 2007: 243). The motives driving senior officers into the insurgency were far more complex, with key actors within the insurgency, including former army generals, 'openly contemptuous of the Shia and demand[ing] the restoration of Sunni power'. Additionally, 'no one admitted they were fighting because they had nothing better to do, or because they were in need of money' (Allawi 2007: 243).

Further, there may have been a more significant set of pre-war conditions and overlap between different Sunni actors, both violent and political, than first assumed, despite some Baathists' cries of innocence. Iraq's insurgency was mobilised before the Americans had entered Iraq. By 2003, the Baath regime had decentralised its grip and the maintenance of order as a result of a set of measures implemented during the 1990s and 2000s, during which they empowered Iraqi tribes and other non-state actors. They gave them caches of arms and ammunition, funds as well as training, all aimed toward ensuring the continued operation and survival of the Baath authorities, which collapsed during the 1991 uprising in the south, a region the regime almost lost. Saddam Hussein also created many private paramilitary and regional armed units which operated with state funding but beyond the remit of the Defence Ministry. Their 'training focused on exactly what the insurgents later used: small arms, small-unit tactics, sabotage, techniques, and military surveillance and reconnaissance tasks' and 'commando or terrorist operations' (Marten 2012: 145). These militias, tribal structures, networks and resources were operational when the US entered Iraq. They continue to be harnessed by the insurgency, with great effect.

The insurgency was, therefore, set in motion before politics and policies in the new Iraq were executed. The argument that there was a pre-existing insurgency of sorts as well as an overlap between the insurgents and their local communities becomes further reinforced when considered against the fact that effective insurgencies and a broader mobilisation of local communities require planning and local support. Baath loyalists and militias, funded by the state in its pre-2003 form and later in the post-2003 Iraq by wealthy Baathist merchants and foreign donors, were organised, had access to arms (Iraqi society at the time was already flooded with weapons) and had the benefit of extensive support and intelligence networks. It is plausible to suggest that these favourable conditions gave militants the capacity to execute their deadliest sectarian attacks as early as March 2004, when, during an Ashura procession millions of Shias were targeted in an operation that killed 270 people and wounded 66.

This pre-war organisation of the insurgency made the task of rebuilding Iraq all the more difficult, particularly when considered in light of its effective mobilisation of one particular and very significant segment of Iraqi society; mobilised, that is, to violently undermine the process of reconstruction. This, in turn, created the space for a Sunni Arab insurrection and provided a conducive environment in which Islamist radicals could operate, given the common goal they shared with the Baath and other indigenous militants, namely the reversal of the new Iraq. As Allawi notes, the ideology of the Baath party also changed to accommodate the increased religiosity of its mainly Sunni base and partly because its own membership had become more pious (Allawi 2007: 241). By 2006, what moderate Sunni Arab leaders there were had been marginalised by extremist elements; those moderates, it should be noted, were under threat from the extreme elements within the Sunni community.

It was against this backdrop of aggravated sectarian tensions that the 2006 sectarian civil war took place. On 22 February 2006, a bomb destroyed the Shia al-Askari shrine in Samarra. The event triggered a concerted response from Shia militias such as the Jaysh al-Mahdi and segments within the Shia community who had formed their own groups of armed men. Some of these militias were integrated into the Iraqi police force. Within days of the bombing, more than 1,200 bodies, mostly of Sunni Arabs, were found. The civil war in 2006 was not a result of the al-Askari attack itself but rather a result of the fact that virtually overnight a well-armed and suddenly marginalised minority (Sunni) confronted a passionate and persecuted majority (Shia) in the context of a brutal military occupation.

The Region

Like the 1979 Iranian Revolution (Nakash 2007), the 2003 intervention in Iraq had an instant impact on the sectarian polarisation of the region. In December 2004, King Abdullah of Jordan coined a phrase that reverberated throughout the world, referring to the dangers of a 'Shia crescent' stretching from Damascus to Tehran and passing through Baghdad, and warning: 'If Iraq goes Islamic republic, then, yes, we've opened ourselves to a whole set of new problems that will not be limited to the borders of Iraq' (quoted in Wright & Baker 2004). The definition of the Iraqi state was still unclear at the time and it was equally unclear whether Iraq would come to be ruled by a Shia alliance. Iraq's neighbours had already made up their mind: the new Iraq represented an Iranian client state. In response came a flood of jihadists using the Arab states as a transit point to enter Iraq and wreak carnage. Militants received active support from either Arab governments or wealthy individuals from Saudi Arabia and the Gulf states.

The transformational impact of the Iraq War on the region is usually examined in terms of its sectarian polarisation of the Middle East, its impact on Iranian–Arab world relations; Iran's influence in the region and, more recently, its impact on the regionalisation of conflicts such as in Syria (Louër 2008; Nakash 2007; Nasr 2007; Potter 2013). Justin Gengler argues that Shia political actors and citizens were previously conceived as local political problems requiring local responses within local political frameworks but their emboldening now requires regional as well as local preventative measures (Gengler 2014: 57). According to this argument, the Arab world shifted its position towards the Shia population and Shia political actors after 2003. The assertion is problematic since the Arab world has always treated Shia political actors as part of a broader regional problem, particularly because of the religious and political ties that exist between the region's different Shia communities. These ties do not necessarily mean that they are conducive to some form of pan-regional Shia alliance but rather that they have constituted the basis on which the Arab world has identified the region's Shia communities as threatening their authority. This regionalised approach to the Shias, which started to crystallise with the advent of the 1979 Iranian Revolution, intensified after the toppling of the Baath regime in Iraq as the state came to be dominated by mostly Shia Islamist political actors. It is in this manner that Shia mobilisation across the region is better described, in that the regional dimension of Shia political mobilisation and the sectarianisation of Middle East geopolitics has intensified, rather than emerged, since 2003.

To better understand how the empowerment of Iraq's Shia population has affected the region it is worth referring back to the Iranian Revolution and the Iran–Iraq War. After 1979 and the emergence of a Shia Islamist republic, the Iranian state embraced an expansionist policy and called for uprisings elsewhere in the region and across the Islamic world. Iraq, like other regimes in the region, feared the emergence of the Islamic Republic of Iran. The Baath regime had a discontented Shia population, with groups such as Da'wa explicitly supporting the Iranian Revolution. Further, the Shias in Iraq had a far more impressive and sophisticated record of protest and mobilisation than their co-religionists elsewhere, starting in the 1960s. That, in turn, prompted the state to resort to the collective suppression of the Shia community. In other words, Iraq already had the foundation on which a Shia revolution could take place. Against this backdrop came the war between Iraq and Iran in 1980. To mobilise the Shias along with the rest of Iraqi society Saddam Hussein emphatically stressed Iraq's Arab and Islamic identities and played on the ethnic divide between Arabs and Persians. Geopolitically, post-revolution Iran was unable to achieve its potential for this reason and, perhaps more importantly, because of Saddam's suppression of any discontent, both within the military and among the civilian population. A seemingly impenetrable divide thus existed between the Iranian and the Iraqi Shia communities.

The question that warrants attention is: what changed after the 2003 intervention? The answer is the position and significance of the Iraqi Shia community and the Arab world's response. What essentially came after 2003 was a bridging of the gaps between the region's various Shia communities. The empowerment of Iraq's Shia community was seen as the empowerment of the Arab world's other marginalised Shia communities. In much the same way as the Iranian Revolution of 1979, the removal of the Baath regime constituted, for some, the deliverance of the Shias as a whole. Straight after the toppling of the Baath regime, one Iraqi Shia expressed the prevailing sentiment at the time: 'We are the first Arab state to be controlled by the Shia since the Fatimids ran Egypt 800 years ago' (quoted in Cockburn 2013b). This perception has proved pivotal in bridging the divides that have existed between different sections of the Shia community both within Iraq and in the region. It has also transformed Shia identity into a powerful galvanising force.

Under the Baath, the Iraqi state was able to contain and manage the impact of the Iranian Revolution and the Iran–Iraq War, with support from the Arab world. However, the democratisation of Iraq in 2003, which the Arab world had to contend with, effectively meant the ascent of Shia political actors into power and the liberation of Shia identity.

Hence, what emerged after 2003, which has had reverberations across the region since, was the liberation of the Shias and their assertion over state and society. The Shias' dominance in the new Iraq concerns the rest of the region because of the considerable extent to which they have organised and mobilised on the basis of their Shia identity. Arab world regimes have historically sought to project a vision and image of unity in the effort to both legitimise their rule and contain internal dissent. Iraq after 2003, like revolutionary Iran in 1979, has undermined this projection to the extent that it may no longer be recoverable, particularly in light of the Arab Spring.

Iraq's Shia political actors also entered the new Iraq with extensive links to Iran, and some of Iraq's most powerful parties (such as the Islamic Supreme Council of Iraq) were formed in and by Iran. The nexus between Iraqi Shia political actors and the Iranian state, on the one hand, and their strong emphasis on their Shia identity, on the other, concerned the region's other Arab states because they had their own restive Shia communities demanding greater political representation and civil rights. At the same time these communities had significant ties to the Iraqi Shia community, as a result of religious pilgrimages, clerical relations and considerable political overlap (Louër 2013: 138–9). This nexus has developed since the toppling of the Baath regime to such an extent that geopolitics are now defined by sectarian identities, bridging the ethnic divide that has historically existed between Arab and Persian Shias. However, this is not necessarily as a matter of faith but, rather, pragmatic realpolitik considerations, including the Arab world's immediate rejection of Iraqi Shia political actors, which has pushed them closer to the Iranian orbit of influence; as well as Iran's assertive campaign to expand its influence in the region, especially and particularly aggressively in Iraq.

The rise of the Shia in Iraq, coupled with the Arab world's historic apprehension towards Iran, means that, since the emergence of the new Iraq, the Arab world, as noted above, finds its projection of cross-sectarian and national unity undermined but, at the same time, it is provided with ample scope to delegitimise and dismiss internal dissent. This was amply illustrated in Bahrain and its Shia-dominated protests that were inspired by events in Tunisia and Egypt, much like the region's other protest movements. Conversely, Iraq's ruling Shia parties vehemently criticised the Bahraini monarchy's suppression of the protests and used this as a means of both delegitimising the monarchy and bolstering their own credentials within the Iraqi Shia community, which by and large supported the protests led by their Bahraini brethren. The notion of a Shia Crescent has, therefore, been reinforced and is a greater reality today than when first asserted by King Abdullah. In other words, it is now more likely that other marginalised Shia communities could emulate their Iraqi counterparts.

Syria

Iraq's impact on the region is further illustrated by the civil war across its border in Syria, an impact that has created a regional disconnect between Sunni and Shia actors to such an extent that even the Syrian state and its Allawite rulers, traditionally considered heretics by the vast majority of Shias, are now considered to be part of an axis of Shia powers comprising Iraq, Iran and Hezbollah. It is questionable whether, but for the emergence of the new Iraq, the conflict in Syria would be a regionalised conflict fought along sectarian boundaries. Aside from the above-mentioned, largely inter-state dynamics driving sectarian politics in the region, there are other dynamics that relate more closely to the inter-personal and intra-communal aspects of sectarian relations. These were fostered and harnessed during the course of events that followed the 2003 toppling of the Baath regime and have given sectarian identity such relevance across the Middle East that it has developed and nurtured a momentum of its own.

These dynamics include the start and continuation of sectarian warfare in Iraq. The mobilisation of Sunni and Shia communities in Iraq has had far-reaching regional consequences because of the cross-border ties that were being developed and forged among different tribal, militant and social groups, particularly in the northern Sunni Arab-dominated border areas that separate Iraq and Syria. Sunni Arab militants from Syria, as well as those foreign militants who used Syria as a transit point into Iraq, fought alongside Iraqis during the insurgency against American and Iraqi armed forces. The favour has been returned during the course of the Syrian civil war: fighters from Iraq's Sunni Arab community have joined rebel forces in Syria, while tribal groups with extensive kinship ties with Syria have provided supplies as well as safe havens for Syrian militants. This cross-border relationship between predominantly Iraqi and Syrian Sunni Arab actors has given Iraq's Sunni Arab militants a momentum that they have capitalised on, particularly in places like Anbar and as portrayed by increasing levels of violence in the country.

The revival of Iraq's insurgency and radical Islamist groups has ramifications for the Iraqi state, in that cross-border ties between Syrian and Iraqi Sunni Arab actors have implications for Iraq's national security. Because of these cross-border relations the Iraqi state, under its Shia-dominated government, regards with unease the potential downfall of the Assad regime lest it provide Iraq's militant groups with momentum and increased leverage and pave the way for a new Syria in which Sunni Arab-dominated groups – the most influential of which are hardline Islamists – offer their Iraqi counterparts state patronage and support. These hardline groups include powerful forces such as the Islamic State of Iraq and Syria (ISIS). ISIS has already transported a wave of suicide bombers to Iraq from Syria, largely because it controls the north-east of Syria and finds a hospitable environment in Iraq's Sunni north-western provinces. The organisation itself originated as an al-Qaeda offshoot in Iraq and fought the Iraqi government and American forces there. This national and geopolitical concern has prompted the Iraqi state, in turn, to support the Assad regime by allowing Syria-bound Iranian cargo flights to pass through Iraqi airspace but also by acquiescing to Shia militias entering Syria to fight alongside the Syrian regime. Like Sunni Arab groups, these Shia militias, including in particular Sadrist movement offshoot groups like Asaib al-Haq, honed their skills in the post-2003 Iraq. Not all of Iraq's Shia militiamen were experienced battle-hardened fighters, with many coming from ordinary backgrounds. Today, they fight in Syria as experienced guerrilla fighters to defend Shia shrines such as the one at Sayyida Zainab, as well as to ensure the Assad regime's survival, ensuring that the conflict in Syria is a holy war as well as a geopolitical battle for the region.

Conclusion

In documenting and analysing the evolution of sectarian politics in the new Iraq, this chapter has identified the complexities related to the post-2003 political process and the nature of sectarian politics in Iraq, while identifying the dynamics that underpinned the atomisation of Iraqi political life and society. Sectarian relations and conflict in the new Iraq have been covered as part of a narrative that looks at them as predominantly post-2003 challenges and issues that originated in and evolved from Western post-conflict reconstruction in the country. This chapter has shown that, while a number of post-2003 events and policies exacerbated sectarian politics and sectarian violence, they did not constitute the predominant source of inter-communal divisions and conflict: firstly, because of the nature of sectarian relations and politics under the Baath regime and then, later, in the new Iraq; and secondly, as a result of the immediate mobilisation of the Sunni Arab community, a mobilisation that pre-dated politics and policies in the new Iraq.

Fundamentally, the post-2003 instability and sectarian violence was underpinned by the pre-2003 militarisation of Iraqi society and the overlap between violent actors and the Sunni Arab community, and also by the Baath Party's empowerment of those non-state actors, who would challenge the new Iraq. This meant that autonomous violent actors were in existence, mobilised and operational before the new Iraq was being reconstructed. This created the space in which sectarian violence could flourish, while also creating an environment the US and its Coalition partners could never come to terms with, let alone remedy as part of its post-conflict reconstruction plans.

It is questionable whether there was ever a chance to remedy pre-existing tensions in the new Iraq, with one community, the Sunni Arabs, mobilised towards rejecting the restructuring of the traditional definition of the state and the other, the Shia Arabs, mobilised to guarantee and sustain this restructuring. Consequently, the Shia identity will continue to assert itself over the state and society as a result of both a sense of insecurity among the Shias and a sense of empowerment. Thus, Iraq's Shia community will remain unified, in so far as sectarian conflict with Arab Sunnis is concerned. This sectarian polarisation in Iraq has had a marked impact on the broader Middle East, to the extent that sectarian relations in Iraq have been mirrored on a regional scale. Iraq's post-2003 sectarian relations have taken on a transnational dimension as a result of inter-state relations since 2003 in response to the new Iraq, which also provoked the emergence of fluid and amorphous cross-border ties forged between disparate sectarian groupings unified primarily by their sectarian identification.

Chapter 13
Humanitarian Intervention after Iraq: The Politics of Protection and Rescue

Binoy Kampmark

This chapter examines the legacy of the 2003 invasion of Iraq, notably the impact it has had on doctrines of humanitarian intervention. Of particular relevance are the contemporary emphases on such events as the intervention in Libya by NATO forces in March 2011, arguably the first instance of what is now termed the responsibility to protect (R2P). The mixed humanitarian rhetoric behind the Iraq intervention provided a template for what to avoid. The intervention in Libya would emphasise the politicisation of the human subject as victim – an individual in need of rescue.

The invasion of Iraq on 19 March 2003 provided an object lesson for supporters of humanitarian intervention: stress the humanitarian agency inherent in the operation and highlight the need to protect civilians at risk. Such focus conceals the fact that armed support is always selective, provided for one group – or groups – in a conflict. The responsibility to protect all too often becomes one to intervene for other motivations, suggesting that the realm of the political cannot be divorced from the exercise of human rights (Rancière 2004; Schaap 2011). Despite seeming plausible, at least initially, the reasoning behind such actions tends to retreat into a realm of ulterior considerations. The humanitarian basis for such engagements risks becoming rhetorical padding, secondary to the logic of power politics. With a sense of chastened awareness, David Rieff's summation may be correct: there are no humanitarian solutions to humanitarian problems (Rieff 2002: 111).

Situating Iraq

The argument around humanitarian intervention has been termed by Michael Walzer (1995) the 'politics of rescue'. The elements of such rescue have been articulated by numerous authorities stretching back to Francisco de Vitoria (1492–1546) and Hugo Grotius (1583–1645), often through the lens of civilising paternalism (Massingham 2009: 810).

John Stuart Mill (1867) considered that there would be 'cases in which it is allowable to go to war, without having ourselves been attacked'. A working rationale for such intervention involves a nation or group of nations that moves troops into another state for philanthropic purposes, be it stopping the oppression of a group, protecting relief efforts, assisting refugees or supporting incipient democratic administrations (Miller 2000: 3). Another clearer formulation is offered by Thomas Hill: the 'forcible interference in the governance of one legitimate state by another for the primary purpose of protecting the latter's subjects from abuse and oppression by its own government' (2009: 222).

According to Mika Aaltola, the very idea of humanitarianism has become 'the key frame through which the multifarious actors of the world evaluate each other's legitimacy and determine their roles in the current world' (2009: 1). Such humanitarianism is underpinned by 'apolitical ethical commitments' and de-territorialised boundaries (Aaltola 2009: 8). Despite such a view, the appetite for humanitarian interventions since the end of the Second World War has been poor. From 1945 to 1967, no UN Security Council resolution makes any mention of humanitarian intervention. References from the 1970s to the 1980s are also sparse, and even the Indian incursion into East Pakistan in 1971 proved to be contradictory in its evocation of humanitarian credentials (Heinze 2006: 23; Weiss 2004). The 1990s saw a challenge to this reluctance to make mention of the concept. By the end of the decade, the UN secretary general, Kofi Annan, was speaking about the necessity to intervene to prevent abuses by governments who could no longer rely on 'state frontiers' as an excuse (Annan 1998).

From the perspective of US foreign policy-makers, the politics of rescue found voice in the intervention in Somalia in 1992, which was, according to Thomas L. Friedman in the *New York Times*, a turning point because it was not based on anything strategic *per se* 'but simply to feed starving people' (Friedman 1992). By the time of NATO's Kosovo intervention in 1999, advocates of intervention such as the Czech Prime Minister, Václav Havel (1999), were suggesting that the nation state had been morally eviscerated. A year later, the international law authority Theodor Meron could confidently say that human rights and principles of humanity had truly influenced the waging of war. But Meron was at pains to point out that a genuine humanitarian law was a contradiction in terms. 'To genuinely humanise humanitarian law, it would be necessary to put an end to all kinds of armed conflict' (Meron 2000: 240).

The invasion of Iraq challenged the humanitarian paradigm. It had, for one, mixed rationales. The codename for the invasion suggested an emancipatory purpose – 'Operation Iraqi Freedom' – but the pro-intervention human rights organisation Human Rights Watch claimed that the intervention was not one of a humanitarian nature. There was no 'ongoing or imminent mass slaughter' (Roth 2004). There were no measures to internationally indict Saddam Hussein, which would have brought a legal tone to actions against him. There was no overriding humanitarian purpose. The overarching claim of the military intervention was to target and punish Saddam's regime for possessing weapons of mass destruction (WMDs) that he was subsequently found not to have. As the weapons became more elusive, the atrocities and war crime credentials of the regime were increasingly highlighted (Kampmark 2004). The theme of liberation came to the fore. Jurists such as Fernando Tesón have gone so far as to suggest that the imposition of a democratic state could itself be considered an act falling within the parameters of humanitarian intervention. For Tesón (2005), Iraq posed two 'humanitarian rationales' – a narrow one, where a tyrant was overthrown, and a 'grand' rationale of US self-defence by democratising the Middle East. Fundamentally, in such a view, an intervention does not lose its humanitarian character even if the primary justification for using force may be non-humanitarian. What matters are the results (Tesón 1997: 103). An even more forceful view of this has been articulated by Nicholas Wheeler: positive humanitarian outcomes, not ignoble rationales, are what matter, because rescuing victims should be the object of the analysis (Wheeler 2000: 38). Terry Nardin suggests by way of reply that such interpretations strain 'the traditional understanding of humanitarian intervention' (Nardin 2005: 21).

Other commentators on the conflict, such as the late progressive critic Christopher Hitchens, have argued since the invasion in 2003 that removing Saddam Hussein was a humanitarian task. What went wrong was the political selling of it – the need on the part of the main instigators to frighten their electorates when they could have just persuaded them (Cottee & Cushman 2008; Robinson 2005). For Hitchens, it was a personal revelation – there was a true liberation narrative at play here: 'Especially in the south – still lining the roads and waving and the children waving, which is always the sign because if the parents don't want them to, they don't.' Hitchens felt like he was riding 'in with the liberation army' (Robinson 2005).

Some literature has examined the invasion of Iraq as a case of abuse where 'moral arguments are used to justify a war that is not primarily motivated by the moral concerns espoused, but by the short-term interests of those instigating violence' (Bellamy 2004: 132). The argument about any humanitarian benefits is also weakened by the persistence of radical sectarianism and high death rates (al-Khalidi & Tanner 2006). Mortality rates in Iraq between 2003 and 2011, calculated by the University Collaborative Mortality Study and based on a cluster sample of 2,000 randomly selected households through Iraq, suggest that the death toll during the period was roughly 450,000 (Hagopian et al. 2013).

But subsequent events have further demonstrated that such abuse was not unique to Iraq and has continued in various guises. Humanitarian military interventions are bedevilled by a fundamental paradox: the illusion of apolitical conditions of intervention, with an emphasis on human security. Such a designation, in ignoring political goals, invariably becomes political. Interventions will favour one cause over another, one group in conflict over another. The consequences of such interventions, while not immediately apparent, usually prove in the long term to be disastrous for the recipient country.

Post-Iraq 'Reform'

In the post-Cold War world, advocates of humanitarian intervention felt that a change of focus was needed to cloak intervention with an appropriate costume – one more acceptable to the practice of human rights and the use of force. The French philosopher Jacques Rancière observed that a legal-political transformation had taken place in the aftermath of the Cold War: the emphasis on nondescript, generalised 'man' had shifted to humanity and in turn to protective humanitarianism, one lifted out of its political context to provide a realm of unscripted 'rights' for the 'powerless'. But, in so doing, it effectively accepted a position of inequality between morally charged elites and oppressed victims. The latter are not seen in terms of solidarity, but as recipients of aid or intervention (May 2008: 152).

Jean Bricmont is less subtle, preferring the term 'humanitarian imperialism' to describe such intervention, of which Iraq was but one example. For him, the human right is a commodity proffered in the name of realpolitik rather than for innate altruistic purposes. According to Bricmont (2006), the humanitarian subject filled the vacuum left by the Cold War, which revolved around US unipolarity and the foundation of a new policing rationale based on democracy and rights.

In 2001, the International Commission on Intervention and State Sovereignty, a grouping of experts commissioned by the Canadian government, issued a seminal report reflecting upon circumstances when human suffering and victimhood within a state's borders justified foreign intervention. Broadly speaking, six criteria for the use of force were articulated: that the motive be primarily humanitarian; that the cause be just (the presence of large-scale violence); that the force used be of last resort; that the intervention have reasonable prospects of success; that it be proportionate; and that it issue from a legal, multilateral framework of decision makers (International Commission on Intervention and State Sovereignty 2001: 32).

New standards justifying breaches to international sovereignty, focused on the globalised concept of the victim, were crafted. In the words of Gareth Evans of the International Crisis Group and Algerian diplomat Mohamed Sahnoun, 'If the international community is to respond to this challenge, the whole debate must be turned on its head. The issue must be reframed not as an argument about the "right to intervene" but about the "responsibility to protect"' (Evans & Sahnoun 2002: 101). In other words, it was better to reshape the argument of military intervention as one of pressing obligations of protection. The sting would thereby be taken out of the violation of a state's sovereignty. 'Changing the terminology from "intervention" to "protection" gets away from the language of "humanitarian intervention"' (Evans & Sahnoun 2002: 101). The authors suggest that such rewording has three benefits: evaluating the intervention from the perspective of those requiring support, not those seeking to intervene; that primary responsibility rests with the state in question; and that the 'responsibility to protect' embraces the 'responsibility to react', the 'responsibility to prevent' and the 'responsibility to rebuild' (Evans & Sahnoun 2002: 101).

After the failings of the Iraq effort, the intervention project became increasingly subtle, if somewhat artificial. What the invasion demonstrated was a loosening of the fetters on how state sovereignty might be violated. As Heinze (2006) argues, the presence of mixed motives behind such violations of sovereignty was justified by the paralysis of the UN Security Council at various points during the post-Cold War era. This stood to reason – the attack on Iraq was the culmination of the view that a variety of motives did not deprive an action of its humanitarian character.

A change in emphasis was suggested behind the dynamics of future humanitarian actions. Greater emphasis was put on placing the welfare of civilians at the core of any military action. In 2005, the United Nations adopted the Responsibility to Protect doctrine (R2P), which reflected the approach suggested by Evans and Sahnoun. The existence of such documents as R2P and the international body of law being drafted around it on the subject of limited sovereignty provided the framework that was adopted in assessing the Libyan engagement. 'What has been emerging [since 1945] is a parallel transition from a culture of sovereign impunity to a culture of national and international accountability' (International Commission on Intervention and State Sovereignty 2001: 14). Where there is a systematic and extensive abuse of human rights, an obligation to intervene may be generated (International Commission on Intervention and State Sovereignty 2001). One author goes so far as to suggest that R2P adds a fourth characteristic to the dimensions of sovereignty – in addition to territory, authority and population comes 'respect for human rights' (Weiss 2004: 138).

The political acumen of state governments that insist on such a course of action remains conflicted. James Kurth has noted a fundamental paradox of humanitarianism in the aftermath of the Iraq invasion: 'Unfortunately, even as the theory and law of humanitarian intervention has ascended to unprecedented heights, the actual practice of humanitarian intervention has been in decline' (Kurth 2006: 88). After the invasion, students of international law conceded that the very idea of humanitarian intervention had been undermined (Massingham 2009: 805).

The Iraq precedent of error and misjudgement has loomed large. It provided an instructive lesson: the humanitarian, rather than the purely strategic or security dimension, was to be emphasised in future in interventions. Obligations to intervene became obligations to protect. Examples of this post-Iraq shift have proliferated. The NATO intervention against Qaddafi's Libya, the French-led intervention in Mali against al-Qaeda-linked insurgents and the debate about intervention in Syria's civil war have all featured humanitarian considerations. Advocates of force in those cases have attempted, in some part, to distinguish themselves from Iraq: the emphasis on the obligation to protect civilians rather than a distinct, full-blown right to intervene, is stressed.

The test case of how far the rhetoric of intervention had come was the intervention in Libya in March 2011. NATO's intervention against the Qaddafi regime, in contrast to the invasion of Iraq, was officially justified as an unvarnished humanitarian effort under R2P principles (Zifcak 2012). UN Security Council Resolution 1970, condemning the systematic attack on civilians and demanding an end to such violence in Libya, and UN Security Council Resolution 1973, imposing the no-fly zone in protecting civilians, are examples of that change in emphasis. This suggested that motives, in a manner that had not played out in Iraq in the same way, mattered. Emphasis was placed on the bloodthirsty barbarity of the Qaddafi regime in response to a rebellion that had started in February 2011, something which initially was not done in the demonisation of Saddam Hussein. The UN high commissioner for human rights emphasised that 'widespread and systematic attacks against the civilian population may amount to crimes against humanity' (Office of the High Commission for Human Rights 2011). Commentators claimed that Qaddafi's language was ominously violent, involving the use of such a term as 'cockroaches' to describe those in the city of Benghazi rising against his rule in February 2011, and the promise to hunt for them from house to house. In late March 2011 United States President Barack Obama spoke of the need to prevent the frustration of democratic aspirations moving through the Middle East, 'eclipsed by the darkest form of dictatorship'. 'To brush aside America's responsibility as a leader and, more profoundly, our responsibilities to our fellow human beings under such circumstances would have been a betrayal of who we are' (quoted in Hall 2011). Efforts were made to underscore the human element while understating the backing of sides. The Libyan operation would protect civilians, but not seek to change the regime (*New York Times* 2011b). The involvement in Iraq loomed large in the disavowal of that purpose – that US-led intervention had taken eight years, had cost thousands of Iraqi and American lives and would not be repeated in Libya. Despite stating such a position, the NATO intervention implied an open repudiation of the Qaddafi regime as a legitimate political force. With its collapse, notions of pure humanitarianism as opposed to regime change became moot points.

An early effort was made to distance the attack on Qaddafi's forces from the previously disastrous effort of the Coalition forces in Iraq. 'A coalition of the willing', explains Daniel Serwer, 'attacks an Arab country; French warplanes strike armoured vehicles; American cruise missiles take down air defenses. It all sounds to some too much like Iraq redux. But it's not.' What then, could be the proper analogy here? For Serwer, it's Srebrenica, a case of military brutality against a local population by a regime that required repulsion. 'This is the international community acting under international law to prevent mass murder' (Serwer 2011). The problem here is that the intervention might well have been authorised by the Security Council, but keeping it within the remit of protective principles was going to prove elusive.

The argument justifying the use of force against Libya was developed in most effective fashion by the French philosopher Bernard-Henri Lévy. Running through his commentaries was an acute fear that a massacre was imminent, and it was a fear he was not shy in promoting. The French philosopher was present in Benghazi in March 2011 to anticipate and predict. His techniques of persuasion, and his overall approach to drumming up attention, were praised. 'Somehow, earlier this year, a philosopher managed to goad the world into vanquishing an evil villain. Perhaps more surprising was the philosopher in question: the man French society loves to mock, Bernard-Henri Lévy' (Wallace-Wells 2011). Hyperbole was never far away from the activist philosopher – he might have been a Lawrence of Arabia, or perhaps an intrepid Don

Quixote. His personal wealth enabled him to travel to Libya, where he found himself in Benghazi. Then came the stretched comparisons: 'Benghazi is the capital not only of Libya but of free men and women all over the world' (Lévy, quoted in Wallace-Wells 2011). To not intervene, he subsequently explained to French President Nicolas Sarkozy, could result in a massacre, whose victims would 'stain the French flag'. Imperial imagery proved fundamental to Lévy's persuasive message.

The passage of UNSCR 1973, with ten votes in favour, none against and five abstentions, became the highpoint of these efforts. It established a no-fly zone as part of the 'necessary measures to protect civilians under threat of attack in the country', stopping short of 'a foreign occupation force of any form on any part of Libyan territory' (United Nations 2011). The introduction of the resolution came from the French minister of foreign affairs, Alain Juppé, who spoke of 'the violent re-conquest of cities that have been released' and the intolerable situation of allowing the Security Council to 'let the warmongers flout international legality' (United Nations 2011). Central to Juppé's language was the brutality visited upon Libyan civilians, a situation that was becoming graver by the hour. The resolution supplemented UNSCR 1970, which involved the imposition of sanctions on the Libyan regime. On 19 March 2011, a largely Anglo-French-led coalition commenced attacks on targets in the country with the launch of Tomahawk cruise missiles and aerial sorties. On 24 March, NATO formally assumed control of enforcing the no-fly zone, with operations formally ending on 31 October.

The Road Travelled: Consequences

The language of UNSCR 1973 ostensibly replicated the R2P doctrine. The intervention was defended by critics of the Iraq invasion as being justifiably humanitarian in character (Pattison 2011: 272; Zifcak 2012: 67–8). But as a circumspect David Rieff (2012) pointed out, it 'left a bitter taste in the mouths of many governments that supported it'. Regime change was not justified (Pattison 2011: 272). To put it another way, the degree of victimhood was not sufficient to warrant intervention. Nor was the intervention free of the matrix of pragmatic considerations that have characterised the approaches of the five permanent members (P5) of the Security Council before, and since, the Libyan conflict (Hehir 2013). What began as a mission for protecting civilians transformed into one of regime change – the old programme of replacing one regime with another. Just-war theory, argues Rieff, precludes intervention where the risk of causing more harm than good is evident. R2P was effectively coopted into the service of the regime change advocates.

A few consequences can be suggested by the interventions in Libya and Mali, much of it to do with the legacy of the Iraq blunder. One is a diminished role for the US in terms of humanitarian military engagements. The sceptical shift in US congressional sentiment to such interventions from the belligerence shown towards Iraq in 2003 was evident. A spokesman for the House Speaker, Republican John Boehner, kept pressing President Obama: 'What does success in Libya look like?' Senator Rand Paul, another Republican, asked what 'imminent threat' the Qaddafi regime posed to the United States (Hall 2011). Such congressional attitudes suggested that the consequences of an intervention, whatever its primary motivation, were vital. Similarly, George F. Will, a veteran writer and commentator for the *New York Times*, suggested how Obama had 'neglected to clarify a few things, such as: Do the armed rebels trying to overthrow that government still count as civilians?' (Will 2011). For Will, the great worry was reducing the US armed forces to a wing of the Red Cross, intervening in a campaign with unknown actors and variables.

The other notable consequence, in line with scepticism from such individuals as Boehner, is how to gauge the success of such actions justified by broad readings of Security Council resolutions. Success in Libya, in fact, was and remains difficult to assess. As a report from Christopher Blanchard for the Congressional Research Service asserted, the transition 'may prove to be as complex and challenging for Libyans and their international counterparts as the 2011 conflict' (Blanchard 2012). Such bland, even disingenuous, language conceals the monumental difficulties that have faced the post-Qaddafi state.

The language of the coalition that responded to the Libyan crisis was obtuse and at times self-contradictory. The British effort was marred by conflicting remarks from the leading commanders on the one hand and the Prime Minister on the other, showing that any coherent reading of 'humanitarian intervention' remains problematic. This has not bothered certain commentators such as Daniel Serwer, who find any contradictions to be inconclusive to the case. Whatever the then US Secretary of State, Hillary Clinton, might have claimed – that the intervention took place to protect civilians, as opposed to regime change – it was 'a distinction without a difference'. 'It is up to [Qaddafi] to convince the coalition that he is prepared to change his behaviour, as he successfully did in 2003 when he gave up his nuclear weapons' (Serwer 2011).

The intervention in Libya can hardly be said to have worked its intended magic. In that sense, it has followed the Iraq example – a project of intervention that resulted in considerable national and regional destabilisation, opening several fronts of radicalised activity

(Byman 2008). The report of the late Anthony Shadid from Libya for the *New York Times* on 9 February 2012 highlighted the role played by the militias and the use of torture. Libya remains deeply divided in a tripartite scheme. Its government has remained blind to the destruction of Sufi shrines and libraries in Benghazi (Burleigh 2012) and law and order is being maintained through a tenuous coopted system of militias that do not necessarily answer to the Libyan army. A critique of the Libyan intervention by Alan Kuperman (2013) suggests that NATO's intervention 'magnified the conflict's duration about sixfold and its death toll at least sevenfold'. This, in addition to 'exacerbating human rights abuses, humanitarian suffering, Islamic radicalism, and weapons proliferation in Libya and its neighbors', made Libya a 'model of failure'.

Such actions demonstrate the dangers of forecasting consequences without adequate knowledge. As Noam Chomsky (1999, 2008) has claimed, the underlying argument for bombing the Serbs in order to pre-empt their plans to expel Kosovar Albanians was a dangerous ploy based on the assumptions of authorities. There is an argument to be made that such attacks intensified the campaign by the Serbs against the Kosovar Albanians, while exposing the Serbian civilian population and infrastructure to NATO attacks (Hayden 2003: 114). Too many hypotheticals were entertained.

The pre-emptive element of humanitarian intervention in the context of Benghazi is similarly problematic, based as it was on the desperate calls of the Transitional National Council, the urgings of such public figures as Lévy, and the perceived need for the UK, France and NATO to show more 'muscle.' Other members of the UN, notably China, Russia and India, suggested that the no-fly zone mandate had been violated, harming the very civilians the measure was designed to protect. The words of a Chinese Foreign Ministry spokeswoman were to the point: 'We've seen reports that the use of armed forces is causing civilian casualties, and we oppose the wanton use of armed force leading to more civilian casualties' (*New York Times* 2011a).

Terms and Consequences: Mali

The language behind the French-led intervention in Mali under the auspices of UN Security Council Resolution 2085 (21 December 2012) echoed the concern expressed for avoiding the rhetorical mistakes made in Iraq. Heavy emphasis was placed on the request for assistance by the Malian President, Dioncounda Traoré, (FIDH 2013) to recapture northern areas of the country controlled by Islamic groups.

The evaluation of Mali's security problems was as inaccurate as the survey of Saddam's regime. Not all were grateful victims. Local specifics were ignored. As Patrick Cockburn, a long-time student of Middle East and African affairs, pointed out, an organisation like al-Qaeda thrives on the false assumption that local disputes have international import. 'Local disputes – in this case between the Tuareg of northern Mali and the government in the capital, Bamako – become internationalised' (Cockburn 2013a). While police actions to restore order might be initially welcomed, the very presence of a great power can prove destructive in the long run.

'Freedom fighters' can morph with effortless ease into rudderless 'militants' whose only purpose is to inflict terror; 'dictatorships' become useful police authorities keeping 'fundamentalism' in check; and 'fundamentalists' in turn can be shape changers. Even after Iraq, such distortions continue, emphasising the false binary between victims and liberators while exaggerating the security threat posed. The French forces fear the workings of Islamic militancy and theocracy in Mali, but have ignored the fact that the Tuareg revolt, led by the National Movement for the Liberation of Azawad, is nationalist in nature. Furthermore, al-Qaeda in the Islamic Maghreb (AQIM), with its origins in the vicious Algerian civil conflict of the 1990s, was tolerated in northern Mali to keep the nationalist Tuareg in check. It has been conveniently ignored for the most part that the Mali government for many years shared in the ill-gotten gains of AQIM's drug and hostage operations. Now the goalposts are being moved again with the return of Tuareg soldiers previously in the employ of Qaddafi's forces.

As May Ying Welsh (2013) has suggested, the region is highly diverse in its range of interests and conflicts. Ansar al-Dine consists of Tuaregs and has a religious bent, but is careful to avoid engaging other Tuareg groups for tribal reasons. It denies links with al-Qaeda. At the behest of a UK–French–US operation, ill-understood fighters and factions have created a security vacuum that threatens considerable parts of the African continent.

This is not to suggest noble aims on part of such individuals as those in Ansar al-Dine, the Movement for Unity and Jihad in West Africa and AQIM. Indeed, there is much to suggest that these groups are despised by the local populace. But it is also dangerous to view external interventions, couched in the language of deceptive humanitarianism, as surgical and altruistic, or that such organisations pose an 'international threat'. A group such as AQIM can hardly be designated a threat to France, let alone Europe, having limited its activities to the drug trade and lucrative hostage-taking. In this, there are shades of Saddam's fictitious WMD threat to the United States and Britain. The humanitarian cover, as ever, proves attractive to apologists for intervention.

The response from Washington and its allies is distinctly troubling. Behind the labels of undifferentiated militancy lie dangerous consequences. The mistake on this occasion has been to equate local troubles with international significance. In this sense, both al-Qaeda and various Western powers share the same goal: to internationalise emergencies, actual or perceived.

End Results: Moving On

In the post-Iraq War climate, the situation on the subject of humanitarian interventions remains unclear, despite visible attempts to distinguish subsequent interventions from Iraq. The focus now is heavily on the idea of the responsibility to protect, which does little to clarify its workability. While some aspects of the R2P doctrine might work, the concept of minimising harm has turned out to be unfeasible in the long run. Even if some variant of the R2P doctrine had been employed in Iraq, it seems reasonable to assume that the country would still have witnessed sectarian violence and been brought to the brink of civil war. Public opinion in the United States has hardened against an active interventionist stance in the wake of the disasters in Iraq, and congressional opinion over Libya suggests that the US is more cautious about such open-ended engagements. 'Tomahawk humanitarianism', exemplified by the attack on Libya, may have had its day (Healy 2013).

The situation in Syria is particularly striking in this regard, with the Obama administration showing reluctance, even in the face of a chemical weapons attack on a civilian population at Ghouta on 21 August 2013, to order strikes against the Assad regime. Geopolitical dangers of destabilisation and political inertia remain the key considerations behind any supposedly clear humanitarian intervention. Iraq continues to be, as ever, the reminder of costly policies of involvement in the Middle East. As with Libya, Congress proved reluctant to commit forces (Clift 2013) when the President sought its approval. A Republican representative, Michele Bachmann, called America 'war weary' (Gentilviso 2013).

Veteran human rights commentator Anne-Marie Slaughter of Princeton University has called for an intervention in Syria based on the principle of protection, adopting the language of Evans and Sahoun (2002). She has proposed the establishment of enclaves ('no-kill zones') around the Turkish, Lebanese and Jordanian borders for members of the population most affected by the Assad regime (Slaughter 2012). Those enclaves would be, in turn, protected by drone aircraft and accessible via humanitarian corridors operated by the Red Cross. What is troubling about Slaughter's analysis is that it slides with little effort into the area of regime change, ignoring the sectarian troubles that Sunni states such as Qatar and Saudi Arabia would cause (and are already causing) in Syria. It is also interesting to note in this regard that Slaughter has previously argued for an extension of R2P to include a forceful 'duty to prevent' the acquisition by certain regimes of WMDs, citing such reasoning as 'entirely humanitarian' (Feinstein & Slaughter 2004: 149; Slaughter 2012). The limitless nature of such humanitarian doctrines would make them untenably dangerous.

The concept of humanitarian intervention after the invasion of Iraq remains inchoate, despite its reframing as a strategy of 'rescue' in the name of a doctrine of protection. The Iraq precedent suggests a note of caution for those advocating humanitarian principles in violating a country's sovereignty: be clear about the rationale to protect; note the urgency of response in the face of actual or impeding atrocity; and limit casualties. In a sense, this inchoate tendency may be the unavoidable outcome of treating human rights as apolitical objects. Philosophers such as Rancière suggest that such identification is false. Human rights are invariably politicised. The invasion of Iraq, for such commentators as Tesón, was no less just for that reason.

The Libyan intervention indicates that military humanitarianism can become a matter of regime change that exceeds dry legal prescripts made in Security Council resolutions. A no-fly zone is a legal redundancy, difficult to police and almost always likely to favour one force over another, as opposed to protecting civilians *in toto*. Asserting such obligations does nothing to eliminate the sheer scope of what is expected – self-interest may well form part of the motivations behind the action, and adopting a lexical trick to refocus the emphasis on intervention ends up being mere sleight of hand. Rieff puts it rather forcefully when he calls into question the idea of 'good intentions' as a basis of making policy:

> It may be a cliché to say that the road to hell is paved with good intentions, but surely it is not too much to insist that good intentions are really not a sound basis for policy, nor do good intentions, or more properly, the wish to do the right thing, mean one is doing the right thing. (Rieff et al. 2001: 102)

A significant legacy of the Iraq War of 2003 is therefore increasing uncertainty on the world stage about 'good intentions' as a basis for humanitarian intervention and the very real prospect that even a desire to 'do the right thing' may end in disaster.

Chapter 14
Iraq, the Illusion of Security and the Limits to Power

Joseph A. Camilleri

The US military intervention in Iraq in March 2003 and the protracted violence it has unleashed constitute a defining moment of the post-Cold War period. Many have analysed this violence primarily in terms of the legality of the use of force (Bellamy 2003; Iwanek 2010; Paulus 2004) and its devastating impact on Iraqi society. Legitimate and important though it is, this line of inquiry is deficient if it does not adequately integrate into its analysis the regional and global ramifications of the violence, which are as enduring as they are wide-ranging. The international dimensions of the Iraq War, US occupation and subsequent US withdrawal are inextricably entwined with the devastating impact that the violence has had on Iraq's economy, environment and politics. With the exception of the unreconstructed political right in the United States, the US decision to intervene is now generally understood to have been illegal[1] and illegitimate (McKeil 2012), but the reasons for the modalities and the consequences of that intervention have yet to be adequately contextualised. If we are to make sense of US actions in Iraq and the blowback effects of invasion and occupation, we need to place them in the context of two decisive tendencies in contemporary international life, namely the 'globalisation of insecurity' and the 'limits to empire' (Camilleri & Falk 2009: 446–65).

The globalisation of insecurity, which refers to the internationalisation of security relations, or to be more precise the transnationalisation of insecurity, is itself the product of several developments, in particular the increasing porosity of national boundaries and the destructiveness and global reach of modern warfare. At first sight the demise of the Cold War suggested a reversal of these trends. On closer inspection, it appears that the trend towards the transnationalisation of insecurity has continued unabated. Regardless of their official rationale, key US policies following the Cold War, notably the maintenance of alliances, the expansion of NATO, the creation of ad-hoc coalitions and military interventionism of various kinds, have powerfully contributed to the internationalisation of conflict.

During the Cold War US military and political elites came to see the global projection of military power as indispensable to the preservation of US interests, values and influence. The end of the Cold War, far from weakening this assumption, gave it renewed impetus. The Soviet threat may have dissipated but the world remained a dangerous place – in Washington's eyes the 'globalisation of insecurity' was here to stay. It was not therefore entirely surprising that the United States should have justified its intervention in Iraq by reference to two existential threats: the actual or potential proliferation of nuclear weapons and the rising intensity of international terrorism. Paradoxically, however, US unilateralism in Iraq, far from stabilising regional or global security and cementing or prolonging the unipolar moment in international relations, fanned the flames of insecurity and in the process demonstrated in stark fashion the 'limits to empire'. Many analysts, notably in the early days of the Iraq War, tended to interpret the new US rhetoric and interventionism in Iraq as evidence of America's unchallenged global supremacy, and were therefore inclined to overlook or seriously underestimate the vulnerabilities of the imperial project (Hinnebusch 2006). Taken at face value US actions and pronouncements appeared to radiate power, yet this was in many respects 'abstracted' or 'virtual' power, not easily convertible into effective political action. With the passage of time few could disregard the resistance to American dominance, although many still sought to explain the US predicament largely by reference to the failings of US statecraft rather than any profound structural changes in the global security system (Nye 2003). What follows is an attempt to trace the logic of empire as it played out in Iraq, its roots in the perception and language of insecurity, and the ongoing fallout – notably the steady and probably irreversible erosion of US power and influence and the trail of hatreds and insecurity both inside Iraq and across its borders which the failed imperial project has left in its wake.

Globalisation of Insecurity

The connection between US military intervention in Iraq and weapons of mass destruction has been the subject of much commentary, but insightful analysis has been much scarcer (Cirincione et al. 2004; Gill & Phythian 2006; Thakur 2007). When it comes to US perceptions of the risks of nuclear proliferation in the Middle East it is necessary to go beyond official declarations and focus on the underlying psychology of US strategic planning. Here two closely interacting elements require our attention: the unresolved contradictions which have beset US policies in the region, and the profound insecurity that inevitably accompanies the actual or potential spread of nuclear weapons. The contradictions arise principally from the virtually unconditional support the United States has extended to the security of the Israeli state in the face of continuing Arab–Israeli tensions and conflict, and from America's reliance on authoritarian regimes for the protection of its strategic and economic interests in the region. Paradoxically, US policy has also been exposed to the vagaries of nuclear insecurity; America faces the threat of nuclear proliferation and unpalatable possibilities should the nuclear weapon fall into hostile hands.

The unilateral US decision to go to war in March 2003 has been variously interpreted as the unfinished business of the First Gulf War, the inevitable consequence of Washington's post-September 11 strategic outlook (Daalder & Lindsay 2003; Purdum 2003), and a reflection of the neo-conservative ascendancy in US policy discourse and practice.[2] All three factors were no doubt influential, but the key lies in the evolution of US counter-proliferation policy under successive US administrations, which centred on preventing, if necessary by force and regime change, the emergence of nuclear-capable regimes deemed hostile to US interests. In the post-Cold War period Iraq became the principal site where the United States sought to apply its policy shift from support for a rules-based multilateral non-proliferation regime to a force-driven unilateral counter-proliferation strategy. The relative weight accorded to economic sanctions, military pressure and diplomatic isolation may have varied from case to case, but the same punitive mix of measures has dominated Washington's response to the WMD crises in Iraq, Iran and Syria. In each instance we can see the deeply felt insecurity of US strategic planners wrestling with the passing of the ephemeral unipolar moment.

If the American state became fixated with the threat posed by recalcitrant regimes pursuing WMD capabilities, it was equally troubled by the terrorist threat, which, not unlike WMD proliferation, raised the spectre of unpredictable and potentially uncontrollable cross-border flows, whether of arms, technologies, materials or personnel. It cannot be stressed enough that in all of this, US strategic and political elites were driven as much by psychological insecurities as by imperial designs. Notwithstanding significant variations in elite thinking – as between the Bush administration and its successor under

Obama – terrorism came to be perceived as a source of danger. In this sense the 'war on terror' was in part an attempt to grapple with a generalised sense of insecurity exacerbated by what was now an increasingly transnational but still poorly understood phenomenon. Paradoxically, terrorism also came to be seen as offering an opportunity to promote important US interests, if necessary by loosening existing restraints on the use of force (Farer 2008), though not necessarily in the simplistic sense often suggested by critics of US policy intent on uncovering secret plots (Hinnebusch 2007).

In the case of Iraq the fact that so much energy was expended, despite the absence of corroborating evidence, on linking Saddam Hussein with al-Qaeda points to a larger political agenda (Camilleri 2008). The horror of September 11 was but a catalyst for a larger strategy in the making for some time, which sought to justify an assault not just on particular terrorist organisations, but on 'radical', 'militant', 'fanatical' Islam more generally, hence the importance of connecting the decision to invade Iraq with the perceived terrorist threat. Political Islam was deemed dangerous not just or even primarily because of the destruction which a number of terrorist groups of Islamic inspiration had already inflicted, or might in future inflict, on the United States. It conjured up images of a more assertive Muslim world, of governments and movements which, acting independently or in concert, might more effectively oppose US strategic, economic and political priorities in the Middle East and beyond. Iraq, Libya, Syria and Iran, though hardly acting in unison, had been troublesome enough in the past. Viewed from the vantage point of America's self-anointed role as guardian and enforcer of global norms, the prospect of such militancy spreading to Egypt, Saudi Arabia, other parts of the Arab world and even Pakistan, Malaysia or Indonesia was deeply disturbing. Particularly troubling for Washington was the prospect that friendly or allied regimes in various parts of the Muslim world would either be toppled or begin to desert the US camp. Hence, the perceived need for a decisive showdown.

Three important strategic principles would guide 'Operation Iraqi Freedom' just as they did 'Operation Enduring Freedom' in Afghanistan. The first of these was reliance on immense military superiority to achieve the desired regime change. The invasion of Iraq would apply the strategic concept of 'rapid dominance' or, as it came to be popularly but mistakenly known, 'shock and awe' (Shimko 2010). The aim was to mount a spectacular, multidimensional and pervasive display of force to paralyse the adversary's perception of the battlefield and destroy its will to fight. But for such a demonstration of military might to be feasible, it was necessary to direct it against a state, an obviously 'recalcitrant' one. It could hardly be directed against terrorist groups comprising a motley band of fighters of no fixed address. Destructive power had to be applied on a spatially constrained political entity that could not escape America's firepower. Having gained physical control of the state, it would then be possible to target any number of hostile groups or individuals whose operations were physically located within or supported by that state. The need to act in Iraq was reinforced by a third principle, namely the belief, widely shared in the United States, that given the incipient tendencies towards a multicentric world system and the challenges posed by the rise of western Europe and China, and potentially Russia and a resurgent Islam, continued dominance required the United States to recreate the kind of bipolar confrontation that had prevailed during the Cold War. Communism and anti-communism were in a sense replaced by terrorism and anti-terrorism, the 'evil empire' by the 'axis of evil'. The aim was essentially the same: to recreate a binary division of the world, in which one side, led by the United States, was engaged in the relentless struggle for the triumph of good over evil. In this sense, Saddam Hussein, like Osama bin Laden or Ayman al-Zawahiri, was crucial to the success of the strategy. Though Saddam could hardly be portrayed as the monolithic embodiment of evil in quite the way that Stalin was, his authoritarian rule could nevertheless assume demonic proportions, especially as in this case the regime, widely regarded as having perpetrated unspeakable crimes, could now be accused of harbouring nuclear ambitions and covertly assisting the work of terrorists. Predictably, the application of these principles in Iraq's fragile political and security environment would over time prove highly destabilising and counterproductive.

Limits to Power

Many observers depicted the US war in Iraq as a dramatic demonstration of US power and of the ineffectiveness of multilateralism generally and the United Nations in particular (Patterson 2010). What subsequently transpired has not borne out this assessment. So far as the United Nations is concerned, the first thing to note is that US and British plans to invade Iraq were strenuously opposed in both the Security Council and the General Assembly. This was the first time since the end of the Cold War that the United States failed to get its own way at the United Nations on an issue which it deemed critical to its security interests. In this sense Iraq represents a major turning point in the dynamics of UN decision-making on matters of regional and global security.

The UN Security Council, it is true, could not stop the unilateral use of force in Iraq. Yet the worldwide opposition to the war, which UN deliberations mirrored and reinforced, severely weakened US capacity to achieve the anticipated quick and decisive victory. No doubt the many political and strategic errors of judgement which afflicted America's conduct of the war and its occupation policy greatly contributed to the duration of the conflict, its high costs and disastrous dénouement. But there is no denying that, having failed to secure the necessary support of the United Nations, the US intervention was effectively deprived of the mantle of legality and legitimacy. The net effect was to diminish the potency and effectiveness of the US-led Coalition, embolden the local insurgency in Iraq, provide al-Qaeda and other foreign terrorist groups with fertile ground for their activities, and make the United States more dependent than it would otherwise have been on the support of Shia political and religious groupings as it went about the excruciatingly difficult task of creating a political base on which to construct a new government.

The failure of US diplomacy at the United Nations accentuated America's isolation, especially after 1 May 2003, the date George W. Bush chose to announce the end to major combat operations in Iraq. Reinforcing the irony of the occasion was the banner displayed on the aircraft carrier USS *Abraham Lincoln* claiming 'mission accomplished', which was shown during the President's televised address. In those initial six weeks of combat the United States incurred 140 fatal casualties. In the eight years that followed US casualties totalled 4,345. By comparison, over the entire duration of the war Britain suffered 179 casualties, and the rest of the Coalition (supposedly comprising forty-six countries) only 139 casualties. By the end of 2011, the number of US personnel wounded in Iraq had reached 32,223.[3] To this should be added the high number of US military personnel who, having served in Operation Iraqi Freedom, were reported to be suffering from severe mental illness. The 2008 Rand inquiry estimated that about one-third of the total number of veterans who had served in the Iraq or Afghanistan wars were suffering from one or more of the following three conditions: post-traumatic stress disorder, depression and traumatic brain injury (Tanielan & Jaycox 2008: xxi). According to another study about 5 per cent reported symptoms of all three conditions (Richardson et al. 2010). As the war unfolded, the Coalition allies became increasingly aware of the high risks involved in fighting in unfamiliar and inhospitable terrain, and of the limited gains this was likely to achieve. Within a year of the US decision to intervene, only Britain was prepared to commit more than 5,000 troops to support the 140,000 US troops now deployed on the ground. Only five other countries (Italy, the Netherlands, Poland, South Korea and Ukraine) had dispatched forces in excess of 1,000, and only thirteen (Australia, Azerbaijan, Bulgaria, the Czech Republic, Denmark, El Salvador, Georgia, Japan, Latvia, Lithuania, Mongolia, Romania and Slovakia) had in excess of 100 troops, almost all in relatively safe, non-combatant roles. By the end of 2006, seventeen countries had withdrawn their forces or announced their imminent withdrawal (GlobalSecurity.org 2007). At the height of the troop surge in October 2007, US military personnel deployed in Iraq numbered 174,000, which accounted for 94 per cent of the total Coalition effort. The burden of the war had fallen almost entirely on US shoulders.

Another indication of America's relative isolation was the heavy financial burden it was obliged to carry for the best part of a decade. The Iraq War proved an extraordinarily expensive operation which would over time contribute significantly to the rapidly rising US budget deficit. As of March 2013, the war in Iraq had cost more than $822 billion in special direct war appropriations to the Department of Defense, the State Department and USAID. To this should be added an additional $1,694 billion for indirect war-related expenses incurred through to 2013 (covering medical, disability and social security payments to veterans, spending by the Department of Homeland Security and interest on loans raised to pay for the war) and an estimated $2,184 billion to cover war-related costs for the period 2014–53 (Rugy 2013; Stiglitz & Bilmes 2008). Over and above these quantifiable costs of the war were the political costs arising from increased public opposition to the war and heightened congressional polarisation. The domestic legitimacy deficit was accompanied by an even greater legitimacy deficit abroad. America's image in the world now stood severely tarnished both among allies and in most parts of the Muslim world.[4]

This cursory examination of the enormous political, diplomatic, financial and military capital the United States had to expend in its prosecution of the war offers compelling evidence of a secular trend that dates back to the wars in Vietnam and Algeria, namely the diminishing utility of military force for preserving imperial interests in the face of determined local resistance. Not only were the costs high, but the gains were conspicuously absent. The use of force in Iraq, far from subduing the terrorist threat, appears to have given it a new lease of life. The war that was meant to be quick and decisive brought a decade of high- and low-intensity conflict that shows no sign of abating.[5] An intervention which set out to remove a brutal dictator, bring human rights violations to an end and introduce democratic governance appears to have produced what can only be described as a failed state. In the midst of chronic instability, sectarianism and polarisation US leverage over Iraq's future trajectory has markedly declined, while Iran's influence has visibly increased.

Of all these unintended but highly adverse repercussions, none has been more vexing to US policy-makers than the resurgence of terrorist activity in Iraq that accompanied the withdrawal of US military forces. From the moment the war got under way, al-Qaeda, until then virtually non-existent in Iraq, set out to capitalise on widespread opposition to US intervention both inside and outside Iraq. As early as 2006 a leaked report prepared by the Defence Academy, a think-tank for the UK Ministry of Defence, could detect the negative impact of the Iraq War on Bush's 'war on terror':

The war in Iraq has acted as a recruiting sergeant for extremists across the Muslim world. The al-Qaeda ideology has taken root across the Muslim world and Muslim populations within Western countries. Iraq has served to radicalise an already disillusioned youth and al-Qaeda has given them the will, intent, purpose and ideology to act. (BBC 2006a)

Al-Qaeda's mobility and flexibility had enabled it to redeploy a number of its fighters from Afghanistan and Pakistan to Iraq and other conflicts in the Middle East and Africa. In a bid to hurt the United States and thwart some if not all of its objectives, al-Qaeda cells embarked upon a four-pronged strategy: (1) isolate US forces by targeting allies; (2) reduce Iraqi willingness to collaborate with the United States by targeting government infrastructure and personnel closely identified with the US interests; (3) undermine reconstruction efforts through high-profile attacks on civilian contractors and aid workers; and (4) fan the flames of sectarian Sunni–Shia hostility. The United States was able to claim a number of victories over al-Qaeda beginning in 2005. In this it was assisted by al-Qaeda's use of Taliban-style controls as well as punishments and killings which alienated the local Sunni tribes. By 2008 the marked fall in al-Qaeda attacks, its drastically diminished capacity to hold territory, and widespread criticism of its methods within both Iraq and other parts of the Muslim world prompted the then CIA director, Michael Hayden, to declare al-Qaeda 'on the verge of strategic defeat in Iraq' (Fox News 2008). Yet, despite losing a large number of its fighters and periodic decapitation, al-Qaeda in Iraq (AQI) recovered by appealing more effectively to the multiple discontents of the Sunni minority.

Well before the last US combat troops left Iraq in December 2011 al-Qaeda was once again making its presence felt. The civilian death toll, which reached its peak in 2006, fell steadily in the following four years, only to resume an upward curve beginning in 2011. According to the United Nations Assistance Mission for Iraq, the total number of civilian fatalities (including police) in 2013 was higher than in 2008, with 7,818 killed (6,787 in 2008), while 17,981 were injured (20,178 in 2008) (United Nations Iraq 2014). What made this a particularly disturbing trend is that the upsurge of terrorist violence was both cause and effect of rising sectarianism and the weakness of the Iraqi state, hence the ability of violent groups to operate virtually with impunity in most parts of the country. Al-Qaeda was now able to strike in areas where it had previously been eliminated, attempting increasingly sophisticated attacks, including raids on prisons to release its personnel (Byman 2014).

Military withdrawal from Iraq, far from signifying 'mission accomplished', had taken place in a context that can only be described as deeply humiliating for the United States. US policy under Obama was overwhelmingly focused on military drawdown, driven as it was by a desire to cut US losses and acceptance of its powerlessness to bring about in Iraq anything resembling the vision of a stable, democratic and prosperous society. As previous chapters indicate, more than a decade after the US invasion, the Iraqi state could not yet provide clean water, regular electricity or adequate health care to the majority of its citizens (Parker 2012). Youth unemployment was estimated to be in excess of 50 per cent, and the oil sector, although it constituted the country's primary asset, accounting for over 90 per cent of government revenues (Index Mundi 2014), remained at the mercy of fierce contestation between the central government and factions in Iraq's oil-rich regions. Iraq's economic and security predicament under Prime Minister Maliki was in large measure the product of a dysfunctional and corrupt political regime that was in many ways the direct legacy of US occupation policy. When the Bush administration planned its invasion it no doubt envisaged the creation of a new political order that would enshrine at least some of the elements of a liberal democratic state: civil liberties, rule of law, free and fair elections, an independent judiciary and free media. Little of this came to pass, in part because the invasion was regarded from the outset by many inside and outside Iraq as illegitimate and illegal. This made the task of establishing order and security – a task that was never fully achieved even at the height of US military deployments – far more difficult than the US President and his closest advisers had anticipated.

As the Obama administration moved closer to the cessation of combat operations in Iraq, attention centred on what future arrangements would govern relations with Iraq. In October 2011, President Obama announced that in line with the November 2008 security agreement, all US troops would leave Iraq at the end of 2011. With the formal end of combat operations in August 2010, US force levels dropped to 47,000, and steadily continued to dwindle thereafter until the departure of the last US troop contingent on 18 December 2011. By this time about 16,000 US personnel were left in the country (mostly contractors), their primary task being to protect the US embassy and consulates, and other US personnel and facilities throughout Iraq.

US energies were now spent primarily on preserving what influence it still had inside the country, and minimising the already considerable strategic advantages that had accrued to Iran as a consequence of the war in Iraq. To this end, the civilian dimension of the post-withdrawal relationship has been forged primarily around the Strategic Framework Agreement, signed in November 2008. It set out guidelines for diplomatic and political relations, as well as cooperation in the key areas of economy, energy, environment, health, culture, information technology and communications, law enforcement and judicial reform. The underlying US interests the agreement sought to protect are not hard to discover. The first, though not necessarily the most important of these, was to provide the United States with at least some leverage to steer the Iraqi political system towards more effective democratic practices and institutions, thereby conferring at least a modicum of *post hoc* legitimacy on the intervention. The other salient interest was to secure a robust Iraqi oil sector that could provide US energy corporations with access to profitable investment opportunities. More importantly, higher levels of Iraqi oil production and export could help ease pressures on the global oil market and stabilise oil prices (McGurk 2013).

The Obama administration was also intent on maintaining a US military presence, centred primarily on the Office of Security Cooperation (OSC-I). Operating under the authority of the US ambassador and with the primary task of administering the foreign military sales programmes (US arms sales to Iraq), OSC-I had some 3,500 personnel (mostly contractors) serving in a security and support capacity, but including about 175 US military personnel and some 45 Defense Department civilians.[6] OSC-I personnel have also been training and mentoring Iraqi security forces for counter-terrorism operations as well as joint military exercises, and performing an advisory role with Iraq's security ministries and command structure (Katzman 2014).

In the absence of a status of forces agreement, the United States was obliged to continue its operations in piecemeal fashion. However, as a consequence of Iraq's changing domestic and external environment in 2012 and especially in 2013, both the Maliki government and the Obama administration had additional though not identical incentives to explore ways of expanding their military cooperation. A critical factor was the resurgence of terrorist activity inside Iraq, led by the Islamic State of Iraq and Syria (ISIS), which by early 2013 appeared to be shifting its personnel, weapons and training from Syria to Iraq. A crucial indicator was the marked increase in the number and sophistication of suicide bombings in Iraq – fifty suicide attacks occurred during November 2013, compared with only three in November 2012 (McGurk 2014). In response to the rising threat, the United States made available to Iraq six C-130J aircraft and a Rapid Avenger surface-to-air missile battery (Griffin 2014). In addition seventy-five Hellfire missiles were delivered in December 2013, with a sale of up to 500 more envisaged for 2014. Other deliveries expected in 2014 included twenty-four Apache attack helicopters, ten Scan Eagle surveillance UAVs (drones) and forty-eight Raven UAVs, intended to strengthen capacity for surveillance of the Jazeera region and the Iraq–Syria border (McGurk 2014). It was anticipated that during a period of a few months the United States would make available to Iraq military equipment valued at more than $6 billion with a large number of defence contractors providing training and related services (Nissenbaum 2014).

Arms sales, the use of US defence contractors in Iraq and the dispatch of US special forces to train elite Iraqi forces in Jordan were just a few of the instruments the United States could employ to maintain a degree of leverage over Iraq's security policies. None of this, however, could obscure Washington's diminishing influence. The US administration repeatedly exhorted the Maliki government to adopt a more inclusive political approach and greater sensitivity to Sunni grievances as part of 'a holistic strategy to isolate and defeat [ISIS] over the long term' (McGurk 2014). Yet the signs that the Maliki government would give effect to these exhortations were less than auspicious. Similarly, frequent US representations made at the highest level urging Iraq to stem the flow of Iranian arms to Syria failed to overcome Iraq's reluctance to inspect aircraft carrying the weapons through its airspace (Gordon et al. 2012). Reports that Iran had signed a deal to sell Iraq arms and ammunition worth $195 million could not but add to US disquiet and frustration (Rasheed 2014).

Conclusion: Geopolitical Fallout

The US decision to bring about regime change in Iraq by the unilateral use of force has been a profoundly painful experience for Iraq, for the entire Middle East, for the United Nations and for the United States itself. More than eleven years after the event the pain remains pervasive and enduring. The reason for this is not hard to discover. The Iraq War and its aftermath of political repression and social dislocation have served as a transmission belt for the production of insecurity – regionally and globally as much as domestically –across four distinct but inter-linked action-reaction syndromes: nuclear proliferation (actual or perceived); great power rivalry; terrorism (actual and feared); and politically driven sectarianism with far-reaching geopolitical ramifications.

Once major powers have acquired nuclear weapons, a dynamic soon takes hold whereby smaller powers dissatisfied with the status quo countenance the acquisition of a nuclear capability. The possibility of proliferation (real, perceived or simply imagined) has prompted the United States to take counteraction in the name of regional and global security, though almost invariably the motive lies rather in the defence of more narrowly defined self-interest. This has been very much the dynamic at work in the Middle East, except that in this case the would-be Arab or Iranian proliferator is seeking immunity from the actions not just of a hostile great power but also of an even more hostile nuclear-armed Israel. This is the backdrop against which the United States viewed the prospect of an Iraqi nuclear programme. The intelligence which prompted the US decision to invade Iraq may have been faulty or even deliberately distorted, but this does not alter the fact that the United States has for the best part of three decades pursued an active and often destabilising counter-proliferation strategy in the Middle East, whether against Iraq one day or Iran the next. The net effect has been to generate a continuing cycle of mistrust and suspicion which, given the Middle East's strategic importance, soon degenerated into a spiral of international sanctions, diplomatic tensions and threatened and actual violence. The United Nations, often ill equipped to control these crises, has nevertheless been brought in to mop up the humanitarian mess which such crises invariably create.

A similar, though distinct, dynamic has been the steady rise in great power tensions. The US decision to go to war in Iraq in defiance of widespread sentiment within the United Nations exacerbated Russian and Chinese grievances, in particular the sense that the United States was still intent on performing a global policing role and on dealing with actual and potential security crises with a view to reinforcing its own alliances and client relationships and containing Russian and Chinese influence. Indicative of the new geopolitical trend was Russia's use of military force in Georgia in August 2008, its subsequent recognition of the two breakaway provinces of South Ossetia and Abkhazia as independent states, and its veto of the 2009 Security Council resolution that would have extended the UN observer mission in Georgia. The bitter recriminations that followed the Western military intervention in Libya in 2011, the subsequent UN Security Council stalemate in Syria, Russia's use of military force in Crimea, and the heightening of maritime disputes in east Asia have made it clear that other powers are now willing to contemplate the use of force without reference to the United Nations and are willing to use their veto power to prevent the United States from using the Security Council to legitimate its own preferred solutions to these and other crises. More than any other factor, the US decision to invade Iraq has set in train a sequence of events which has reduced Washington's capacity to dictate the UN's security agenda, but has at the same time reduced the UN's capacity for crisis management and dissipated any lingering hope of a less polarised world order.

A somewhat different but not unconnected dynamic has been at work in the US-led war on terror. A good deal of dissimulation no doubt informed initial US claims of Saddam's links with or support for terrorist groups. But in many ways the claims turned out to be a self-fulfilling prophecy. As we have seen, the Iraq War provided al-Qaeda with a golden opportunity to expand its field of operations away from Afghanistan into Iraq, and despite numerous setbacks resulting in part from the brutality of its methods, al-Qaeda has managed to gain a substantial foothold in the Sunni provinces of Iraq and to use its experience in Iraq as a symbolic and material catalyst for the diffusion of al-Qaeda-affiliated or inspired jihadism to other parts of the Arab world, including Yemen, Somalia, Algeria, Libya and Mali. The US role in Iraq appears to have given rise to a remarkable paradox. The fall of Muammar Qaddafi has enabled al-Qaeda groups to establish well-armed, well-trained, and combat-experienced militias which the Libyan government is ill equipped to control. The same trend has emerged in Syria, where al-Qaeda, though constituting only a part of the rebel forces, has been able to make good use of its unique skills in bomb-making and suicide operations as well as significant sources of external assistance. Using bases in Iraq, it has become steadily stronger and better armed.

This brings us to the third phenomenon, namely the upsurge of sectarian divisions that followed the removal of the Saddam regime. The ensuing ascendancy of the Shia majority and the relative exclusion of the Sunni minority has become inextricably linked to radical extremism on both sides and has given an added lease of life to al-Qaeda jihadism, with the consequent polarisation spilling over to neighbouring countries, notably Syria, and fuelling the regional rivalry between Iran and Saudi Arabia and their respective followers in the region.

The Iraq War and the ensuing terrorism and sectarian violence have inevitably given rise to sudden, large-scale population movements both within Iraq and between Iraq and other countries. Though a number of refugees have in recent years returned to Iraq, many are still provisionally settled in neighbouring countries, thereby exacerbating local and regional tensions. The resurgence of terrorist activity following the withdrawal of US troops, especially in Anbar province, has sent hundreds of thousands of Iraqis fleeing once again, thereby compounding the destabilising influences bearing upon neighbouring countries. The widespread political violence and sectarianism of the last decade has also provoked the mass exodus of Iraq's religious and ethnic minorities, notably Christians (predominantly Assyrian, Chaldean, Armenian and Syriac), Turkmens, Feyli Kurds (ethnically Kurdish Shias) and Kaka'is (who speak their own dialect and adhere to a syncretic religious tradition).

To put it simply, but not inaccurately, the Iraq War has nurtured the *transnational confluence* of localised grievance and unrest, Islamic jihadism and rising geopolitical tensions, which US power has been at a loss to comprehend, let alone manage or control. In the process the capacity of the United States to shape political outcomes, both in Iraq and other parts of the Middle East, has steadily diminished. The trials and tribulations of interventionism may have sharply circumscribed the US drive to power and paradoxically highlighted the enduring need for multilateral solutions, but it is too early to tell whether they have paved the way for greater wisdom and circumspection.

Notes

1. United Nations secretary general Kofi Annan stated in an interview on BBC News (16 September 2004) that the US-led invasion of Iraq was an illegal act that contravened the UN Charter.
2. See the Statement of Principles published by the Project for a New American Century in 1997 (http://cf.linnbenton.edu/artcom/social_science/clarkd/upload/PNAC—statement%20of%20principles.pdf, accessed 23 October 2014).

3. Iraq Coalition Casualty Count, available at icasualties.org (accessed 23 October 2014).
4. A Pew survey conducted in 2005 found America's approval rating to have fallen to 43 per cent in France, 41 per cent in Spain and Germany, 42 per cent in Lebanon, 38 per cent in Indonesia, 23 per cent in Turkey and Pakistan and 21 per cent in Jordan. In several countries a clear majority of the electorate now supported greater independence from the United States (53 per cent in Britain, 59 per cent in Germany and 73 per cent in France) and considered that it would be 'better if another rivalled US military power' (58 per cent in Britain, 68 per cent in Poland, 73 per cent in Germany, 74 per cent in China and Russia, 81 per cent in India and Turkey, 82 per cent in Jordan and 85 per cent in France). See Pew Research Center (2005).
5. According to the estimate provided by Iraq Body Count (widely regarded as highly conservative), civilian deaths caused by political violence between March 2003 and March 2013 numbered in excess of 110,000 (Iraq Body Count 2013).
6. Between 2010 and 2012 the United States provided Iraq with a total of 140 M1A1 tanks.

Conclusion

The Iraq Legacies and the Roots of the 'Islamic State'

Benjamin Isakhan

In June 2014 the Sunni fundamentalist terrorist organisation the Islamic State of Iraq and Syria (ISIS) expanded rapidly across parts of central and northern Iraq.[1] They captured significant cities such as Mosul and Tikrit, adding them to their existing strongholds in a number of restive Sunni-majority towns and cities in Iraq (including Ramadi and Fallujah, which they had held since January 2014) and in Syria (such as Raqqa, which they controlled from March 2013). Their stated goal was to create a new Islamic caliphate across the Arab world by smashing the borders imposed on the Middle East nearly a century ago by the British and French following the collapse of the Ottoman Empire at the end of the First World War. In a matter of days, ISIS had in fact bulldozed key parts of the border between Iraq and Syria and declared their new 'Islamic State'. Having seized such large swathes of territory, they began to impose their strict fundamentalist vision: they set up makeshift sharia law courts in which 'infidels' (non-Muslims, those who refused to publicly endorse their ideology and even those accused of petty crimes like drinking alcohol) were tried and, in many cases, executed; women were forced into marriages and then raped; Christians were publicly crucified and left to die slowly over the course of several days; mass graves were hastily dug and filled with the (mostly Shia) corpses of Iraqi Security Forces (ISF), who had fought against the sudden advance of ISIS. With every victory ISIS increased in strength, money, military equipment and prestige among their fellow militant Sunni jihadists. They also increased in confidence. ISIS spokesman Abu Muhammad al-Adnani threatened not only to topple the Maliki government and to settle debts in Samarra and Baghdad (both of which have significant Shia shrines), but also to push further south to destroy Shia Islam's two holiest cities, which he referred to as *'Karbala al-munajjasah* [Karbala the defiled]' and *'Najaf al-ashrak* [Najaf the most polytheistic]' (quoted in Aghlani 2014).

Not surprisingly, Iraq's Shia majority reacted with fury. An unfortunate turning point came when a spokesman for Iraq's most senior Shia cleric, Grand Ayatollah Ali al-Sistani – who is typically understood as a strong voice for moderation and restraint – issued a statement in which he asserted that it is 'the legal and national responsibility of whoever can hold a weapon to hold it to defend the country, the citizens and the holy sites' (Sheikh Abdul Mahdi al-Karbalaei, quoted in Rubin et al. 2014). Shia militias held impromptu recruitment drives across the south of the country. Thousands of men enlisted, were hastily armed and were packed into trucks and buses that sped north to stem the ISIS advance. The radical firebrand Shia cleric Moqtada al-Sadr suddenly announced the re-formation of his Mahdi Army, which had been responsible for some of the worst sectarian violence of 2006–8 before being defeated and disbanded by the ISF. Other militias with close ties to Maliki's government, such as Asaib Ahl al-Haq and the Badr Brigade, also surged north fighting alongside the ISF in key battles – a worrying sign that the already cloudy distinction between the national army and the Shia militias was becoming much murkier (Al Jazeera 2014). At best, the ISIS advance has reignited the sharp Sunni–Shia divide and is likely to provoke a protracted and bloody fight; at worst it may have marked the beginning of a sectarian bloodbath that would make the 2006–8 civil war look tame by comparison.

Meanwhile, in a rapid turn of events the Kurds exploited the mayhem that emerged from the ISIS advance to move closer to their goal of secession from Iraq and towards an independent Kurdish nation. Indeed, within days of the ISIS attack on Mosul Shoresh Haji, a Kurdish member of parliament, referred to the events as a 'golden opportunity to bring Kurdish lands in the disputed territories back under Kurdish control' (quoted in Goudsouzian & Fatah 2014). The Kurdish armed forces (Peshmerga) did exactly that, seizing parts of the disputed territories, including the oil-rich city of Kirkuk, which the Kurds have long coveted in the belief that it is the rightful capital of a larger Kurdistan. The Iraqi Kurdish President and former guerrilla leader, Massoud Barzani, appeared on CNN using perhaps the strongest rhetoric by a prominent Kurdish statesman to date. Barzani argued that the Iraq the world had known for almost 100 years was falling apart, that Maliki had squandered his opportunity to build a democratic future and that his Shia-dominated government had lost control of the country. He went on to argue that the Kurdish people 'cannot remain hostages to the unknown ... After the recent events in Iraq, it has been proved that the Kurdish people should seize the opportunity now – the Kurdistan people should now determine their future' (quoted in Krever 2014). Although they have little else in common, in a very real sense the Kurds and ISIS do share a desire to redraw the borders imposed by Western imperialism nearly a century ago and create entirely new states premised on ethnic/religious homogeneity. Given the strength and loyalty of the Pershmerga and the passion of the Kurdish people for their own state, it is very difficult to imagine that they would give up Kirkuk or the disputed territories willingly or take a step backwards on their long journey towards independence.

With the deadly ISIS advance, the sudden rousing of Shia militias and the threat of Kurdish secession, Iraq faces a host of deep-seated and intractable problems. Together, these events raise a number of serious questions, not just for Iraq and its future but also for the broader Middle East, the United States and its Coalition partners and the international community. While these challenges and questions will drive much academic debate, political analysis and media discussion in the months and years ahead, they are not the central purpose of this conclusion chapter. While there is always a risk in commenting on unfolding events, including the potential to overstate their significance and likely long-term impact, it is difficult to ignore the fact that the chapters collected in this volume have taken on a new significance in light of the rapid advance of ISIS and all that has happened since. While the chapters did not predict the turn of events outlined above, it is worth highlighting that the themes addressed in this volume not only point to the deeply troubling and overlapping legacies of the 2003 Iraq War, but are also often prescient in their argument that such legacies set in train a sequence of events that have served as the collective catalyst for the crisis of mid-2014. In drawing together the key arguments of this volume and offering comments by way of a conclusion, this chapter will reflect briefly on the three central legacies addressed in this volume and their relationship to contemporary events in Iraq, pointing the way forward for future research on these and the many other legacies of the Iraq War.

The first central legacy of the Iraq War is the ongoing consequences of several critical mistakes made by the US-led Coalition before, during and immediately after the 2003 intervention. These mistakes were driven by a broader neo-conservative ideology in which key US administration officials believed that they could simply topple the Baathist regime, impose the institutions and mechanisms of modern representative democracy and watch Iraq transform from a quasi-socialist dictatorship to a society driven by a free-market economy under the auspices of an inclusive government. This ideology manifested itself in several inter-connected ways – each of which has had important consequences for Iraq. One example is the Coalition Provisional Authority's (CPA) extensive project to de-Baathify Iraq. De-Baathification has had a number of dramatic consequences for Iraq but, as various chapters in this volume demonstrate, three critical dimensions all converged to marginalise the Sunnis and thereby underpin the current crisis. Firstly, in designing their de-Baathification process, the CPA failed to include a 'truth and reconciliation' dimension that would have allowed the Iraqi people to publicly purge the grievances of the past and might have stemmed the rapid descent into sectarianism after 2006 – especially between Sunni Arabs and Shia Arabs. Secondly, de-Baathification forced many Sunni Arab members of the military, police and other elements of the security apparatus out of work. As Iraqi politics become increasingly sectarian, several violent groups including al-Qaeda in Iraq (AQI) seized on the popular resentment of the marginalised Sunni Arabs in their recruitment campaigns. Thirdly, de-Baathification also had sharp political consequences. Indeed, the twinning of de-Baathification and the US-imposed model of representative democracy (which has privileged the Shia Arab majority) has meant that prominent Sunni politicians have been undermined or excluded from the political process – even those with only the most tenuous relationship to the former regime. The CPA's de-Baathification programme therefore failed to heal old wounds, marginalised well-trained Sunni Arab security personnel and drove an ever-widening political wedge between Sunni Arab interests and the Shia Arab-dominated government in Baghdad. In 2014, the consequences of this could not be clearer: ISIS – who are the direct descendants of AQI (see below) – were able to capitalise on popular Sunni Arab dissatisfaction with the Maliki government to take over large swathes of the country and threaten to destabilise the region.

Another key mistake made by the US-led occupation was demanding that Iraqi politicians hastily design a new constitution. Although, as several chapters in this volume demonstrate, the Iraqi constitution was ratified by popular referendum in October 2005, it does not speak to a united Iraqi people wishing to work together towards a cohesive and peaceful future. Instead it entrenches sharp divisions, is incomplete on several complex issues and presents many steep challenges which continue to plague Iraq. Two inter-related challenges are worth dwelling on here because they underpin chapters in this book and also cut to the heart of the key problems with the constitution, namely oil and the status of the Kurdish region. After arriving in Baghdad, the US pushed hard for the privatisation of the Iraqi oil sector after decades of state control. This led to an Iraqi constitution that had the stated intention of opening up Iraq's oil sector to foreign oil companies and evenly distributing the revenues from Iraq's oil wealth to the people. In reality, however, Iraq's oil was unevenly spread across an increasingly sectarian country and the constitution lacked the clarity needed to stipulate how the revenues should be distributed and to determine the precise nature of relations between the federal government and various regional authorities when it came to signing lucrative contracts with international oil companies. This not only opened up the oil sector to billions of dollars' worth of corruption, it also enabled the Kurds to aggressively pursue oil deals with major firms independent of Baghdad, greatly antagonising the central government. Key to such moves by the Kurds has not just been their quest for independence but also the lack of clarity over the relationship between Erbil and Baghdad with regard to natural resources. While the 2005 Iraqi constitution guarantees Kurdish autonomy it remains unclear about the future status of the so-called disputed territories and especially the oil-rich city of Kirkuk. It is little wonder that in the face of the deadly advance of ISIS and the failings of the Baghdad government to restore order, the Kurds have seized this 'golden opportunity' to advance their goals.

The US's haphazard imposition of imperfect democratic mechanisms has not only seen Sunni Arab marginalisation, generated deep constitutional weaknesses and exacerbated already fractious relations between the Kurds and Baghdad, it has also provided an opportunity for members of the Shia Arab political elite to dominate Iraqi politics. As has been documented in several chapters throughout this volume, the Shia Arabs sought to utilise their majority status to catapult themselves to an unprecedented degree of power. Such cynical majoritarianism paved the way for the increasingly dictatorial style of Prime Minister Nouri al-Maliki and his government. Having come to power in 2006 on the back of both domestic and international good will in the hope that he would create a democratic, inclusive and peaceful Iraq, Maliki soon showed his true colours. He used his incumbency to create a shadow state loyal to himself, tightened his grip on political and military power, undermined the autonomy of key state institutions, actively persecuted his political opponents and waged a blatantly populist sectarian campaign, especially against the Sunni minority. In addition, as is documented in this volume, Maliki has also taken a hardline approach to Iraq's fledgling civil society, which speaks both for and to a broad cross-section of Iraqi people. Also documented here is Maliki's sustained strategy to fracture any vestige of political cohesion between political opponents from within his own Shia Arab ethno-religious group – in the fear that they might band together and effectively oust him via an election. It is therefore of little surprise that, since the ISIS advance of mid-2014, many Iraqi politicians and world leaders have ranged from subtle calls for a more inclusive political arrangement (often a code word for Maliki's resignation) to passionate pleas for the ousting of Maliki from Iraqi politics by any means. However, while removing Maliki might be a step towards a more positive political future, it would not be a panacea for Iraq's many deep-seated and intractable problems.

The legacies of the 2003 Iraq War cannot, however, simply be distilled down to the failings of de-Baathification and democracy, disputes over oil or the series of grievances between the Sunni Arabs, the Kurds and the Shia Arabs. Iraq is – and always has been – a fragile cultural mosaic with a rich and complex history of overlapping and intersecting communities, ideologies and narratives. The second central legacy of the 2003 Iraq War addressed by several chapters in this volume is that while this mosaic has not been shattered completely it has lost – possibly forever – many of its pieces and much of its colour and warmth. With all its trumpeting about bringing democracy and freedom, the US-led Coalition profoundly underestimated the complexity and fragility of modern Iraq and failed to make allowances for those places and people made most vulnerable by the war and everything it would unleash. One example of this is the damage to Iraq's sensitive historical sites – many of which date back to the earliest iterations of human civilisation across the plains of ancient Mesopotamia, through the rise and fall of several grand empires, to the wondrous achievements of Iraq under the Abbasid caliphate. While the failure of the US-led occupation to protect the Iraq National Museum from mass devastation immediately after the fall of the Baathist regime is well known, less attention has been paid to the use of key heritage sites (such as the ancient city of Babylon) as military bases for Coalition forces, the wanton looting of archaeological locations across the country and the deliberate destruction of many important sites of Islamic heritage due to their specific sectarian lineage. As discussed in this book, beyond the immediate concern such heritage destruction raises about the loss of some of humankind's greatest historical sites, there is the deeper existential question of what happens to notions of social cohesion when the collective past of a people is so systematically destroyed (Isakhan 2011b, 2013b, 2015a).

Iraq's cultural diversity and fragility is not just a product of its rich history, it is a lived reality for contemporary Iraqis. As several of the chapters in this volume attest, Iraq's most vulnerable citizens, the women and children and the nation's smaller religious and ethnic groups ('ultra-minorities'), have been routinely caught in the figurative and literal cross-fire since the onset of the Iraq War. By engaging Iraq as if it was constituted exclusively by the three main groups (Sunni Arab, Kurds and Shia Arab) and specifically the men in these groups, the US set in motion a sequence of events that would have grim consequences for all those excluded from this simplistic frame. Since the invasion many of Iraq's women and ultra-minorities have been routinely ignored or marginalised by the political process, been systematically discriminated against or harassed and, in the worst instances, become the victims of deadly attacks motivated by fundamentalist and sectarian agendas. Understandably, many of Iraq's most vulnerable have fled such dire circumstances on a previously unthinkable scale. Some – the internally displaced – have fled Iraq's previously diverse regions for those in which peace (and often homogeneity) prevail. Others – the refugees – have crossed borders, clutching their loved ones and few material possessions to find themselves crammed into makeshift tent cities. Still others – the migrants – have packed up everything and boarded planes bound for countries where they hope to make a new life for themselves free from the threat of discrimination and violence. Given Iraq's current situation and the dim prospects of a stable and secure future, it is hard to know when or if their homeland will ever be safe enough for their return.

This ripping apart of Iraq's delicate socio-cultural fabric has been brought into sharp relief with the rapid advance of ISIS and the subsequent chaos in Iraq. In both Syria and Iraq, ISIS have been responsible for the destruction of some of the world's most sensitive cultural heritage sites, including the mass looting of archaeological zones and the destruction of ancient buildings and statues. They have also destroyed untold numbers of religious sites that do not conform to their strict vision including churches, mosques, shrines and temples. In July 2014 they bombed and destroyed the tomb of Jonah in Mosul – the biblical prophet most famous for having been swallowed by a whale. As noted above, ISIS have threatened to extend such attacks to the holy sites of Shia Islam – conjuring sharp memories of the 2006 bombing of the al-Askari mosque (a revered Shia shrine in Samarra), which unleashed a cataclysmic wave of sectarian bloodshed. Beyond their threat to places, the ISIS advance has posed a very real threat to Iraq's many peoples. Christians and other non-Muslims have fled again in droves from cities like Mosul; Shia Turkmens in Kirkuk have taken up arms against both ISIS and the Kurds; Yazidis and Shabaks have fortified their tiny communities, fearing for their lives; women have been ordered to stay indoors unless accompanied by a man and untold numbers have been forced into marriage and raped.

The fracturing of Iraq's fragile cultural mosaic has been so systemic and profound that it has had serious effects well beyond its borders. The third and final central legacy of the 2003 Iraq War detailed in this book is its significant regional and global consequences. The ascension of a

Shia Arab-dominated government in Baghdad not only ended nearly a century of Sunni rule over the modern Iraqi state, it also destroyed the delicate sectarian balance of the region, perhaps irreversibly. Along with other nations and non-state actors, two devoutly religious Middle Eastern powerhouses – Iran's Shia theocracy and the Sunni absolute monarchy of Saudi Arabia – fought proxy wars in Iraq, covertly funding, training and abetting militias, terrorist networks and insurgents. The sectarian bloodbath that followed, and which continues in new forms today, spilled over borders and quickly contaminated religious rhetoric and divided neighbourhoods across the region. The most dramatic example is that of Syria, in which a civil war escalated from relatively peaceful protests against the regime of Bashar al-Assad (dominated by Alawites, a sub-sect of Shia Islam) into a protracted and complex fight with important sectarian dimensions. It is precisely the sectarian dimension of such regional turmoil and lawlessness that provided the perfect opportunity for the aggressive spread of ISIS. Funded by private donors from Saudi Arabia, Kuwait and Qatar (Fisk 2014), ISIS has fought against Assad's Alawite-dominated government in Damascus and Maliki's Shia-dominated government in Baghdad, both of whom continue to receive significant support from the Iranian government and Shia movements such as Hezbollah. The sectarianism unleashed by the 2003 Iraq War has dramatically changed the Middle East and, with regional powers having invested so heavily in this divide, it is difficult to see how it can be contained.

All of this raises questions about the legacy of the US decision to stage the Iraq War in 2003 and about what the US, its Coalition partners and the international community ought to do in Iraq today. The key questions confronting Washington in mid-2014 are to what extent America has a moral obligation or a political responsibility to oust ISIS; what, if any, assistance it should offer the ISF; and whether it should support Maliki's troubled government. In attempting to answer these questions, the US has been confronted by the legacies of the difficult, costly and protracted nature of the Iraq War of 2003 as well as Obama's 2008 campaign pledge to end the war and the general distaste for 'going back in' across America and the world. Beyond such factors, as several chapters in this volume detail, US caution regarding confronting the ISIS threat in Iraq also stems from the fact that the war not only exposed the costly nature of military intervention, it also unveiled the limitations of using force to advance humanitarianism on the one hand and fight terrorism on the other.

In terms of humanitarianism, the Iraq War has brought home the irony of staging a supposedly 'humanitarian intervention' that led to so much death and destruction. This is especially true when one considers the enormous civilian death toll of the war but also the graphic images of torture that emerged from Abu Ghraib prison. The failure to thoroughly investigate and prosecute those who ordered or were complicit in such acts puts the lie to the 'humanitarian' *raison d'être* of the war and has left behind a complex legacy of uncertainty over how to deal with civilian casualties and human rights abuses in the context of armed conflict. These issues converged to raise deeper questions about the very notion of humanitarian intervention and, while 'responsibility to protect' has emerged as the new security and human rights norm (Bellamy 2008; Evans 2008), it seems little has changed in terms of its selective application, its use to further other motives and its capacity to prevent the deaths of those it aims to save. What has changed is the US distaste for such interventions – as evidenced by their light hand in Libya (2011), their distance from the French intervention in Mali (2013) and their indecisive and ineffective reaction to the ongoing situation in Syria since 2011.

Recent US reluctance to get involved in major military interventions also extends to their obvious distaste for fighting 'terrorism'. Although the 'War on Terror' dictated US foreign policy for more than a decade after the events of 11 September 2001, in more recent years the US has shown little enthusiasm for countering the ever-increasing threat of militant jihadists. Both the spread of such groups and the US reluctance to address their stranglehold date back to the Iraq War of 2003. As is now widely understood, despite claims by the Bush administration and its allies, there were no links between Saddam Hussein's Baathist regime and al-Qaeda at the time of the intervention. Ironically, the lawlessness and chaos that engulfed Iraq in the wake of the US-led intervention provided the ideal environment for the emergence of the terrorist group al-Qaeda in Iraq (AQI), under the leadership of Abu Musab al-Zarqawi. This group not only waged a number of brutal attacks on US and Coalition forces, but also used sectarian violence to trigger the 2006–8 civil war. Following the assassination of Zarqawi by the US in 2006 and the troop surge of 2007, AQI rebranded themselves the Islamic State in Iraq (ISI) and bided their time. In 2011 the outbreak of civil war in neighbouring Syria, coupled with the withdrawal of all US troops from Iraq later that same year, enabled the group to unleash an ambitious expansion on a scale they could not have imagined only a year earlier. Several hard-won victories and clever military manoeuvres later, ISIS (as ISI became) had realised their goal of an 'Islamic State' (for however long). To reiterate: in 2003 there was no al-Qaeda presence in either Iraq or Syria; by mid-2014 large parts of both countries are under the direct control of

ISIS – a group whose ideological and physical roots are in al-Qaeda but whose practices are so extreme and cruel that it has been completely disowned by the official al-Qaeda leadership. More to the point, ISIS are now the poster boys for a whole new generation of militant Islamists who are spreading like wildfire across the Middle East and north and central Africa, terrorising civilian populations and threatening Western interests, with few concerted efforts being made to halt their frightening advance or nefarious ideology.

The distaste in the US for either military intervention or direct confrontation with such Islamic extremism is also born of a broader legacy of the 2003 Iraq War: the challenge to their global hegemony. The architects of the Iraq War set about designing a dramatic display of US power. Like all imperial projects, it was driven by both their military superiority and their ideological zeal. Beyond the 'shock and awe' campaign was a resounding belief in the implicit merits of liberal democracy and a free market. Once the Baathist regime had been obliterated and the nation decimated and defeated, Iraqis were expected to dust themselves off and get on with the job of building a robust and inclusive democracy underpinned by a newly created capitalist economy. The many failings on the path to this simplistic vision led to a dramatic loss of prestige for the US, exposing the limited reach of the world's last remaining superpower and ushering in a new era of slow and probably irreversible erosion in US strength and influence. As the US is forced to confront these legacies in the light of the ISIS threat, it is worth remembering that a key lesson of the entire Iraq War, and one which is brought to the fore several times throughout this volume, is that peace and democracy cannot be imposed with the barrel of a gun (or at the end of a drone strike for that matter). Consequently, it seems clear that further US military intervention in Iraq – especially if it led to mass Sunni civilian casualties – would add fuel to the already global ISIS propaganda fire. Even senior US military figures such as the former commander of all Coalition forces in Iraq, General David Petraeus, have argued that US military intervention would be unwise, especially if it is perceived as supporting the Shia-dominated government and its associated militias (Lamothe 2014).

Given that military intervention is neither desired by the US nor likely to result in a more stable and secure future for Iraq, much political debate in Washington and elsewhere has shifted to the need for a 'political solution'. In its simplest form, this solution has been reduced to the need to oust Prime Minister Maliki and his apparatchiks and include the Sunni Arabs and Kurds in a new power-sharing agreement. However, Iraqi politics and the future of democracy in the country face problems that cannot simply be solved by removing Maliki and imposing an ad-hoc inclusive government; the crisis is much deeper and is underpinned by two key issues. Firstly, Iraq must address the understandable malaise about the capacity of democracy to meet and resolve the nation's many urgent needs. Superficial reforms and token gestures are unlikely to satisfy the demands of the Sunni Arabs or the Kurds; the ousting of the Maliki government will not automatically cure Iraq's many ills or energise its citizens. The question therefore remains as to how exactly *any* democratic political arrangement could move Iraq forward. Secondly, assuming that such a political arrangement can be developed to the satisfaction of all concerned, Iraq is left with a larger question about whether it is in the best interests of its many diverse peoples to stand united under the banner of one cohesive nation state or to devolve into several separate and independent regions (Isakhan 2012b). These two questions – the democratic malaise and the devolution of Iraq – lie at the heart of the crisis facing Iraq in 2014 and must be addressed if the country is to withstand the ISIS threat.

As the chapters in this volume also reveal, the magnitude of the challenges ahead cannot be overstated given the fact that a prolonged period of violence, economic stagnation and political instability has followed the 2003 Iraq War and looks set to continue. To name just a few of the biggest challenges yet to be faced: there are various complex issues embedded into the Iraqi constitution that need calm and non-partisan clarification, especially that of regional autonomy; de-Baathification needs to be scaled back and a robust 'truth and reconciliation' measure put in place that is privileged over simple punitive and exclusionary approaches; oil laws need urgent revisions leading to the fairer distribution of wealth; and Iraq's governmental and bureaucratic institutions (the judiciary, electoral and integrity commissions etc.) need to be given genuine autonomy and encouraged to do their important work. Beyond this, and perhaps most critically, Iraq needs a fresh and inclusive political arrangement which can strike a delicate balance: representing the interests of all the nation's religions, ethnicities and peoples, but without permanently enshrining a sectarian quota that can too easily serve as a crutch for division and stagnation. Even if Iraq does resort to some form of devolution to separate autonomous zones, Iraqi politics ought to be premised not on sectarian identity, but on strong policy, coherent political ideology and a willingness to embrace economic and social reform. The Iraqi political elite should aspire to transparency, accountability and electoral legitimacy in a system where personal ambition, graft, nepotism and violent vendettas have too often served as the drivers. As ambitious as all this is, it is the only real way to counter the short and long-term threat of groups like ISIS and their terrifying vision.

To assist in meeting and overcoming these enormous challenges, Iraq needs the encouragement and support of the international community, and especially the US, rather than condescending lectures, simplistic political models or military interventions. Indeed, the US ought to be held to their initial promise to the Iraqi people at the time of the 2003 invasion: to bring peace, democracy and prosperity to Iraq. As the legacy of the Iraq War demonstrates, this will be much more difficult than at first conceived. It will take a concerted, multi-pronged and multi-level effort from the US and they cannot do it alone. The US will need to form new and goal-oriented partnerships with key regional powers who will need to put aside petty political grievances and sectarian grudges to aid their floundering and troubled neighbour towards a more peaceful Middle East. The role of other international and multilateral institutions will also be vital, including the UN, the IMF and the World Bank – but also, crucially, the Arab League.

However, while the international community certainly has an important role to play, the future of Iraq is in the hands of the Iraqi people. While the catastrophic turn of events brought on by the 2003 Iraq War and the aggressive expansion of ISIS in mid-2014 has led to climacteric change, in a very real sense the nature and scope of this change will depend on the Iraqis: will they choose years of protracted ethno-religious violence and the complete disintegration of Iraq or will this moment serve as the unlikely catalyst for Iraq and its leaders to address the nation's key structural and political problems and finally move forward? It is worth remembering that Iraq has endured a great deal of suffering. In the past half-century alone, it has seen thirty-five years of repressive Baathist rule, nearly a decade of war with Iran in the 1980s, over a decade of crippling international sanctions after the 1991 Gulf War, a further near-decade of US military occupation following the 2003 Iraq War, and years of bloody sectarianism and new forms of authoritarianism since then. And yet, somehow, Iraq and the Iraqi people have withstood it all. The spirit of the Iraqi people and their resilience to even the most heinous politics and deadly ideologies provides some glimmer of hope. Several times throughout this volume we have seen this spirit in action: political leaders of all sects who have stood up against military occupation, corruption and sectarianism despite the high personal cost; persecuted minorities who have agitated for political diversity and a recognition of Iraq's complexity; female bloggers who have advocated for women's basic rights and freedoms; civil society movements and peaceful protestors who are neither ideologically nor ethno-religiously exclusive; heritage workers who are restoring access to Iraq's important historical sites in the hope of inculcating mutual respect via a shared past; Iraq's wide diaspora, who can play a vital role in connecting their homeland to the international community, thereby serving as transnational catalysts for economic, social and political reform; and religious figures who have utilised key tenets of their theology to argue that the central principles of all religious doctrines are those of human dignity and mutual respect. All of this provides hope that the future legacy of Iraq is not one in which we are forced to reflect on a state that failed to stand up to seemingly insurmountable problems, but rather a population who stood together and showed the world that even the biggest challenges can be overcome.

Note

1. This chapter, written in July 2014, reflects a very specific and rapidly evolving sequence of events triggered by the expansion of ISIS across western and central Iraq. No doubt the situation will have changed dramatically by the time of publication. What will not have changed is the connection between this rapid turn of events and the legacies of the Iraq War of 2003 documented in this volume. In a very real sense, then, this chapter is both a conclusion to this volume in which the editor contemplates the broader themes of the chapters contained herein and a postscript documenting events that have taken place after the contributors finalised their respective chapters. To separate them into two distinct documents is to ignore the intimate relationship between the two. To put it another way, this chapter argues that the recent advance of ISIS, the establishment of their 'Islamic State' and everything that this has unleashed in Iraq cannot be understood without due consideration of the various complex legacies of the 2003 intervention. The chapters collected here have therefore not only taken on grave significance in light of recent events but have also often been prescient in their argument that the catastrophic failures of the US-led war and the Iraqi political elite have triggered a sequence of events – the full extent of which is only now being appreciated. To ignore the legacies of the Iraq War of 2003 in confronting ISIS today is to make certain that old mistakes are repeated and vital lessons ignored.

References

AAA Commission on the Engagement of Anthropology with the US Security and Intelligence Committees (2009), 'Final Report on The Army's Human Terrain System Proof of Concept Program', 14 October.

Aaltola, M. (2009), *Western Spectacle of Governance and the Emergence of Humanitarian World Politics*, New York: Palgrave Macmillan.

AAP (2004), 'PM "appalled" by torture pics', *Sydney Morning Herald*, 30 April.

Abbas, M. (2014a), 'Disqualified candidates spark controversy in Iraq', *Al-Monitor*, 19 March.

Abbas, M. (2014b), 'Is ISIS planning for new Fallujahs?', *Al-Monitor*, 13 March.

Abbas, M. (2014c), 'ISIS expands in areas around Baghdad', *Al-Monitor*, 4 April.

Abbas, M. (2014d), 'The political roots of the Anbar crisis', *Al-Monitor*, 12 February.

Abd-Al-Amir, A. (2013), 'Maliki's sectarian populism working among Iraqi Shiites', *Al-Hayat*, 17 May.

Adelman, H. & E. Barkan (2011), *No Return, No Refuge: Rites and Rights in Minority Repatriation*, New York: Columbia University Press.

Adnan, A. (2005), *Al-Shi'a wal-Dawla al-'Iraqiya al-Haditha*, Beirut & Najaf: al-Arif.

Adnan, D. (2014), 'Iraqi cleric, exiting politics, urges others to keep serving', *New York Times*, 18 February.

AFL-CIO (2006), 'Iraqi unions condemn move to give oil production to foreign multinationals', *American Federation of Labor and Congress of Industrial Organizations News*, 19 December.

AFP (2009), 'Tiny Christian community stays put in Iraq', AFP News website, 18 March.

AFP (2010), 'Iraq reinstates 59 election candidates', AFP, 25 January.

Aghlani, S. (2014), 'The power of sacred geography in Iraq', Chatham House website, 18 June.

A'idoun Group (2007), 'Palestinian Refugees in Iraq: Missing Protection', 5 March.

AINA (2005), 'Kurdish gunmen open fire on demonstrators in north Iraq', AINA website, 16 August.

AINA (2013), 'Assyrian businesses, church attacked in Baghdad, 2 killed', AINA website, 25 June.

Al Jazeera (2009), 'Acute tension between the Iraqi Government and Oil Unions', Al Jazeera website, 23 July.

Al Jazeera (2011a), 'Deadly protests rock Iraq', Al Jazeera website, 26 February.

Al Jazeera (2011b), 'Fresh protests hit Iraqi cities', Al Jazeera website, 18 February.

Al Jazeera (2014), 'Iraqi army claims gains against rebels', Al Jazeera website, 15 June.

Ali, T. (2003), 'Re-colonizing Iraq', *New Left Review* 21: 5–19.

Al-Ali, Z. (2014), *The Struggle for Iraq's Future: How Corruption, Incompetence and Sectarianism Have Undermined Democracy*, New Haven, CT: Yale University Press.

Al-Ali, N. & N. Pratt (2006), 'Women in Iraq: Beyond the Rhetoric', *Middle East Report* 239.

Al-Ali, N. & N. Pratt (2009), *What Kind of Liberation?: Women and the Occupation of Iraq*, Berkeley: University of California Press.

Alkadiri, R. (2010), 'Oil and the Question of Federalism in Iraq', *International Affairs* 86(6): 1315–28.

Allawi, A. (2007), *The Occupation of Iraq: Winning the War, Losing the Peace*, New Haven, CT: Yale University Press.

Alnasrawi, A. (1994), *The Economy of Iraq: Oil, Wars, Destruction of Development and Prospectus, 1950–2010*, Westport, CT: Greenwood Press.

Alsumaria (2009), 'Iraqi Federation of Oil Unions in South Oil Company threatens escalation', Alsumaria TV, 17 July.

'Alyan, A. (2005), *Al-Shi'a wal-Dawla al-'Iraqiya al-Haditha* ('The Shia and the Modern Iraqi State'), Beirut and Najaf: al-'Arif.

American Civil Liberties Union (n.d), *Accountability for Torture*, American Civil Liberties Union website.

Amos, D. (2010), 'Dancing for their lives', *Foreign Policy*, 9 March.

Anderson, L. (2013), *Federal Solutions to Ethnic Problems: Accommodating Diversity*, Abingdon: Routledge.

Anderson, L. & G. Stansfield (eds) (2004), *The Future of Iraq: Dictatorship, Democracy, or Division?*, New York: Palgrave Macmillan.

Anderson, L. & G. Stansfield (2009), *Crisis in Kirkuk: The Ethnopolitics of Conflict and Compromise*, Philadelphia: University of Pennsylvania Press.

Annan, K. (1998), 'Reflections on Intervention', speech delivered at Ditchley Park for the Ditchley Foundation, Oxfordshire, 26 June.

Al-Araji, F. (2004a), A Family in Baghdad blog, 14 January.

Al-Araji, F. (2004b), A Family in Baghdad blog, 27 January.

Al-Araji, F. (2004c), A Family in Baghdad blog, 12 August.

Al-Araji, F. (2005a), A Family in Baghdad blog, 3 February.

Al-Araji, F. (2005b), A Family in Baghdad blog, 6 February.

Al-Araji, F. (2005c), A Family in Baghdad blog, 10 April.

Al-Araji, F. (2010), 'Overview on Iraq now ...', A Family in Baghdad blog, 13 September.

Al-Araji, F. (2013), A Family in Baghdad blog, 24 March.

Al-Araji, F., R. Jarrar & K. Jarrar (2008), *The Iraq War Blog: An Iraqi Family's Inside View of the First Year of the Occupation*, Nashville: Second Chance Publishing.

Arato, A. (2009) *Constitution Making under Occupation: The Politics of Imposed Revolution in Iraq*, New York: Columbia University Press.

Archer, L. (2013), 'Iraq "on the cusp" as spike in brutal sectarian violence threatens civil war', ABC News (Australia) website, 5 July.

ARTE (2011), 'ARTE Reportage', ARTE, 22 January.

Al-Asady, H. (2007), 'Iraqi oil workers claim tactical victory as negotiations resume and Ministry of Oil rebuked', *Naftana*, 11 June.

Al-Asady, H. (2008), 'Statement by Iraqi Federation of Oil Unions to 2008 Chevron and ExxonMobil Shareholder Meetings', Iraqi Federation of Oil Unions, 28 May.

Asia News (2013), 'Christian teacher has throat cut in Mosul, plunging city in fear again', Asia News website, 7 January.

Asia Pacific Forum on National Human Rights Institutions, Association for the Prevention of Torture & Office of the High Commissioner for Human Rights (2010), *Preventing Torture: An Operational Guide for National Human Rights Institutions*, Sydney: Asia Pacific Forum on National Human Rights Institutions / Geneva: Association for the Prevention of Torture / Geneva: Office of the High Commissioner for Human Rights.

Associated Press (2007), 'Tension on the rise between Kurds, Turkmen and Arabs over Kirkuk's fate', *International Herald Tribune*, 28 January.

Assyria Council of Europe (2012), 'Human Rights Report on Assyrians in Iraq: The Exodus from Iraq', March.

Assyria Council of Europe & Hammurabi Human Rights Organisation (2010), 'The Struggle to Exist, Part II: Violence against Assyrian Communities in Nineveh Province's Disputed Territories'.

Assyria Council of Europe, Finland–Assyria Association and Unrepresented Nations and Peoples Organization (2011), 'The Last Generation? The Situation of Assyrians in Northern Iraq', April.

Atarodi, H. (2003), *Great Powers, Oil and the Kurds in Mosul: Southern Kurdistan/Northern Iraq, 1910–1925*, Lanham, MD: University Press of America.

Al-Atraqchi, F. (2005), 'Iraqi blogger on martial law', Al Jazeera website, 31 March.

Australian Red Cross (2009), People on War survey.

Aylwin-Foster, N. (2005), 'Changing the Army for Counterinsurgency Operations', *Military Review*, November–December, p. 2.

Al-Azzawi, S. (2007), 'Deterioration of Iraqi women's rights and living conditions under occupation', Brussells Tribunal, 19 December.

Bacon, D. (2013), 'Iraq's oil workers walk off drilling rigs and take to the streets', *Truthout*, 19 December.

Bahrani, Z. (1998), 'Conjuring Mesopotamia: Imaginative Geography and a World Past', in L. Meskell (ed.), *Archaeology under Fire: Nationalism, Politics and Heritage in the Eastern Mediterranean and Middle East*, London: Routledge, pp. 159–74.

Bahrani, Z. (2008), 'The Battle for Babylon', in P. Stone & J. Bajjaly (eds), *The Destruction of Cultural Heritage in Iraq*, Woodbridge: Boydell Press, pp. 165–71.

Ballard, J. (2010), *From Storm to Freedom: America's Long War with Iraq*, Annapolis, MD: Naval Institute Press.

Barakat, S. (2005), 'Post-Saddam Iraq: Deconstructing a Regime, Reconstructing a Nation', *Third World Quarterly* 26(4–5): 571–91.

Barwari, D. (2013), 'Iraqi women victimized by tribal marriage customs', *Al-Monitor*, 12 September.

Başoğlu, M. (1993), 'Prevention of Torture and Care of Survivors: An Integrated Approach', *Journal of the American Medical Association*, 4 August, 606–11.

Bassem, W. (2013), 'In Iraq, honor crimes spread to cities', *Al-Monitor*, 11 October.

Batatu, H. (1978), *The Old Social Classes and the Revolutionary Movements of Iraq: A Study of Iraq's Old Landed and Commercial Classes and of Its Communists, Ba'thists, and Free Officers*, Princeton, NJ: Princeton University Press.

Bauman, M. (2011), 'As Iraq war winds down, Christian community finds itself "devastated"', Catholic News Agency, 20 December.

BBC (2003), 'Iraq halts Russian and Chinese oil deals', BBC News website, 26 May.

BBC (2005), 'Iraqis differ on charter progress', BBC News website, August 27.

BBC (2006a), 'Iraq war "recruiting extremists"', BBC News website, 27 September.

BBC (2006b), 'World citizens reject torture, global poll reveals', BBC World Service website, 19 October.

BBC (2012), 'Iraq hit by deadly attacks on Eid al-Adha holiday', BBC News website, 17 October.

BBC (2013), 'Christian areas hit by Baghdad bombs', BBC News website, 25 December.

Bechler, R. (2006), 'Fighting Iraq's new Taliban', Open Democracy website, 8 June.

Bedford, D. (2011), 'Iraqi oil workers' wildcat strike', Workers' Liberty website, 11 May.

Bell, J. & C. Saunders (2007), 'Iraqi Oil Policy: Constitutional Issues Regarding Federal and Regional Authority', legal memorandum, 7 July, available at National Resource Governance Institute website (www.resourcegovernance.org).

Bellamy, A. (2003), 'International Law and the War with Iraq', *Melbourne Journal of International Law* 4(2): 497–520.

Bellamy, A. (2004), 'Ethics and Intervention: The "Humanitarian Exception" and the Problem of Abuse in the Case of Iraq', *Journal of Peace Research* 41(2): 131–47.

Bellamy, A. (2008), 'The Responsibility to Protect and the Problem of Military Intervention', *International Affairs* 84(4): 615–39.

Bending Truth (2003), 'Team Troy scores (yet) another own goal', Bending Truth blog, 11 December.

Bennett, W., R. Lawrence & S. Livingston (2006), 'None Dare Call It Torture: Indexing and the Limits of Press Independence in the Abu Ghraib Scandal', *Journal of Communication* 56(3): 467–85.

Bensahel, N., O. Olga, C. Keith, R. Brennan, H. Gregg, T. Sullivan & R. Andrew (2008), *After Saddam: Prewar Planning and the Occupation of Iraq*, Santa Monica, CA: RAND Corporation.

Benvenuto, J., R. Jacobs & J. Lim (2013), 'The Assyrian Genocide, 1914 to 1923 and 1933 up to the Present', Center for the Study of Genocide and Human Rights, Newark College of Arts and Sciences, Rutgers University.

Bertman, S. (2003), *Handbook to Life in Ancient Mesopotamia*, New York: Facts on File.

BetBasoo, P. (2012), *Incipient Genocide: The Ethnic Cleansing of the Assyrians of Iraq*, Chicago: Assyrian International News Agency.

Billig, M. (1995), *Banal Nationalism*, London: Sage.

Blair, T. (2003), Prime Minister's statement to Parliament following his meeting with President Bush, London, 3 February.

Blanchard, C. (2014), 'Libya: Transition and US Policy', Congressional Research Service, 28 March.

Bremer, L. P. (2003a), Coalition Provisional Authority Order Number 1: De-Baathification of Iraqi Society, 16 May.

Bremer, L. P. (2003b), Coalition Provisional Authority Order Number 2: Dissolution of Entities, 23 May.

Bremer, L. P. (2003c), Coalition Provisional Authority Order Number 5: Establishment of the Iraqi De-Baathification Council, 25 May.

Bremer, L. P. (2006), *My Year in Iraq: The Struggle to Build a Future of Hope*, New York: Simon & Schuster.

Bricmont, J. (2006), *Humanitarian Imperialism: Using Human Rights to Sell War*, New York: Monthly Review Press.

Brubaker, R. (1996), *Nationalism Reframed: Nationhood and the National Question in the New Europe*, Cambridge: Cambridge University Press.

Bruinessen, M. van (2000), *Mullas, Sufis and Heretics: The Role of Religion in Kurdish Society – Collected Articles*, Istanbul: Isis Press.

Bryan, D. (2007), 'Abu Ghraib whistleblower's ordeal', BBC News website, 5 August.

Bull, B. (2007), 'Mission Accomplished', *Prospect*, October.

Bunce, V. (1999), *Subversive Institutions: The Design and the Destruction of Socialism and the State*, Cambridge: Cambridge University Press.

Bunkall, A. (2014), 'Iraq: government rejects torture allegations', Sky News website, 12 January.

Bureau of Democracy, Human Rights, and Labor (2008), 'Iraq: Country Report on Human Rights Practices 2007,' US Department of State website, 11 March.

Burleigh, M. (2012), 'Nato's meddling in Libya destabilised Africa', *The Commentator*, 26 September.

Bush, G. (2002), 'Transcript: George Bush's speech on Iraq', *The Guardian*, 7 October.

Bush, G. (2003a), 'Major Combat Operations in Iraq Have Ended', Remarks by the President from USS *Abraham Lincoln*, 1 May.

Bush, G. (2003b), 'President Bush Discusses Freedom in Iraq and Middle East: Remarks by the President at the 20th Anniversary of the National Endowment for Democracy', Office of the Press Secretary, White House, 6 November.

Bush, G. (2003c), State of the Union address, Congress of the United States of America, 29 January.

Butler, J. (2009), *Frames of War: When Is Life Grievable?*, London: Verso.

Byman, D. (2008), *The Five Front War: The Better Way to Fight Global Jihad*, Hoboken, NJ: John Wiley.

Byman, D. (2014), 'The Foreign Policy Essay: "2013 – The Year We Lost Iraq?"', Lawfare blog, 5 January.

Cameron, P. (2011), 'Contracts and Constitutions: The Kurdish Factor in the Development of Oil in Iraq', *International Journal of Contemporary Iraqi Studies* 5(1): 81–99.

Camilleri, J. (2008), 'The "War on Terror": Reassessing Its Rationale and Efficacy', in Hans Köchler (ed.), *The 'Global War on Terror' and the Question of World Order*, Vienna: International Progress Organization, pp. 61–8.

Camilleri, J. & J. Falk (2009), *Worlds in Transition: Evolving Governance across a Stressed Planet'*, London: Edward Elgar, pp. 446–65.

Campbell, P. & P. Kelly (2013), 'In/Between Feminism and Foucault: Iraqi Women's War Blogs and Intellectual Practices of the Self', *Critical Sociology* 39(2): 183–99.

Carr, M. (2008), 'The Barbarians of Fallujah', *Race & Class* 50(1): 21–36.

Casey, M. & J. Haber (2014), 'Iraqi forces free hostages after firefight in ministry building', *Foreign Policy*, 30 January.

Center for Torture Accountability (2013), 'Larry James', Center for Torture Accountability website.

Cevik, I (2006), 'Talabani: Autonomy for Turkmen in Kurdistan', *Kurdistan Weekly*, 30 January.

Chaffee, D. (2008), 'Rehabilitating the U.S. Ban on Torture: A Call for Transparent Treatment Policy', American Constitution Society for Law and Policy.

Chapman, C. & P. Taneja (2009), *Uncertain Refuge, Dangerous Return: Iraq's Uprooted Minorities*, London: Minority Rights Group International.

Chatty, D. (2010), 'Iraqi refugees: problems and prospects', Open Democracy website, 24 November.

China Daily (2007), 'Sadrist group quits ruling Shiite parliament bloc', *China Daily*, 16 September.

Chomsky, N. (1999), *The New Military Humanism: Lessons from Kosovo*, Monroe, ME: Common Courage Press.

Chomsky, N. (2008), 'Humanitarian Imperialism: The New Doctrine of Imperial Right', *Monthly Review*, September.

Christian Peacemaker Teams in Iraq (2005), 'Iraq's Yezidis: A Religious and Ethnic Minority Group Faces Repression and Assimilation', 25 September, available at AINA website (accessed 20 October 2014).

Chung, C. (2012), 'The Yazidis of Iraq: A Litmus Test for Democratic Progress', *Georgetown Journal of International Affairs*, 6 August.

Cirincione, J., J. Mathews & G. Perkovich (2004), *WMD in Iraq: Evidence and Implications*, Washington, DC: Carnegie Endowment for International Peace.

Clarion (2013), 'Charges dismissed against Iraq oil union leader', *PSC-CUNY Clarion*, 30 November.

Clift, E. (2013), 'The reluctant salesman: how President Obama can win enough votes on Syria', *Daily Beast*, 9 September.

Coalition Provisional Authority (2004), Law of Administration for the State of Iraq for the Transitional Period, 8 March.

Cochetel, V. (2007), 'Resettlement', *Forced Migration Review*, June, 21–2.

Cockburn, P. (2013a), 'The Mali trap', *CounterPunch*, 21 January.

Cockburn, P. (2013b), 'The war against the Shia catches all in its crossfire', *The Independent*, 13 January.

Cogan, J. (2007), 'Iraqi oil workers strike in Basra', World Socialist Web Site, 9 June.

Cogan, J. (2010), 'With US backing, court rejects candidate ban in Iraq', World Socialist Web Site, 6 February.

Cohen, A. (2013), 'Torture memo author, now a federal judge, still justifying torture', *The Atlantic*, 9 February.

Cohen, R. & A. al-Khalidi (2007), 'Time for the United States to Recognize Iraq's Humanitarian Crisis', Brookings website, 4 January.

Cole, J. (2006), *The Ayatollahs and Democracy in Iraq*, Amsterdam: Amsterdam University Press.

Common Dreams (2007), 'Iraq government orders arrest of oil workers' leaders', *Common Dreams*, 6 June.

Contrera, R. (2009), 'Saving the people, killing the faith', *Holland Sentinel*, 8 August.

Cordesman, A. & A. Mausner (2009), *Withdrawal from Iraq: Assessing the Readiness of Iraqi Security Forces*, Washington, DC: Center for Strategic & International Studies.

Cornell, S. (2002), 'Autonomy as a Source of Conflict: Caucasian Conflicts in Theoretical Perspective', *World Politics* 54: 245–76.

Cottee, S. & T. Cushman (eds) (2008), *Christopher Hitchens and His Critics: Terror, Iraq, and the Left*, New York: New York University Press.

Crawford, A. (2007), 'Iraq's Mandaeans "face extinction"', BBC News website, 4 March.

Crawford, N. (2013), 'US Costs of Wars through 2013: $3.1 Trillion and Counting – Summary of Costs for the US Wars in Iraq, Afghanistan and Pakistan', Costs of War Project.

Crocker, B. (2004), 'Reconstructing Iraq's Economy', *Washington Quarterly* 27(4), 73–93.

Currier, C. (2013), 'Charting Obama's crackdown on national security leaks', *ProPublica*, 30 July.

Curtis, J. (2005), 'Report on Meeting at Babylon 11–13 December 2004', London: British Museum.

Curtis, J. (2009), 'Relations between Archaeologists and the Military in the Case of Iraq', *Papers from the Institute of Archaeology* 19: 2–8.

Curtis, J. (2011), 'Relations between Archaeologists and the Military in the Case of Iraq', in P. Stone (ed.), *Cultural Heritage, Ethics and the Military*, Woodbridge: Boydell Press, pp. 193–213.

Daalder, I. & J. Lindsay (2003), *America Unbound: The Bush Revolution in Foreign Policy*, Washington, DC: Brookings Institution Press.

Daily Telegraph (2009), 'Iraq PM set to break with Shiite coalition in January polls', *Daily Telegraph,* 13 August.

Dam, N. van (1980), 'Middle Eastern Political Cliches: Takriti and Sunni Rule in Iraq; Alawi Rule in Syria', *Orient* 21(1): 42–57.

Davis, E. (2007), 'The Formation of Political Identities in Ethnically Divided Societies: Implications for a Democratic Transition in Iraq', *American Academic Research Institute in Iraq Newsletter* 2(1): 3–4.

Dawisha, A. (2005), 'The Prospects for Democracy in Iraq: Challenges and Opportunities', *Third World Quarterly* 26(4–5): 723–37.

Dawisha, A. (2009), *Iraq: A Political History from Independence to Occupation*, Princeton, NJ: Princeton University Press.

Deeks, A. & M. Burton (2007), 'Iraq's Constitution: A Drafting History', *Cornell International Law Journal* 40(1).

Defterios, J. (2013), 'Why violence will not derail Iraq's oil production', CNN website, 26 September.

Deisher, J. (2013), 'Military contractor sues Abu Ghraib detainees for legal expenses', *Jurist*, 16 August.

Diamond, L. (2005a), 'Lessons from Iraq', *Journal of Democracy* 16(1): 9–23.

Diamond, L. (2005b), *Squandered Victory: The American Occupation and the Bungled Effort to Bring Democracy to Iraq*, New York: Times Books.

Diamond, L. (2011), 'Iraqi Kurdistan is booming. Will it ever be a separate state?', *New Republic*, 22 December.

Dodge, T. (2005), *Iraq's Future: The Aftermath of Regime Change*, Abingdon: Routledge.

Dodge, T. (2012a), 'Enemy Images, Coercive Socio-engineering and Civil War in Iraq', *International Peacekeeping* 19(4): 461–77.

Dodge, T. (2012b), *Iraq: From War to New Authoritarianism*, Abingdon: Routledge.

Dodge, T. (2013), 'State and Society in Iraq Ten Years after Regime Change: The Rise of a New Authoritarianism', *International Affairs* 89(2): 241–57.

Doucette, J. (2010), 'The Social Construction of a Torture Sustaining Reality: A Rhetorical Analysis of Claims-making about Terrorism as a Social Problem in the United States post 9/11', MA thesis, University of Ottawa.

Duffield, J. (2012), 'Oil and the Decision to Invade Iraq', in J. Cramer & A. T. Thrall (eds), *Why Did the United States Invade Iraq?*, Abingdon: Routledge, pp. 145–66.

Duffy, H. (2005), *The 'War on Terror' and the Framework of International Law*, Cambridge: Cambridge University Press.

Duss, M. & P. Juul (2009), *The Fractured Shia of Iraq: Understanding the Tensions within Iraq's Majority*, Washington, DC: Center for American Progress.

Efrati, N. (2004), 'The Other "Awakening" in Iraq: The Women's Movement in the First Half of the Twentieth Century', *British Journal of Middle Eastern Studies* 31(2): 153–73.

EIA (2013), 'Iraq Country Analysis', US Energy Information Administration.

Eibner, J. (2008), 'Terror reigns over Mosul's Christians: CSI & Hamorabi deliver emergency relief', Christian Solidarity International, 24 November.

Eisenstein, Z. (2013), '"Leaning in" in Iraq: Women's rights and war?', Al Jazeera website, 23 March.

Elsea, J. (2010), *Private Security Contractors in Iraq and Afghanistan: Legal Issues*, Washington, DC: Congressional Research Service.

Emmerson, B. (2013), 'Report of the Special Rapporteur on the Promotion and Protection of Human Rights and Fundamental Freedoms while Countering Terrorism', UN Office of the High Commissioner for Human Rights.

Evans, G. (2008), *The Responsibility to Protect: Ending Mass Atrocity Crimes Once and for All*, Washington, DC: Brookings Institution Press.

Evans, G. & M. Sahnoun (2002), 'The Responsibility to Protect', *Foreign Affairs*, November–December, pp. 99–110.

Fallows, J. (2005), 'Why Iraq has no army', *Atlantic Monthly*, December, pp. 60–77.

Fallows, J. (2006), *Blind into Baghdad: America's War in Iraq*, New York: Vintage.

Fang, B. (2007), 'The Talibanization of Iraq', *Ms. Magazine*, Spring.

Fantappie, M. (2013), *Contested Consolidation on Power in Iraq*, Washington, DC: Carnegie Middle East Center.

Farer, T. (2008), *Confronting Global Terrorism and American Neo-conservatism: The Framework of a Liberal Grand Strategy*, Oxford: Oxford University Press, pp. 29–66.

Farouk-Sluglett, M. & P. Sluglett (2003), *Iraq since 1958: From Revolution to Dictatorship*, London: I. B. Tauris.

Farr, W. (1999), *The Third Temple's Holy of Holies: Israel's Nuclear Weapons*, Montgomery, AL: USAF Counterproliferation Center.

Farrell, S. (2008), 'Baghdad Jews have become a fearful few', *New York Times*, 1 June.

Fawcett, J. & R. Cohen (2002), 'The Internally Displaced People of Iraq', Brookings–Bern Project on Internal Displacement, 20 November.

Fay, G. (2004), *AR 15–6 Investigation of the Abu Ghraib Detention Facility and 205th Military Intelligence Brigade*, Washington, DC: Department of Defense.

Fearon, J. (2007), 'Iraq's Civil War', *Foreign Affairs*, March–April, pp. 2–15.

Federation of Workers' Councils and Unions in Iraq (2011), 'Minister of Oil punishes refinery employees with heavy penalties', press release, 28 May.

Feinstein, L. & A. Slaughter (2004), 'Duty to Prevent', *Foreign Affairs*, January–February, pp. 136–50.

Ferris, E. (2007a), 'Humanitarian Issues and Politics in Iraq', Brookings website, February 14.

Ferris, E. (2007b), 'Iraqi refugees: our problem or Sweden's?', *Washington Post*, June 18.

Ferris, E. (2007c), 'Security, Displacement and Iraq: A Deadly Combination', Brookings–Bern Project on Internal Displacement, 27 August.

Ferris, E. & M. Hall (2007), 'Update on Humanitarian Issues and Politics in Iraq', Brookings–Bern Project on Internal Displacement, 6 July.

Ferris, E. & K. Stoltz (2008), *Minorities, Displacement and Iraq's Future*, Washington, DC: Brookings Institution/Universität Bern.

FIDH (2003), 'Continuous and Silent Ethnic Cleansing', 6 January.

FIDH (2013), 'Military Intervention in Mali: "Human Rights and Humanitarian Law Compliance Is Crucial to Fighting Terrorism"', 15 January.

Filkins, D. (2014), 'What we left behind', *New Yorker*, 28 April.

Fisk, R. (2014), 'Iraq crisis: Sunni caliphate has been bankrolled by Saudi Arabia', *The Independent*, 12 June.

Forsyth, M. (2004), 'Casualties of War: The Destruction of Iraq's Cultural Heritage as a Result of US Action during and after the 1991 Gulf War', *DePaul-LCA Journal of Art & Entertainment Law* 14: 73.

Foucault, M. (1982a), 'On the Genealogy of Ethics: An Overview of Work in Progress', in H. Dreyfus & P. Rabinow (eds), *Michel Foucault: Beyond Structuralism and Hermeneutics*, Chicago: University of Chicago Press, pp. 229–53.

Foucault, M. (1982b), 'The Subject and Power: An Afterword', in H. Dreyfus & P. Rainbow (eds), *Michel Foucault: Beyond Structuralism and Hermeneutics*, Chicago: University of Chicago Press, pp. 208–29.

Fox News (2008), 'CIA director Michael Hayden says al-Qaeda is on "verge of defeat in Iraq"', Fox News website, 30 May.

Freeman, C. (2013), 'Iraq's battle to save its Christian souls: "Christians are finished here"', *Sunday Telegraph*, 15 December.

Frelick, B. (2007a), 'Iraqis Denied Right to Asylum', *Forced Migration Review*, June, pp. 24–6.

Frelick, B. (2007b), 'Iraq's other surge', *Wall Street Journal*, 14 February.

Friedman, T. (1992), 'In Somalia, new criteria for US role', *New York Times*, 5 December.

Frow, J. (2007), 'Unaustralia: Strangeness and Value', *Cultural Studies Review* 13: 38–52.

Galbraith, P. (2006), *The End of Iraq: How American Incompetence Created a War without End*, New York: Simon & Schuster.

Gallagher, K. (2009) 'Universal Jurisdiction in Practice: Efforts to Hold Donald Rumsfeld and Other High-level United States Officials Accountable for Torture', *Journal of International Criminal Justice* 7: 1087–1116.

General Federation of Iraqi Workers (2007), 'Statement issued by the General Federation of Iraqi Workers on the draft Oil and Gas Law', Iraqi Trade Unions website, 26 July.

General Federation of Iraqi Workers (2012), 'Appeal: stop government interference in workers elections', 8 July.

General Federation of Trade Unions and Workers Councils in Iraq (2012), 'Break-in at Basra Office of General Federation of Iraqi Unions and Councils', 16 September.

Gengler, J. (2014), 'Understanding Sectarianism in the Persian Gulf', in L. Potter (ed.), *Sectarian Politics in the Persian Gulf*, London: Hurst, pp. 31–66.

Gentile, C. (2010), 'Union leaders taken to court for oil sector dissent', *Iraq Oil Report*, 2 July.

Gentilviso, C. (2013), 'Michele Bachmann: Syria strike would be "a very bad call"', *Huffington Post*, 6 September .

George, D. (2008), 'The Looting of the Iraq Museum', in P. Stone & J. Bajjaly (eds), *The Destruction of Cultural Heritage in Iraq*, Woodbridge: Boydell Press, pp. 97–107.

Gerstenblith, P. (2008), 'Legal Aspects of Protecting Archaeological Heritage in Time of War: The Paradigm of Iraq', in G. Emberling & K. Hanson (eds), *Catastrophe! The Looting and Destruction of Iraq's Past*, Chicago: Oriental Institute of the University of Chicago, pp. 81–7.

Gerstenblith, P. (2009), 'Archaeology in the Context of War: Legal Frameworks for Protecting Cultural Heritage during Armed Conflict', *Archaeologies* 5(1): 18–31.

Gerstenblith, P. (2010), 'The Obligations Contained in International Treaties of Armed Forces to Protect Cultural Heritage in Times of Armed Conflict', in L. Rush (ed.), *Archaeology, Cultural Property, and the Military*, Woodbridge: Boydell Press, pp. 4–14.

Ghanim, D. (2011), *Iraq's Dysfunctional Democracy*, Santa Barbara, CA: Praeger.

Ghanim, W. (2013), 'Back on the street in Basra: oil workers demonstrate again', *Niqash*, 29 August.

Ghazi, Y. (2013), 'Worshipers are targeted at a Christmas service in Baghdad,' *New York Times*, 25 December.

Gibson, M. (2009), 'Culture as Afterthought: US Planning and Non-planning in the Invasion of Iraq', *Conservation and Management of Archaeological Sites* 11(3–4): 333–9.

Gill, P. & M. Phythian (2006), *Intelligence in an Insecure World*, Cambridge: Polity Press, pp. 125–47.

Glanz, J. & W. Gibbs (2009), 'US adviser to Kurds stands to reap oil profits', *New York Times*, 11 November.

GlobalSecurity.org (2007), 'Iraq coalition troops: non-US forces in Iraq – February 2007'.

González, R. (2008), '"Human Terrain"', *Anthropology Today* 24(1): 21–6.

Goode, E. (2008), 'Kidnapped Iraqi archbishop is dead', *New York Times*, 14 March.

Gordon, M., E. Schmitt & T. Arango (2012), 'Flow of arms to Syria through Iraq persists, to US dismay', *New York Times*, 1 December.

Goudsouzian, T. & L. Fatah (2014), 'Fall of Mosul: what's at stake for the Kurds?', Al Jazeera website, 12 June.

Gourevitch, P. & E. Morris (2008), *Standard Operating Procedure: A War Story*, New York: Penguin Press.

Graff, P. (2008), 'Reminiscences of old Baghdad by one of last Jews', Reuters, 9 November.

Gray, T. & B. Martin (2007), 'Abu Ghraib', in B. Martin (ed.) *Justice Ignited: The Dynamics of Backfire*, New York: Rowman & Littlefield, pp. 129–41.

Green, P. (2013), 'Catalyzing Cultural Heritage Data for Mission Success: Project ORCHID', *Archaeologies* 9(1): 267–77.

Greenwald, G. (2011), 'Top Bush-era GITMO and Abu Ghraib psychologist is WH's newest appointment', *Salon*, 25 March.

Griffin, J. (2014), 'US agrees to send new arms, artillery to Iraq to fight al-Qaeda', Fox News website, 17 January.

Griswold, E. (2010), 'Al Qaeda turns to the Church', *Daily Beast*, 6 November.

Gronke, P., D. Rejali, D. Drenguis, J. Hicks, P. Miller & B. Nakayama (2010), 'US Public Opinion on Torture, 2001–2009', *PS: Political Science and Politics* 43(3): 437–44.

Guardian (2006), 'Torture in Iraq "worse than under Saddam"', *The Guardian*, 22 September.

Habib, M. (2013a), 'Changing alliances for 2014: a new leader for Iraq's Sunni Muslims', *Niqash*, 13 December.

Habib, M. (2013b), 'Dangerous times ahead: Al Qaeda to annex one third of Iraq', *Niqash*, 27 December

Haddad, F. (2011), *Sectarianism in Iraq: Antagonistic Visions of Unity*, New York: Columbia University Press.

Haddad, F. (2013), 'Sectarian Relations and Sunni Identity in Post-Civil War Iraq', in L. Potter (ed.), *Sectarian Politics in the Persian Gulf*, London: Hurst.

Hagopian, A., A. Flaxman, T. Takaro, S. Esa Al Shatari, J. Rajaratnam, S. Becker, A. Levin-Rector, L. Galway, B. Hadi al-Yasseri, W. Weiss, C. Murray & G. Burnham (2013), 'Mortality in Iraq Associated with the 2003–2011 War and Occupation: Findings from a National Cluster Sample by the University Collaborative Iraq Mortality Study', *PLOS Medicine*, 15 October.

Al-Haidari, N. (2012), 'The redacted Iraqi Jews', Gatestone Institute website, 27 December.

Hall, M. (2011), 'Obama cites "responsibility" of US in Libya intervention', *USA Today*, 28 March.

Al-Hamdani, A. (2008a), 'The Damage Sustained to the Ancient City of Ur', in P. Stone & J. Bajjaly (eds), *The Destruction of Cultural Heritage in Iraq*, Woodbridge: Boydell Press, pp. 151–5.

Al-Hamdani, A. (2008b), 'Protecting and Recording our Archaeological Heritage in Southern Iraq', *Near Eastern Archaeology* 71(4), 221–30.

Hamilakis, Y. (2010), 'From Ethics to Politics', in Y. Hamilakis & P. Duke (eds), *Archaeology and Capitalism: From Ethics to Politics*, Walnut Creek, CA: Left Coast Press, pp. 15–40.

Hamoudi, H. (2007), 'My Perceptions on the Iraqi Constitutional Process', *Stanford Law Review* 59(5): 1315–20.

Hamoudi, H. (2013), *Negotiating in Civil Conflict: Constitutional Construction and Imperfect Bargaining in Iraq*, Chicago: University of Chicago Press.

Hanna, B. (2013), 'Decade of violence threatens to uproot Iraq's Christians', *Al-Monitor*, 21 August.

Hannikainen, L. (1997), 'The International Legal Basis of the Autonomy and Swedish Character of the Åland Islands', in L. Hannikainen & F. Horn (eds), *Autonomy and Demilitarisation in International Law:*

The Åland Islands in a Changing Europe, The Hague: Kluwer Law International.

Hans Wehr Dictionary of Modern Written Arabic (1976), 3rd edn, Ithaca, NY: Spoken Language Services.

Haraway, D. (2008), *When Species Meet*, Minneapolis: Minnesota University Press.

Harper, A. (2008), 'Iraq's refugees: ignored and unwanted', *International Review of the Red Cross* 90(869).

Hasan, H. (2014a), 'Iraqi judiciary accused of bias, failure', *Al-Monitor*, 28 March.

Hasan, H. (2014b), 'Maliki goes on offense as elections approach', *Al-Monitor*, 25 April.

Hashim, A. (2006), *Insurgency and Counter-insurgency in Iraq*, London: Hurst.

Hatch, R. (2005), 'A Year of De-Baathification in Post-conflict Iraq: Time for Mid-course Corrections and a Long-term Strategy', *Journal of Human Rights* 4(1), 103–12.

Havel, V. (1999), 'Kosovo and the end of the nation state', *New York Review of Books*, 10 June, pp. 4–6.

Hayden, R. (2003), 'Biased "Justice": Humanrightism and the International Tribunal for the Former Yugoslavia', in A. Jokic (ed.), *Lessons of Kosovo: The Dangers of Humanitarian Intervention*, Peterborough, ON: Broadview Press, pp. 93–120.

Healey, G. (2013), 'Counting the high cost of Obama's Libya, Syria debacles', *Washington Examiner*, 17 September.

Hehir, A. (2013), 'The Permanence of Inconsistency: Libya, the Security Council, and the Responsibility to Protect', *International Security* 38(1): 137–59.

Heinze, E. (2006), 'Humanitarian Intervention and the War in Iraq: Norms, Discourse and State Practice', *Parameters*, Spring, pp. 20–34.

Helbig, Z. (2007), 'Personal Perspective on the Human Terrain Systems Program', in American Anthropological Association Annual Conference, Washington, DC.

Hendrickson, D. & R. Tucker (2005), 'Revisions in Need of Revising: What Went Wrong in the Iraq War', *Survival: Global Politics and Strategy* 47(2): 7–32.

Hersh, S. (2004), 'Torture at Abu Ghraib', *New Yorker*, 10 May.

Heuvelen, B. & A. Iraq (2013), 'Oil union unrest continues over unmet demands', *Iraq Oil Report*, 5 September.

Hibbitts, B. (2005), 'Dead Iraqi prisoner in Abu Ghraib photos died during CIA "torture"', AP, 17 February.

Hil, R. (2008), 'Civil Society, Public Protest and the Invasion of Iraq', *Social Alternatives* 27(1): 29–33.

Hill, T. (2009), 'Kant and Humanitarian Intervention', *Philosophical Perspectives* 23(1): 221–40.

Hinnebusch, R. (2006), 'The Iraq War and International Relations: Implications for Small States', *Cambridge Review of International Affairs* 19(3): 451–64.

Hinnebusch, R. (2007), 'The American Invasion of Iraq: Causes and Consequences', *Perceptions*, Spring, pp. 9–27.

Hobson, J. (2013), 'Iraq's Exiled Jews Fight to Keep Memorabilia', *Here & Now with Robin Young and Jeremy Hobson*, WBUR Boston, 12 December.

Hourani, A. (1991), *A History of the Arab Peoples*, London: Faber & Faber.

Hovannisian, R. (1997), *The Armenian People from Ancient to Modern Times, vol. 2: Foreign Dominion to Statehood – The Fifteenth Century to the Twentieth Century*, New York: Palgrave Macmillan.

Howard, J. (2003), Ministerial Statement to Parliament on Iraq, Commonwealth of Australia, 4 February.

Howie, L. (2011), *Terror on the Screen: Witnesses and the Re-animation of 9/11 as Image-event, Popular Culture and Pornography*, Washington, DC: New Academia.

Human Rights Watch (1993), 'Genocide in Iraq: the Anfal campaign against the Kurds', July.

Human Rights Watch (2006), 'Nowhere to flee: the perilous situation of Palestinians in Iraq', 10 September.

Human Rights Watch (2009), *On Vulnerable Ground: Violence against Minority Communities in Nineveh Province's Disputed Territories*, New York: Human Rights Watch.

Human Rights Watch (2010), 'Secret order, government regulations a setback for freedom of assembly', 17 September.

Human Rights Watch (2013a), 'Iraq: abusive commander linked to Mosul killings', 11 June.

Human Rights Watch (2013b), 'The persecution of Iraqi women', February.

Human Rights Watch (2014a), 'Iraq', in *World Report 2014: Events of 2013*, New York: Human Rights Watch.

Human Rights Watch (2014b), '"No one is safe"', Human Rights Watch website, February.

Humphrey, M. (2002), *The Politics of Atrocity and Reconciliation: From Terror to Trauma*, London: Routledge.

Al-Hurmezi, A. (2010), 'The human rights situation of the Turkmen community in Iraq', Middle East Online, 9 December.

Hussein, A. (2013), 'Iraqi religious leaders nix Maliki's electoral plans', *Al-Monitor*, 21 July.

Index Mundi (2014), 'Iraq Economy Profile 2014', 23 August.

IndustriALL (2013), 'Union victory! Basra court finally drops charges against Hassan Juma'a', *IndustriALL*, 2 July.

Ingrams, D. (1983), *The Awakened: Women in Iraq*, London: Third World Centre.

International Commission on Intervention and State Sovereignty (2001), *The Responsibility to Protect*, Ottawa: International Development Research Centre.

International Coordination Committee for the Safeguarding of the Cultural Heritage of Iraq (2009), *Final Report on Damage Assessment in Babylon*, Paris: UNESCO.

International Crisis Group (2005), 'Unmaking Iraq: A Constitutional Process Gone Awry', September.

International Crisis Group (2006a), 'Iraq and the Kurds: The Brewing Battle over Kirkuk', 18 July.

International Crisis Group (2006b), 'Iraq's Muqtada al-Sadr: spoiler or stabilizer', July 11.

International Crisis Group (2008), 'Failed Responsibility: Iraqi Refugees in Syria, Jordan, and Lebanon', 10 July.

International Crisis Group (2009), 'Iraq's New Battlefront: The Struggle over Ninewa', 28 September.

International Crisis Group (2011), *Failing Oversight: Iraq's Unchecked Government*, New York: International Crisis Group.

International Crisis Group (2012), 'Iraq and the Kurds: The High-stakes Hydrocarbon Gambit', 19 April.

International Federation of Chemical, Energy, Mine and General Workers' Unions (2011), 'Iraqi government moves to end free trade unions, remove recognition of national centre', 18 May.

International Monetary Fund (2007), 'Iraqi request for stand-by arrangement and cancellation of current arrangement', 5 December.

Iraq, A. (2013a), 'Basra farmers protest Exxon encroachment', *Iraq Oil Report*, 12 February.

Iraq, A. (2013b), 'Protestors attack West Qurna 2 field', *Iraq Oil Report*, 4 March.

Iraq, A. (2013c), 'South oil workers heighten protests over jobs, pay', *Iraq Oil Report*, 13 February.

Iraq, A. & B. Lando (2013), 'Oil workers start new protests despite reprisals', *Iraq Oil Report*, 9 April.

'Iraq: oil workers on strike in Basra' (2007), *On the Barricades*, 4 June.

Iraq Body Count (2012a), 'Iraqi deaths from violence, 2003–2011', 2 January.

Iraq Body Count (2012b), 'Iraqi Deaths from Violence in 2012', 1 January.

Iraq Body Count (2013), 'The war in Iraq: 10 years and counting – analysis of deaths in a decade of violence', press release, 19 March.

Iraq Body Count (2014), 'The Trenching of Faults: Iraq 2013', 1 January.

Iraqi Civil Society Solidarity Initiative (2012), 'Iraqi trade union office attacked by government thugs seeking to take over union', 1 October.

Iraqi Civil Society Solidarity Initiative (2013), 'An Open Letter to the International Oil Companies Operating in Iraq, a Decade after the US Invasion of Iraq', 18 February.

Iraqi Federation of Oil Unions (2007), 'Iraqi Federation of Oil Unions strike demands', press release, *IFOU*, 5 May.

Iraqi Federation of Oil Unions (2010) 'Oil for All', 30 July.

Ireland, M. (2007), 'Assyrian and Chaldean Christians flee Iraq to neighbouring Jordan', ASSIST News Service, 29 May.

IRIN (2006), 'Iraq: Christians live in fear of death squads', IRIN News website, 19 October.

IRIN (2007), 'Iraq–Syria: UNHCR highlights Palestinian refugees' plight in desert camp', 17 May.

Isakhan, B. (2006), 'Read All about It: The Free Press, the Public Sphere and Democracy in Iraq', *Bulletin of the Royal Institute for Inter-Faith Studies* 8(1–2): 119–54.

Isakhan, B. (2008), 'The Post-Saddam Iraqi Media: Reporting the Democratic Developments of 2005', *Global Media Journal* 7(13).

Isakhan, B. (2009), 'Manufacturing Consent in Iraq: Interference in the Post-Saddam Media Sector', *International Journal of Contemporary Iraqi Studies* 3(1): 7–26.

Isakhan, B. (2011a), 'The Streets of Iraq: Protests and Democracy after Saddam', in B. Isakhan & S. Stockwell (eds), *The Secret History of Democracy*, Basingstoke: Palgrave Macmillan, pp. 191–203.

Isakhan, B. (2011b), 'Targeting the Symbolic Dimension of Baathist Iraq: Cultural Destruction, Historical Memory and National Identity', *Middle East Journal of Culture and Communication* 4(3): 257–81.

Isakhan, B. (2012a), 'The Complex and Contested History of Democracy', in B. Isakhan & S. Stockwell (eds), *The Edinburgh Companion to the History of Democracy*, Edinburgh: Edinburgh University Press, pp. 1–26.

Isakhan, B. (2012b), *Democracy in Iraq: History, Politics, Discourse*, London: Ashgate.

Isakhan, B. (2012c), 'Iraq', in B. Isakhan & S. Stockwell (eds), *The Edinburgh Companion to the History of Democracy*, Edinburgh: Edinburgh University Press, pp. 407–417.

Isakhan, B. (2013a), 'Despots or Democrats?: Sistani, Sadr and Shia Politics in Post-Saddam Iraq', in R. Kumar & N. Nizar (eds), *Islam, Islamist Movements and Democracy in the Middle East: Challenges, Opportunities and Responses*, Delhi: Global Vision, pp. 167–88.

Isakhan, B. (2013b), 'Heritage Destruction and Spikes in Violence: The Case of Iraq', in J. Kila & J. Zeidler (eds), *Cultural Heritage in the Crosshairs: Protecting Cultural Property during Conflict*, Leiden: Brill, pp. 219–48.

Isakhan, B. (2014a), 'Democratising Governance after the Arab Revolutions: The People, the Muslim Brotherhood and the Governance Networks of Egypt', in B. Isakhan & S. Slaughter (eds.), *Democracy and Crisis: Democratizing Governance in the Twenty-First Century*, Basingstoke: Palgrave Macmillan, pp. 149–65.

Isakhan, B. (2014b), 'The Politics of Australia's Withdrawal from Iraq', *Australian Journal of Political Science* 29(4): 647–61.

Isakhan, B. (2014c), 'Protests and Public Power in Post-Saddam Iraq: The Case of the Iraqi Federation of Oil Unions', in L. Anceschi, G. Gervasio & A. Teti (eds), *Informal Power in the Greater Middle East: Hidden Geographies*, Abingdon: Routledge, pp. 117–28.

Isakhan, B. (2015a), 'Creating the Iraqi Cultural Property Destruction Database: Calculating a Heritage Destruction Index', *International Journal of Heritage Studies* 21(1): 1–21.

Isakhan, B. (2015b), 'Succeeding and Seceding in Iraq: The Case for a Shiite State', in D. Kingsbury & C. Laoutides (eds), *Territorial Separatism in Global Politics: Cases, Outcomes and Resolution*, Abingdon: Routledge.

Isakhan, B. & S. Slaughter (2014), 'Crisis and Democracy in the Twenty-First Century', in B. Isakhan & S. Slaughter (eds), *Democracy and Crisis: Democratizing Governance in the Twenty-first Century*, Basingstoke: Palgrave Macmillan, pp. 1–22.

Isakhan, B. & S. Stockwell (2011), 'Democracy and History', in B. Isakhan & S. Stockwell (eds), *The Secret History of Democracy*, Basingstoke: Palgrave Macmillan, pp. 1–16.

Isakhan, B., F. Mansouri & S. Akbarzadeh (eds) (2012), *The Arab Revolutions in Context: Civil Society and Democracy in a Changing Middle East*, Carlton, VIC: Melbourne University.

ISCI Bulletin (2011), 'The Challenges of the Political Arena', *ISCI Bulletin* 4(13): 6–7.

Al-Issawi, R. (2009), Al-Sharqiya TV, 30 November.

Al-Istrabadi, F. (2009), 'A Constitution without Constitutionalism: Reflections on Iraq's Failed Constitutional Process', *Texas Law Review* 87: 1627–55.

Iwanek, T. (2010), 'The 2003 Invasion of Iraq: How the System Failed', *Journal of Conflict & Security Law* 15(1): 89–116.

Jabar, F. (2003), *The Shi'ite Movement in Iraq*, London: Saqi.

Jawad, S. (2013), *The Iraqi Constitution: Structural Flaws and Political Implications*, London: Middle East Centre, London School of Economics and Political Science.

Al-Jawaheri, Y. (2008), *Women in Iraq: The Gender Impact of International Sanctions*, London: I. B. Tauris.

Jawhar, R. (2010), 'The Iraqi Turkmen Front', in M. Catusse & K. Karam (eds), *Returning to Political Parties? Partisan Logic and Political Transformations in the Arab World*, Beirut: Lebanese Centre for Policy Studies, pp. 313–28.

Jenkins, G. (2008), *Turkey and Northern Iraq: An Overview*, Washington DC: Jamestown Foundation.

Jiyad, A. (2010a), 'Oil in Iraq: Basic Issues, Development and Discourse', *International Journal of Contemporary Iraqi Studies* 4(1–2): 155–95.

Jiyad, A. (2010b), 'Oil Upstream Development: The Feasibility of a Fast-tempo, Big-push Strategy', *International Journal of Contemporary Iraqi Studies* 5(1): 11–46.

Johnson, D. (2008), '2007 in Iraq: The Surge and Benchmarks – A New Way Forward', *American University International Law Review* 24(2): 248–73.

Joint Analysis Policy Unit (2013), 'Iraq Budget 2013: Background Paper', January.

Joint Analysis Unit (2014), 'Iraqi Budget Execution', February.

Joseph, S. (ed.) (2000), *Gender and Citizenship in the Middle East*, Syracuse, NY: Syracuse University Press.

Kadhim, A. (2013), *Reclaiming Iraq: The 1920 Revolution and the Founding of the Modern State*, Austin: University of Texas Press.

Kalin, W. (2007), 'A tragedy of increasing proportions: internal displacement in Iraq', Brookings website, 20 June.

Kampmark, B. (2004), 'From Security to Liberation: Shifting Pro-war Discourses on the Iraq War', *Electronic Journal of Australian and New Zealand History*, 1 August.

Kane, S. (2010), *Iraq's Oil Politics: Where Agreement Might Be Found*, Washington, DC: United States Institute of Peace.

Kar, D. & B. LeBlanc (2013), *Illicit Financial Flows from Developing Countries, 2002–2011*, Washington, DC: Global Financial Integrity.

Karon, T. (2004), 'How the prison scandal sabotages the US in Iraq', *Time*, 4 May.

Karpinski, J. (2004), interview, *On the Ropes*, BBC Radio 4.

Karpinski, J. & S. Strasser (2005), *One Woman's Army: The Commanding General of Abu Ghraib Tells Her Story*, New York: Miramax Press.

Katzman, K. (2010), *Iraq: Politics, Elections, and Benchmarks*, Washington, DC: Congressional Research Service.

Katzman, K. (2014), 'Iraq: Politics, Governance, and Human Rights', Congressional Research Service, 15 September, pp. 35–7.

Keane, J. (1998a), *Civil Society: Old Images, New Visions*, Cambridge: Polity.

Keane, J. (1998b), *Democracy and Civil Society*, rev. edn, London: University of Westminster Press.

Keegan, J. (2004), *The Iraq War: The Military Offensive, from Victory in 21 Days to the Insurgent Aftermath*, New York: Knopf.

Khadduri, W. (2010), 'Iraq Grand-upstream Opening: Alternatives and Challenges', *International Journal of Contemporary Iraqi Studies* 5(1): 101–11.

Al-Khalidi, D. (2012), *Qatala*, Beirut: Tanwir.

Al-Khalidi, A. & V. Tanner (2006), 'Sectarian Violence: Radical Groups Drive Internal Displacement in Iraq', Brookings–Bern Project on Internal Displacement, October.

Al-Khalidi, A. & V. Tanner (2007), 'The Remorseless Rise of Violence and Displacement in Iraq', *Refugees* 146(2).

Al-Khalidi, A., V. Tanner & S. Hoffmann (2007), 'Iraqi Refugees in the Syrian Arab Republic: A Field-based Snapshot', Brookings–Bern Project on Internal Displacement, 11 June.

El-Khawas, M. (2008), 'Nation Building in a War Zone: The US Record in Iraq, 2003–2007', *Mediterranean Quarterly* 19(1): 42–62.

Krepinevich, A. Jr (2005), 'How to Win in Iraq', *Foreign Affairs*, September–October.

Krever, M. (2014), 'Iraqi Kurdistan leader Massoud Barzani says "the time is here" for self-determination', CNN website, 23 June.

Kroker, A. (2012), *Body Drift: Butler, Hayles, Haraway*, Minneapolis: University of Minnesota Press.

Kukis, M. (2011), *Voices from Iraq: A People's History, 2003–2009*, New York: Columbia University Press.

Kulwin, N. (2013), 'The hypocrisy of Berkeley professor John Yoo', *Daily Californian*, 21 April.

Kuperman, A. (2013), 'Lessons from Libya: how not to intervene', Belfer Center for Science and International Affairs, Harvard Kennedy School, September.

Kurdish Globe (2013), 'Region's budget share is lower than expected', *Kurdish Globe*, 10 February.

Kurth, J. (2006), 'Humanitarian Intervention after Iraq: Legal Ideals vs Military Realities', *Orbis* 50(1): 87–101.

LaFranchi, H. (2013), 'John Kerry urges Iraq to inspect Iranian overflights to Syria', *Christian Science Monitor*, 25 March.

Al-Laithi, N. (2008), 'As Iraq moves towards provincial elections, minority sects further marginalized', *Azzaman*, 29 September.

Laizer, S. (1996), *Martyrs, Traitors and Patriots: Kurdistan after the Gulf War*, London: Zed.

Lalani, M. (2010), *Still Targeted: Continued Persecution of Iraq's Minorities*, London: Minority Rights Group International.

Lamani, M. (2009), *Minorities in Iraq: The Other Victims*, Waterloo, ON: Centre for International Governance Innovation.

Lamassu, N. (2007), 'The Plight of the Iraqi Christians', *Forced Migration Review*, June, p. 44.

Lamothe, D. (2014), 'David Petraeus issues warning about US military involvement in Iraq', *Washington Post*, 18 June.

Lando, B. (2014), interview, *Morning Edition*, NPR, 19 February.

Lattimer, M. (2006), '"In 20 years, there will be no more Christians in Iraq"', *The Guardian*, 6 October.

Law of the Supreme National Commission for Accountability and Justice (2010), in J. Ehrenberg, J. McSherry, J. Sanchez & C. Sayej (eds), *The Iraq Papers*, Oxford: Oxford University Press, pp. 327–33.

Lazreg, M. (2008), *Torture and the Twilight of Empire: From Algiers to Baghdad*, Princeton, NJ: Princeton University Press.

Le Billon, P. (2005), 'Corruption, Reconstruction and Oil Governance in Iraq', *Third World Quarterly* 26(4–5): 685–703.

Le Billon, P. (2012), *Wars of Plunder: Conflicts, Profits and the Politics of Resources*, New York: Columbia University Press.

Le Billon, P. & F. El Khatib (2004), 'From Free Oil to "Freedom Oil": Terrorism, War and US Geopolitics in the Persian Gulf', *Geopolitics* 9(1): 109–37.

Legislative Election of 7 March (2010), Independent High Electoral Commission.

Leichman, A. (2010), 'Christians pick up more seats in Iraqi parliament', *Christian Post*, 4 June.

Leo, B. & R. Thuotte (2011), 'MDG Progress Index 2011: The Good (Country Progress), the Bad (Slippage), and the Ugly (Fickle Data)', Washington, DC: Center for Global Development.

Lewis, J. (2003), 'Iraqi Assyrians: Barometer of Pluralism', *Middle East Quarterly* 10(3): 49–57.

Linnartz, I. (2008), 'The Siren Song of Interrogational Torture: Evaluating the US Implementation of the UN Convention against Torture', *Duke Law Journal* 57: 1485–1516.

Loewenstein, A. (2008), *The Blogging Revolution*, Carlton, VIC: Melbourne University.

Londoño, E. (2010), 'Shiite bloc suspends talks, undermining Maliki's chances to remain Iraq's leader', *Washington Post*, 2 August.

Londoño, E. (2012), 'In Iraq, growing gap sets Kurds apart', *Washington Post*, 10 March.

Looney, R. (2006), 'The IMF Returns to Iraq', *Challenge* 49(3): 26–47.

Looney, R. (2008), 'Reconstruction and Peacebuilding under Extreme Adversity: The Problem of Pervasive Corruption in Iraq', *International Peacekeeping* 15(3): 424–40.

Louër, L. (2008), *Transnational Shia Politics: Religious and Political Networks in the Gulf*, London: Hurst.

Loughry, M. & J. Duncan (2008), 'Iraqi Refugees in Syria: A Report of the ICMC–USCCB Mission to Assess the Protection Needs of Iraqi refugees in Syria', International Catholic Migration Commission/United States Conference of Catholic Bishops, April.

Lupieri, E. (2002), *The Mandaeans: The Last Gnostics*, Grand Rapids, MI: Eerdmans.

Lutz, C. (2013), 'US and Coalition Casualties in Iraq and Afghanistan', Costs of War Project.

McDowall, D. (2004), *A Modern History of the Kurds*, 3rd edn, London: I. B. Tauris.

McFate, M. & S. Fondacaro (2008), 'Cultural Knowledge and Common Sense', *Anthropology Today* 24(1): 27.

McGeough, P. (2014), 'As violence grows, Iraq faces threat of disintegration', *The Age*, 16 February.

McGovern, G. & W. Polk (2006), *Out of Iraq: A Practical Plan for Withdrawal Now*, New York: Simon & Schuster.

McGurk, B. (2013), US Deputy Assistant Secretary, testimony before the hearing of the House Foreign Affairs Committee, Subcommittee on the Middle East and North Africa, 13 November.

McGurk, B. (2014), US Deputy Assistant Secretary, testimony before the House Foreign Affairs Committee hearing on Iraq, 5 February.

McKeil, A. (2012), 'The Iraq War in International Society', *E-International Relations*, 25 July.

Macuch, R. (1965), *Handbook of Classical and Modern Mandaic*, Berlin: Walter de Gruyter.

Mahdi, K. (2007a), 'Iraq's Oil Law: Parsing the Fine Print', *World Policy Journal*, June, pp. 11–23.

Mahdi, K. (2007b), 'Neoliberalism, Conflict and an Oil Economy: The Case of Iraq', *Arab Studies Quarterly* 29(1): 1–20.

Mahdi, O. (2011), 'Dulaimi calls for a Sunni province', *Niqash*, 3 February.

Maher, A. (2013), 'Iraq 10 years on: good times in Kurdish Irbil', BBC News website, 23 March.

Maisel, S. (2008), 'Social Change amidst Terror and Discrimination: Yezidis in the New Iraq', *Middle East Institute Policy Brief* 18.

Makan, A. & N. Hume (2014), 'Iraq eyes return to Opec quota system', *Financial Times*, 28 January.

Makiya, K. (1998), *Republic of Fear: The Politics of Modern Iraq*, rev. edn, Berkeley: University of California Press.

Mamouri, A. (2014a), 'Iraqi media also characterized by political, sectarian bias', *Al-Monitor*, 9 January.

Mamouri, A. (2014b), 'Iraqi secularists under attack ahead of elections', *Al-Monitor*, 11 April.

Mamouri, A. (2014c), 'What is Sistani's position on the Iraqi elections', *Al-Monitor*, 13 March.

Mandaean Human Rights Group (2009), *Mandaean Human Rights Annual Report*, Morristown, NJ: Mandaean Associations Union.

Al-Marashi, I. (2005), 'Iraq's Constitutional Debate,' *The Middle East Review of International Affairs* 9(3): 1–41.

Al-Marashi, I. (2007), 'The Dynamics of Iraq's Media: Ethno-sectarian Violence, Political Islam, Public Advocacy, and Globalization', *Cardozo Arts and Entertainment Law Journal* 25(1): 96–140.

Al-Marashi, I. & A. Keskin (2008), 'Reconciliation Dilemmas in Post-Ba'athist Iraq: Truth Commissions, Media and Ethno-sectarian Conflicts', *Mediterranean Politics* 13(2): 243–59.

Margesson, R., A. Bruno & J. Sharp (2009), 'Iraqi Refugees and Internally Displaced Persons: A Deepening Humanitarian Crisis?', Washington, DC: Congressional Research Service.

Marr, P. (2006), *Who Are Iraq's New Leaders? What Do They Want?*, Washington, DC: United States Institute for Peace.

Marr, P. (2007), *Iraq's New Political Map*, Washington, DC: United States Institute for Peace.

Marten, K. (2012), *Warlords: Strong-arm Brokers in Weak States*, Ithaca, NY: Cornell University Press.

Massingham, E. (2009), 'Military Intervention for Humanitarian Purposes: Does the Responsibility to Protect Doctrine Advance the Legality of the Use of Force For Humanitarian Ends?', *International Review of the Red Cross* 91(876): 803–31.

Mastroianni, G. (2013), 'Looking Back: Understanding Abu Ghraib', *Parameters* 42.

May, T. (2008), *The Political Thought of Jacques Rancière: Creating Equality*, Edinburgh: Edinburgh University Press.

Mayer, J. (2008), *The Dark Side: The Inside Story of How the War on Terror Turned into a War on American Ideals*, New York: Doubleday.

Mernissi, F. (1991), *Women and Islam: An Historical and Theological Enquiry*, New Delhi: Women Unlimited.

Meron, T. (2000), 'The Humanization of Humanitarian Law', *American Journal of International Law* 94(2): 239–78.

Mill, J. S. (1867), 'A Few Words on Non-Intervention', in *Dissertations and Discussions*, vol. 3, 2nd edn, London: Longmans, Green, Reader & Dyer.

Miller, R. (2000), 'Humanitarian Intervention: Altruism and the Limits of Casuistry', *Journal of Religious Ethics* 28(1): 3–35.

Mills, R. (2013), 'Northern Iraq's Oil Chessboard: Energy, Politics, and Power', *Insight Turkey* 15(1): 51–62.

Al-Miqdad, F. (2007), 'Iraqi refugees in Syria', *Forced Migration Review*, June, 6–9, 19–20.

Mitchell, T. (2011), *Carbon Democracy: Political Power in the Age of Oil*, New York: Verso.

Moghadam, V. (2003), *Modernizing Women: Gender and Social Change in the Middle East*, 2nd edn, Boulder, CO: Lynne Rienner.

Mohammed, M. (2010), 'Iraq election officials confirm Sunni candidate ban', Reuters, 13 February.

Morrow, J. (2005), *Iraq's Constitutional Process II: An Opportunity Lost*, Washington, DC: United States Institute for Peace.

Al Moumin, M. (2012), 'The Legal Framework for Managing Oil in Post-conflict Iraq: A Pattern of Abuse and Violence over Natural Resources', in P. Lujala & S. Rustad (eds), *High-value Natural Resources and Post-conflict Peacebuilding*, Abingdon: Earthscan, pp. 413–35.

Mourad, T. (2010), 'An Ethical Archaeology in the Near East: Confronting Empire, War and Colonialism', in Y. Hamilakis & P. Duke (eds), *Archaeology and Capitalism: From Ethics to Politics*, Walnut Creek, CA: Left Coast Press, pp. 161–7.

Moussa, M. (2008), 'The Damages Sustained to the Ancient City of Babylon as a Consequence of the Military Presence of Coalition Forces in 2003', in

P. Stone & J. Bajjaly (eds), *The Destruction of Cultural Heritage in Iraq*, Woodbridge: Boydell Press, pp. 143–50.

MRS/RE (2010), 'Maliki "won't allow US meddling in election row"', Press TV website, 5 February.

Munson, P. (2009), *Iraq in Transition: The Legacy of Dictatorship and the Prospects for Democracy*, Washington, DC: Potomac.

Musings on Iraq (2014), 'How faults with Iraq's constitution undermines the country, interview with constitutional scholar Zaid al-Ali', Musings on Iraq blog, 24 February.

Muttitt, G. (2012), *Fuel on the Fire: Oil and Politics in Occupied Iraq*, London: Vintage.

Myers, S. (2010), 'Crossroads of antiquity can't decide on new path', *New York Times*, 19 October.

Nakash, Y. (2007), *Reaching for Power: The Shi'a in the Modern Arab World*, Princeton, NJ: Princeton University Press.

Namey, G. (2011a), 'Military Detention: Uncovering the Truth, Story 3 – Australia's Knowledge of and Role in Hiding Detainees from the International Committee of the Red Cross at Abu Ghraib', Public Interest Advocacy Centre website.

Namey, G. (2011b) 'Military Detention: Uncovering the Truth, Story 4 – Australian Military Lawyer's Advice on Interrogation Techniques at Abu Ghraib', Public Interest Advocacy Centre website.

Namey, G. (2011c) 'Military Detention: Uncovering the Truth, Story 5 – Australian Knowledge of, and Role in Investigating Torture and Abuse at Abu Ghraib', Public Interest Advocacy Centre website.

Naqishbendi, R. (2005), 'Iraq: its demography and geography as impediments to peace and stability', KurdishMedia website, 3 November.

Nardin, T. (2005), 'Humanitarian Imperialism', *Ethics and International Affairs* 19(2): 21–6.

Nasr, V. (2007), *The Shia Revival: How Conflicts within Islam Will Shape the Future*, New York: W. W. Norton.

Nasrawi, S. (2013), 'Iraq without its Christians', *Al-Ahram Weekly*, 28 November.

New York Times (2011a), 'China blasts Obama's Libya war as humanitarian catastrophe', 22 March.

New York Times (2011b), 'The goal in Libya is not regime change', interview with Amr Moussa, 23 March.

Niqash Special Correspondent (2014), 'Banned for bad behaviour: criticising Iraqi PM enough to get MPs banned from elections?', *Niqash*, 20 March.

Nissenbaum, D. (2014), 'Role of US contractors grows as Iraq fights insurgents', *Wall Street Journal*, 3 February.

Norton-Taylor, R. (2008), 'Iraq: alarm at forced transfer of Basra union activists', *The Guardian*, 25 July.

Nye, J. Jr (2003), 'US Power and Strategy after Iraq', *Foreign Affairs*, July–August, pp. 60–73.

Obama, B. (2009a), 'Responsibly ending the war in Iraq', Camp Lejeune, North Carolina, 27 February.

Obama, B. (2009b), 'Text: Obama's speech in Cairo', *New York Times*, 4 June.

Obama, B. (2011), 'Transcript: President Obama Iraq speech', BBC News website, 15 December.

Office for the Coordination of Humanitarian Affairs (2011), *Regional Response Plan for Iraqi refugees – 2011 Mid-year Review*, New York & Geneva: United Nations.

Office of the High Commissioner for Human Rights (2011), 'Pillay calls for international inquiry into Libyan violence and justice for victims', press release, 22 February.

Office of the High Commissioner for Human Rights (2013), 'CIA rendition programme: UN expert in human rights and counter-terrorism expert asks for truth and accountability', press release, 6 March.

Oğuzlu, H. (2004), 'Endangered Community: The Turkoman Identity in Iraq', *Journal of Muslim Minority Affairs* 24(2): 309–25.

Oil Workers' Rights Defense Committee (2013), 'Report on the oil workers demonstrations on the 13th of February, 2013'.

O'Leary, B. (2009), *How to Get Out of Iraq with Integrity*, Philadelphia: University of Pennsylvania Press.

Omestad, T. (2012), 'Vulnerable Iraqi minorities making gains with USIP help', United States Institute of Peace website, 26 December.

Open Society Justice Initiative (2013), *Globalizing Torture: CIA Secret Detention and Extraordinary Rendition*, New York: Open Society Justice Initiative.

Organisation of Women's Freedom in Iraq (2011), 'The Day of Iraqi Rage', 6 March.

Ottaway, M. & D. Kaysi (2010a), 'Can Iraq's Political Agreement Be Implemented?', Carnegie Endowment for International Peace, 15 November.

Ottaway, M. & D. Kaysi (2010b), 'De-Baathification as a Political Tool: Commission Riling Bans Political Parties and Leaders', Carnegie Endowment for International Peace, 26 January.

Ottaway, M. & D. Kaysi (2010c), 'Iraq's Long Road to a Government', Carnegie Endowment for International Peace, 26 May.

Ottaway, M. & D. Kaysi (2010d), 'Post-election Maneuvering: Rule of Law Is the Casualty', Carnegie Endowment for International Peace, 30 April.

Ottaway, M. & D. Kaysi (2010e), 'Who Will Be the Next Prime Minister of Iraq?', Carnegie Endowment for International Peace, 5 April.

Palumbo, G. (2005), 'The State of Iraq's Cultural Heritage in the Aftermath of the 2003 War', *Brown Journal of World Affairs* 12(1): 225–38.

PanArmenian.Net (2007), '28 Armenians died during 4 years in Iraq', 24 March.

Parker, N. (2012), 'The Iraq We Left Behind: Welcome to the World's Next Failed State', *Foreign Affairs*, March–April, pp. 94–110.

Parker, N. (2014), 'Iraq: the road to chaos', *New York Review of Books*, 15 April.

Parker, N. & R. Salman (2014), 'Maliki faces struggle to secure third term as Iraqi PM', Reuters, 29 April.

Patterson, W. (2010), 'Irrelevant or Indispensable? The State of the UN in the Aftermath of Iraq', *Virginia Social Science Journal* 45: 48–66.

Pattison, J. (2011), 'The Ethics of Humanitarian Intervention in Libya', *Ethics and International Affairs* 25(3): 271–7.

Paulus, A. (2004), 'The War against Iraq and the Future of International Law: Hegemony or Pluralism?', *Michigan Journal of International Law* 25(3): 691–734.

Perry, W., S. Johnson, K. Crane, D. Gompert, J. Gordon, R. Hunter & H. Shatz (2009), *Withdrawing from Iraq: Alternative Schedules, Associated Risks, and Mitigating Strategies*, Santa Monica, CA: RAND Corporation.

Persecution (2014), 'Iraq moves to preserve Christian heritage, Syriac language', Persecution: International Christian Concern website, 20 February.

Pew Research Center (2005), 'Global Opinion: The Spread of Anti-Americanism', 24 January.

Pfiffner, J. (2010), 'US Blunders in Iraq: De-Baathification and Disbanding the Army', *Intelligence and National Security* 25(1): 76–85.

Phillips, A. (2009), 'How Al Qaeda Lost Iraq', *Australian Journal of International Affairs* 63(1): 64–84.

Pinckney, D. (2010), 'Time Is Not on My Side: Cultural Resource Management in Kirkuk, Iraq', in L. Rush (ed.), *Archaeology, Cultural Property and the Military*, Woodbridge: Boydell Press, pp. 117–25.

Porch, D. (2003), 'Germany, Japan and the "De-Baathification" of Iraq', *Strategic Insight* 2(3).

Potter, L. (2013), *Sectarian Politics in the Persian Gulf*, New York: Oxford University Press.

Purdum, T. (2003), *A Time of Our Choosing: America's War in Iraq*, New York: Times Books.

Rabkin, N. (2014), 'Iraq's Sunni Clerical Establishment', *Inside Iraqi Politics* 60.

Rafaat, A. (2012), 'Kurdish Islam and the Question of Kurdish Integration into the Iraqi State', *Journal of Social, Political, and Economic Studies* 37(1): 3–37.

Rahimi, B. (2004), 'Ayatollah Ali al-Sistani and the Democratization of Post-Saddam Iraq', *Middle East Review of International Affairs* 8(4).

Rampton, S. (2003), *Weapons of Mass Deception: The Uses of Propaganda in Bush's War on Iraq*, New York: Penguin.

Rancière, J. (2004), 'Who Is the Subject of the Rights of Man?', *South Atlantic Quarterly*, Spring–Summer, pp. 297–310.

Rasheed, A. (2014), 'Exclusive: Iraq signs deal to buy arms, ammunition from Iran – documents', Reuters, 24 February.

Rathmell, A. (2005), 'Planning Post-conflict Reconstruction in Iraq: What Can We Learn?', *International Affairs* 81(5): 1013–38.

Rejali, D. (2007), *Torture and Democracy*, Princeton, NJ: Princeton University Press.

Republic of Iraq (2005), Iraqi Constitution, General Directorate for Nationality, Ministry of Interior.

Reuters (2001), 'Saddam praises Sabaeans, pledges to build temple', *Gulf News*, 12 February.

Reuters (2008), 'Iraqi lawmakers approve seats for religious minorities in '09 polls', Radio Free Europe/Radio Liberty website, 3 November.

Reuters (2013a), 'Deadly bombing hits Iraqi funeral', *New York Times*, 14 September.

Reuters (2013b), 'Protestors break into Iraq's West Qurna-2 oilfield', 4 March.

Richardson, L., C. Frueh & R. Acierno (2010), 'Prevalence Estimates of Combat-related Post-traumatic Stress Disorder: Critical Review', *Australian and New Zealand Journal of Psychiatry* 44(1):4–19.

Richelson, J. (ed.) (2004), 'Iraq and Weapons of Mass Destruction', National Security Archive website, 11 February.

Rieff, D. (2002), 'Humanitarianism in Crisis', *Foreign Affairs*, November–December, pp. 111–21.

Rieff, D. (2012), 'As Syrians suffer, do we stand by or send in the troops?', *Sydney Morning Herald*, 5 March.

Rieff, D., S. Tharoor & S. Daws (2001), 'Humanitarian Intervention', *World Policy Journal* 18(3): 101–2.

Riverbend (2003a), 'Cousins and veils ...', Baghdad Burning blog, 1 October.

Riverbend (2003b), 'Latest developments ...', Baghdad Burning blog, 6 December.

Riverbend (2003c), 'The opposite direction', Baghdad Burning blog, 28 August.

Riverbend (2004), 'American elections 2004 ...', Baghdad Burning blog, 25 October.

Riverbend (2005), *Baghdad Burning: Girl Blog from Iraq*, New York: Feminist Press.

Riverbend (2006a), *Baghdad Burning II: More Girl Blog from Iraq*, New York: Feminist Press.

Riverbend (2006b), 'Summer of goodbyes ...', Baghdad Burning blog, 5 August.

Riverbend (2006c), 'Viva Muqtada ...', Baghdad Burning blog, 31 May.

Riverbend (2007a), 'Bloggers without borders ...', Baghdad Burning blog, 22 October.

Riverbend (2007b), 'The rape of Sabrine', Baghdad Burning blog, 20 February.

Riverbend (2013), 'Ten years on ...', Baghdad Burning blog, 9 April.

Roberts, B. & G. Roberts (2013), 'A Case Study in Cultural Heritage Protection in a Time of War', in J. Kila & J. Zeidler (eds), *Cultural Heritage in the Crosshairs: Protecting Cultural Property During Conflict*, Leiden: Brill, pp. 169–93.

Robinson, P. (2005), 'Hitch-cocked: a Conversation with Christopher Hitchens', *Uncommon Knowledge*, Hoover Institution, 25 March .

Roeder, P. (1991), 'Soviet Federalism and Ethnic Mobilization', *World Politics* 43(2): 196–232.

Roeder, P. (2009), 'Ethnofederalism and the Mismanagement of Conflicting Nationalisms', *Regional and Federal Studies* 19(2): 203–19.

Rose, B. (2007), 'Talking to the Troops about the Archaeology of Iraq and Afghanistan', in R. Rhodes (ed.), *The Acquisition and Exhibition of Classical Antiquities: Professional, Legal, and Ethical Perspectives*, Notre Dame, IN: University of Notre Dame Press, pp. 139–54.

Rosen, N. (2008), *The Triumph of the Martyrs: A Reporter's Journey into Occupied Iraq*, Washington, DC: Potomac.

Ross, M. (2012), *The Oil Curse: How Petroleum Wealth Shapes the Development of Nations*, Princeton, NJ: Princeton University Press.

Roth, K. (2004), *Human Rights Watch World Report 2004: Human Rights and Armed Conflict*, Human Rights Watch.

Rothfield, L. (2009), *Rape of Mesopotamia: Behind the Looting of the Iraq Museum*, Chicago: University of Chicago Press.

Roux, G. (1992), *Ancient Iraq*, 3rd edn, London: Penguin.

Al-Rubaie, M., A. Allawi & S. al-Hakim (2010), 'Declaration of the Shia of Iraq', in J. Ehrenberg, J. McSherry, J. Sanchez & C. Sayej (eds), *The Iraq Papers*, Oxford: Oxford University Press, pp. 313–15.

Rubin, A., S. al-Salhy & R. Gladstone (2014), 'Iraqi Shiite cleric issues call to arms', *New York Times*, 13 June.

Rugy, V. de (2013), 'The Budgetary Impact of Recent US Wars', George Mason University, 10 September.

Rush, L. (2011), 'Military Archaeology in the US: A Complex Ethical Decision', in P. Stone (ed.), *Cultural Heritage, Ethics and the Military*, Woodbridge: Boydell Press, pp. 139–51.

Rush, L. (2012), 'Working with the Military to Protect Archaeological Sites and Other Forms of Cultural Property', *World Archaeology* 44(3): 359–77.

Russell, J. (2001), 'Robbing the Archaeological Cradle', *Natural History* 110(1): 44–55.

Russell, J. (2008), 'Efforts to Protect Archaeological Sites and Monuments in Iraq, 2003–2004', in G. Emberling & K. Hanson (eds), *Catastrophe! The Looting and Destruction of Iraq's Past*, Chicago: Oriental Institute of the University of Chicago, pp. 29–43.

Rutherglen, S. (2006), 'The Sack of Baghdad: The US Invasion of Iraq Has Turned Icons into Loot and Archaeological Sites into Ruins', *American Scholar* 75(3): 33–40.

Sabah, Z. & R. Jervis (2007), 'Christians, targeted and suffering, flee Iraq', *USA Today*, 23 March.

Sadah, A. (2013a), 'Maliki faces tough political choices ahead of elections', *Al-Monitor*, 11 April.

Sadah, A. (2013b), 'Maliki makes concessions on de-Baathification', *Al-Monitor*, 18 January.

Sadah, A. (2013c), 'Maliki wields "de-Baathification" in Iraqi power struggle', *Al-Monitor*, 21 February.

Sadah, A. (2013d), 'Maliki's own party urges him not to run', *Al-Monitor*, 23 August.

Sadah, A. (2013e), 'Speaker accuses Maliki of meddling in Iraq's independent commissions', *Al-Monitor*, 7 March.

Salaheddin, S. (2012), 'Iraq officially retreats from ambitious oil plans', Associated Press, 10 October.

Salloum, S. (ed.) (2013), *Al-Aqalliyat fi al-'Iraq*, Baghdad & Beirut: Masarat.

Samaraweera, V. (2007), 'Identifying the Federal Supreme Court of Iraq', USAID, 1 November.

Santora, M. (2007), 'Militia nearly overran Iraqi troops', *Globe and Mail*, 30 January.

Saroyan, W. (1934), 'Seventy Thousand Assyrians', in W. Saroyan, *The Daring Young Man on the Flying Trapeze and Other Stories*, New York: Random House.

Sarson, J. & L. MacDonald (2009), 'Torturing by Non-state Actors Invisibilized, a Patriarchal Divide and Spillover Violence from the Military Sphere into the Domestic Sphere', *Peace Studies Journal* 2: 17–38.

Sassoon, J. (2009), *Iraqi Refugees: The New Crisis in the Middle East*, London: I. B. Tauris.

Sassoon, J. (2012), *Saddam Hussein's Ba'th Party: Inside an Authoritarian Regime*, Cambridge: Cambridge University Press.

Savage, J. (2014), *Reconstructing Iraq's Budgetary Institutions: Coalition State Building after Saddam*, Cambridge: Cambridge University Press.

Scahill, J. (2009), 'New UN report shows the US combo of torture and impunity thrives in Iraqi prisons', Common Dreams website, 1 May.

Schaap, A. (2011), 'Enacting the Rights to Have Rights: Jacques Rancière's Critique of Hannah Arendt', *European Journal of Political Theory* 10(1): 22–45.

Schipper, F., F. Schuller, K. von Habsburg-Lothringen, H. Eichberger, E. Frank & N. Fürstenhofer (2010), 'Cultural Property Protection in the Event of Armed Conflict: Austrian Experiences', in L. Rush (ed.), *Archaeology, Cultural Property, and the Military*, Woodbridge: Boydell Press, pp. 145–57.

Schmidt, M. & J. Healy (2011), 'Iraq shuts office of protest organizers', *New York Times*, 7 March.

Schwenkel, C. (2009), 'From John McCain to Abu Ghraib: Tortured Bodies and Historical Unaccountability of US Empire', *American Anthropologist* 111(1): 30–42.

Scott, J. (2007), *The Politics of the Veil*, Princeton, NJ: Princeton University Press.

Serwer, D. (2011), 'The strikes on Libya: humanitarian intervention, not imperial aggression', *The Atlantic*, 19 March.

Shadid, A. (2012), 'Libya struggles to curb militias as chaos grows', *New York Times*, 8 February.

Shafiq, T. (2014), 'PSAs vs Service Contracts: The Case of Iraq', *Middle East Economic Survey* 57(8).

Shimko, K. (2010), *The Iraq Wars and America's Military Revolution*, Cambridge: Cambridge University Press, pp. 164–8.

Siebrandt, D. (2009), *Assessment of the Archaeological Site of Ur*, Baghdad: US Embassy.

Siebrandt, D. (2010), 'US Military Support of Cultural Heritage Awareness and Preservation in Post-conflict Iraq', in L. Rush (ed.), *Archaeology, Cultural Property, and the Military*, Woodbridge: Boydell Press, pp. 126–37.

Siebrandt, D. (2012), *Al-Hurriyah Air Base Site Survey*, Baghdad: US Embassy.

Simon, R., & E. Tejirian (2005), *The Creation of Iraq, 1914–1921*, New York: Columbia University Press.

Sirkeci, I. (2005), *Turkmen in Iraq and International Migration of Turkmen*, Ankara: Global Strategy Institute.

Sirkeci, I. (2011), *Turkmen in Iraq and Their Flight: A Demographic Question*, Ankara: Center for Middle Eastern Strategic Studies.

Sissons, M. (2008), 'Briefing Paper: Iraq's New "Accountability and Justice" Law', International Center for Transitional Justice, 22 January.

Sissons, M. & A. al-Saiedi (2013), *A Bitter Legacy: Lessons of De-Baathification in Iraq*, New York: International Center for Transitional Justice.

Al-Sistani, A. (2010), 'Collection of Fatwas', in J. Ehrenberg, J. McSherry, J. Sanchez & C. Sayej (eds), *The Iraq Papers*, Oxford: Oxford University Press, pp. 320–4.

Slaughter, A. (2012), 'How to halt the butchery in Syria', *New York Times*, 23 February.

Smith, M., M. Habboush & L. Maghribi (2013), 'Iraq faces chronic housing shortage, needs foreign investment – minister', Reuters, 16 September.

SOITM: Iraqi Turkmen Human Rights Research Foundation (2011), 'The human rights situation of the Turkmen of Iraq (after the fall of Ba'ath regime at 10 April 2003)', SOITM website, 4 December.

Solidarity Center (2007), 'US unions rally to support Iraqi worker rights, protest oil law', Solidarity Center website, 18 August.

Solidarity Center (2010), 'Solidarity Center decries anti-union moves in an Iraqi refinery', Solidarity Center website, 5 April.

Sontag, S. (2003), *Regarding the Pain of Others*, London: Hamish Hamilton.

Spencer, R. (2014), 'Syria's al-Qaeda threatens rival in letter, video', *National Post*, 26 February.

Spiegel, P. (2006), 'Army lets general in prison scandal retire', *Los Angeles Times*, 1 August.

Stansfield, G. (2003), *Iraqi Kurdistan: Political Development and Emergent Democracy*, London: RoutledgeCurzon.

Stansfield, G. (2007), *Iraq: People, History, Politics*, Cambridge: Polity.

Stansfield, G. & L. Anderson (2009), 'Kurds in Iraq: The Struggle between Baghdad and Erbil', *Middle East Policy* 16(1): 134–45.

Stiglitz, J. & L Bilmes (2008), *The Three Trillion Dollar War: The True Cost of the Iraq Conflict*, New York: W. W. Norton.

Stone, E. (2008), 'Patterns of Looting in SOUTHERN IRAQ', *Antiquity* 82(315): 125–38.

Stone, P. (2009), 'Protecting Cultural Heritage in Times of Conflict: Lessons from Iraq', *Archaeologies* 5(1): 32–8.

Stone, P. & J. Bajjaly (eds) (2008), *The Destruction of Cultural Heritage in Iraq*, Woodbridge: Boydell Press.

Stover, E., H. Megally & H. Mufti (2005), 'Bremer's "Gordian Knot": Transitional Justice and the US Occupation of Iraq', *Human Rights Quarterly* 27(3): 830–57.

Surk, B. & L. Jakes (2010), 'Iraqi Christians mourn after church siege kills 58', Associated Press, 1 November.

Taguba, A. (2004), 'Article 15–6 Investigation of the 800th Military Police Brigade', Washington, DC: US Department of Defense.

Taneja, P. (2007), *Assimilation, Exodus, Eradication: Iraq's Minority Communities since 2003*, London: Minority Rights Group International.

Taneja, P. (2011a), *Iraq's Minorities: Participation in Public Life*, London: Minority Rights Group International.

Taneja, P. (2011b), 'Middle East and North Africa', in J. Hoare (ed.), *State of the World's Minorities and Indigenous Peoples 2011: Events of 2010, Focus on Women's Rights*, London: Minority Rights Group International, pp. 208–30.

Tanielian, T. & L. Jaycox (eds) (2008), *Invisible Wounds of War: Psychological and Cognitive Injuries, Their Consequences, and Services to Assist Recovery*, Santa Monica, CA: RAND Corporation.

Taylor, S. (2004), *Among the 'Others': Encounters with the Forgotten Turkmen of Iraq*, Ottawa: Esprit de Corps.

Taylor Martin, S. (2003), 'Her job: lock up Iraq's bad guys', *St Petersburg Times*, 14 December.

Teijgeler, R. (2011), Response to "Relations between Archaeologists and the Military in the Case of Iraq"', in P. Stone (ed.), *Cultural Heritage, Ethics, and the Military*, Woodbridge: Boydell, pp. 210–13.

Telaferli, Y. (2007), 'Summary of the real story of Telafer disaster: How the sectarian hatred was introduced in to the city and the role of Kurdish militants', SOITM website, 13 April.

Tesón, F. (1997), *Humanitarian Intervention: An Inquiry into Law and Morality*, 2nd edn, Dobbs Ferry, NY: Transnational.

Tesón, F. (2005), 'Ending Tyranny in Iraq', *Ethics and International Affairs* 19(2): 1–20.

Tessier, J. (2007), 'Shake & Bake: Dual-use Chemicals, Contexts, and the Illegality of American White Phosphorus Attacks in Iraq', *Pierce Law Review* 6: 323–64.

Thakur, R. (2007), *War in Our Time: Reflections on Iraq, Terrorism, and Weapons of Mass Destruction*, Tokyo: United Nations University Press.

Thumim, N. (2010), 'Self-representation in Museums: Therapy or Democracy?', *Critical Discourse Studies* 7(4): 291–304.

Thurlow, M. (2005), 'Protecting Cultural Property in Iraq: How American Military Policy Comports with International Law', *Yale Human Rights and Development Law Journal* 8: 153–87.

Transparency International (2014), 'Corruption by Country: Iraq', Transparency International.

Tremlett, G. (2010), 'WikiLeaks: "US pressured Spain over CIA rendition and Guantanamo torture"', *The Guardian*, 1 December.

Torre, M. & M. Fine (2008), 'Participatory Action Research in the Contact Zone', in J. Cammarota & M. Fine (eds), *Revolutionizing Education: Youth Participatory Action Research in Motion*, New York: Routledge, pp. 23–44.

Tripp, C. (2007), *A History of Iraq*, 3rd edn, Cambridge: Cambridge University Press.

Turkle, S. (1999), 'An Interview with Sherry Turkle', *Hedgehog Review*, Fall.

Ullman, H. & J. Wade (1996), 'Shock and Awe: Achieving Rapid Dominance', Institute for National Strategic Studies.

UNAMI Human Rights Office & Office of High Commissioner for Human Rights (2012), *Report on Human Rights in Iraq: January to June 2012*, Baghdad: UNAMI Human Rights Office/OHCHR.

UNESCO (1954), Convention for the Protection of Cultural Property in the Event of Armed Conflict.

UNHCR (2004), 'Country of Origin Information – Iraq', August.

UNHCR (2007a), 'Asylum Levels and Trends in Industrialised Countries, 2006', UNHCR's Field Information and Coordination Support Section, 23 March.

UNHCR (2007b), 'Government Assessment Report – Erbil, Sulaymaniyah', 1 September.

UNHCR (2007c), 'Terrified Palestinians flee Baghdad for Syrian border', 24 January.

UNHCR (2010), 'Syria at a Glance', August.

UNHCR (2012a), 'Exodus continues from Syria, including some 10,000 Iraqis', 24 July.

UNHCR (2012b), 'UNHCR reports more Syrian refugees in all neighbouring countries', 17 August.

UNHCR (2013), 'UNHCR Syria Refugee Fact Sheet', December.

United Nations (1966), International Covenant on Economic, Social and Cultural Rights.

United Nations (2011), 'Security Council approves "no-fly Zone" over Libya', press release, 17 March.

United Nations Assistance Mission for Iraq (2008), 'Human Rights Report 1 July–31 December 2008', United Nations Assistance Mission for Iraq.

United Nations General Assembly (2012), 'Report of the Special Rapporteur on Extrajudicial, Summary or Arbitrary Executions, Christof Heyns: Follow-up to Country Recommendations – United States of America', Human Rights Council: Twentieth Session, 30 March.

United Nations Iraq (2010), 'The United Nations in Iraq calls on Iraq to ratify the Convention against Torture', press release, 26 June.

United Nations Iraq (2014), 'UN casualty figures for December, 2013 deadliest since 2008 in Iraq', 1 January.

United Nations Security Council (2004), letter dated 23 February from Secretary-General to President of Security Council.

United States Commission on International Religious Freedom (2006), 'Iraq's Permanent Constitution: Analysis and Recommendations', March.

United States Commission on International Religious Freedom (2008), *USCIRF Report on Iraq*, Washington, DC: United States Commission on International Religious Freedom.

United States Commission on International Religious Freedom (2009), *Annual Report of the United States Commission on International Religious Freedom*, Washington, DC: United States Commission on International Religious Freedom.

United States Commission on International Religious Freedom (2013), *Iraq: USCIRF 2013 Annual Report*, Washington, DC: United States Commission on International Religious Freedom.

UPI (2010), 'Iraq wants to lead oil world', UPI, 30 December.

Uqaili, T. (2008), 'Iraqi Border Fields: Politics and Realities', *Middle East Economic Survey* 51(12): 26–29.

US Department of State (2004), 'Iraq's successes and challenges as it rebuilds its economy and rejoins the world marketplace', news conference, 21 December.

US Labor against the War (2012a), 'Iraqi union federation condemns government interference in the internal affairs of unions', 8 July.

US Labor against the War (2012b), 'Joint statement: Iraqi trade unions in Basra denounce sham elections', 29 June.

Vahidmanesh, P. (2010), 'As old as water itself: the Mandaeans of Iran, followers of John the Baptist', *Payvand Iran News*, 31 July.

Valanis, J. (2013), 'Developing a Cultural Property Protection Training Program for ROTC: Methodology, Content, and Structure', in J. Kila & J. Zeidler (eds), *Cultural Heritage in the Crosshairs: Protecting Cultural Property During Conflict*, Leiden: Brill, pp. 93–111.

Vervaet, L. (2010), 'The Violence of Incarceration: A Response from Mainland Europe', *Race & Class* 51(4): 27–38.

Vieth, W. (2003), 'Powell: US won't claim Iraq's oil', *Los Angeles Times*, 23 January.

Visser, R. (2010), *A Responsible End? The United States and the Iraqi Transition, 2005–2010*, Charlottesville, VA: Just World.

Visser, R. (2013a), 'Anti-Maliki forces reach another milestone', *Iraq Business News*, 26 July.

Visser, R. (2013b), 'De-Baathification in the Iraqi provincial elections by governorate and political entity', Iraq and Gulf Analysis blog, 10 March.

Visser, R. (2014a), 'Analysis of IHEC Resignation' *Iraq Business News*, 28 March.

Visser, R. (2014b), 'Details of coalitions contesting April elections', *Iraq Business News*, 3 February.

Visser, R. (2014c), 'Full list of election candidates', *Iraq Business News*, 7 April.

Visser, R. (2014d), 'Jumping ship? Defections ahead of the elections', *Iraq Business News*, 8 April.

Voller, Y. (2013), 'Kurdish Oil Politics in Iraq: Contested Sovereignty and Unilateralism', *Middle East Policy* 20(1): 68–82.

Wallace-Wells, B. (2011), 'European Superhero Quashes Libyan Dictator', *New York Magazine*, 26 December.

Walzer, M. (1995), 'The Politics of Rescue', *Social Research* 62(1): 53–66.

Weiss, T. (2004), 'The Sunset of Humanitarian Intervention? The Responsibility to Protect in a Unipolar Era', *Security Dialogue* 35(2): 135–53.

Welsh, M. (2013), 'Making sense of Mali's armed groups', Al Jazeera website, 17 January.

Wenski, T. (2006), 'Bishops, commission plead for help for Iraqi Assyrian Christians', Assyrian International News Agency, 11 November.

Wheeler, N. (2000), *Saving Strangers: Humanitarian Intervention in International Society*, Oxford: Oxford University Press.

Whitaker, J. & A. Varghese (2009), 'Online Discourse in the Arab World: Dispelling the Myths', United States Institute of Peace, December.

WikiLeaks (2010), 'The Iraq War Logs', 22 October.

Will, G. (2011), 'Obama's humanitarian imperialism in Libya', *National Post*, 7 April.

Wilmshurst, D. (2000), *The Ecclesiastical Organisation of the Church of the East, 1318–1913*, Leuven: Peeters.

Wolfowitz, P. (2003), House Committee on Appropriations hearing on a supplemental war regulation, 27 March.

World Factbook (2007), 'World Factbook: Iraq Economic Data, 1989–2003', Washington: Central Intelligence Agency.

World Factbook (2014), *World Factbook: Iraq*, Washington: Central Intelligence Agency.

Wright, H., T. Wilkinson, E. Stone & M. Gibson (2003), 'The National Geographic Society's Cultural Assessment of Iraq', National Geographic Society, May.

Wright, R. & P. Baker (2004), 'Iraq, Jordan see threat to election from Iran', *Washington Post*, December 8.

Xu, C. & L. Bell (2013), 'Worldwide reserves, oil production post modest rise', *Oil and Gas Journal*, 2 December.

Yaphe, J. (2003), 'Iraq's Sunni Arabs: Part of the Past, Part of the Future?', Carnegie Endowment for International Peace, 25 November.

Yildiz, K. & T. Blass (2004), *The Kurds in Iraq: The Past, Present and Future*, London: Pluto Press.

Zahra, H. (2010), 'Top cleric warns Iraq leaders on coalition talks', AFP, 18 June.

Zangana, H. (2013), 'For Iraqi women, America's promise of democracy is anything but liberation', *The Guardian*, 26 February.

Zedalis, R. (2008), 'Foundations of Baghdad's Argument that Regions Lack Constitutional Authority over Oil and Gas Development Agreements', *Journal of Energy & Natural Resources Law* 26(2): 303–16.

Zeidel, R. (2008), 'A Harsh Readjustment: The Sunnis and the Political Process in Iraq', *Middle East Review of International Affairs* 12(1): 40–50.

Zeidel, R. (2009), 'The Association of Muslim Scholars: The Rise and (Temporary) Fall of a Sunni Arab Political Organization in Iraq', *Journal of South Asian and Middle Eastern Studies* 33(1): 20–35.

Zeidel, R. (2010), 'On Servility and Survival: The Sunni Opposition to Saddam and the Origins of the Current Sunni Leadership in Iraq', in A. Baram, A. Rohde & R. Zeidel (eds), *Iraq between Occupations: Perspectives from 1920 to the Present*, New York: Palgrave Macmillan, pp. 159–73.

Zeidel, R. (2014), 'From Deba'athification to "Justice and Accountability": Iraqi Reform in a Wider Context', in B. Friedman & B. Maddy-Weitzman (eds), *The Cohesion of the Middle East States: A Reassessment*, Tel Aviv: Moshe Dayan Center.

Al-Zeidi, M. (2013), 'Iraq's premiership needs reform', *Al-Monitor*, 5 September.

Zeidler, J. & L. Rush (2010), 'In-theatre Soldier Training through Cultural Heritage Playing Cards: A US Department of Defense Example', in L. Rush (ed.), *Archaeology, Cultural Property, and the Military*, Woodbridge: Boydell Press, pp. 73–85.

Zhao, S. (2005), 'The Digital Self: Through the Looking Glass of Telecopresent Others', *Symbolic Interaction* 28(3): 387–405.

Zifcak, S. (2012), 'The Responsibility to Protect after Libya and Syria', *Melbourne Journal of International Law* 13(1): 59–93.

Zoepf, K. (2004), 'Many Christians flee Iraq, with Syria the haven of choice', *New York Times*, 5 August.

Index